BEYOND CORTÉS AND MONTEZUMA

INSTITUTE FOR MESOAMERICAN STUDIES MONOGRAPH SERIES

PUBLICATION NO. 1
Archaeology and Ethnohistory of the Central Quiche, edited by Dwight T. Wallace and Robert M. Carmack

PUBLICATION NO. 2
Basic Quiche Grammar, by James L. Mondloch

PUBLICATION NO. 3
Bibliography of Mayan Languages and Linguistics, by Lyle Campbell with Pierre Ventur, Russell Stewart, and Brant Gardner

PUBLICATION NO. 4
Codex Vindobonensis Mexicanus 1: A Commentary, by Jill Leslie Furst, with a preface by Mary Elizabeth Smith

PUBLICATION NO. 5
Migration Across Frontiers: Mexico and the United States, Vol. 3, edited by Fernando Camara and Robert Van Kemper

PUBLICATION NO. 6
The Historical Demography of Highland Guatemala, edited by Robert Carmack, John Early, and Christopher Lutz

PUBLICATION NO. 7
Aztec Sorcerers in Seventeenth Century Mexico: The Treatise on Superstitions, by Hernando Ruiz de Alarcón, edited and translated by Michael D. Coe and Gordon Whittaker

PUBLICATION NO. 8
Maya Hieroglyphic Codices, by Yuri Knorosov, translated by Sophie Coe

PUBLICATION NO. 9
Phoneticism in Mayan Hieroglyphic Writing, edited by John Justeson and Lyle Campbell

PUBLICATION NO. 10
A Consideration of the Early Classic Period in the Maya Lowlands, edited by Gordon R. Willey and Peter Mathews

PUBLICATION NO. 11
Hach Winik: The Lacandon Maya of Chiapas, Southern Mexico, by Didier Boremanse

PUBLICATION NO. 12
Classic Period Mixtequilla, Veracruz, Mexico: Diachronic Inferences from Residential Investigations, by Barbara Stark

PUBLICATION NO. 13
Before Guadalupe: The Virgin Mary in Early Colonial Nahuatl Literature, by Louise Burkhart

PUBLICATION NO. 14
Postclassic Soconusco Society: The Late Prehistory of Chiapas, Mexico, edited by Barbara Voorhies and Janine Gasco

PUBLICATION NO. 15
Utatlán: The Constituted Community of the K'iche' Maya of Q'umarkaj, by Thomas F. Babcock

PUBLICATION NO. 16
Aztec Antichrist: Performing the Apocalypse in Early Colonial Mexico, by Ben Leeming

PUBLICATION NO. 17
Staging Christ's Passion in Eighteenth-Century Nahua Mexico, by Louise M. Burkhart

PUBLICATION NO. 18
Beyond Cortés and Montezuma: The Conquest of Mexico Revisited, edited by Vitus Huber and John F. Schwaller

BEYOND CORTÉS AND MONTEZUMA

The Conquest of Mexico Revisited

EDITED BY

Vitus Huber and John F. Schwaller

UNIVERSITY PRESS OF COLORADO
Denver

© 2025 by University Press of Colorado

Published by University Press of Colorado
1580 North Logan Street, Suite 660
PMB 39883
Denver, Colorado 80203-1942

All rights reserved

The University Press of Colorado is a proud member of Association of University Presses.

The University Press of Colorado is a cooperative publishing enterprise supported, in part, by Adams State University, Colorado State University, Fort Lewis College, Metropolitan State University of Denver, University of Alaska Fairbanks, University of Colorado, University of Denver, University of Northern Colorado, University of Wyoming, Utah State University, and Western Colorado University.

ISBN: 978-1-64642-664-5 (hardcover)
ISBN: 978-1-64642-665-2 (paperback)
ISBN: 978-1-64642-666-9 (ebook)
https://doi.org/10.5876/9781646426669

Library of Congress Cataloging-in-Publication Data

Names: Huber, Vitus, editor. | Schwaller, John Frederick, editor.
Title: Beyond Cortés and Montezuma : the conquest of Mexico revisited / edited by Vitus Huber and John F. Schwaller.
Other titles: Institute for Mesoamerican Studies Monograph Series ; volume 18
Description: Denver, Colorado : University Press of Colorado, [2024] | Series: Institute for Mesoamerican Studies Monograph Series ; volume 18 | Includes bibliographical references and index.
Identifiers: LCCN 2024011474 (print) | LCCN 2024011475 (ebook) | ISBN 9781646426645 (hardcover) | ISBN 9781646426652 (paperback) | ISBN 9781646426669 (ebook)
Subjects: LCSH: Nahuas—Mexico—History. | Mexico—History—Conquest, 1519–1540—Historiography. | Mexico—History—Conquest, 1519–1540—Sources.
Classification: LCC F1230 .B53 2024 (print) | LCC F1230 (ebook) | DDC 972/.0200497452—dc23/eng/20240410
LC record available at https://lccn.loc.gov/2024011474
LC ebook record available at https://lccn.loc.gov/2024011475

This book will be made open access within three years of publication thanks to Path to Open, a program developed in partnership between JSTOR, the American Council of Learned Societies (ACLS), University of Michigan Press, and The University of North Carolina Press to bring about equitable access and impact for the entire scholarly community, including authors, researchers, libraries, and university presses around the world. Learn more at https://about.jstor.org/path-to-open/.

This work is licensed under CC BY-NC-ND 4.0.

Cover art: Mural by Desiderio Hernandez Xochitiotzin in the Palacio de Gobierno in Tlaxcala city. Photograph by Wolfgang Sauber. Public domain image from Wikimedia Commons.

Contents

Foreword
    Kevin Terraciano   vii

Preface
    Vitus Huber and John F. Schwaller   xi

Introduction
Beyond Cortés and Moteuczoma: Revisiting the *Conquista* of Mexico
    Vitus Huber   3

PART I: SEMANTICS AND EFFECTS

1. The Language of "Conquest" in Colonial Nahuatl Manuscripts
    Stephanie Wood   17

2. "Perpetuating Lands": The Crucial Transition from War to Colonial Settlement in the *Conquista* of Mexico
    Vitus Huber   45

3. The *Conquista* of Mexico Today: Hyperactive Memory, National Identity, and Symbolic Violence
    Justyna Olko   69

Part II: Narratives and Memories

4. The Last Journey of Cuauhtemoc: Models for the *Anales de Tlatelolco*'s Version of Cuauhtemoc's Death
   Julia Madajczak   99

5. Zacarías de Santiago: A Tlaxcalteca Conquistador in the Evolution of Nahua Historical Memories
   Robert Haskett   125

6. How to Read Native Accounts of the *Conquista* of Mexico
   María Castañeda de la Paz   161

Part III: Power and Negotiations

7. Moteuczoma's Surrender of Power: A Critical Proposal
   Miguel Pastrana Flores   191

8. The Forty *Teteuctin*: Nahua Bodies in the Mediterranean
   Erika Escutia   215

Part IV: Representations and Iconic Figures

9. Beyond Malinche: Other Native Women in the *Conquista*
   Lori Boornazian Diel   243

10. Between Victor and Vanquished: The Metamorphosis of Moteuczoma in a Painted *Biombo*
    Patrick Hajovsky   272

Epilogue
Conclusions
   John F. Schwaller   305

Index   315
About the Authors   325

Foreword

KEVIN TERRACIANO

The corpus of books, manuscripts, archival documents, and images on the Spanish-led invasion of Mexico is so extensive and dispersed in libraries, archives, and museums on both sides of the Atlantic that scholars continue to make original contributions to a deep historiography on the topic. The war that the Spaniards called *la conquista de México* (or *Nueva España*) is easily the most documented series of events in the history of the early Americas. The topic has inspired European, Indigenous, Mestizo, and Creole writers and artists for centuries, but scholarship on the topic has surged in recent years with the quincentennial commemoration of the war. Matthew Restall's reinterpretation of the encounter between Montezuma and Cortés (2018) was among the first and most impressive books to appear in relation to the anniversary. Two excellent anthologies were published in 2022: *500 años de la conquista de México: Resistencias y apropiaciones*, edited by Valeria Añón, and *The Conquest of Mexico: Five Centuries of Reinvention*, edited by Peter Villella and Pablo García Loaeza. A weekly series in Mexico titled Noticonquista, organized by Federico Navarrete and colleagues at UNAM, exemplified how to present concise and well-curated historical essays to a public audience. These are but a few of many recent studies of the topic, and no doubt there are more to come. The present volume is a welcome addition to this literature.

Most of the interdisciplinary chapters in *Beyond Cortés and Montezuma* seek to look beyond the dramatic encounter between Moteuczoma Xocoyotzin and Hernando Cortés and the invasion of Tenochtitlan and Tlatelolco by examining texts and images that shed light on a complex narrative of contact and conflict, negotiation and cooperation, that continued well after 1521 into Mexico's viceregal or "colonial" period. I think of the "conquest" as an extended, incomplete, transformative process rather than a finite military event, and I would argue that the systemic exploitation and marginalization of Indigenous peoples of the Americas that began in the late fifteenth century continues to the present, not only in Mexico but in many nations throughout North and South America. Justyna Olko makes this point very clearly in her compelling contribution to this volume. Olko exposes the painful legacy of the *Conquista* and colonial rule, and the current Mexican government's continued inability or unwillingness to make sense of the past despite all the new historical research on the topic. National leaders fail to recognize the legacy of violence and to implement policies to address many of the problems that the Zapatista rebellion in Chiapas brought to the world's attention more than three decades ago.

But many chapters in this volume also document a spectrum of active and creative Indigenous responses to colonial rule, thereby demonstrating the limits of colonial and postcolonial domination, the vitality of Indigenous cultures, and the agency of individuals and communities. Stephanie Wood examines Nahuatl-language sources for insights into how people spoke of the war in all types of texts from both the early and later colonial periods, and finds little evidence that Nahuas thought of themselves as a conquered people. Julia Madajczak revisits a fascinating Nahuatl manuscript associated with the *Anales de Tlatelolco*, likely written in the late seventeenth century by Don Diego García de Mendoza Moctezuma, who drew on a vivid oral tradition to narrate how Cuauhtemoc was betrayed and unjustly executed by Cortés en route to Honduras. Madajczak skillfully unpacks the narrative's many symbolic cultural references and its complex mixture of fact and fable. María Castañeda de la Paz reminds us that Indigenous texts such as the *Anales de Tlatelolco*, like all sources, have their implicit biases and objectives. In fact, many Native writings mimic Spanish strategies in the viceregal period, when the king's rule and favor was paramount. Robert Haskett addresses a similar theme by analyzing local memories of the conquest preserved in pictorial and alphabetic records that highlight the heroic figure of Don Zacarías de Santiago, a noble who went with a Tlaxcalan delegation to visit King Philip II in 1584 and obtained a coat of arms and other privileges for himself and his *altepetl* (city-province). Many late colonial documents from the region go so far as to cast Don Zacarías in the impossible role of a conquistador who greeted Cortés in 1519. Like a skilled detective, Haskett sifts through a trove of discursive, difficult sources that represent collective responses to late colonial changes in land tenure, typical of the *títulos primordial* genre of colonial-era Indigenous writing. In fact Don Zacarías was not a conquistador and did not greet Cortés, but people from several nearby communities remembered or imagined him in such a role, in part because it served their present interests. In other words, the encounter and war remained relevant historical reference points for many Indigenous pueblos in the eighteenth century. Of course, descendants of Spanish conquistadors also tried to benefit from claims of their ancestors' services to the crown. Vitus Huber considers the concerns and strategies of an ordinary if not obscure Spaniard who fought in Mexico and other parts of New Spain, and who sought to procure rewards from the crown in the rapid transitional period between *entradas* and settlement.

Despite the volume's provocative "beyond" title, many chapters do not stray too far from the meeting between Moteuczoma and Cortés and the war in Mexico Tenochtitlan. After all, these were momentous events. Miguel Pastrana Flores surveys a wide range of sources to scrutinize Moteuczoma's alleged submission to King Charles, the idea of a *translatio imperii* constructed by Cortés and advanced by nearly all Spanish accounts of the encounter. According to most Spanish narratives, Mexica rebels rejected the pact by revolting against their leader and the Spaniards, an act of treason that necessitated a "just war." Pastrana considers how the Mexicah would have conceived of such an act of self-deposition, based on Nahua practices and institutions of governance. Erika Escutia explores what can be known about the forty *teteuctin*, or Nahua lords, Cortés brought with him to the court in Spain in 1528, and especially how these performatively displayed political subjects were represented and interpreted by European observers. Lori Boornazian Diel goes beyond the usual focus on Malintzin to consider the representation and roles of other Native women in narratives of the encounter and war: as slaves, as marriage alliance or "gifting" partners, and as battle participants and victims. Diel's discussion of Tecuichpotzin, one of Moteuczoma's daughters who was later named Doña Isabel, is especially interesting. Last but certainly not least, Patrick Hajovsky identifies a painting in the Museo de Américas in Madrid as a missing panel from a conquest *biombo* (screen-fold painting) that is now preserved in a private collection in Mexico. The panel depicts a familiar scene in many biombos and *enconchados* (paintings encrusted with mother-of-pearl) produced in Mexico in the late seventeenth century: Moteuczoma standing on his balcony, assaulted by Mexica rebels who reject his call for peace after war has broken out. Hajovsky's find is a significant contribution to the literature on history paintings of the conquest and visual representations of Moteuczoma.

John F. Schwaller deserves a good deal of credit for bringing this edition to fruition, along with coeditor Vitus Huber. I know that Schwaller organized and participated in several conference panels and meetings on the broadly defined and inclusive topic of the conquest, war, invasion, and so on. His concluding chapter makes clear the complexity and enduring significance of this history. I congratulate Fritz and Vitus and all the authors on their valuable contributions to an extensive, interdisciplinary literature.

Preface

VITUS HUBER AND JOHN F. SCHWALLER

From 2019 to 2021 the commemoration of the 500th anniversary of the so-called *Conquista* of Mexico has once again raised public interest, provoked polemic debates, and stimulated scholarly discussion. We consider the time at the close of the intensified responsiveness as an appropriate moment to take stock and organize the various arguments. The fertilizing conversation especially in Mexico and Spain as well as among the specialists across the globe has been very inspiring and informative. The chapters of this volume not only originate from this discussion but are an effort to continue it as well. Most of them stem from a double panel held online at the triannual meeting of the Asociación de Historiadores Latinoamericanistas Europeos (AHILA) in Paris in August 2021. With this international and interdisciplinary book, we not only aim at reflecting upon the state of the art but even more so at mapping out cutting-edge approaches, materials, and questions. We are hoping to open—or at least point toward—some paths that we regard as fruitful for future scholarship on the subject.

We extend our gratitude to University Press of Colorado and the Institute for Mesoamerican Studies of the University at Albany for the acceptance to the IMS Monograph series, as well as to the anonymous reviewers for their insightful comments. We would like to thank Rachael Levay, Walter Little, Allegra Martschenko, Dan Pratt, and Darrin Pratt for their support in the publishing process and Stanislaw Pawlowski and Héloïse Stritt for their help in proofreading the manuscript.

Furthermore, we are grateful to Kevin Terraciano for honoring this book with his foreword and to all the contributors for their cooperation.

We would like to dedicate this volume to Luis Fernando Granados Salinas (1968–2021). Our dear friend and colleague from the Universidad Veracruzana in Xalapa passed away unexpectedly. As this happened shortly before the conference of AHILA, we lack even a working paper and are unable to publish his planned contribution to this volume. Nevertheless, the book intends to honor Luis's work by uniting some of the most renowned experts in the studies of Nahua culture and of colonial Spanish America from Europe, Mexico, and the US.

The volume's international and interdisciplinary group seeks fresh insights from historical as well as philological, gender, and art historical perspectives. Moreover, the decades-old revisionism still generates new questions, and it is still necessary to continue dismantling sturdy narratives that distort both Mesoamerican and European history. Within the boundaries of a collective volume, we hence endeavor to revisit the historiography of the *Conquista* of Mexico and to suggest examples for new approaches that go beyond Cortés and Moteuczoma.

BEYOND CORTÉS AND MONTEZUMA

Introduction

Beyond Cortés and Moteuczoma

Revisiting the Conquista *of Mexico*

VITUS HUBER

The events commonly known as the "Conquest of Mexico" still arouse great interest, even roughly half a millennium after they unfolded. The main reasons for this are twofold: on the one hand, these events have a world-historical significance and, on the other hand, they have constantly provoked controversies. Basically, since the beginning, the interpretation and depiction of these incidents have been strongly loaded with interests. Not only Indigenous people or Spaniards defended their interests, which were moreover often erroneously perceived as respectively homogenous. The field of actors and their points of view were ultimately much more disparate. After missionaries and clerics had challenged conquistadors' accounts starting in the early sixteenth century, other European powers picked up the criticism against the Spanish Crown. Alongside further voices from women, Africans, merchants, settlers, and others, the wide range of sources mirrors the phenomenon's polyphony.

For a long time in the 500 years of historiography, the more strident tones were given preferential consideration. Complexity was often reduced. This volume aims to take into account more subtle tones and contribute to a more detailed picture. By including neglected sources and aspects, this book expands on single facets of the events and their historiographies. Simultaneously, it encourages thorough reflections upon the methodological approaches by asking what implications the selection of empirical material and the framing of the subject have on the outcome and narrative of the inquiry. Furthermore, it examines the proper language to discuss the events. The essays offer a variety of options: "conquest," "invasion," "encounter," "war," among others. The use of certain categories like "soldiers" or *hueste* had and continues to have a distortive impact on the evaluation of the object or subject they are describing. One should therefore reflect upon the question, to put it in the semiotician Ferdinand de Saussure's terms, how the signifier influences the signified. Indeed, the choices made regarding topics, sources, time frame, and terminology heavily influence the results of the analysis.

Reassessing the semantics of key terms is definitely necessary. In many ways language has been instrumental in the construction of narratives; hence, using adequate terminology is essential. Admittedly, considering the different tongues and cultures as well as the complex situation of the moment under scrutiny, cultural translations and simplifications impose themselves. Telling the story of such a multifarious process is challenging. Nevertheless, language usage dictates the message, whether implicitly or explicitly. We should thus start by revisiting the term "conquest."

Scholars have grappled with finding adequate expressions for the so-called *Conquista*. On the eve of the 500th anniversary of the voyage of Columbus in 1992, following the initiative of Mexico, most members of the Organization of American States declared in the 1980s to replace the terms of "discovery and conquest" with "encounter of cultures." The goal was to underscore the agency of Indigenous people and to eliminate the heroic semantic of a lopsided European achievement.[1] It certainly encouraged the ongoing debate about the active role of Indigenous people. The shortcoming of the word "encounter," though, lies in its neutrality. It appears somewhat innocuous. Reacting to criticism against Spanish conquistadors' and settlers' brutal treatment of the local population in the Americas, in 1573 Philip II had already commissioned that the clearly euphemistic term of "pacification" replaces the word "conquest."[2] "Pacification" had already circulated before his decree. On the other hand, "conquest" never disappeared entirely. In the nineteenth and twentieth century the latter was applied again with pride, especially by nationalist Spanish historiography.[3]

Depending on the sources one uses or the group of actors one discusses, scholars prefer to call the *Conquista* of Mexico a "war" or an "invasion."[4] The latter is certainly a valid description. Nonetheless, it is not necessarily a more precise term than "conquest." It mainly marks a different *perspective*, the one from the people and places attacked instead of that from the attackers' point of view. Consequently, it makes sense to use the term "invasion" in those situations when the narrative's focus lies on the attacked locals and their homelands. Additionally, the expression judges the action as something negative just in the same manner as "conquest" implied a positive meaning until the late twentieth century. In fact, since the latter is the established term in historiography and common public perception, the demonstrative distancing from it makes the former more judgmental. Finally, in contrast to "conquest," an invasion does not automatically end in a lasting occupation of the territory (or parts thereof) invaded. We therefore think, depending on the perspective, "invasion" is an apt description but only for specific phases of the process.

A similar verdict applies to the term "war." The renowned historian Matthew Restall has started to promote the use of "Spanish-Aztec War (1519–21)" and, regarding the larger conflict, "Spanish-Mesoamerican War (1517–50)."[5] The problem here is that—certainly against the inventor's idea—the adjectives exclude the Tlaxcaltecah and other Indigenous allies to the Spaniards. This seems incompatible with the last approximatively five decades of scholarship that has worked on giving the "subaltern" a voice.[6] After we have emphasized their decisive contributions, we should eschew falling behind this level of differentiation again. Furthermore, the term "war" hides the fact of the succeeding Spanish colonial presence for roughly 300 years. Without claiming that this presence meant area-wide colonial rule, it was clearly more than a common "war."[7]

Our suggestion is to use the most precise terms at hand for individual events within the bigger process (like invasion/attack, conquest, battle, siege, looting of an individual place, etc.) and call the larger phenomenon *Conquista* in italics, indicating that one refers to the complex historic encounters of the Old and New World. This way, even in Italian and the Iberian tongues the italics and capitalized spelling—instead of aggrandizing the word—mark the distance from a naive use of the term. In all other languages, it furthermore stands out through the application of a foreign word. This solution is far from perfect, since the expression translates as the problematic "conquest," yet makes clear that it represents a controversial issue. It furthermore stands out from other famous conquests, for example, the one of Constantinople by the Ottomans or the Mughal conquest of Gujarat. This holds true even in Spanish, as the conquests of Seville or Granada and so forth are always mentioned specifying the place. Thus, in the American context too, adding the toponyms helps to distinguish what part of the larger process of the *Conquista* one is referring to: for example, the "*Conquista* of Guatemala." No additional geographic specification means simply the "*Conquista* of the Americas" in general. For ease of finding in digital research and in library catalogues, we have privileged the traditional monikers "Montezuma" and "Conquest" in the title of this volume. Notwithstanding this, the authors strive to be as precise as possible in the chapters, applying the Andrews-Campbell-Karttunen's orthographic conventions regarding "Moteuczoma,"[8] and the italicized *Conquista*, as suggested by us. However, a certain terminological heterogeneity remains throughout the volume, which perfectly represents the contested nature of the significance of this history and the often fragmentary documentation underlying it. Whether or not one accepts our terminology, the next question concerns the meanings of the matter described by it.

Without a doubt, *Conquista* stands for a complex phenomenon. It included not only a myriad of different institutions and actors with a varying degree of agency but also a whole range of interactions that ran from peaceful conversations and gift-giving to cultural, commercial, and biological exchange—however coercive—and political or military maneuvers. All of this unfolded under the influence of the environment (topographic, climatic, and meteorological conditions) as well as further contingent factors like the disastrously lethal effect of European diseases such as smallpox on the local population.[9] Politically, its result led—albeit not linearly—to Spanish colonial rule in a vast yet porous area of the Americas. This rule was fragile, inconsistent, and flexible indeed, but this "domination without dominance," as Gonzalo Lamana described the early colonial situation in Peru, was arguably an important factor for its undeniable longevity.[10] Indeed, the effects of colonial rule differed from place to place and depended on social status. They could impact the daily life of a lord's son educated in the Franciscan Colegio de Santa Cruz in Tlatelolco more profoundly than the one of a commoner (*macehualli*) working in the cultivation of beans, to cite two examples. This variety of experiences makes it harder to define the most accurate terminology.[11]

The discourses of the *Conquista*, in general, and of the *Conquista* of Mexico, in particular, have shaped these events and our perceptions of them since day one. For the *Conquista* of Mexico, Cortés with his letters to King Charles created a seemingly compelling story, which for roughly five centuries has been eagerly followed and retold.[12] His letters give the reader the rare opportunity to follow Cortés and his men and experience the whole "adventure" as it allegedly unfolds. By inviting the reader to be his witness, Cortés "made history" in both senses of the term: with his deeds and with the narrative he constructed around them, however accurate or aberrant it might be. In any case, it is a thrilling plot indeed, including the constituents you find in many intriguing novels and films today: the protagonist (and allies) go(es) to a foreign land for a noble cause, where they get into great danger and an almost hopeless situation, but instead of surrendering, they overcome the seemingly unsurpassable obstacle, master the challenge, or defeat the overpowering enemy in the end. No wonder many scholars, novelists, screenwriters, and others essentially followed this—or Bernal Díaz del Castillo's similar—storyline. Yet, repeating the same tale does not make that tale any truer. Undeniably, it makes it harder to revisit.

The methodological choices of perspective, of focus, and of framing have great implications for the analysis and depend greatly on the selection of sources. Deconstructing various myths about the *Conquista*, Restall—and lately also Nancy van Deusen—cited the Haitian anthropologist Michel-Rolph Trouillot, who had pointed out that the scarcity of sources from marginalized groups is in fact one of the main reasons we regard their members as marginalized in the first place. Their past and their history have been "silenced."[13] With substantial efforts, scholars since Miguel León-Portilla in Mexico and James Lockhart in the US have studied Nahuatl, Maya, Quechua, and other Indigenous languages using written records in the Native languages along with their pictorial codices and their material culture of quipus and further artifacts. The access to more sources has broadened our knowledge about pre-Hispanic cultures, and the linguistic approaches have informed generations of scholars.[14] At the advent of the twenty-first century, Restall has renewed Lockhart's plea for a new philology, an approach that has been instructive for the former's conceptualization of the New Conquest History. It aims at deconstructing Eurocentrically glorifying narratives and at shedding light on actors who were neglected until recently: namely, women, Indigenous people, Africans, enslaved people, and others.[15] This welcome approach has decisively contributed to a more complete picture of that history.

A challenge that remains is the fact that all surviving textual Indigenous sources treating the *Conquista* were produced *after* the events—most of them even decades later—and hence in the colonial setting. One must thus read them with this new power constellation in mind, which certainly influenced their narratives too.[16] Several of the chapters in this volume touch on this methodological challenge. Meanwhile, contextual rhetoric and hidden agendas have also been detected in Spanish sources, most famously in works like Cortés's epistolary reports to King Charles or in Bernal Díaz del Castillo's so-called *True History* (*Historia verdadera de la conquista de la Nueva España*), published posthumously in 1632.[17]

Regardless of the empirical basis on which scholars ground their work and the vagaries they imply, it is imperative to reflect upon the weight one attributes to a topic or to a specific voice. The *Conquista* is too complex to simply depict in black-and-white contrasts. Take for instance the balance between coercive and peaceful encounters. Focusing one's story on the violent battles does not necessarily paint the "legend" clearly black or white. On the one hand, the carnage could present the Spanish as reckless villains. On the other, it could also mark the logic of conquest, crediting the latter with political rights and military glory. If, on the contrary, one highlights the many peaceful encounters in which the parties came to agreements without fighting each other ferociously, it could be regarded as an attempt to trivialize the brutality and bloodshed of the conflict. Equally biased are perspectives that praise the pre-Hispanic cultures to an extent that they seemingly forget or at least downplay the gory rituals of human sacrifice. Even the nature of sacrifice can be presented in opposing manners. Some argue that it was deeply rooted in the religious life of the culture, an extreme form of public execution. Traditionally, it was seen as a sufficient justification for European colonization.

Whatever the author's point of view, it is a narrow path, and one always runs the risk of overemphasizing one side or another. When recognizing the importance of the Nahua and other Indigenous participants who cooperated with the Spanish, one lessens to some degree the latter of the harm caused by the Spanish arrival. Even though one intended to deconstruct the myth of the small, brave group of Spaniards allegedly conquering a whole empire on their own, one ends up blaming local fractions to have grievously enabled the European invaders to colonize parts of the Americas. Similarly, when further reducing the aggrandizing plot of the small cohort against an entire empire by rendering the Triple Alliance as a mere empire of tribute, one automatically questions the greatness of that alliance or even the pre-Hispanic cultural achievements in general. These are but a few examples of how delicate it is to pursue a balanced stand. Every small shift away from common opinions on a certain issue can be interpreted as denying the Mexicah's or Tlaxcaltecah's and others Indigenous groups' agencies or the Spaniards' responsibility when in fact one tries to adjust to the latest scholarship or one's own findings. Then again, not adapting is also not an option, as this would perpetuate outdated views.[18]

The selected time frame is another factor that largely dictates the chronology and narrative of a story. Comparable to graphic illustrations of mathematical diagrams, for example, for stocks, the graph might dramatically point up or down, depending on the section of the chart chosen. When one adjusts the parameter of either the x- or y-axis, sharp peaks can flatten out or, vice versa, relatively low horizontal waves gain in verticality. Even though far from the illustrated linearity of mathematical charts, historical narratives are also strongly shaped by the selected period and by the analytical *Flughöhe*, the cruising altitude of the analysis. From a distance, the *Conquista* might seem like a bilateral confrontation between the so-called Old and New World. Zooming in on the scene, one finds that the multifaceted conflicts and interactions become more visible. Clearly, these interactions could take place between Spaniards and Nahuas, and others, but also within different representatives of Indigenous groups or within European ones. While a narrow understanding of the *Conquista* of Mexico refers to the time of Spanish arrival at the Totonac coast in spring 1519 until the fall of Tenochtitlan on August 13, 1521, the conquering phase of Central Mexico was far from being over by then. As Julia Madajczak's chapter shows, four years later, in 1525, when Cortés had Cuauhtemoc executed in Itzamkanac in today's Guatemala, the Spaniards and their Nahua allies were still far from having full control over the region.

Defining a time frame comes with another choice to make, that of the *geographic* scope. For the *Conquista* with its "encounter" of two worlds—admittingly neither of them was a monolithic one—the difficulty of storytelling lies in the (at least) two distinct beginnings. If one starts with the Mexicah or Tlaxcaltecah, for example, and introduces the Spaniards only at their arrival, the scholar misses an important part of why and how the Spanish had decided to set sail from the Iberian Peninsula in the first place. Yet again, starting with the Europeans, one would easily earn criticism for a Eurocentric framing, as it might foster a glorifying narrative. While the classic Eurocentric narrative maintains its long tradition, new literature often includes both perspectives by jumping back and forth, weaving the multiple threads to a more integrative storyline.[19]

The commemoration of 500 years since the fall of Tenochtitlan has given rise to a number of related publications—especially in Mexico and Spain.[20] On the one hand, some offer edited sources or focus on principal figures and events, spanning genres from new editions of biographies or reevaluations of Hernán Cortés to updated narratives of the *Conquista* of Mexico.[21] On the other hand, the approaches from Indigenous perspectives have strongly increased, even though their main focus seldom lies on the *Conquista* itself but rather on topics from the time before or after.[22]

Arguably more important, scholarship on the *Conquista* had already advanced before the attention had been raised, stimulated by the quincentenary. The edition of the so-called *Petición al cabildo*, the earliest Spanish document from today's Mexican lands, contains the rubrics and signatures of 346 participants of Cortés's expedition, eighty of whom had been unknown beforehand.[23] Furthermore, new research has analyzed the Spanish Crown's politics of European enslavement and also the related strategies and practices both in the Caribbean and in New Spain.[24] Finally, the importance of booty was highlighted, describing the dynamics of the *Conquista* as a "spiral of spoils" that not only emerged from pre-Hispanic and Iberian rewarding practices but moreover played a decisive role in the establishment of Spanish colonial rule in the Americas.[25] Hence, the latest studies on both sides of the Atlantic have not only provided new insights but also offered new narratives of the whole process. This dynamic scholarship has also informed the discussion presented in this volume.

With the aspiration to continue to revisit the *Conquista*, the book is structured in four parts, including (1) Semantics and Effects, (2) Narratives and Memories, (3) Power and Negotiations, and (4) Representations and Iconic Figures. The first part illustrates how the words people use(d) to speak of the *Conquista* of Mexico matter(ed) in these people's own historical contexts: Stephanie Wood scrutinizes the term "conquest" in colonial Nahuatl manuscripts as well as additional key vocabulary regarding warfare. Wood dismisses the term "conquest" as an imported one that would inadequately undermine the Nahuas' perspective on their histories, rendering them rather histories of victimhood than of survivance.

Vitus Huber assesses the tipping point when war turns into colonialism and when conquistadors become settlers. Huber argues that the characteristics of the specific warfare—including the practices of alliances—were foundational for the colonial rule. Justyna Olko reflects on the aftermath of the *Conquista* in Indigenous communities of the twenty-first century. Olko reveals how histories and its forms of commemoration shape social reality and vice versa.

The second part deals with two different concepts of Nahua history telling. Julia Madajczak examines three narrative tropes of Cuauhtemoc's death in Nahuatl sources that also appear in the late colonial *Anales de Tlatelolco*. Even though these motives were of a symbolic rather than a historical nature, they still helped Nahuas conceptualize their ruler and the passage to the Otherworld. Robert Haskett dissects the layers of Nahua historical memories that had led Don Zacarías de Santiago, a man from the Tlaxcalteca elite, to the erroneous honor of being celebrated in late colonial times as a Nahua conquistador allied with Hernando Cortés. María Castañeda de la Paz demonstrates how a number of Spanish and especially Nahua authors constructed colonial narratives. With a focus on the events in the Hibueras that led to the hanging of the lords of the Triple Alliance, she describes—in a complementary way to Madajczak—the modes of copying, altering, and composing the historical accounts according to the authors' interests.

The third part consists of two chapters about the question of power and how it can be gained, maintained, or lost within both the Nahua and colonial settings. Miguel Pastrana Flores analyzes the critical moment of the surrender of power from Moteuczoma to the Spanish Crown. He argues that the way in which the transfer of power was presented in Spanish sources, namely, as a submission to the Crown, was incompatible with Nahua political concepts. Erika Escutia focuses on the intercultural readings of the forty Nahua dignitaries' bodies that accompanied Cortés on his journey to Europe in 1528. Escutia highlights that these Nahuas did not merely serve Cortés to consolidate his power by exhibiting his success. Rather, the Nahua delegation benefitted from the trip to negotiate and enhance their own social and political position in their homelands. Escutia's emphasis on the body and its representation points at the approaches chosen for both of the following chapters.

The fourth part includes two chapters on iconic figures and issues of representation. Lori Boornazian Diel invites the reader to look beyond the famous Marina or Malinche for additional women in Nahuatl accounts of the *Conquista* of Mexico. According to Diel, women played different roles in the encounters with the Spaniards that corresponded to their social status and ethnicity. Patrick Hajovsky studies a little-known portrait of Moteuczoma and his physical features painted on a folding screen (*biombo*). This extraordinary depiction of the great speaker (*huey tlahtoani*) illustrates him in a rather passive and tragic posture, evoking associations with the Noble Savage. As this chapter, as well as that of Pastrana Flores, demonstrate, the title of our book does not imply that we erase the major figures from the picture but that we push beyond their usual images.

In an epilogue, John F. Schwaller sums up by commenting on each chapter of this volume and on the vagaries of the term "Conquest."

* * *

Regarding orthography of terms in Nahuatl, we have followed the Andrews-Campbell-Karttunen standards. Different spellings of terms like Mexicah, Tlaxcaltecah, or Tlatelolcah versus Mexica, Tlaxcalteca, or Tlatelolca abide to Nahuatl grammar: The final *-h* is used for nouns in plural, for example, Tlatelolcah stands for the people from Tlatelolco; without the final *-h*, it is used as an adjective, for example, a Tlatelolca lord. Furthermore, the ending on *-tl* stands for a noun in singular, for example, Mexicatl, Tlaxcaltecatl, Tlatelolcatl. Finally, as an exception, we use the common English spelling "Nahuas," for the noun in plural. When the final *-s* is missing, it indicates an adjective use, for example, "Nahua culture." The adjective "Nahuatl" is only applied when referring to the language, like a "Nahuatl text," not the culture or ethnic group more generally, for example, "Nahua world."

NOTES

1. Horst Pietschmann, "Bilanz der Diskussionen und Initiativen zum 'Quinto Centenario' in Spanien und Amerika," in *Fünfhundert Jahre Evangelisierung Lateinamerikas: Geschichte—Kontroversen—Perspektiven*, ed. Michael Sievernich and Dieter Spelthahn (Frankfurt: Vervuert, 1995), 162–71, here 162–63.

2. Archivo General de las Indias (henceforth AGI), Indiferente, 427, leg. 29, fols. 67r–93v, Ordenanzas de descubrimiento y población, July 13, 1573.

3. See, e.g., Marcelino Menéndez y Pelayo, *La ciencia española: Polémicas, proyectos y bibliografía*, 3 vols. (Madrid: Imprenta Central a Cargo de Victor Saiz, 1887–89).

4. See, e.g., Guillermo López Varela et al., eds., *A más de 500 años de la invasión de Mesoamérica: Memorias y resistencias de esperanza ngigua, antropología e historia* (Puebla: El Errante, 2021). For "war," see the following note.

5. Matthew Restall, *When Montezuma Met Cortés: The True Story of the Meeting That Changed History* (New York: ECCO, 2019), 40. On the controversial use of the term "Aztec," see Schwaller in this volume.

6. Restall himself must be credited for his remarkable achievements in advancing research of many marginalized participants of the *Conquista*. See, e.g., Matthew Restall, *The Black Middle: Africans, Mayas, and Spaniards in Colonial Yucatan* (Stanford, CA: Stanford University Press, 2009); pathbreaking on the Indigenous' participation was Laura Matthew

and Michel Oudijk, eds., *Indian Conquistadors: Indigenous Allies in the Conquest of Mesoamerica* (Norman: University of Oklahoma Press, 2007).

7. On the colonial transformations see, e.g., Serge Gruzinski, *La colonisation de l'imaginaire: Sociétés indigènes et occidentalisation dans le Mexique espagnol XVIe–XVIIIe siècle* (Paris: Gallimard, 1988); Felix Hinz, *"Hispanisierung" in Neu-Spanien 1519–1568: Transformation kollektiver Identitäten von Mexica, Tlaxkalteken und Spaniern*, 3 vols. (Hamburg: Dr. Kovač, 2005); Bradley Benton, *The Lords of Tetzcoco: The Transformation of Indigenous Rule in Postconquest Central Mexico* (New York: Cambridge University Press, 2017).

8. For these conventions that are commonly abbreviated as ACK after the authors who have contributed to them, see J. Richard Andrews, *Introduction to Classical Nahuatl*, rev. ed. (Norman: University of Oklahoma Press, 2003); Joe Campbell and Frances Karttunen, *Foundation Course in Nahuatl Grammar* (Missoula: University of Montana, 1989); and Frances Karttunen, *An Analytical Dictionary of Nahuatl* (Norman: University of Oklahoma Press, 1992).

9. For the certainly difficult calculations regarding the demographic catastrophe, see Esteban Mira Caballos, *El indio antillano: Repartimiento, encomienda y esclavitud (1492–1542)* (Seville: Múñoz Moya, 1997), 33–47; and Vågene Åshild et al., "Salmonella Enterica Genomes from Victims of a Major Sixteenth-Century Epidemic in Mexico," in *Nature Ecology and Evolution* 2 (2018): 520–28.

10. Gonzalo Lamana, *Domination without Dominance: Inca-Spanish Encounters in Early Colonial Peru* (Durham, NC: Duke University Press, 2008), esp. 125–25. On the functionality of the "inefficiency" of the Spanish empire, see Arndt Brendecke, *The Empirical Empire: Spanish Colonial Rule and the Politics of Knowledge* (Berlin: De Gruyter, 2016), esp. 235–78.

11. The literature on early colonial life is vast; see, for e.g., James Lockhart, *The Nahuas after the Conquest: A Social and Cultural History of the Indians of Central Mexico, Sixteenth through Eighteenth Centuries* (Stanford, CA: Stanford University Press, 1992); Rebecca Horn, *Postconquest Coyoacan: Nahua-Spanish Relations in Central Mexico, 1519–1650* (Stanford, CA: Stanford University Press, 1997); Stephanie Wood, *Transcending Conquest: Nahua Views of Spanish Colonial Mexico* (Norman: University of Oklahoma Press, 2003); Benjamin Johnson, *Pueblos within Pueblos: Tlaxilacalli Communities in Acolhuacan, Mexico, ca. 1272–1692* (Boulder: University Press of Colorado, 2017); Lidia Gómez García, *Los anales nahuas de la ciudad de Puebla de los Ángeles, siglos XVI y XVIII: Escribiendo historia indígena como aliados del rey católico de España* (Puebla: Ayuntamiento de Puebla–Gerencia del Centro Histórico, UNESCO, Universidad de Rutgers, 2018).

12. Cf. Hernán Cortés, *Cartas de relación*, ed. Mario Hernández Sánchez-Barba (Madrid: Historia 16, 1985); Francisco López de Gómara, *Historia general de las Indias: "Hispania victrix" cuya segunda parte corresponde a la conquista de Méjico*, ed. Pilar Guibelalde, 2 vols. (Barcelona: Iberia, 1966); William Prescott, *The Conquest of Mexico: With a Preliminary View of Ancient Mexican Civilization, and the Life of the Conqueror Hernando*

Cortés, 2 vols. (New York: Harper, 1843); Hugh Thomas, *The Conquest of Mexico* (London: Hutchinson, 1993).

13. Michel-Rolph Trouillot, *Silencing the Past: Power and the Production of History* (Boston: Beacon, 1995); Matthew Restall, *Seven Myths of the Spanish Conquest* (New York: Oxford University Press, 2003), 16; Nancy van Deusen, "Indigenous Slavery's Archive in Seventeenth-Century Chile," *Hispanic American Historical Review* 101, no. 1 (2021): 2–4.

14. Out of their vast opus see, e.g., James Lockhart, Arthur Anderson, and Frances Berdan, eds., *Beyond the Codices: The Nahua View of Colonial Mexico* (Berkeley: University of California Press, 1976); or Miguel León-Portilla, *The Broken Spears: The Aztec Account of the Conquest of Mexico* (Boston: Beacon, extended and rev. ed. 2009). For one of the latest books on Nahuatl hieroglyphs, see Gordon Whittaker, *Deciphering Aztec Hieroglyphs: A Guide to Nahuatl Writing* (Berkeley: University of California Press, 2021); or on Nahuatl loans, see Justyna Olko et al., eds., *Loans in Colonial and Modern Nahuatl: A Contextual Dictionary* (Berlin: De Gruyter, 2020). Stephanie Wood has led the creation of an online Nahuatl dictionary and Laura Matthew that of a repository for Nahua-related colonial documents. Accessed October 23, 2023. https://nahuatl.uoregon.edu; and http://nahuatl-nawat.org.

15. Matthew Restall, "A History of the New Philology and the New Philology in History," *Latin American Research Review* 38, no. 1 (2003): 113–34.

16. Nancy van Deusen has artfully described the Indigenous people's adaption of rhetoric in their petitions to the Spanish Crown. See Nancy van Deusen, *Global Indios: The Indigenous Struggle for Justice in Sixteenth-Century Spain* (Durham, NC: Duke University Press, 2015). See also the contributions in this volume by Castañeda de la Paz, Haskett, or Huber.

17. Rolena Adorno, *The Polemics of Possession in Spanish American Narrative* (New Haven, CT: Yale University Press, 2007), esp. 10–11; Cortés, *Cartas de relación*; Bernal Díaz del Castillo, *Historia verdadera de la conquista de la Nueva España*, with an introduction by Felipe Castro Gutiérrez (Mexico City: Editores Mexicanos Unidos, 2005; orig. pub. 1632).

18. I have similarly articulated the arguments of this paragraph in Vitus Huber, *Die Konquistadoren: Cortés, Pizarro und die Eroberung Amerikas* (Munich: C. H. Beck, 2019), 115–16.

19. For the latter style, see lately David Carballo, *Collision of Worlds: A Deep History of the Fall of Aztec Mexico and the Forging of New Spain* (New York: Oxford University Press, 2020); for the former, Fernando Cervantes, *Conquistadores: A New History* (London: Penguin Books, 2020).

20. Cf., e.g., two different approaches in the special issues of a Spanish and a Mexican journal: "Hernán Cortés: V Centenario de su llegada a México," *Revista de historia militar* 64, no. 2 (2020); versus "Nuevas miradas sobre la Conquista española: Sucesos, significados, efectos y controversias," *Antropología: Revista interdisciplinaria del INAH* 8 (2021). Cf., furthermore, the fifteen short biographies in the series *1521: Un atado de vidas* and other

numerous publications in relation to the *Conquista* of Mexico in the *Catálogo México 500: México 200* from the UNAM. accessed October 23, 2023, https://catalogomexico500.unam.mx; e.g., Alejandro Salafranca Vázquez, ed., *1521: La conquista de México en el arte* (Mexico City: Publicaciones & Fomento, 2020); or Ana Carolina Ibarra and Pedro Marañón Hernández, eds., *1519: Los europeos en Mesoamérica*, Colección México 500 (Mexico City: Publicaciones & Fomento, 2021).

21. For a rather hagiographic approach on Cortés, see José Ángel Carretero Calero and Tomás García Muñoz, eds., *Hernán Cortés en el siglo XXI: V centenario de la llegada de Corté* (Medellín: Fundación Academia Europea e Iberoamericana de Yuste, 2020); for a more critical one, see Felix Hinz and Xavier López Medellín, eds., *Hernán Cortés revisado: 500 años de conquista española de México (1521–2021)* (Madrid: Iberoamericana-Vervuert, 2021). A reedition of his biography from 2010 provides Esteban Mira Caballos, *Hernán Cortés: Una biografía para el siglo XXI* (Barcelona: Crítica, 2021). See, furthermore, Martín Ríos Saloma, ed., *Conquistas: Actores, escenarios y reflexiones: Nueva España (1519–1550)* (Madrid: Sílex Ediciones, 2021); or Stefan Rinke, *Conquistadors and Aztecs: A History of the Fall of Tenochtitlan* (Oxford: Oxford University Press, 2023).

22. Some of the latest exceptions here are Camilla Townsend, who discusses the *Conquista* thoroughly: Camilla Townsend, *Fifth Sun: A New History of the Aztecs* (Oxford: Oxford University Press, 2020); and Obregón Cervera and Antonio Marco, "Conquistadores indígenas: Planteamientos tácticos y armamento durante la conquista de México," special issue: "Hernán Cortés: V Centenario de su llegada a México," *Revista de historia militar* 64, no. 2 (2020): 89–114. For a focus on multiple aspects, see Frances Berdan and Michael Smith, *Everyday Life in the Aztec World* (Cambridge: Cambridge University Press, 2020); and Frances Berdan, *The Aztecs: Lost Civilizations* (London: Reaktion Books, 2021).

23. It was first edited in 2005 and almost simultaneously again in 2013 and 2014: Rodrigo Martínez Baracs, "El primer documento conocido escrito en México por los conquistadores españoles," *Cartones y cosas vistas* 60 (2005): 113–23; María del Carmen Martínez Martínez, *Veracruz 1519: Los hombres de Cortés* (León: Universidad de León, 2013); John F. Schwaller and Helen Nader, *The First Letter from New Spain: The Lost Petition of Cortés and His Company, June 20, 1519* (Austin: University of Texas Press, 2014).

24. Jonas Schirrmacher, *Die politik der sklaverei: Praxis und konflikt in Kastilien und Spanisch-Amerika im 16. jahrhundert* (Paderborn, Germany: Ferdinand Schöningh, 2018); Erin Stone, *Captives of Conquest: Slavery in the Early Modern Spanish Caribbean* (Philadelphia: University of Pennsylvania Press, 2021).

25. Vitus Huber, *Beute und Conquista: Die politische ökonomie der eroberung Neuspaniens* (Frankfurt: Campus, 2018); Vitus Huber, "The Spiral of Spoils: Booty, Distributive Justice, and Empire Formation in the *Conquista* of Mexico," *Colonial Latin American Review* 31, no. 1 (2022), 133–57.

Part I

Semantics and Effects

1

The Language of "Conquest" in Colonial Nahuatl Manuscripts

STEPHANIE WOOD

> Survivance is an active sense of presence, the continuance of native stories, not a mere reaction, or a survivable name. Native survivance stories are renunciations of dominance, tragedy, and victimry.
> —GERALD VIZENOR (ANISHINAABE), *MANIFEST MANNERS* (1999)

In recent years, a few scholars have called out for transcending the word "conquest" to describe what happened in Mexico in the early sixteenth century. Historian Susan Schroeder decried "the conquest as loser history."[1] More attention to this recent approach is warranted, and in this moment of observing 500 years of history, the timing is propitious. The new approach is *not* an apology for colonialism—far from it. It can recognize violence, death, and the injustice of invasive settlement and imperialism without deleting or minimizing Native resistance and survival (or the more proactive, "survivance"). It can support the approach of Gerald Vizenor, who, in concert with a number of scholars who have studied the Mesoamerican experience of and response to supposed "conquest," favors narratives that uncover the active presence and agency of Indigenous communities, concerned that tales of victimhood only reify that status. Indeed, reading the words of Indigenous historians provides important material for reassessing the view of a cataclysmic and massively destructive invasion and colonization of Mexico by the Spaniards, showing that the original pueblos of New Spain were able to transcend that vision.[2] Outdated perspectives, including even the expression "conquest" itself, exaggerate the powerful role of the leaders of the Spanish expeditions and leave the impression that the Indigenous people and their cultures were fully destroyed (in the worst of cases) or that those who were not killed were fully subjugated and converted into passive victims (in the "best" of cases).

After more than a generation of research in Mexican archives and abroad—and the probing of thousands of manuscripts from between approximately 1540 and 1820 and written in Indigenous languages—scholars have been clarifying the important participation of Indigenous peoples in giving shape to the realities of New Spain. This more active role would lead to the preservation of a certain measure of political autonomy in their local town councils (cabildos)[3] and some powerful social and cultural continuities[4]—such as a vitality in their agricultural methods, their cuisine, their dress, their natural medicines, and their religious beliefs and practices, among many more ways of knowing.

Regarding Indigenous points of view in the transcending of "conquest," one place to begin is with the way survivors and their descendants looked upon the Spanish invasion and colonization enterprise. Indigenous narratives of the Spanish conquest of Mexico, translated into English and other languages, have been global bestsellers. Miguel León-Portilla's *Visión de los vencidos* ("Vision of the Vanquished" or *Broken Spears*), first published in 1959, has been translated into English, German, French, Polish, Catalan, and Otomí, and it has been a staple of college Mexican history courses for two generations.[5] James Lockhart's *We People Here: Nahuatl Accounts of the Conquest of Mexico* (1994), offers valuable alternative translations of some of the same sources, such as Book 12 of the *Florentine Codex*. Such publications of "indigenous perceptions of the wars, sometimes based on analysis of accounts in Mesoamerican languages," represent a prominent strain in what Matthew Restall terms "New Conquest History." This is a growing body of revisionist scholarship, fed to a notable extent by both Lockhart and some of his former students, including Restall himself. This new direction in historiography challenges the "traditional triumphalist narrative of the invasion wars," as Restall notes, not only elevating Native perspectives but giving "increased attention to the experience of black conquistadors," women, and Indigenous allies. It also revisits Spanish sources with a more critical eye.[6]

The project at hand strives to contribute to New Conquest History by employing an ethnohistorical method of text analysis with a focus on Indigenous-language manuscripts. The aim is to track about a dozen words relating to themes of war, including terms for conquest, in the Nahuatl language. It seeks to understand Nahua forms of expression when reflecting on the upheaval that came with the Spanish invasion and colonization of what was the Mexica realm of influence and beyond. Nahuatl was the lingua franca among Indigenous languages in colonial

Mexico, and the one for which we have the greatest number of known, surviving manuscripts. A close examination of the vocabulary for war, and its particular expression "conquest," may provide insight into ways the Nahuas might have reflected on their relative situation as both conquerors of other Indigenous groups[7] and as a people supposedly vanquished by the Spanish, if they entertained such a view of themselves at all.

The Nahuatl terms relating to warfare under investigation here come from quotidian documents as well as from historical narratives, such as annals and primordial titles. Typical of the New Philological approach, this cataloguing and cross-examination of the language of war among Nahuas includes not only a consideration of genre but also close attention to context and the varying shades of meaning that we might identify with a given time or place.[8] Studying the meaning of terms in an Indigenous language such as Nahuatl and trying to understand Indigenous perspectives are endeavors complicated by the fact that European influences found their way into Native texts, and all alphabetic texts are post-contact. Thus, if we seek to understand Nahua conceptualizations of war and conquest through their own language, we must be on the lookout for potential neologisms, calques, and other evidence of adopted/adapted ideas and expressions.[9] We must also survey a broad range of sources, casting as wide a net as possible, and we must be wary of translations that distort Nahua expressions through a European or European-American lens.

This intensive, ethnohistorical research has reached the point where some scholars have begun calling the events launched in 1519 the "invasion and colonization" in lieu of "conquest." This type of reformulation opens the door to Native points of view and the mechanisms for cultural conservation. Exploitation, degradation, and losses were real, and the epidemics decimated the population, which no one wishes to deny, but the documents in Indigenous languages reveal notable examples of vivacity and lasting continuities in the face of these serious obstacles. A history that recognizes the stamina and creativity of the *pueblos originarios* can be a more just and balanced history.

In her book *The Conquest All Over Again*,[10] Susan Schroeder mentions that the Spanish Word *conquista* was "never used by the Nahuas"—although, later, she admits its use in primordial titles (late-colonial manuscripts).[11] Schroeder notes that the transitive verb *pehua*—in Nahuatl—had preference in the annals for speaking about the conflicts initiated by the Spanish invasion. *Pehua* was the historical term, the familiar and the preferred term, and it sufficed for this discussion. Furthermore, for Schroeder, *pehua* could imply a profound loss of people and property and yet not be "the Armageddon suggested by the Spanish when they referred to the fall of Tenochtitlan."[12]

Despite this new interpretation, which demonstrated the need to reevaluate the language for speaking of the "conquest," Schroeder still translated *pehua* as "to conquer," something worthy of revisiting, along with my own earlier translation of *tlalmaceuhqui* as "conqueror." It is relevant to reexamine the use of terms and translations that many historians have employed when considering the seizure of power in 1521, language that continues to have important implications up to the present day.

PEHUA/TEPEHUA/TEPEHUALIZTLI

The word most often used in Nahua vocabulary of the sixteenth century—and most often translated as "conquest," or *conquista*—is *tepehualiztli*.[13] Alonso de Molina translated *tepehualiztli* as "conquista o vencimiento de los enemigos" (conquest or the overcoming of the enemy).[14] But, one may ask, is *conquista* an accurate equivalent? The term *tepehualiztli* has at its root *pehua*, and the intransitive of *pehua* means "to start" or "to begin." The transitive of *pehua*, according to the linguist Frances Karttunen, is something akin to "to start at someone," or in other words, to "provoke."[15] This idea to provoke coincides with *tepehualtiani* (the person who practices *tepehua*),[16] which Molina translates as a "provocador o principiador de bregas y contiendas" (a provocateur or initiator of quarrels and disputes). Although clearly, and with reason, one sees aggression in these root words, it is a huge jump from there to arrive at "conquest," "conquer," and "conqueror" based on the Nahua terminology. Might it be that Molina was injecting his own interpretation, emphasizing something more aggressive and destructive with *conquistar* than what *pehua* pretends? Or perhaps Molina had a way of thinking about conquest that was somewhat less destructive than what many imagine today.

The *Codex Mendoza*, an impressive pictorial manuscript in the Nahua tradition possibly made in 1541 (but no later than 1553), provides an accounting of the extensions of the pre-contact Mexica tributary realm and the tributes in kind and labor that were extracted from the affected pueblos. The *Codex* includes more than 200 hieroglyphs of what the glosses and texts explain to be *tepehualiztli*, the specific word in the Mendoza referencing the conquests of pueblos such as Tehuantepec, Coyolapan, Iztactlalocan, Huipillan, and Xiuhhuacan.[17] In Figure 1.1, temples (symbolizing the towns) have been set afire and are tipping over.[18] While presenting this inventory of towns that have been defeated by the Mexicah in pre-Hispanic times, the *Codex* goes on to dedicate twice that amount of space to describe the tributes extracted from these same towns in the wake of those attacks.[19] The significant implication is that if the townspeople were paying tributes, they were surviving. They may have been defeated militarily, but they could not have been destroyed. They were folded into the empire for their productive value.

Figure 1.1. *Codex Mendoza*, details showing *tepehualiztli* glyph, folio 6r. Bodleian Libraries, University of Oxford, MS. Arch. Selden. A. 1.

From the point of view of the Spaniards in the sixteenth century, they saw the Mexica dominion as something that confirmed their own objectives in desiring to create an empire: a demonstration of power and domination, followed by the acquisition of laborers, the extraction of tributes in kind, and, about a century or more later on, the accumulation of supposed "vacant lands," all the while leaving intact many preexisting structures that helped facilitate economic extraction. Contrary to the Black Legend emphasized by British observers of Spanish colonialism, complete destruction was not the Spaniards' desire, because if it were, the colonists would not have been able to extract labor and goods from their new subjects. Granted, epidemic diseases would reduce that colonized population and cause immeasurable hardship in the people's provisioning of tribute goods and labor to the colonizers. But a critical mass survived, and more than that, the people practiced survivance: active responses to colonization.

Perhaps in the thinking of Alonso de Molina, the provocation to war (with the intent of defeating other towns and then bringing them into the empire) was the "conquest" that *tepehualiztli* implied, and not a total erasure of peoples. But the self-satisfied narratives of power, audacity, and genius written by the invaders have shaped history and the meaning of terms. With the passage of decades and centuries, history has given a privileged place to the chronicles of the Spanish "conquerors," as they called themselves. This has contributed to the evolution of the term "conquest," generally impregnating the thought and the language of the early-modern world and beyond, even affecting the minds and language of the Nahuas over time.

The anthology *Vision of the Vanquished*, or *Broken Spears*, with its collection of early texts translated from Nahuatl, for sixty years now has left its global audience of readers with a focus on the flashpoint of contact and confrontation—at the expense of later testimonies and provincial perspectives. This is true too of Book 12 of the famous *Florentine Codex* (a major source for *Broken Spears*), showing the dramatic Spanish advance, battles, and betrayals leading up to the seizure of power, but leaving us without much of a sense of the *longue durée* of colonialism or its more nuanced impact on Native communities that lived on within the emerging "New Spain"—so called despite the colonizers still being in the minority by the time the yoke of Spanish colonialism was thrown off. Lockhart has estimated that people with a Spanish ethnicity comprised less than 20 percent of the Mexican population in 1810.[20]

TEOATL TLACHINOLLI / ATL TLACHINOLLI

The Nahuas had a rich metaphor for speaking of devastation, which was *teoatl tlachinolli* or, more simply, *atl tlachinolli*, both expressions sometimes translated as "flood and conflagration." But Alonso de Molina translates *atl tlachinolli* as "batalla o guerra," battle or war, given the absence of the *teo-* (which adds a divine aspect to the water). One finds "flood and conflagration" to be widespread in Old World beliefs about potential apocalyptic expressions of God's judgment, which raises the specter of European influences in sixteenth-century texts. The *Florentine Codex*, produced under a friar's supervision, uses *teoatl tlachinolli*, the more religious phrase.[21] Despite these possible influences, early carvings of atl tlachinolli support that it was a pre-contact concept. These carvings include a carved drum from Malinalco and a stone bas-relief associated with the founding of Mexico Tenochtitlan (in the National Museum of Anthropology and History).[22] In these two examples, the symbols for water and fire take the form of speech scrolls emerging from a jaguar and an eagle, suggesting the interpretation of their being war cries, which takes us back to Molina's sixteenth-century definition.

We must proceed carefully to grasp the full implications of these metaphors as they may have been perceived by Nahuas. If we consider the context and the history of Mexico, we recall how the capital city was originally built on lakes and suffered from periodic floods (see figure 1.2). Over the years, dikes and sluices were built with the intention not only to separate saline from fresh water but also to try to control flooding.[23] The specter of flooding could cause great apprehension.

Just as the Nahuas knew floods, we can assume that they also knew the potential devastation of fire, given the pictorial representation of their attacks on the many towns or city-states they would bring into their tributary domain as a temple burning and tipping over, pictured in the *Codex Mendoza*. The concept of "scorched earth" warfare may capture something of the *tlachinolli* component of the metaphor atl or teoatl tlachinolli. David Wright Carr points out that the root of *tlachinolli* is *ichinoa*, which Alonso Urbano translated in the early seventeenth century as "quemar los campos o montes" (to burn the fields or woods). Such controlled burning was practiced by Native peoples in many parts of North America, but it could be something very different when it was not intentional and when it got out

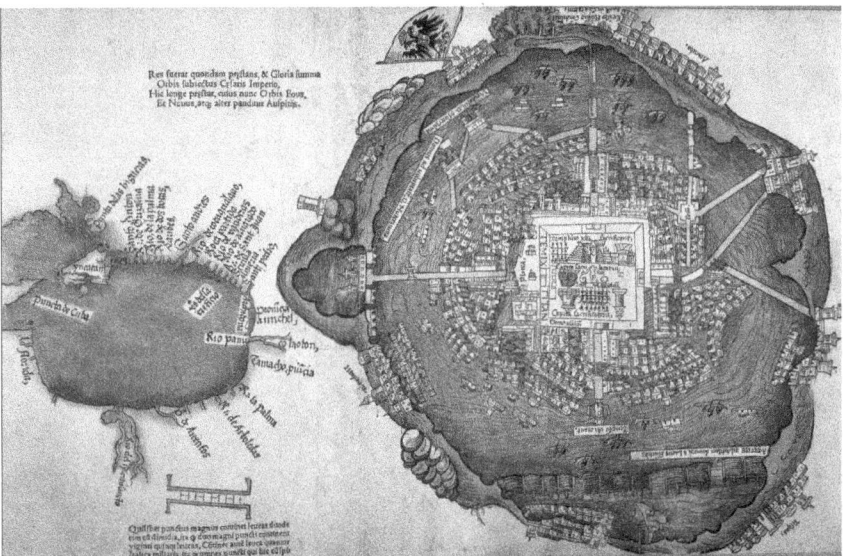

Figure 1.2. Mexico-Tenochtitlan Map, ca. 1524, from Nuremberg. Courtesy of Wikimedia Commons.

Figure 1.3. The *tlalli* (agricultural land) element of the Teotlalpan compound hieroglyph. *Codex Mendoza*, folio 51r, The Bodleian Libraries, University of Oxford, MS. Arch. Selden. A. 1.

of control. Wright also recognizes the sideways *u* shapes on the tlachinolli visual in the hieroglyph for the metaphor, the same ones that appear on glyphs for cultivated lands (see figure 1.3), concluding that the fields of the metaphor of scorched earth were agricultural.[24] This represents a specter of a much greater threat to human life, not just to combatants but also for elders, women, and children, who could perish from hunger if cultivated fields were burned in war.[25]

The atl tlachinolli (flood, conflagration) metaphor conjures up a situation that could put the Nahuas on the brink of apocalypse, requiring their diligent attention to serving their deities and maintaining a balance at home. It could also represent a war waged against distant provinces to bring new peoples into the expanding empire. At this point, the flood and conflagration of this Nahua metaphor for war do not appear greatly different from European imperial aggression, but the pairing of fire and water symbols reaches back to at least Teotihuacan, such as on the murals of Totometla, where it is further associated with the birds and butterflies that would accompany warriors in their afterlife.[26] Despite these early roots, one has yet to find Nahua historical narratives that reach forward in time and employ the expression in relation to the Spanish invasion and seizure of power in Mexico.

YAOTL/YAOYOTL

Going beyond metaphors, one seeks a more direct way of saying "war" in Nahuatl. The best documented terminology involves variations on *yaotl* (enemy, hostilities, battle, and, in compounds, war) and *yaoyotl* (the practice or inherent nature of yaotl, i.e., war, warfare, battles, or fighting). Such vocabulary and its usage illuminate how Nahua authors elucidated a wide range of conflict. One may also draw substantiation from this language for the metaphors already mentioned. For example, in Sahagún's *Primeros memoriales*, the word *yaoc* (in war) is equated with *in teoatl in tlachinolli*.[27]

Vocabulary with a *yao-* root is extensive in Molina's lexicon of 1571.[28] On folio 31 recto, for example, the following terms appear (with my added English translations of Molina's Spanish):

yaoana, "captivar en guerra" (to capture in war; or literally to "enemy-take")

yaoc niloti, "retirarse en la guerra" (to retreat in war)

yaoc nitlayecoa, "batallar, o pelear fuertemente en la guerra" (to battle or fight strongly in war)

yaocalli, "fusta artillada, o cosa assi para pelear en la mar; fortaleza, el edificio" (a gunboat with artillery, or the like, for fighting by sea; a fort, a building)

yaoitacatl, "victuallas, o mantenimiento para la guerra" (victuals or the sustenance for wars)

yaoimati, "ser diestro y entendido en las cosas de la guerra" (to be skillful and educated or knowledgeable in the things of war)

This is but a fraction of the *yao* word list in Molina's vocabulary. One is hard pressed to find anything particularly Nahua in the list. Many of the concepts represented could pertain to a universal practice of war—any time, any place. Indeed, some may be translations of Spanish words, such as the gunboat with artillery, called literally "war-house."

If we turn to manuscript attestations and beginning with searches in sixteenth-century Nahuatl texts for terms involving the root -*yao*- that would clarify cultural differences regarding war, nothing definitive immediately meets the eye. Sahagún's *Primeros memoriales* make it clear that, in pre-Hispanic times, Nahua warriors had to go to war and be brave and valiant captains in *yaoyotl*.[29] In Sahagún's *Florentine Codex* we learn that Moteuczoma rewarded "all the seasoned warriors, who had entered the field of battle" (with both warriors and battle having the -*yao*- element).[30]

Showing a lasting preference for the *yao* terminology into the seventeenth century, Chimalpahin refers to a thwarted rebellion (*yaoyotl*) against the Crown by Spaniards.[31] Another seventeenth-century Nahua annalist, from the Tlaxcala-Puebla Valley, recalled how secular priests (Spaniards) "armed themselves for war" (*omoyaochichiuhqueh*) with "swords, daggers, and carbines."[32] Afro-Mexicans could also threaten rebellion (*yaoyotl*), according to this same annalist.[33]

Yet another Tlaxcalan annalist, Juan Buenaventura Zapata y Mendoza, writing in Nahuatl later in the seventeenth century, speaks of Spaniards who went to the coast to exercise a military vigilance (*yaotlapialoto*). Zapata y Mendoza further describes a "true war" between Nahuas and Spaniards, the former throwing stones and the latter getting out their swords.[34] Stone throwing was common in Nahua riots, and small uprisings relating to town boundaries that occurred all through the Spanish colonial period.[35] The use of "true" war raises the specter of a possible division in Nahua thinking between battles with destructive intent versus perhaps ritual battles.[36]

The *tlacuilo* (scribe) of Huejotzingo (Huexotzinco) actually paired the verb *tepehua* (to provoke) with *yaochihua* (to make war), which suggests a war-like provocation. This was in the famous letter to the king of Spain written in 1560 about the help the Huexotzinca gave to the Spaniards in the creation of the empire called New Spain. In the translation made by Lockhart, the reader will find "to conquer" and "conquests" where "to provoke" and "attacks" could easily serve, as shown in the following quote:

> "ça ce yn ya ic nica nueva España in tepeuhque in teyaochiuhque inic quitzonquixtique in intepevaliz ayc tiquintlalcavique amo no itla tiquimitlacalhuique in inyaotiliz yn manel tiçeme yc ticpololoque" (all over New Spain here where they [the Spaniards] *conquered* and made war until they finished their *conquests*, we never abandoned them, nor did we do anything detracting from their war making, though some of us were destroyed in it).[37]

The letter was definitely referring back to the Spanish invasion and seizure of power (with the help of allies), which may explain Lockhart's choices in the translations, but descriptions of war making would actually have sufficed. This is an example where the language of "conquest" has become imbedded in historians' thinking, conditioning its use to discuss warfare in that particular time frame.

POLOA/POLIHUI/TLALPOLOA/TLALPOLOANI

The Huexotzinco tlacuilo also uses the verb *poloa* in the passive voice, first-person plural in this passage. For *poloa* Molina gives "perder o destruir," which in the tlacuilo's conjugation would be "we were lost or destroyed." Another example, from 1552, connects *poloa* to losses relating to something akin to *atl tlachinolli*: "Perhaps his house burned [down] or perhaps fertile lands came to an end, if the river took his property away, so that he lost what he made a living with."³⁸ It is reasonable to recognize that there are losses and destruction in war, and that individuals will perish, without concluding that there was an apocalypse, as Schroeder noted. The Huexotzinca scribe wanted to infuse an empathy in his readers when writing about some of the losses incurred in that period. It is also important to remember that he was petitioning for privileges on behalf of the many survivors—new subjects of the Crown—for having fought on the side of the Spanish invaders. A recognition of their capacity for recuperation changes the panorama considerably in the new evaluation of "conquest."

The use of *poloa* as a transitive verb also appears in documents of Nahua authorship. Molina gives "destruir a otros con guerra o conquistarlos" (to destroy others with war or conquer them). Frances Karttunen offers an alternative, saying that *poloa* is understood as "to destroy, squander, or spend something, to lay waste something or someone."³⁹ An example from a manuscript could be where the *Historia Tolteca-Chichimeca* quotes, "Yeuatl quimati quenin techonpoloz" ("¡Él sabe cómo nos destruirá!," or, "He knows how he will destroy us!").⁴⁰ But writers typically preferred other forms of *poloa* in reference to losses and destruction in war.

In some seventeenth-century annals left by a Tlaxcalteca tlacuilo, the defeat of the Mexicah is described using a plural, third-person preterit conjugation of the intransitive *polihui* ("perecer o desaparecer"—to perish or to disappear—according to Molina). The sentence is "1521 3 Calli xihuitli yhquac poliuhque Mexica" (1521 3 House year. At this time the Mexicah were defeated). Perhaps this Indigenous Spanish ally also wished to exaggerate the achievement of Tlaxcala, because, of course, many Mexicah died but not everyone disappeared. Furthermore, in the following phrase the scribe mentions how "yhquac tlalpolo marques," and Camila Townsend translates this as "At this time the Marqués [i.e., Hernando Cortés] conquered the land."⁴¹ But, literally, one could say that Cortés caused the Mexicah to lose land (*tlalpoloa*). The *Codex Cozcatzin* also uses *tlalpoloa* to discuss military defeat: "Ca zan achto yn ocan tocac tonatiuh yn oquinpopolo tlatilulca otlalpoloto" ("Hasta entonces no [se había] visto, solo apareció el sol cuando ya [Axayácatl] había vencido y derrotado a los tlatelolcas," or "The sun was not seen until then, it only appeared after [Axayacatl] had overcome and defeated the Tlatelolca").[42] Two forms of *poloa* appear in this sentence, in fact: *popoloa* (which Molina translates as "to destroy through combat") and *tlalpoloa* (destroy the land).[43] The fact of making an enemy lose lands has serious consequences, but it was not necessarily apocalyptic. The Tlatelolcah were still clearly present in the capital after their defeat by Axayacatl in 1473; they had become payers of tributes and provisioners of labor to Tenochtitlan.[44]

The term *tlalpoloani* (literally, one who makes others lose land) appears in Book 10 of the *Florentine Codex*, translated by Anderson and Dibble as "conqueror,"[45] again showing how easily US historians embraced the Spanish terminology for the seizure of power in Mexico. In other documents one will find *tlalpoloa* used in association with Cortés and *tlalpoloani* with Moteuczoma, making them flip sides of a coin. For *tlalpoloani*, Molina gives "conquistador o un asolador" (a conqueror, or one who causes devastation). It is interesting that, outside of these few examples, the term *tlalpoloani* is not very common in Nahuatl documents. The question arises as to whether it was a neologism or a type of calque that was utilized to say "conqueror" in Nahuatl. If so, that might suggest that a neat equivalent did not exist in the Indigenous language already or it was employed only rarely.

CONQUISTADOR/CONQUISTAR/CONQUISTA

The term *conquistador*—an indisputable loan in Nahuatl manuscripts—is much more common than *tlalpoloani*. One explanation could be that the calque *tlalpoloani* was not a good fit. Furthermore, Nahua notaries near the Spanish colonial settlements were more accustomed to hearing the word *conquistador*—such an ingrained part of the colonizers' vocabulary as they sought privileges related to their levels of investment of goods and aggression, recalled in their self-aggrandizing tales called *probanzas de méritos y servicios* (proofs of merits and service).[46] Such literature circulated about the so-called conquest, and the Nahua intellectuals were very familiar with the narratives. The *Historia tolteca-chichimeca* refers in Nahuatl to a "lipro [*sic*] de conquista" (book about the conquest) of fifty-two pages.[47]

At first, when Nahuas used *conquistador*, this was to speak only of Spaniards. Examples appear in the letter from Huexotzinco to the king (literally, the scribe wrote awkwardly: "conguitadores," "conguistadores").[48] In about 1582, annalist Juan Bautista recalled an imprisonment of judges, *conquistadorme* (a Nahuatlized plural), and many additional "honorable Spanish persons."⁴⁹ Chimalpahin used a double plural in recalling Spanish *conquistadoresme* when he took the loanword into his vocabulary. In his annals he writes: "Tlacat. nican tepiltzin. criyoyo mitohua yntech quiça yn pipiltin conquistadoresme" (the child of people here, called a *criollo*; he comes from the noble conquerors).⁵⁰ This creole was a Spaniard born in Mexico, descended from the earliest settlers. In another part of his annals, Chimalpahin mentions a "Mestiço conquistador."⁵¹ Thus, the term that was originally associated with Spaniards was evolving in the seventeenth century, hand in hand with the evolution of Mexican ethnicities.

Eventually, Nahuas began to refer to their own ancestors as "conquistadores," using the loanword for this new purpose. The earliest known example may be the use of the abbreviation "cōqstores. guatemaltecos" (Guatemalan conquerors) in a petition of 1572.⁵² In this example, some Caqchiquel petitioners of San Miguel Escobar were seeking a legal status akin to that of the Mexican and Tlaxcalan allies of the Spanish settlers there.⁵³ Apparently, those Indigenous allies from central Mexico were already calling themselves conquistadores, and some Caqchiqueles were envious of the privileges they had earned. Certainly, the Native allies were more numerous than the intruders, and they had played a role similar to that of the Spanish invader-occupiers. The flaunting of such involvement underscores how Indigenous individuals could choose the alliance with the foreign invaders as not only a means of survival but also a means to increase their authority and status and get their taxes reduced, embracing the opportunity for agency. Also, a Spaniard calling himself a conquistador and a Nahua taking on the same identifier could read different meanings into that term given their cultural differences.

Not only were Spanish chronicles becoming known but the language of "conquest" was becoming encoded in unique ways in the Nahua folklore of central Mexico in the process. We learn from the annalist Juan Buenaventura Zapata y Mendoza in the second half of the seventeenth century that the Spanish governor of Tlaxcala approved a renovation of a theatrical event he called "Yn Conquista" in Nahuatl ("La Conquista," or "The Conquest"). It was a reenactment of the arrival of Cortés and his welcome reception by the famous local "four *tlahtoque*" (Nahua rulers). Zapata y Mendoza recalls how the Spanish governor and his wife (and he knew both of their names) paid generously for those who organized the event.⁵⁴ Apparently, the Tlaxcaltecah and the foreign settlers alike enjoyed the drama and the mythification of the "conquest," helping imbed it in the vernacular. The highest authorities were probably gratified to see people they would consider their colonial subjects performing the events of 1519–21 in a celebratory way, while the Tlaxcalteca performers were imagining a different history, where the Spaniards actually *helped them* thwart their Mexica enemies.

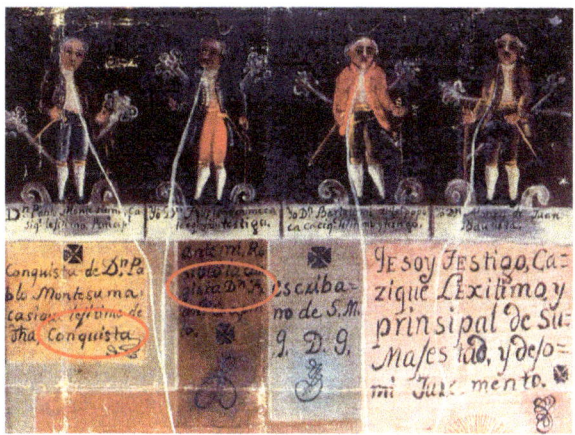

Figure 1.4. Part of the *Lienzo de Tepatlaxco*, with details showing *conquista*. Archivo General de la Nación, México, Tierras 3362, exp. 3, fol. 10.

Spanish loanwords relating to "conquest" can be found in pictorials such as *lienzos* and *mapas* and in late colonial (ca. post-1640) primordial titles in alphabetic Nahuatl. A testament from San Marcos Tlayacac, Morelos, dated "1546" (but seemingly no earlier than 1666, putting it right in the period of primordial title production), uses the expression "ypa coquista" (in the time of the conquest), showing an unusual consciousness of the evolving periodization.[55] Another example appears in a mapa originally created in 1671 but that exists today though only in a copy and translation made in 1801.[56] This pictorial comes from the pueblo called San Sebastián Tepatlaxco, a *sujeto* (attached, smaller community) of Tepeaca, Puebla. In the first place, the text mentions the "Rei de España Dⁿ. Luis de Velasco Carlos Quinto, *conquistador* Jeneral" (King of Spain, Don Luis de Velasco Carlos Quinto, Conqueror General), confusing the viceroy with the king. This reveals a typical haziness in Nahuatl texts that were looking back upon foreign powerholders.[57] Then, the author/artist mentions five caciques (Indigenous leaders)—but only four shown in portraits on the canvas—as "conquistadores q^e. conquistaron" (conquerors who conquered), employing an unnecessary redundancy.

The uncomfortable handling of the Spanish in the short texts on the painted scene in the mapa suggests that an Indigenous *nahuatlahto* probably translated the original Nahuatl into Spanish. The original texts hammer home the "conquering" role, exaggerating it to convince the audience that these ancestors clearly deserved any privileges they would receive. Note how, in the image in figure 1.4, they are dressed like Spaniards. They are all baptized, have Christian given names and the borrowed titles of nobility, "Don," but most still have Nahua names, too—Montesuma, Chichimeca, Xitlalpopoca, and Coapinto (preserving the spellings as given in 1801).

The Spanish noun *conquista* (conquest) and the verb *conquistar* (to conquer) found their way into additional Nahuatl-language narratives in the seventeenth century. The primordial titles of San Bartolomé Capulhuac (in the Valley of Toluca), for example, employed the Nahuatlized verb *conquistarhui* in recalling a friar of the sixteenth century, "can yehuatzin mohuicas quinmoconquistarhuis auh huel amo quinequisque" (who would come to conquer [the local people], and they will really not want it). According to this historical account and paraphrasing the Nahua *fundador* (town founder), the friar made multiple visits trying to win people over, but they were frightened away. The friar then recruited the Nahua founder to speak kindly to his people, explaining his words in Nahuatl and helping the evangelizer to convince them to accept the new faith. This narrative also recalls the founder helping the friar "destroy that which they [his people] had been worshiping," and it remembers his son assisting with "breaking up the gods [representations of pre-Hispanic divinities]," eventually winning the local folks over to Christianity.[58] In this Nahuatl account, these were the actions associated with the term "to conquer," showing how broadly the label could be applied. It became an etiquette implying any activity that would advance colonization, whether it involved destructive battles or cajoling.

The *amatlacuilolli* (literally, fig-bark paper writings, i.e., primordial titles) from Metepec (ca. 1640s) also make a reference to early Spanish colonial changes, involving the borrowed vintage language *conquisstacion y congregacion* (a "conquering" and a "congregation") in the Nahuatl narrative. Ironically, the local female Indigenous leader (called a *tzontecomatl*, head, and a widow), Doña Ana Cortés Acaxochitl, ordered these changes in "1526." In a gesture of appreciation from the local people, her subjects asked God that this *nantzintli* (revered mother) and town founder be blessed with a pregnancy. As with so many titles, the emphasis of this narrative is not on destruction but on the acceptance of Christianity, procreation, and the strengthening of the *altepetl* (Native pueblo or city-state), all of which came with a more concentrated settlement, the construction of a new temple, and the recognition of local leadership and authority.[59]

The fundador of Capulhuac and the tzontecomatl Doña Ana of Metepec were Indigenous allies to the colonizers, active in the advancement of Christianity, and described at least in part with the language of "conquest." Elsewhere in this volume, Robert Haskett provides the example of Don Zacarías as a Native "conquistador." Various books from recent years highlight this phenomenon too.[60] These numerous examples show how not only Spanish chronicles but also Nahuatl narratives were contributing to the solidification of the terminology of "conquest," simultaneously in the minds of the people and in the historical record, even while its cultural meanings and local interpretations could range widely.

TLALMACEHUA/TLALMACEUHQUI/ALTEPEMANQUI

In the second half of the Spanish colonial period—when the loanwords *conquista*, *conquistar*, and *conquistadores* appear with some frequency in Nahuatl texts—they nevertheless do so with lesser frequency than the terms *tlalmacehua* (to deserve land) and *tlalmaceuhqui* (one who wins land by being deserving). *Tlalmaceuhqueh*, in the plural, are literally "people deserving of land."[61] These vocabulary words may have also served as calques of the Spanish terminology of conquest, appearing where the reader might expect to see *conquistador* or—perhaps better yet—*fundador* (founder) and *poblador* (settler). The popularity of *tlalmaceuhqui* in place of the loanword *conquistador* may suggest a preference for the meaning of the term in Nahuatl, "to be deserving of land," which was more humble, appreciative, and productive than "conqueror," with its more aggressive and destructive behavioral associations.[62] While one has yet to see a direct relationship between these Nahua word choices and those of the colonizers, it is worth noting that Vitus Huber has detected a similar shift in the Spanish language, whereby Philip II preferred "pacificación y población" (pacification and population) over "conquista" and "conquistador" in a ruling of 1573.[63]

While Nahuas' land-deserving terminology might be expected in primordial titles, it can also be found a few times in the writings of Chimalpahin, from before the second half of the Spanish colonial period. For example, his annals include the use of *tlalmaceuhqui* in reference to a Chichimec king, Quahuitzatzin, who had a role in re-founding the Tolteca town of Tzaqualtitlan as Tenanco (in the Chalco area). Susan Schroeder translates the label as "conqueror."[64] Apparently it was an imperialistic move on the part of the Chichimec king, but the action was less one of destruction and more one of starting or creating something. Also, elsewhere Schroeder translates a reference by Chimalpahin to the "eighty-two years and two months" (but who's counting?) of the Spanish appearance: "Since they arrived in Mexico, coming to acquire the land" (*tlalmacehuaco*). Here, Chimalpahin (and Schroeder) may be intending something like "came to colonize the land," if not literally to be deserving of land (see figure 1.5). But Chimalpahin also writes about a friar who "went to get really settled and to acquire land there [in Xochimilco]" (using the conjugated verb, *tlalmacehuato*).[65] Again, he uses the term to speak about another Spaniard, one who could have been helping to colonize that community but not conquering it in a military sense.

In various attestations of *tlalmacehua* (to be deserving of land), there is an emphasis on *huehuetqueh* (ancestors) of pre-sedentary times becoming the earliest or "first" settlers of a community, establishing (sometimes using the verb *centlalia*) the altepetl, which may push the meaning more toward town founding than subjugating and colonizing someone else's town. A story about the very first people of

Figure 1.5. Primordial titles of Atlautla and Texinca (Chalco), detail of "totlalmaceuhcauh" (our land deserver), a Chichimeca lord, wearing a crown and a hide, and carrying a bow and arrow. Archivo General de la Nación, México, Tierras 1663, exp. 1. (This manuscript is dated "1606," but it is surely decades later than that, as suggested by the orthography and vocabulary.)

Jonacatepec (originally Xonacatepec), in Morelos, states that they "settled [here] and obtained land for the very first time."[66] Finally, it is worth mentioning that the similar late-colonial term *altepemanqueh* (town founders; see figure 1.6) may be a calque for *fundadores*, in Spanish, as it literally refers to the people who established (the verb here is *mana*) an altepetl. The term is also prominent in the Techialoyan group, where founders either appear as semi-sedentary hunters with bows and arrows (e.g., in the manuscript associated with Mimiapan) or robed sedentary leaders (e.g., in the manuscript associated with Texcalucan and Chichicaspa, originally Tetzcalocan and Chichicazpan?).[67]

Primordial titles from Zempoala (dated 1610 but surely from many decades later) refer to the acquisition of a house and territory that were bequeathed to the testator. The person credited with bringing these possessions into the community was "yn huey pili ça notachcocoltzin Yxtlixuchitl tlalmaceuhqui" (translated to Spanish as "nuestro bisabuelo, el gran señor Ixtlilxochitl, que lo conquistó y ganó," or, "our great-grandfather, the great lord Ixtlilxochitl, who conquered and won it"). Here, the translators of the colonial period (quoted by the editors of the publication) use the language of conquest, but they also add the concept of *ganar*, an age-old term from Iberia, the Spanish Caribbean, Mexico, and Peru, associated with winning or gaining ground. *Ganar* is closer to the Nahuatl verb *tlalmacehua*, but one can see the associations that led to the equation of conqueror with *tlalmaceuhqui*, as imperfect as that was. The testator also refers to his ancestors as *tlalmaceuhqueh*, saying that he makes his living from what they left him and that he had distributed some of the lands to his people so that they could pay tributes. He remembers one

Figure 1.6. Techialoyan manuscript associated with Texcalucan and Chichicaspa, details showing the *altepemanqueh* of neighboring Huixquilucan. The *Mapas Project*, ed. Stephanie Wood, University of Oregon.

of his ancestors, Don Diego de Mendoza Moteuczoma, for having come to deserve/win/acquire land (*omotlalmacehuilico*) and engender human beings (*omotlacaxinachotzino*), that is, populate the town.[68]

The Zempoala narrative has a similar orthography to the Techialoyan texts[69]—a subgroup of Nahua primordial titles, being more pictorial and painted on native fig-bark paper (*amatl*). Techialoyan manuscripts are also replete with the terms *tlalmaceuhqui* and *tlalmaceuhqueh*, people deserving of land. See figure 1.7 for details of a Techialoyan manuscript associated with Mimiahuapan (also known as Mimiapan), another Toluca valley town. Here, the ancestor of choice is "yn tlazo pili Acolnahuatl, tlalmazeuhqui," "the precious nobleman Acolnahuatl, land deserver" (perhaps intending Acolnahuacatl, a ruler of Azcapotzalco).[70] In this image he holds a *macuahuitl* (obsidian blade-studded club) and may have a feather on his head, emphasizing his life in pre-contact times.

In this context, memories of forebears, often of Chichimec heritage, can be hazy when recalled in the second half of the Spanish colonial period. What is known today as the "Map of Chichimec History," reproduced in the *Handbook of Middle American Indians* as a nineteenth-century copy, speaks of Chichimeca Nepopoalca tlalmaceuhqueh from the year 1466, without explaining what was meant by the term or what happened at that time.[71] Tlalmaceuhqueh are also mentioned in the annals associated with "Anónimo Mexicano" as living in the time of Xolotl, a thirteenth-century Chichimec ruler. The author pairs *tlalmaceuhqueh* with *tlalequeh* (land possessors) in a diphrasis, as though being equivalent terms, which sheds

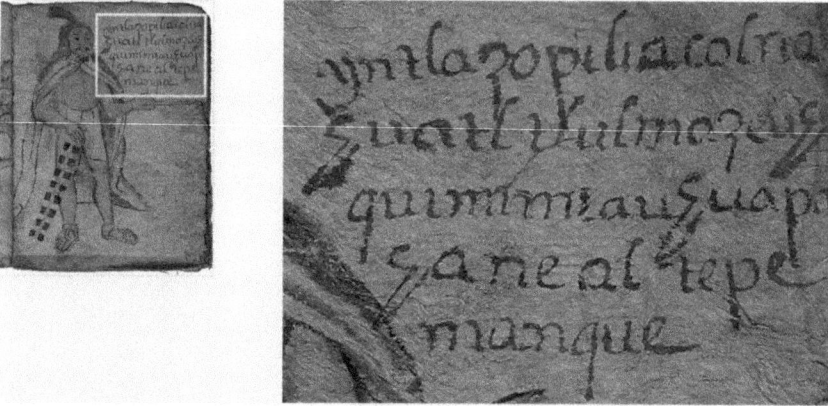

Figure 1.7. Techialoyan manuscript of Mimiahuapan, details showing *tlalmaceuhqui* term, folio 9r. The *Mapas Project*, ed. Stephanie Wood, University of Oregon.

some additional light on the meaning of this important concept.⁷² The now-lost original Nahuatl version of the "Fundación de Cuacuauzentlalpan" in the Chalco region, allegedly written by the grandsons of Xolotl, was translated to Spanish in 1930 and published in 1962. Lacking the original makes it difficult to know, but this narrative may have also used the same language as the author called Anónimo Mexicano, as there are various expressions using the Spanish verb *ganar* (*tlalmacehua*?) and references to "nosotros los poseedores de tierra" ("we the possessors of land," i.e., *tlalequeh*?).⁷³ Interestingly, the various terms relating to *tlalmacehua*, to be deserving of land, are rarely linked or paired with *tepehua* or *popoloa*.

Whether wielding loanwords, calques, or their own pre-contact language for war, Nahua writers do present a somewhat different picture of early sixteenth-century encounters than the image many modern-day observers of those events might imagine. Being in close contact with the Spanish language for centuries, Nahua authors both absorbed some foreign concepts and shared some of their own with the colonizers. The resulting colonization process in New Spain had a distinct Indigenous stamp upon it, as Spaniards leaned on Native allies, built their own veneer upon existing structures of the Aztec empire, followed Nahua patterns of tapping tributes and labor, replaced temples with churches, and overlooked many ancient practices and beliefs living on after contact. Indigenous towns were (re)founded with much pomp and circumstance, keeping local leaders in positions of authority, recognizing and marking towns' territorial extensions (ironically, "granting" land to them that was already theirs), and trying to uphold population density as epidemics ravaged these communities.⁷⁴

Outside of the narratives from the capital or from their principal allies, and beyond the flashpoint of contact, historical memories in Nahuatl of those early events only begin to abound after about 1640. From that point through the end of the Spanish colonial period was when workshops stepped up to provide Nahuatl-language textual and pictorial records—what we now call "primordial titles" and "Techialoyan manuscripts," along with lienzos, mapas, testaments, genealogies, and coats of arms—to individuals and towns that were actively working up to defend their positions. Having suffered terrible losses as a result of the epidemics and seeing the rise of the hacienda (large, landed estate) in their midst, town leaders recognized the dire need for documentation, not just to present in the courts but to provide a narrative for youth to use to protect their towns in the future. Survivance required a proactive approach to educating the future generations with stories about the important contributions of ancestors in the defense of community.

CONCLUSIONS

Early Nahua leaders—being viewed in retrospect from a later vantage point—are men and women who sometimes fought with the invaders and otherwise cooperated with some changes, securing their ability to represent and defend their towns. These ancestors are remembered as meritorious persons for winning lands for their pueblos, acting as town founders and populators. Narrators speak of them with pride and invest them with a communitarian consciousness (even if they were not always altruistic but also seeking an advantageous position for their own lineages). Techialoyan manuscripts, which use this language about ancestors especially liberally, and sometimes refer to leader's parcels, still emphasize group-held land.[75] Primordial titles do merge somewhat with cacique testaments, but even in such cases they show a strong concern for the well-being of their towns.[76] These late historical narratives undergird the concept of the strength and longevity of the altepetl. They reveal a depth of understanding about how to work the colonial system that was, nevertheless, alienating their pueblos' original territories and demanding onerous taxes and labor.

The result is that early ancestors were—far from being conquered by Spaniards—accommodating the intrusion of new overlords and their faith in exchange for having been allowed to (re)found their towns, build their churches, create their town councils, and see their minimum land bases measured and marked. Accepting the façade of a Spanish-style town on their pueblos (while still being Indigenous run), they could continue to maintain many of the original activities of the altepetl (agriculture, craft making, marketing, etc.), on at least part of their ancestral lands.

No one denies that the Nahuas created their own imperialist tributary domains. No one denies that they defeated other Indigenous communities in the process. And, clearly, they often remembered their own forebears as strong warriors who subjugated people while extending their hegemony. But the argument here is that there is no need to translate all their language of war into versions of the term "conquest" (an imported term), especially if one is to come to a moderated understanding of the term *conquista* in Spanish and "conquest" in English, at least in the context of the history of New Spain. While there are kernels of truth to the lore about Spanish and Indigenous conquistadores, the full story is much more nuanced. Like the legends of the battles between "cowboys and Indians" that supposedly wiped out all Native peoples of the US West, imaginings of the full obliteration of Nahuas in central Mexico erase important truths about resistance and accommodation.

Although the Nahuas began, little by little, to embrace the European language, they pushed back against it at the same time. They chose to spread the story of their forebears as more positive actors, people who could be recalled and leaned upon in the late-colonial struggle to defend the sovereignty of their pueblos' territories as Spanish colonists gained momentum in creating haciendas. Nahua authors after about 1650 (given the timing of demographic decimation, hacienda expansion, fading oral traditions, and the lack of sufficient documentation of claims) worked hard to harness the more positive and assertive memories in defense of their agricultural lands, pastures, and woodlands, plus the ongoing semiautonomous leadership that lived on for centuries. They chose narratives of pride about their Chichimec roots, about expanding their imperial reach, and then, after the Spanish invasion and occupation, upholding survivance over victimhood. These were anything but visions of the "vanquished."

NOTES

Epigraph: Gerald Vizenor, *Manifest Manners: Narratives on Postindian Survivance* (Lincoln: University of Nebraska Press, 1999), 7.

1. Susan Schroeder, "Introduction: The Genre of Conquest Studies," in *Indian Conquistadors: Indigenous Allies in the Conquest of Mesoamerica*, ed. Laura E. Matthew and Michel Oudijk (Norman: University of Oklahoma Press, 2007), 1–28, here 5.

2. See Stephanie Wood, *Transcending Conquest: Nahua Views of Spanish Colonial Mexico* (Norman: University of Oklahoma Press, 2003), 1–212, esp. x–xi, 21–22, and 142–43, for arguments against the use of the term "conquest." A few notable works (in order of their publication) are *Beyond the Codices: The Nahua View of Colonial Mexico*, ed. and trans. Arthur J. O. Anderson, Frances Berdan, and James Lockhart (Berkeley: University of

California Press, 1976), 1–290; James Lockhart, *Nahuas and Spaniards: Postconquest Central Mexican History and Philology* (Stanford, CA: Stanford University Press, 1991); James Lockhart, *The Nahuas after the Conquest: A Social and Cultural History of the Indians of Central Mexico: Sixteenth through Eighteenth Centuries* (Stanford, CA: Stanford University Press, 1992); and *We People Here: Nahuatl Accounts of the Conquest of Mexico*, ed. and trans. James Lockhart (Berkeley: University of California Press, 1993).

3. See, e.g., Robert Haskett, *Indigenous Rulers: An Ethnohistory of Town Government in Colonial Cuernavaca* (Albuquerque: University of New Mexico Press, 1991); and William F. Connell, *After Moctezuma: Indigenous Politics and Self-Government in Mexico City, 1524–1730* (Norman: University of Oklahoma Press, 2011). This latter study concludes that even in Mexico City, in the heart of the Spanish population of New Spain, "natives effectively created a political system based on native political traditions within a Spanish institutional structure" (186) and that this lasted until the end of the eighteenth century.

4. See, e.g., Caterina Pizzigoni, *Testaments of Toluca* (Stanford, CA: Stanford University Press, 2006), quote from page 45. And consider the conclusion reached by Camila Townsend in *Malintzin's Choices: An Indian Woman in the Conquest of Mexico* (Albuquerque: University of New Mexico Press, 2006), who writes that "Malintzin came from a long line of survivors, people who wrested their lives from the land in good years and bad" (212). Granted, Doña Marina lived in the epic moment of contact, but the instinct for survival was vitally strong even then and it would be long lasting in her ethnic group.

5. For a chart of the various editions, see http://en.wikipedia.org/wiki/The_Broken_Spears. See also John F. Schwaller's article "Broken Spears or Broken Bones: Evolution of the Most Famous Line in Nahuatl," *Americas* 66, no. 2 (2009): 241–54, for his elaboration on Lockhart's discovery of the misreading of *omitl* (bones) as *mitl* ("spear," which is actually better as "arrow").

6. Matthew Restall and Micaela Wiehe, "The New Conquest History and the New Philology in Colonial Mesoamerica," *Oxford Bibliographies*, August 2023, https://www.oxfordbibliographies.com/view/document/obo-9780199766581/obo-9780199766581-0113.xml; see also Matthew Restall, "The New Conquest History," *History Compass* 10, no. 2 (2012): 151–60.

7. Laura Matthew and Michel Oudijk, eds., *Indian Conquistadors: Indigenous Allies in the Conquest of Mesoamerica* (Norman: University of Oklahoma Press, 2007) provides a wealth of information on this phenomenon.

8. Restall and Martin, "The New Conquest."

9. See Thomas C. Smith-Stark, "Lexicography in New Spain (1492–1611)," in *Missionary Linguistics IV / Lingüística misionera: Lexicography*, ed. Otto Zwartjes, Ramón Arzápalo Marín, and Thomas C. Smith-Stark (Amsterdam: John Benjamins, 2009), 3–82, here 66–67.

10. Susan Schroeder, ed., *The Conquest All Over Again: Nahuas and Zapotecs Thinking, Writing and Painting Spanish Colonialism* (Brighton, UK: Sussex Academic Press, 2011).

11. One example of the term in a primordial title is located in Lisa Sousa and Kevin Terraciano, "The 'Original Conquest' of Oaxaca: Nahua and Mixtec Accounts of the Spanish Conquest," *Ethnohistory* 50, no. 2 (2005): 349–400.

12. Schroeder, *Conquest*, 104.

13. This evaluation of the popularity of certain words derives from a close examination of the attestations of their use found in the *Online Nahuatl Dictionary*, ed. Stephanie Wood (Eugene: Wired Humanities Projects, University of Oregon, 2000–present), accessed May 1, 2023, https://nahuatl.wired-humanities.org.

14. Alonso de Molina, *Vocabulario en lengua castellana y mexicana y mexicana y castellana* (Mexico City: Antonio de Spinosa, 1571), pt. 2: Nahuatl to Spanish, fol. 102v, col. 2. The English is my translation.

15. Personal communication, May 24, 2014.

16. In bk. 12 of the *Florentine Codex*, one will see the use of "tepehua" (*ontepevaloia cana*), speaking of some conquest in a place as yet to be identified. See the translation made by Lockhart, published in the *Early Nahuatl Library*, ed. Stephanie Wood (Eugene: Wired Humanities Projects, University of Oregon, 2000–2018), accessed May 1, 2023, https://enl.wired-humanities.org/fcbk12ch41/elements/fcbk12ch41f86v/00.

17. Antonio Perri, *Il Codex Mendoza e le due paleografie* (Bologna: Ed. CLUEB, 1994), 300–303.

18. *Codex Mendoza: Mexican Pictorial Manuscript, MS. Arch. Selden. A. 1* (Oxford: Bodleian Library, Digital Bodleian, Oxford University, 2018), https://digital.bodleian.ox.ac.uk/objects/2fea788e-2aa2-4f08-b6d9-648c00486220/surfaces/68210492-1fd1-499e-acee-188fa1226ca1/.

19. Daniela Bleichmar, "Painting the Aztec Past in Early Colonial Mexico: Translation and Knowledge Production in the Codex Mendoza," *Renaissance Quarterly* 72, no. 4 (2019): 1362–1415, here 1370.

20. James Lockhart and Stuart B. Schwartz, *Early Latin America: A History of Colonial Spanish America and Brazil* (Cambridge: Cambridge University Press, 1984), 320.

21. Anderson and Dibble translate *teoatl tlachinolli* in bk. 6 of the *Florentine Codex* as "divine liquid, fire." This is quoted in Willard Gingerich, "Heidegger and the Aztecs: The Poetics of Knowing in Pre-Hispanic Nahuatl Poetry," in *Recovering the Word: Essays on Native American Literature*, ed. Brian Swann and Arnold Krupat (Berkeley: University of California Press, 1987), 85–112, here 95. For discussions of Old World expressions, see, e.g., Rodney R. Hutton, *Fortress Introduction to the Prophets* (Minneapolis: Fortress Press, 2004), 55–56. Furthermore, Psalm 29:10 refers to the flood waters (http://biblehub.com/psalms/29-10.htm) and Isaiah 66:16 refers to the Lord punishing the world by fire (http://biblehub.com/isaiah/66-16.htm). The English Baptist and biblical scholar John Gill (1697–1771) put them together in his "Exposition of the New Testament" (http://biblehub.com/2_peter/3-7.htm, all accessed May 1, 2023), saying that the Lord would bring a "flood of fire."

22. See Ian Mursell, "Was the Mexica War Cry 'atl tlachinolli'?" *Mexicolore*, accessed May 1, 2023 https://www.mexicolore.co.uk/aztecs/ask-us/was-atl-tlachinolli-the-mexica-war-cry.

23. See, e.g., a reference to Mexico City being flooded during the reign of Ahuitzotl. Fray Bernardino de Sahagún, *Florentine Codex: General History of the Things of New Spain*, ed. and trans. Arthur J. O. Anderson and Charles E. Dibble (Santa Fe and Salt Lake City: School of American Research and the University of Utah, 1951), bk. 8, no. 14, pt. IX, 2. We also see a reference to floods in Mexico City in 1499 in Don Domingo de San Antón Muñón Chimalpahin Quauhtlehuanitzin, *Annals of His Time: Don Domingo de San Antón Muñón Chimalpahin Quauhtlehuanitzin*, ed. and trans. James Lockhart, Susan Schroeder, and Doris Namala (Stanford, CA: Stanford University Press, 2006), 130–31.

24. See Wright Carr, "Teoatl tlachinolli: Una metáfora marcial del centro de México," *Dimensión Antropológica* 19, no. 55 (2012): 11–37. In the *Codex Mendoza* (passim), this same element with dots and *u*'s also appears in place-names that have *milli* (field), *tlalli* (land, parcel), *chinamitl* (chinampa), and *ixtlahuatl* (plain), and all but ixtlahuatl appear in testaments in association with agricultural uses. The visual typically includes lines that seem to divide the cultivated lands into usufruct parcels in both pre-Columbian carvings, such as the head of Coyolxauhqui (Wright's fig. 6), and in manuscripts (Wright's figs. 8, 12, 13; see also the place-names in the *Codex Mendoza*, e.g., fols. 7v and 42r). The *Codex Mendoza* offers another key to the interpretation of cultivation, or at least fertility. On fol. 60r we see a youth on the ground, and the ground has these *u*s and dots. The gloss says it is "tierra humeda y mojada" (humid, wet land).

25. One also finds *tlachinoa* in Molina, "quemar los campos o montes" (117v). And in modern Nahuatl, the scholars at IDIEZ in Zacatecas tell us that *tlachinoā* means "to burn dead plant matter after harvest or after clearing a wooded area for planting." This appears in our *Online Nahuatl Dictionary*, accessed May 1, 2023, https://nahuatl.wired-humanities.org/content/tlachinoa.

26. Alberto Juárez Osnaya, *El desarrollo arquitectónico de Totometla en el marco del sistema urbano de Teotihuacan* (Mexico City: Instituto Nacional de Antropología e Historia, 2017), 249–51.

27. Fray Bernardino de Sahagún, *Primeros memoriales*, ed. Henry B. Nicholson and Thelma D. Sullivan (Norman: University of Oklahoma Press, 1997), 235.

28. Molina, *Vocabulario*, fol. 31r, col. 1.

29. Thelma D. Sullivan, *Nahuatl Proverbs, Conundrums, and Metaphors, Collected by Sahagún* (Mexico City: Universidad Nacional Autónoma, 1963), 168–69.

30. Sahagún, *Florentine Codex*, 87.

31. Chimalpahin, *Annals of His Time*, 138–39.

32. Camilla Townsend, ed. and trans., *Here in This Year: Seventeenth-Century Nahuatl Annals of the Tlaxcala-Puebla Valley* (Stanford, CA: Stanford University Press, 2010), 126–27.

33. Townsend, *Here in This Year*, 88–89.

34. Juan Buenaventura Zapata y Mendoza, *Historia cronológica de la Noble Ciudad de Tlaxcala*, trans. Luis Reyes García and Andrea Martínez Baracs (Tlaxcala: Universidad Autónoma de Tlaxcala, Secretaría de Extensión Universitaria y Difusión Cultural, 1995), 482–83. What seems to be an eighteenth-century Nahuatl text, the *Tlalamatl of Huauhquilpan* (Hidalgo), recounts a time when the local people made war on a bishop ("yaochihuilique yn teopiscatlatoani"). Rocío Cortés, *El "nahuatlato Alvarado" y el Tlalamatl Huauhquilpan: Mecanismos de la memoria colectiva de una comunidad indígena* (New York: Hispanic Seminary of Medieval Studies, 2011), 34, 46.

35. See William B. Taylor, *Landlord and Peasant in Colonial Oaxaca* (Stanford, CA: Stanford University Press, 1972), 84–85, who refers to numerous uprisings across the eighteenth century involving Indigenous communities trying to sabotage land surveys by Spanish colonial authorities, including rock throwing.

36. Ritual wars included *xochiyaoyotl*, translated to Spanish as *guerra florida*, and to English, as "flower" or "flowery" war. See Ross Hassig, *Aztec Warfare: Imperial Expansion and Political Control* (Norman: University of Oklahoma Press, 1988), 254–55.

37. Lockhart, *People*, 292–93. Emphasis mine.

38. Fray Alonso de Molina, *Nahua Confraternities in Early Colonial Mexico: The 1552 Nahuatl Ordinances of fray Alonso de Molina, OFM*, ed. and trans. Barry D. Sell (Berkeley: Academy of American Franciscan History, 2002), 130–31. Polihui is seen in references to being hungry, lacking food. See Hernando Ruiz de Alarcón, *Treatise on the Heathen Superstitions That Today Live among the Indians Native to this New Spain, 1629*, ed. and trans. James Richard Andrews and Ross Hassig (Norman: University of Oklahoma Press, 1987), 98.

39. Frances Karttunen, *An Analytical Dictionary of Nahuatl* (Norman: University of Oklahoma Press, 1992), 202. Karttunen has worked with both early Nahuatl and the language as spoken in the twentieth century.

40. Paul Kirchhoff, Lina Odena Güemes, and Luis Reyes García, *Historia Tolteca-Chichimeca* (Mexico City: CISINAH, INAH-SEP, 1976), 130, 152. The English translation is mine.

41. Townsend, *Year*, 160–61.

42. Ana Rita Valero de García Lascuráin and Rafael Tena, *Códice Cozcatzin* (Mexico City: Instituto Nacional de Antropología e Historia, Benemérita Universidad Autónoma de Puebla, 1994), 104. The authors' translations here seem reasonable. The English is my translation.

43. Molina, *Vocabulario*, fol. 83r col. 2, and fol. 124v, col. 1. The English is my translation.

44. Diego Durán, *The History of the Indies of New Spain*, trans. Doris Heyden (Norman: University of Oklahoma Press, 1994). Restall also sees a somewhat distinct identity remaining for the city of Tlatelolco after 1473, where the scholars participating in creating

the *Florentine Codex* continued to hold a grudge against Moteuczoma after the capital fell to the Spanish. See his *Seven Myths of the Spanish Conquest* (Oxford: Oxford University Press, 2003), 113–14.

45. Sahagún, *Florentine Codex*, bk. 10, 23.
46. Restall, *Seven Myths*, 13.
47. Kirchhoff et al., *Historia tolteca-chichimeca*, 131.
48. Anderson and Berdan, *Beyond the Codices*, 182–83.
49. Luis Reyes García, *¿Como te confundes? ¿Acaso no somos conquistados? Anales de Juan Bautista* (Mexico City: Centro de Investigaciones y Estudios Superiores en Antropología Social, Biblioteca Lorenzo Boturini Insigne y Nacional Basílica de Guadalupe, 2001), 1–343, here 162–63.
50. Chimalpahin, *Annals of His Time*, 110–11. The relatively light familiarity with the loanword in the first half of the Spanish colonial period may explain these awkward spellings and plurals.
51. My emphasis. Chimalpahin, *Annals of His Time*, 110–11, 228–29, and 234–35.
52. Caroline Cunill actually writes about a probanza put forward apparently in 1552 by the Indigenous *gobernador* named Don Francisco on behalf of the people Xicalango, Tabasco, who had helped the Spanish seize power in the Yucatan. It is just not clear whether he called himself a conquistador. See her article "El uso indígena de las probanzas de méritos y servicios: Su dimensión política (Yucatán, siglo XVI)," *Signos Históricos* 16, no. 32 (2014): 1–34.
53. See Laura E. Matthew, *Memories of Conquest: Becoming Mexicano in Colonial Guatemala* (Chapel Hill: University of North Carolina Press, 2012), 250, and *Nuestro pesar, nuestra aflicción: Tunetuliniliz, tucucuca, memorias en lengua náhuatl enviadas a Felipe II por indígenas del Valle de Guatemala hacia 1572*, ed. and trans. Karen Dakin and Christopher Lutz (Mexico City: Universidad Nacional Autónoma de México, Centro de Investigaciones Regionales de Mesoamérica, Plumsock Mesoamerican Studies, 1996), 34.
54. Zapata y Mendoza, *Historia cronológica*, 484–87.
55. Teresa Rojas Rabiela, Elsa Leticia Rea López, and Constantino Medina Lima, eds., *Vidas y bienes olvidados: Testamentos indígenas novohispanos* (Mexico City: Centro de Investigaciones y Estudios Superiores en Antropología Social, 1999), 2: 72–73. Lockhart writes that most primordial titles do not show a clear consciousness of a period of conquest or a pre- and post-contact divide: "The authors of the titles had often lost nearly all sense of any distinction between things of Spanish origin and things of indigenous origin as long as they belonged to the local tradition. Lost, too, was an awareness of the difference between the pre- and postconquest periods." Lockhart, *The Nahuas after the Conquest*, 418.
56. Archivo General de la Nación, Mexico (henceforth AGN), Tierras, 3362, exp. 3, fol. 10.
57. For the common confusion of kings and viceroys in the primordial titles of the Chalco region, see Lockhart, *Nahuas*, 60.

58. AGN, Tierras, 2860, exp. 1, cuad. 2, fols. 65r–68v.

59. Ángel María Garibay Kintana, *Códice de Metepec: Estado de México* (Mexico City: publisher not identified, 1949), fols. 1, recto through 4 recto. See also a discussion of civil congregations in Stephanie Wood, *Transcending Conquest: Nahua Views of Spanish Colonial Mexico* (Norman: University of Oklahoma Press, 2003), 121–24.

60. See Florine Asselbergs, *Conquered Conquistadors: The Lienzo de Quauhquechollan. A Nahua Vision of the Conquest of Guatemala* (Boulder: University Press of Colorado, 2004); Yanna Yannakakis, *The Art of Being In-Between: Native Intermediaries, Indian Identity, and Local Rule in Colonial Oaxaca* (Durham, NC: Duke University Press, 2008); Laura E. Matthew and Michel Oudijk, eds., *Indian Conquistadors: Indigenous Allies in the Conquest of Mesoamerica* (Norman: University of Oklahoma Press, 2014); *The Native Conquistador: Alva Ixtlilxochitl's Account of the Conquest of New Spain*, ed. and trans. Amber Brian, Bradley Benton, and Pablo García Loaeza (University Park: Pennsylvania State University Press, 2015).

61. This word appears in many primordial titles, in Techialoyan manuscripts, and in at least one lienzo or mapa. For examples, see the *Online Nahuatl Dictionary*, https://nahuatl.wired-humanities.org/content/tlalmaceuhqui, accessed May 1, 2023. Perhaps one should be aware that the use of this term was mainly popular with a small number of workshops that produced the titles and not necessarily something in broad usage among a range of *escribanos*. But the manuscripts still could have impacted the thinking in the many Nahua pueblos that were served by the workshops.

62. At first, I accepted the translation of *tlalmaceuhqui* as conqueror, but I am rethinking this thanks to Kelly S. McDonough. She has studied the concept of *macehua* (to be deserving or to obtain what is desired) in colonial Nahua culture, and she correctly rejects the translation of "conqueror" for *tlalmaceuhqui*. See Kelly S. McDonough, "Primordial Titles and Narrative Mapping in Colonial Mexico," *Journal for Early Modern Cultural Studies* 17, no. 1 (2017): 24n17. It is also significant to see the term *macehua* (to be deserving) associated with being a part of an *altepetl* in the *Historia Tolteca-Chichimeca* (132): "Ynic quitlatlamaceuito yn imaltepeuh = por lo que cada uno fue a merecer su pueblo" (so that each one became deserving of their town). My translation to English.

63. Vitus Huber found this shift in the *Ordenanzas de descubrimiento y población* of July 13, 1573, in the Recopilación 2: bk. 4, tít. 6, ley 6, citing it in his book: Vitus Huber, *Beute und Conquista: Die politische Ökonomie der Eroberung Neuspaniens* (Frankfurt: Campus, 2018), 313 and passim.

64. Susan Schroeder, *Chimalpahin and the Kingdoms of Chalco* (Tucson: University of Arizona Press, 1991), 122.

65. Chimalpahin, *Annals of His Time*, 52–53.

66. Townsend, *Year*, 84–85.

67. See the *Mapas Project* (open-access digital collection), ed. Stephanie Wood (Eugene: Wired Humanities Projects, University of Oregon, 2000–2018), https://mapas.wired-humanities.org/search/node/altepemanque#overlay=mimi/elements/mimi07v/001, accessed May 1, 2023. *Altepemanqueh*, like *tlalmaceuhqueh*, does appear in some records from the sixteenth and early seventeenth centuries, but it was promoted in a significant way by the workshop production of manuscripts aiming to defend indigenous towns ca. 1640–1720.

68. This is not how the colonial translators rendered these two verbs. They gave: "por haber conquistado, y allí fue la fundación de el pueblo" ("for having conquered, and there [*sic—niz* means here] was the foundation of the town"). But *tlacaxinachtli* is semen, and the related verb is literally to procreate. Teresa Rojas Rabiela, Elsa Leticia Rea López, and Constantino Medina Lima, eds., *Vidas y bienes olvidados: Testamentos indígenas novohispanos* (Mexico City: Centro de Investigaciones y Estudios Superiores en Antropología Social, 2000), 3: 76–77, 88–89. The Techialoyan manuscript associated with Tepotzotlan uses *onmotlacaxinachyotzinotiah*, which Byron McAfee translated as "here the settlers started multiplying." See Donald Robertson, "The Techialoyan Codex of Tepotzotlan: Codex X (Rylands Mexican Ms. 1)," *Bulletin of the John Rylands Library* 43, no. 1 (1960): 109–30, here 127.

69. Assuring the placement of this manuscript in the Techialoyan corpus is a reference to "ton Tieco te Mentoça Motecçoçoma" (77), i.e., Don Diego de Mendoza Moctezuma. See Stephanie Wood, "Don Diego García de Mendoza Moctezuma: A Techialoyan Mastermind?" *Estudios de Cultura Náhuatl* 19 (1989): 245–68. This association has been further substantiated by María Castañeda de la Paz, *Verdades y mentiras en torno a don Diego de Mendoza Austria Moctezuma* (Mexico City: Universidad Nacional Autónoma de México, Instituto de Investigaciones Antropológicas, 2017).

70. See Fernando Horcasitas and Wanda Tommasi de Magrelli, "El códice de Tzictepec: Una nueva fuente pictórica indígena," *Anales de Antropología* 12 (1975): 243–72.

71. Howard F. Cline, Charles Gibson, and H. B. Nicholson, eds., *Handbook of Middle American Indians*, vols. 14 and 15, *Guide to Ethnohistorical Sources, Parts Three and Four* (Austin: University of Texas Press, 1975), fig. 26.

72. *Anales del Museo de México*, vol. 7 (Mexico City: Imprenta del Museo Nacional, 1903), 120.

73. R. H. Barlow, "La Fundación de Cuacuauzentlalpan [región de Chalco, México]," *Tlalocan* 4 (1962): 64–73. See, e.g., the mention of "ganar la tierra" (to gain ground, win land, or advance settlement) in association with struggle, fighting, and spilling blood (66). The Spanish concept of ganar can thus overlap with conquistar, although it probably originated with the winning of territory during the Reconquista of Iberia. This narrative from the Chalco area is heavily influenced by Christianity, but it is critical of the "armed" Spanish invasion (67). Similar to the narrative from Zempoala already mentioned, this one from

Cuacuauzentlalpan blurs the line between primordial titles and testaments, and this one does refer (at least in Spanish) to a cacicazgo.

74. This interpretation about how the colonization of central Mexico played out is not new. See Charles Gibson, *The Aztecs under Spanish Rule: A History of the Indians of the Valley of Mexico, 1519–1810* (Stanford, CA: Stanford University Press, 1964); and Lockhart, *The Nahuas after the Conquest*.

75. Terms such as *altepetlalli* and *altepetlatquitl* convey the concern with group-held lands. The Techialoyan from Cuajimalpa (originally, Cuauhximalpan) has some pages where landholdings appear in rectangular form and are labeled as *altepetlatquitl* (town property) and *yntlal altepehuaque* (the land of the people of the altepetl). See https://artsandculture.google.com/story/techialoyan-de-cuajimalpa-codice/3AVhpJMc2P3pJg, accessed May 1, 2023. The original is in the AGN.

76. For further exploration of the relationships between caciques' testaments and primordial titles, see Stephanie Wood, "Testaments and Títulos: Conflict and Coincidence of Cacique and Community Interests [in Colonial Mexico]," in *Dead Giveaways: Indigenous Testaments of Colonial Mesoamerica and the Andes*, ed. Matthew Restall and Susan Kellogg (Salt Lake City: University of Utah Press, 1998), 85–111.

2

"Perpetuating Lands"

The Crucial Transition from War to Colonial Settlement in the Conquista of Mexico

VITUS HUBER

On January 4, 1529, Francisco de Granada, an average Spanish conquistador in his mid-thirties, presented a petition and a questionnaire to a judge (*alcalde ordinario*) of Mexico-Tenochtitlan and a royal scribe. In the five subsequent days eight witnesses answered seventeen questions in front of these officials, confirming Granada's services to the Crown. Granada had served under several military leaders (*capitanes*) in multiple expeditions: He claims to have arrived in "New Spain" from Cuba with Hernán Cortés, with whom he fought in the wars (*guerras*) against Tlaxcala and entered Tenochtitlan, before they were forced to leave again. Until the following conquest (*conquista*) of the mighty city, he served four captains consecutively in several provinces. Afterward, he joined four new *capitanías* going as far southwest as Guatemala, before settling again in Mexico-Tenochtitlan.[1] Certainly, many other fellow Spaniards traveled far longer distances and participated in more battles, yet one still wonders what determined such itineraries and especially their ending.

This chapter addresses the issue of when and why a looting or conquering expedition, a so-called *entrada*, stopped and under what circumstances an entrada turned into colonialism. It also asks how the individual member ended up where he—and in fewer cases she—did and what made them walk away from the hazards of an entrada and decide to settle in a certain place in the Americas. These questions not only shed light on the way in which expansive warfare shifted to "peaceful" or colonial settlement. They furthermore help understand the mechanisms that supported a long-term Spanish presence in the Americas.

Recent scholarship has introduced a great number of aspects about the events that came to be known as the *Conquista* of Mexico.[2] Roughly at the dawn of the twenty-first century, the New Conquest History has started to extensively deconstruct former narratives that glorified European "achievements" and to bring previously marginalized actors to historians' attention.[3] This study has improved our knowledge significantly. Focus has shifted from white male European participants, previously the "heroes" of the adventure. As a consequence, the large majority of the Spanish conquistadors still needs to be revisited.[4] What is more, one of the turning points, the moment when conquistadors became settlers, was decisive for the establishment of colonialism. Nonetheless, studies of this phase normally only date back to the twentieth century and concentrate primarily on models of state formation or on collecting (geo-)biographical data, as important as that may be.[5] Focusing on the transition between expansion and persistence or retreat—linguistically from the aggressors' perspective—allows us to better grasp that the bridging negotiations that mark the difference of war vis-à-vis warfare that turns into conquest by colonizing the territory.

After briefly looking at the dynamics of conquest in the first section and the foundations of colonialism, including the participation of the local Indigenous people, in the second, the chapter then focuses on the contemporaries' arguments in favor of Spanish settlement. The way former conquistadors or their heirs and other European settlers campaigned for long-term settlement is particularly revelatory. By analyzing this discourse and these practices, one not only deciphers the specific semantics of colonialism but also maps the influence of archival knowledge production on the historiographical perspective. While this latter point has recently received growing scholarly attention, its combination with the former topic still promises new insights. My hypothesis is that the Spaniards' rhetoric provides important but only lopsided evidence. By scrutinizing its logic and by putting it into context, we get a more complete picture of this crucial, and by no means linear, transition from war to colonial settlement.

DYNAMICS OF CONQUEST

The dynamics of conquest in the Americas were influenced by various factors, though often sparked by the Spaniards' zeal to achieve something. In the second question of his questionnaire, Francisco de Granada asked the witnesses to answer the following: "Whether they know that I came to these lands at my own expense and voluntarily without anybody paying me a salary nor did I come in any interest other than to serve Your Majesty [the Spanish Crown] and to value more."[6] This holds true for the majority of the Spanish participants of what came to be known as the *Conquista*, as the first witness confirmed: "No conquistador was given subsistence nor salary and all were going at their own expense and ... the majority of the people go and work to value more."[7] Joining an entrada at one's own expense and hoping to improve one's reputation (and one's standard of living) formed the basic structure of these endeavors that we may call "booty communities."[8] These groups constituted themselves to collect booty and/or possibly colonize a place.

The fact is that Francisco de Granada carried on signing up for new campaigns, after Cortés had dissolved the capitanías in Coyoacán following the victory over Tenochtitlan. Defeating the Triple Alliance of Tetzcoco, Tlacopan, and Tenochtitlan-Tlatelolco (*yexcan tlatoloyan*) drastically increased the power of the league led by the Spaniards and Tlaxcaltecah. Furthermore, the newly won but fragile hegemony had to be consolidated and defended. Beyond these political necessities, the individual Spanish participants needed to find resources to make a living according to their aspirations. Granada went with Gonzalo de Sandoval to Tutepec and Coatzacoalcos; from there with Pedro de Briones to the provinces of Zapotecas; and then with Pedro de Alvarado to Utatlan, Guatemala, Cuzcatlan, and other provinces. He stated in his petition that he also helped Vasco Porcallo to put down local opposition in Guatemala.[9]

On the individual level, even though the motivations are generally too complex to grasp, lacking riches would force Spanish conquistadors to move on. After the year and a half that Granada had served in Guatemala, he left the city of Santiago and returned to Mexico-Tenochtitlan. Justifying his departure from Guatemala, he said that there he had felt "lost and without any benefit."[10] Consequently, the lack of means to live according to one's expectations functioned as a push factor on the Spaniards. Complementary to this, places about which they heard promising stories and where they hoped to make a fortune, or at least a living, acted as pull factors.[11]

Besides these push and pull factors, newly acquired resources—such as the distribution of booty, the allotment of estates and encomiendas, or promotion to offices and higher military ranks—usually led to settlement and the provisioning of new entradas at the same time. Those who were indebted or disappointed, or simply aspired for more, joined new expeditions, as Granada did. The regular fresh supply of newly arrived Spaniards supported the expansive expeditions, allowing the war engine to restart continuously. New lands and tax revenues were needed, and new glory aspired to.[12]

This spiral of spoils, the recurrent process of plundering and dividing the booty with the expansive operating range of the entradas, was furthermore influenced by Indigenous agency. Local or regional rivalries had a long pre-Hispanic tradition in the area and were fought or negotiated, against or despite the presence of the Spaniards. It is well known, for example, that the so-called Aztec Triple Alliance had been founded in 1430 and established its hegemonic power until the arrival of the Spaniards. Other leagues were more transient and only occasionally forged, for instance, the one between Tlaxcallan, Huexotzinco, and Chololan. As has been shown by James Lockhart and multiple other historians, Cortés entered this "game" of alliance forging and, in the end, benefitted decisively from it. Scholars have disputed whether this "success" was due to his alleged military strategic genius and personal charisma or was merely coincidence.[13]

It is undisputed that the copious Indigenous warriors who were mobilized for the military alliances with the Spaniards outnumbered the latter by far. The current scholarly assessment is similarly unanimous in the importance of this support. Simply put: it was indispensable.[14] Less clear are the reasons *why* the local lords decided to ally with the strangers. All textual and visual sources from the immediate time of the events in the early 1520s stem from Europeans. Later sources did include Indigenous voices, but they have to be interpreted in the context of the new colonial setting. Evaluating the intercultural negotiations for the forging of leagues is hence a difficult task.[15]

We do know, though, that many Indigenous lords had their warriors, porters, and other servants accompany the Spaniards either to simply subjugate or to conquer and settle other towns and provinces. In a lawsuit about the distribution of *indios* arranged by Francisco de Montejo and Alonso de Ávila after they had "conquered and pacified" the province of Acalan in today's Campeche, Pedro González testified the following:

> He said that he saw how Alonso de Ávila went with his people with many peaceful indios from the province of Acalan to Mazatlan and conquered that province of Mazatlan. Many lords from there served them or gave tributes or came with the accountant [Ávila] in peace until Cochiztlan which lays at the north coast. From there they returned to their homes.[16]

This is a representative example of the way in which the spiral of spoils functioned regarding Indigenous participation. After the Spaniards came to terms with the lords of the province of Acalan, whether the means of "conquering and pacifying" it were violent or peaceful, the local leaders supplied the invaders with food and manpower for the next entrada. In this case, they supplied and helped the Spanish conquistadors and their allies and joined them but after a while returned home again. Nevertheless, their support functioned as a steppingstone, allowing for the expansive conquest to continue. In other campaigns, like those that historian Yanna Yannakakis described, Indigenous auxiliaries from Oaxaca would not return to their places of origin but instead helped settle and colonize the newly conquered territories with their own people.[17] It would be interesting to know more about the reasons for such behavior, and maybe archaeological or environmental methodologies could bring new insights to this enigma.

What has already become sufficiently palpable beyond the Spanish conquistadors' pressure to "succeed" is the important role Indigenous support played in this historic process. Also, *after* the conquering entradas, cooperation with the Indigenous inhabitants remained a decisive factor for the transition from warfare to colonialism.

INDIGENOUS COOPERATION AND FOUNDATIONS OF COLONIALISM

The essence of colonialism is the persisting presence of foreign people with a certain amount of power. Granada's decision to become one of the first European settlers of Mexico-Tenochtitlan can therefore be seen as a limited but fundamental step toward colonialism, but it was far from being the only one. Needless to say, without Spaniards who were willing to settle in these lands that later came to be called New Spain, these colonial structures would not have been installed. And in many cases, they definitely did *not* materialize, because, for different reasons, no Spanish presence or representation via Indigenous allies was established. Hence, examining the constellations that led to European settlements is crucial for understanding this important phase that could turn into colonialism.

Support from Indigenous elites was another essential precondition, even in times after the conquering entradas, as already seen. From the earliest days after their landing at the Totonac coast in today's state of Veracruz, the Spaniards depended heavily on help from the native inhabitants. An extensive list of local rulers received Cortés and his men along their journey through their territories. Others sent their emissaries, most famously Moteuczoma's ad hoc ambassadors Cuitlalpitoc and Teulitlilli (or Tlilancalqui), lord of Cuetlaxtlan, who conversed with the Spaniards at their arrival at the Totonac coast. Whether the local leaders offered the foreigners gifts; traded some goods with them; received them in their towns providing food and shelter; or supplied them with local guides, information, porters, cooks, women, or military auxiliaries, the Spaniards benefitted substantially from these encounters.[18] It is hard to judge, but arguably one of the most effective gifts for Cortés came in the person of the enslaved woman known as Marina or Malintzin. Through her language skills, she facilitated intercultural communication and most probably gave the Spanish conquistadors some advantage through her advice as a cultural translator.[19]

The Spaniards' dependency on the locals' hospitality and cooperation became especially evident in these things' absence. For instance, when the Mexicah sieged the Spaniards' camp in June 1520, they had also cut the food supplies for their foreign "guests," increasing the pressure on them to leave Tenochtitlan. The fleeing Spaniards apparently suffered thirst and hunger until they could buy food from the people of Hueyotlipan in the province of Tlaxcala.[20] In other cases, when the native inhabitants denied the invaders food supplies, the latter tried to violently seize it: either by secretly stealing it, by taking hostages, or by attacking the town.[21] Coercion was typically a more arduous, troublesome, and precarious way than peaceful agreement.

Despite the image of martial conquests often painted in textual or iconographic depictions of the *Conquista*, besides the ferocious battles and wars, many encounters between the opponents were peaceful. The historians Michel Oudijk and Matthew Restall have already shown this and pointed at the special term coined for "peaceful conquest": "conquista de buenas palabras," meaning "conquest of good words."[22] Calling it a (violent) conquest implied greater risks taken by the conquistador and hence, in the logic of the economy of mercy, a more honorable service to the Crown. The rhetoric generally minded complying with legal preconditions for a Just War and consequently for a righteous claim to the conquered lands and riches. With growing criticism against the killing and mistreatment of the people of the Americas, the term "pacification" quickly appeared more frequently in the sources. In 1573 Philip II even ordered substitution of the word "conquest" with this euphemistic term.[23]

Rhetoric aside, the Spaniards genuinely preferred peaceful agreements with the locals. One reason for this can be found, for example, in a later experience in Venezuela. Here the conquistadors argued that they favored nonviolent subjugation, because otherwise the "indios" would burn down their villages and flee the place. Obviously, this would leave the invaders without anyone to work for them in the fields and mines.[24] Cortés was experienced enough to recommend that his captains try to win over the Indigenous rulers peacefully. He told his men to promise the local lords certain advantages, like helping them against their enemies or exempting them from tributary payments.[25] While this might give the impression of cagey tactical maneuvering, the local lords had their own reasons too. It is simply harder to deduce their options for agency from the sources. Also, we know less about the negotiations and conquests that led to *no* treaty or to a military loss for the attacking party. Nonetheless, often enough the conquistadors achieved an agreement, whether arranged peacefully or through coercion.[26]

Having come to an understanding, the Spanish leaders would distribute the acquired spoils, parcels of land, and indios (*repartimiento de indios/encomiendas*) among their men. Aside from indios, this practice was a custom in military conduct that was common in the so-called Reconquista of the Iberian Peninsula.[27] At the same time, Nahua and other Indigenous societies habitually took captives in wars and used them as rewards as well. In the *Conquista*, groups of indios were distributed in allotments (*repartimientos*) to Spanish settlers since the beginning, in the Caribbean phase.²⁸ Later the encomiendas were often based on pre-Hispanic tribute entities, and local elites banded with the Spaniards to collect the tributes. Beyond labor, the foundation of colonialism was the allotment of parcels of land. Cortés allotted the urban land of Tenochtitlan together with agricultural lots outside the town to his men in 1522 in Coyocan.²⁹

The repartimiento of spoils including the distribution of riches and, more important, of land represented an essential step toward the colonization of newly occupied territory. To claim and guarantee the Spanish hegemonic position and to stabilize it, Cortés formulated certain preconditions for Spaniards to possess land in the *Ordenanzas de buen gobierno* of 1524. There he prescribed that everyone possessing indios or estates in New Spain had to promise to settle there for at least eight years. Further duties for settlers included keeping defensive arms and possibly a horse; cultivating European agricultural plants, especially vines; treating the indios benevolently and assuring their evangelization; getting married or calling for their wives in Europe; and building a house. Moreover, Cortés encouraged dissatisfied conquistadors to send the Spanish Crown an account of merits and services (*información de méritos y servicios*) and to ask for royal favors.³⁰

As introduced earlier, Francisco de Granada had such a petition produced in 1529. He not only boasted in it about all the expeditions he had served but also tried to stand out from the anonymous mass of conquistadors. He highlighted, for instance, that he had killed more than twenty "very brave indios," that he had caught a local leader of the Valle del Tuerto in Guatemala, and that he had suffered injuries to his face and leg when chased out of Tenochtitlan by the Mexicah.³¹ Openly admitting to having slain someone is rather rare in the genre of informaciones de méritos y servicios. Capturing a hostile leader or spilling one's blood caused by war injuries, on the other hand, had been regarded as extraordinary services to the king for a long time. Already the famous medieval code of law called Las Siete Partidas (ca. 1256–65) had prescribed special gratifications for such "achievements" and sacrifices.³²

This tradition reflects the king's obligation to reward his vassals for their loyalty according to the principle of distributive justice (*iustitia distributiva*).³³ What the Portuguese historian Manuel António Hespanha termed the "economy of mercy" guided the rhetoric in these petitions from former conquistadors.³⁴ Granada stated that no one had paid him for his services to the Crown and that he even had lost his probably biggest investment: his horse. It had fallen into a trap, a big hole with pickets set up inside by Indigenous enemies in Guatemala.³⁵ In the logic of economy of mercy, Granada's services morally obliged the king to grant him royal favors. These could include a pension, an office, encomiendas, or symbolic titles. Granada's petition was successful, and he was rewarded with a personal coat of arms.[36] As we will see, this remuneration was not enough for Granada, though.

SERVING THE KING BY SETTLING THE LAND

Francisco de Granada's "merits and services," which he mentioned in his petition of 1529, included the fact that he belonged to "the first [Spanish, V.H.] citizens and dwellers" of Mexico-Tenochtitlan. He also said: "I have my house in [that city] and am one of the first to have it [the house] inhabited."[37] This statement not only shows that Cortés had allotted him a parcel of land in Mexico-Tenochtitlan. It furthermore points out that Granada ostensibly complied with Cortés's requirements for conquistadors to settle in New Spain over several years and to maintain an inhabited household. It seems obvious why Cortés would demand that his people stay in the area: he feared otherwise quickly losing his recently gained power. To some extent, the Spanish conquistadors and settlers, as well as the Crown, all shared, at least collectively, this position about the necessity of remaining physically present in the conquered territories. Despite the apparent unanimity, the arguments for this fundamental precondition for colonialism differed and are worth analyzing.

From a macro point of view, it is apparent that if too many Spanish conquistadors or early settlers left the so-called New World, the Spanish Crown could barely establish its power in that area. Wherever the Spaniards withdrew or where the local elites denied their cooperation, colonial institutions could not materialize. As discussed, it is difficult to trace the reasons for local leaders to partner up with the invading Spaniards, unless they were forced to, or they saw personal advantages in doing so. From the Crown's perspective, the conquered lands were considered its overseas territories. With the aim of preventing feudal structures, the Crown granted the lands to the settlers for usufruct only (*donativos graciosos* or *mercedes reales*). This thin line between seeking control via a centralized administration and binding the Spaniards to the new territories left space for debate.[38]

The Spaniards in the Americas were often granted lands immediately by their captain. They habitually received two lots: the first for their deeds as conquistadors and the second for becoming a citizen (*vecino*) of the town. These allotments of land parcels formed part of the political economy of conquest, meaning the entangled political and economic mechanisms that shaped the dynamic of the *Conquista*. Contrary to mobile goods, such as precious metals and stones and the like, the lots could not be relocated to Europe or other places. Hence, the distribution of lands forced the Spaniards to stay in the area if they wanted to enjoy the benefits thereof. Even though this was not strategically planned by the Crown, it nevertheless played out to its advantage.[39]

Then again, the incentives to linger in a place had to be strong enough. Otherwise, as described in this chapter's first section, the Spaniards would seek their goals somewhere else. When Cortés famously prepared an expedition to explore the South Sea (Pacific Ocean) aiming for the Moluccas at the end of the 1520s, the Crown felt pressured. The Council of the Indies and the Council of State feared that the Spanish settlers would leave New Spain behind and follow Cortés to the Moluccas. Such a depopulation of Europeans would have been detrimental to the Spanish defense of New Spain. However, as they knew Cortés was almost ready to set sail and they probably hoped for great opportunities if he opened the sea route via the South Sea to the Spice Islands, they let him try.[40] A few years later, the settlers' eagerness to leave the area grew again, as news from Peru spread. The Spanish authorities had to convince them to stay to maintain the towns and provinces that they had won only a few years before.[41]

Francisco de Granada, as mentioned, apparently knew about the value remaining in the region and maintaining a house and household. He and his fellow early conquistadors listed it in their reports of merits and services and highlighted that they belonged to the *first* who inhabited their houses. Following the principle of distributive justice, being one of the pioneers in doing something of this kind deserved extraordinary royal mercies. Moreover, since the division of goods often caused lawsuits, having witnesses testifying in support of one's claim and the Crown confirming it could help corroborate one's possessions. Producing notarial or archival documents would shape reality.[42]

Granada added another requirement Cortés had ordered to his list of services that would entitle the conquistadors to royal favors: the keeping of one's arms and possibly horses ready to defend the lands. In this spirit, Granada claimed the following: "I have and have had my armaments and horse and have helped in the service of Your Majesty to maintain what was won until now." The formulation is very typical for the genre, and it shows the awareness of the perceived necessity of a physical presence in the newly acquired lands. The Crown and the individual Spaniard would otherwise lose part of what had been "won" in the New World. Granada continued, saying: "Since I entered into this New Spain with Cortés, the captain who was governor, I have never left this land."[43] He furthermore stressed never having done anything against the service of the Crown for which he would have been castigated. The latter limitation leaves the door open for speculation, but what is more important, lingering in the New World entitled the Spaniards to ask for royal favors. Even though this was beneficial to them personally, they presented it as if it were primarily the Crown who profited from their presence.[44]

Then again, Spanish settlers still had to convince the king to grant them land that they could pass on to their heirs. Otherwise, the parcel would go back to the

Crown. A group of former conquistadors in 1544, for example, petitioned exactly that. Their argument for allocating the land in perpetuity was that otherwise "we will not be able to maintain ourselves in the perpetuation of the land to leave in it our children." Therefore, they asked the Crown for royal mercies "for our maintenance and perpetuation so we can, in your royal service, maintain and perpetuate this land that we have won with so much work."[45] The Crown, being dependent on the Spanish settlers to hold the land, approved their request. Here we see the common interest in establishing a long-term presence in the area: to "perpetuate this land."

Several initiatives were launched with the aim of increasing the profits from the newly occupied soil. One famous example is Juan Garrido, the Black conquistador who praised himself for having been the first to plant wheat in New Spain. He boasted that this brought benefit to the region. As mentioned earlier, being a pioneer in something makes these deeds extraordinary. Witnesses confirmed that they saw how Garrido sowed two seeds of wheat in a garden. While one witness concluded that from these two grains 160 ears were harvested, being the beginning of wheat growing, the other claimed that all the wheat in New Spain stemmed from these two seeds.[46] While this claim might have been slightly exaggerated and must be understood in the logic of the petitions for royal favors, it is less relevant *if* Garrido eventually was the first to cultivate wheat than the fact that somebody was and that henceforth this crop thrived and prospered in the New World too.

Another initiative to improve revenues from the colonized lands remained rather hypothetical during its creator's lifetime. Diego de Ocaña was a notary from Seville who arrived in New Spain in 1525. He acted as a public notary in Tenochtitlan, when he heard that a ship off course on the New Spanish coast reported rich islands in the Southern Sea. In one of his two letters written to the Casa de la Contratación in 1526, he criticized Cortés and encouraged the Crown to introduce seeds and seedlings from Moluccas across the Pacific. He wrote:

> Your Majesty should give order to equip a couple of ships from here that should go there [Spice Islands] to bring plants and seeds from the Spicery to these parts [New Spain], as all these islands and lands [of New Spain] are apt for it. This will spread over all these lands ... and all these lands will ennoble themselves and become a lot more populated. Your Majesty could have very large revenues from it.[47]

Moreover, the Crown should send good ship pilots and botanical experts. With cagey rhetoric he added that if the Crown was unwilling to arm and pay to send these ships, someone else would be at hand to do so. In order to prevent the Crown from having to trade with such third parties, Ocaña recommended hiring royal officials to take care of it directly. All of this happened during the time when, after the famous Magellan voyage, the House of Trade for the Commerce of the Spicery (Casa de contratación del comercio para la Especiería) was established in La Coruña (1522–29) and still before the Castilian Crown had conceded the claim to the Moluccas to Portugal in the Treaty of Zaragoza of 1529.

Ocaña's suggestion went nevertheless a step further, as he not only envisioned the long-sought-after sea route to the Spice Islands. Ocaña combined a potential trading route with the opportunity to enhance the amenity of New Spain. Its value would not only increase on an agricultural and botanical level but also by attracting more settlers. This environmental development plan sounds like a case of proto-*arbitrismo*, since Ocaña suggests the Crown to take action to "ennoble its lands." Yet, perhaps similarly interested in "ennobling" himself, Ocaña proposed this project at the same time as presenting himself as a loyal servant to the Crown.[48]

The Spaniards undertook multiple steps, as briefly outlined here, that aimed at guaranteeing a long-term presence in the area. At the same time, they searched for ways to increase the profitability of the lands, either with livestock, agriculture, plantations, or mines. Some of this information stems from the communication with the Crown when its vassals simultaneously demonstrated their alleged merits and services. Further data are stored in lawsuits, accounts, or contracts that can be found in municipal or notary archives. The Archivo General de Notarías de México, for example, holds "company contracts" (*compañías*) in which individual Spaniards agree to run mines together, sell or borrow land parcels, enslave people, and care for livestock.[49] We will delve deeper into the issue of archives in the chapter's last section, but another critical point must be made beforehand. The diverse and conflicting interests regarding incentives to settle versus keeping the local ambitions of Spanish subjects in check required permanent negotiations between the parties involved. Those Indigenous who cooperated with the Spaniards were key factors in that calculation.

NEGOTIATING COLONIAL STRUCTURES

The sixteenth-century debate about the Spaniards' role in settling in the New World was especially delicate apropos the treatment of the local people. This topic has attracted much research, with studies especially focusing on the legal dimension around the Junta de Valladolid or on the socioeconomic impact of forced labor, enslavement, and tribute systems.[50] As these macro perspectives from theological, legal, or economic perspectives are familiar, the following section focuses instead on the arguments to justify encomiendas, allotment and alienation of lands, and slave ownership put forward by the actors in situ. This should help understand a vital aspect of the reasons for the transition from conquest to colonialism.

As the entradas were organized as booty communities, their members generally expected to receive a share of the spoils. Despite many tales about gold and silver in the Americas, indios, their lands, and products quickly became the more relevant "goods" that were distributed among the conquistadors. They were also less "fugitive assets" than precious metals and provided a continuous, or at least recurring, source of revenue instead of a one-time gain. Conquistadors not only expected a share of the booty but also hoped for rewards granted as royal favors. Such royal grants (mercedes) included mainly encomiendas, offices, pensions, or noble titles. We have seen that Francisco de Granada, for example, received in acknowledgment of his "merits and services" stated in his petition of 1529 a personal coat of arms in 1532. This allowed him to display a banner with his crest, for instance, on the outside of his house and evidenced his social status of a hidalgo, the lowest rank of the Spanish nobility.[51]

Most Spanish conquistadors and settlers searched for a better life than the one they had in Europe, and they aspired to social ascendance. Since the vast majority of participants did not get rich "overnight" by finding abundant treasures of precious metals and stones or by making a lucrative slave raid, the possession of encomiendas, of plots of land, or of enslaved people could enable one to improve one's personal standard of living. What is more, not having to work with one's own hands was a sought-after privilege, mainly reserved for the nobility. Europeans in the Americas therefore tried to avoid physical labor themselves. Having indios in an encomienda or receiving a royal pension was each a popular way to circumvent manual labor. It allowed for an ostensibly noble way of living. Nonetheless, for Francisco de Granada the symbolic capital of owning his own noble crest did not automatically free him from physical toil. Reputation was not everything. In 1541, he joined the collective petition of a group of so-called first conquistadors presented by Francisco Téllez, asking the Crown for encomiendas. In it the petitioners expressed their hopes to be rewarded for their services according to the customs. Moreover, they felt they *merited* remuneration in the form of sinecures, namely, encomiendas and lands.[52]

Conquistadors like the group around Téllez argued that they not only deserved but even *needed* the allotments of indios to sustain themselves. They depicted it as a necessity to persevere in the area.[53] This is where the common interest with the Crown culminated and the conflicts began at the same time: the presence of Spaniards was a precondition to maintaining the Crown's hegemonic claim to these lands and peoples. On the other hand, the Crown feared that these encomenderos and landowners could become too powerful and possibly act too independently. Simultaneously, cooperating Indigenous elite and common indios tried to defend their collective and individual interests as well. What made everything even more complex was that soon many other actors such as Franciscan missionaries, Catholic clergy, and Spanish settlers and merchants pursued their own goals.[54]

Common ground from the perspectives of the European players lay in striving for a persisting presence of Christians in the New World and to some degree for securing or even increasing colonial revenues. Hernán Cortés touched exactly on these points when he argued for the encomiendas to be granted in perpetuity (able to be bequeathed) to the Spaniards. In a letter reserved for King Charles V from 1524, he described his experience from the Caribbean phase of the *Conquista* when the local population drastically declined after the encounter with the Spanish. Cortés now promoted the hereditary award of indios, stating that this way the encomenderos would treat their indios more gently. If the Spaniards could maintain their encomiendas and pass them on to their children they would, according to Cortés, be more sustainable with the indios. That, in turn, would increase the incentives for Spaniards to stay in the Americas, the basis for longtime presence and colonization.[55]

The value of maintaining a healthy Indigenous population was already noticed. While missionaries famously criticized the maltreatment of the indios and campaigned for their protection for moral reasons, Spanish laypeople argued on economic grounds. The royal official on Hispaniola, *licenciado* Alonso de Zuazo, for example, wrote in a letter to Charles's influential chief tutor and first chamberlain, William II de Croÿ, lord of Chièvres, in 1518 that the enslavement and abuse of the island's natives would be detrimental to the Spanish cause. He argued as follows: "Because the good of all these wide and spacious realms is that they are populated by indios, and if they would be missing everything would be missing."[56] Thus alongside ethical and religious motivations were secular and pecuniary ones, basically arguing for the same cause. Discursive front lines in the conflict regarding the adequate treatment of the Indigenous people did not simply divide missionaries/clergymen on the one side and settlers/encomenderos on the other. It was more multisided than that.

Whatever the crucial reasons for the Crown's decision, we only know that in the sixteenth century encomenderos in New Spain could inherit their encomiendas at least over one or two generations and occasionally even perpetually. The main and probably most convincing argument was that perpetuity would give the Spaniards an inducement to settle and remain in the conquered lands. For example, in an earlier collective petition thirty-six conquistadors presented by Gutierre de Badajoz in 1536 made this argument of longtime settlement: that they should be allowed to bequeath their encomiendas to their descendants.[57] It is well known that this practice continued even after the New Laws (Leyes Nuevas) of 1542/43, with which the Crown had intended to centralize its control in the Americas by banning the institution of the encomienda. Other measures proved equally difficult to implement. For instance, in 1549 the Crown prohibited encomenderos from sending indios to work in the mines. However, these regulations did not prevent the practice.[58]

This suggests three points: first, that the Indigenous population played a key role in the process of colonization, both as the valuable "good" that had to be protected and preserved and as the exploitable source of manpower and thus of revenue; second, that hereditary encomiendas and related offices and incomes acted as incentives that kept their owners in the colonies; third, that the Crown depended heavily on its Spanish vassals on the ground. The degree to which cooperating Indigenous benefitted from the Spanish presence is difficult to evaluate and requires further research. In addition, the Spaniards in New Spain enjoyed a fair amount of leeway from the Crown in regard to exploiting the native population.

A similar situation can be traced in the context of land ownership. Studying the process of land alienation in the municipalities of Tecamachalco and Quecholac in today's Puebla, historian Hildeberto Martínez concluded that protective Spanish legislation barely retarded this process. For at least half a decade, Spaniards were relatively free in expropriating lands from the Indigenous. They took it either violently or through manipulated documents of land ownership, by releasing livestock on the coveted lands, by founding congregations, or by marrying a local woman. The Indigenous elite suffered as well, since their former laborers (*terrazgueros*) now left their fields to work for Spanish settlers or Franciscan friars. Martínez calculated that in total the inhabitants of Tecamachalco and Quecholac were deprived of over 137,000 hectares of land in the years from 1521 to 1644. These numbers represent a rather severe case. Nonetheless, the example illustrates well the diverse mechanisms of appropriation of land and Indigenous labor force by the Spaniards.[59]

Even after several attempts by the Crown to regulate and to limit the power of Spanish encomenderos, the latter blithely ignored the laws or at least found a way to skirt around them. This holds equally true for the Spaniards' access to local workforce. As has been shown in different studies, despite the repeated ban of the enslavement of indios by Isabella I and Charles V, exceptional circumstances still allowed such practices. These might include well-known reasons like justifying it by pointing to the indios' practice of anthropophagy or a so-called Just War, including rebellion against Christians, that self-righteously legitimized the Spanish enslaving local people. The possession of mills for wheat or sugar cane production was another excuse the Crown accepted to keep enslaved indios.[60] Apparently, as mentioned previously, ventures that helped feed the settlers or promised to enhance the value of the soil could count on the Crown's support. Whether this support goes back to the latter's interest in maintaining the presence of its vassals in the New World or due to successful "lobbying" is hard to tell.

To sum up this section, the multitude of divergent interests required constant negotiations. The historian Jonas Schirrmacher recently demonstrated this in regard of the Crown's policy concerning indio-slavery. Rather than a "chaotic policy," the ubiquitous exceptions granted, or at least tolerated, symbolize the political flexibility the Crown applied to reach compromises.[61] Similar negotiations between local actors (Indigenous lords, Spanish encomenderos or settlers, friars, and clergymen) and royal officials took place regarding the maintenance of encomiendas, the treatment of the indios, or the alienation of lands. Almost omnipresent workarounds to prohibitions do not prove an asserted inefficiency of the Crown's rule. Quite the contrary, they manifest the necessary flexibility in praxis to find a middle ground. In turn, this flexibility stemmed less from a strategic policy than from pragmatic negotiations in a contingent setting.[62] The debates and concessions granted to the Spaniards settling in New Spain evidence the ways in which the latter were attracted to stay in the area because of their access to local resources in people, goods, or lands.

SEMANTICS OF COLONIALISM

To receive an encomienda, land, pension, office, or symbolic titles, the Spanish had to either secure it in the immediate dividing of the spoils or ask the Crown via the petitioning procedure. The semantics of this process is particularly revelatory, as it gives insights not only into the personal claims of the conquistadors or the legal and administrative contexts but moreover into the powerful mechanisms of knowledge production and the establishment of archives.

The language in the Spanish sources regarding the *Conquista* is usually adapted to the legal, political, and social context in which the speech act is embedded. Referring to the act of conquering the lands the conquistadors spoke of *conquistar* but synonymously used the terms "to win land" (*ganar tierra*), "to pacify" (*pacificar*), as already mentioned, and "to put the provinces/towns/people/lands under Your Majesty's yoke" ("poner so el yugo de su magestad las prouinçias," etc.). Speaking of "settling" (*poblar*), they also used the expression "to perpetuate land" (*perpetuar tierra*). And by doing so or by cultivating the soil, they would, in their view, "ennoble land" (*ennoblecer tierra*), as discussed. The adaptation of language to the source's context has become particularly clear in the case of Philip II's replacement of the term "conquest" by "pacification" and their corresponding verbs.[63] Such semantic polyvalency and ambiguities make the heuristic reading of the sources a delicate task.

A certain uniformity of a series of expressions and phrases provide, in turn, helpful hints in the interpretation of sources. They are due to the widespread use of scribes and, depending on the type of source, due to the quite uniform production and organization of the documents. The administrative procedures often required redundant formulations, and the scribes followed common patterns applying set phrases. This practice resulted in the development or adaptation of topoi that can be found in many of the corresponding sources. For the very same reason, petitions from members of Indigenous elites normally contain the same characteristic style as those from Spaniards. Identical scribes or at least identical topoi and semantic gestures led to a shared language in the sources.[64] It remains unknown to what degree it was the scribes' habits and the administrative procedures that distorted the Indigenous voices or the latter's ability to shape their rhetoric according to European requirements. Moreover, the new power relations influenced ways of thinking and speaking. The colonial sources of Indigenous people are also adapted to this novel situation. They should be read accordingly in this colonial context.[65]

For the most part, though, the archives reflect the views of the Spanish and explicitly or implicitly degrade other actors to a minor position. For example, the Spaniards' conception of law obviously often excluded Amerindians regarding the possibility of suffering damage from certain actions. The clause that a certain contract or agreement should not be to the detriment of a third party customarily referred to other Spanish or at least European subjects. For instance, when the Crown allowed Cortés to explore the South Sea, it included this clause to avoid potentially clashing promises it had made to other contract explorers for nearby regions. In these cases, the Indigenous people were simply ignored, which suggests that they did not count as a potential third party according to Castilian law.[66]

Such an omission or other diminutions to minor roles have been noted and repeatedly lamented by scholars since the 1960s. Writ large, this is nothing new, but recent research has shown how productive and how necessary it is to integrate the aspect of the production of archives into historical analysis.[67] To a significant yet undefinable degree, the missing sources from marginalized actors are themselves the reason for these actors to be considered today as marginal.

This study hopes to have sufficiently pointed out wherever the compositions of the archives are "silencing," as the anthropologist Michel-Rolph Trouillot would call it, the contributions of allegedly minor participants. It has become clear how essential the Indigenous actors were both in cooperating with the Spaniards and in attracting and maintaining them in the New World, while at the same time how the Indigenous presence in the Spanish sources is mainly of a passive nature. Exactly in this style, Francisco de Granada mentions them concerning his military "deeds" of killing more than twenty Indigenous persons and capturing an opponent leader. In addition to these passive positions, he also assigns them a more active, but clearly negative, role, when mentioning "them" to have killed his horse with a trap as well as a Christian in a battle and to have taken a couple of Spaniards as prisoners.[68]

CONCLUSION

This chapter has analyzed the turning point of when conquistadors became settlers or, to phrase it differently, when expansive warfare turned into colonialism. By examining the dynamics of the entradas as well as the negotiations with the Indigenous allies and the royal officials, the following factors have crystalized as particularly influential for this transitional phase.

First, the participants' customs of dividing the booty generated their expectations to include receiving a share of the spoils. Since the Spanish conquistadors had joined these ventures at their own expenses and had frequently been indebted, they were under high pressure to "succeed" and had to continue till they found an appealing alternative. Furthermore, the distributed spoils consisted mainly of "goods" that could only be enjoyed locally, which fostered the incentives to settle.

This leads us to the second factor: the Spaniards' decision to settle was foundational. Even if this seems banal, it encapsulates a multifaceted interplay of negotiation processes and measures that proved vital for the dynamics of the *Conquista* as demonstrated here. In fact, it was an important step toward the emerging colonial institutions. Such steps were nevertheless for the most part only possible if support from the local people permitted them.

Hence, the third factor consists in the Indigenous' cooperation with the Spaniards. The Indigenous people's readiness to support the Spanish and to unite forces with them was critical. The reasons to do so are hard to extract from the sources, as the biased contemporary production of archives neglected or minimized their roles. The actions the Indigenous undertook still display a wide range of different forms of help, which provided the Spaniards with the necessary means to persevere in the area.

In conclusion and always on the basis of contingent and environmental influences, these factors shaped the multifarious transition from conquering entradas to colonialism. Francisco de Granada has served here as a random example to personify this process. Apart from his award of a personal coat of arms, which elevated him socially above the average conquistador, he makes a representative case. Just like him, most of his fellow Spaniards attempted in one way or another to claim some source of revenue that allowed them to establish themselves in the New World. By doing so, they often produced the archival evidence that has influenced the narrative about this process to this day.

NOTES

1. Granada's leaders were Cortés, Diego de Ordaz, Jorge de Alvarado, and Bernardino Vázquez de Tapia, then Gonzalo de Sandoval, Pedro de Briones, Pedro de Alvarado, and Vasco Porcallo. Archivo General de Indias (henceforth AGI), Patronato, 54, n. 6, r. 1, fols.

1r–9v, Información de méritos y servicios (henceforth IMS) de Francisco de Granada, 1529. I am grateful to John F. Schwaller, Benjamin Steiner, and the anonymous reviewers for their insightful comments on earlier versions of this text.

2. See the discussion and references in my introduction to this volume.

3. Matthew Restall, *Maya Conquistador* (Boston: Beacon Press, 1998); Matthew Restall, "Black Conquistadors: Armed Africans in Early Spanish America," *Americas* 57, no. 2 (2003a): 171–205; Matthew Restall, "A History of the New Philology and the New Philology in History," *Latin American Research Review* 38, no. 1 (2003b): 113–34.

4. Some exceptions have been doing exactly this. See, e.g., Richard Flint and Shirley Flint, *A Most Splendid Company: The Coronado Expedition in Global Perspective* (Albuquerque: University of New Mexico Press, 2019); Vitus Huber, *Die Konquistadoren: Cortés, Pizarro und die Eroberung Amerikas* (Munich: C. H. Beck, 2019); or George Lovell, Christopher Lutz, and Wendy Kramer, *Strike Fear in the Land: Pedro de Alvarado and the Conquest of Guatemala, 1520–1541* (Norman: Oklahoma University Press, 2020).

5. See, e.g., Horst Pietschmann, *Die staatliche Organisation des kolonialen Iberoamerika* (Stuttgart: Klett-Cotta, 1980); Peter Boyd-Bowman, *Indice geobiográfico de más de 56 mil pobladores de la América Hispánica* (Mexico City: Instituto de Investigaciones Históricas Fondo de Cultura Económica, 1985); or Robert Himmerich y Valencia, *The Encomenderos of New Spain, 1521–1555* (Austin: University of Texas Press, 1991).

6. "Sy saben q*ue* pase a estas partes a mi costa e misyo*n* syn me dar nadie sueldo ni otro ynterese salvo por servir a su mag*estad* e por mas valer." (All translations by V. H. Citations are not modernized, abbreviations are spelled out in italics, and "[*sic*]" is not used for common contemporary orthographic variations, like "y" for "i," etc.). AGI, Patronato, 54, n. 6, r. 1, fol. 2r, IMS Francisco de Granada, 1529.

7. Juan de Nájera's testimony: "No se daba acostami*en*to ni salario a ningun conq*ui*stador e q*ue* todos andaban a su costa e q*ue* . . . la mayor p*ar*te de la gente andan e trabajan por mas valer." AGI, Patronato, 54, n. 6, r. 1, fol. 3v, IMS Francisco de Granada, 1529.

8. For an in-depth analysis of this structure, see Vitus Huber, *Beute und Conquista: Die politische Ökonomie der Eroberung Neuspaniens* (Frankfurt: Campus, 2018); and Vitus Huber, "The Spiral of Spoils: Booty, Distributive Justice, and Empire Formation in the *Conquista* of Mexico," *Colonial Latin American Review* 31, no. 1 (2022): 133–57.

9. AGI, Patronato, 54, n. 6, r. 1, fol. 2v, IMS Francisco de Granada, 1529.

10. "Me vine a esta çibdad biendome p*er*dido e syn probecho ninguno despues de año e medio pasado q*ue* andaba en aquellas p*ro*vincias sirviendo al rey n*ue*stro señor e dexe hecha la villa en guatemalan q*ue* llamaban santiago." AGI, Patronato, 54, n. 6, r. 1, fol. 3r, IMS Francisco de Granada, 1529.

11. See later in chapter on Cortés's expedition to the South Sea.

12. Huber, *Beute und Conquista*, 235–57.

13. For the spiral of spoils, see Huber, "The Spiral of Spoils"; for the pre-Hispanic martial culture, see Ross Hassig, *War and Society in Ancient Mesoamerica* (Berkeley: University of California Press, 1992); and Marco Antonio Cervera Obregón, *El armamento entre los mexicas* (Madrid: Ediciones Polifemo, 2007). For Cortés and his alliances, see John Elliott, "The Mental World of Hernán Cortés," *Transactions of the Royal Historical Society* 17 (1967): 41–58; and James Lockhart, *We People Here: Nahuatl Accounts of the Conquest of Mexico* (Berkeley: University of California Press, 1993).

14. On the mobilization of Indigenous conquistadors, see, e.g., AGI, Patronato, 54, n. 3, r. 1, 2, fol. 41r; furthermore, see Laura Matthew and Michel Oudijk, eds., *Indian Conquistadors. Indigenous Allies in the Conquest of Mesoamerica* (Norman: University of Oklahoma Press, 2007); and Marco Antonio Cervera Obregón, *Guerreros aztecas: Armas, técnicas de combate e historia militar del implacable ejército que conquistó Mesoamérica* (Madrid: Ediciones Nowtilus, 2011), ch. X.

15. See, e.g., Michel Oudijk and Matthew Restall, *Conquista de buenas palabras y de guerra: Una visión indígena de la conquista* (Mexico City: Beacon Press, 2013); Camilla Townsend, *Fifth Sun: A New History of the Aztecs* (Oxford: Oxford University Press, 2020); and Robert Haskett's chapter in this volume.

16. "Salio con la gente que a maçatlan con muchos yndios de paz de la provinçia de acalan e conquisto la dicha provinçia de maçatlan con muchos señores della syrvieron o dieron tributos e binieron con el dicho contador de paz fasta cochiztlan que es en la costa del norte e desde alli se bolvieron para sus casas." AGI, Justicia, 1005, n. 3, r. 1, fol. 30r–v.

17. See Yanna Yannakakis, "The Indios Conquistadores of Oaxaca's Sierra Norte: From Indian Conquerors to Local Indians," in *Indian Conquistadors. Indigenous Allies in the Conquest of Mesoamerica*, ed. Laura Matthew and Michel Oudijk (Norman: University of Oklahoma Press, 2007), 227–53. Furthermore, a lawsuit between the fiscal and the Mexicah, Tlaxcaltecah, and Zapotecah from 1564–78 is arguably the most informative—though heavily loaden with particular interests—source regarding their participation at the conquest of Guatemala. AGI, Justicia, 291, n. 1, r. 1, esp. fols. 68r, 144v–148r, 156r, 174r–v, 178r, and 181r.

18. Evidence can be found in all kinds of sources, most famously in Cortés's letters or various chronicles like Diego Durán's *Historia*, etc. See Hernán Cortés, *Cartas de relación*, ed. Mario Hernández Sánchez-Barba (Madrid: Historia 16, 1985); and Diego Durán, *Historia de las Indias de Nueva-España y islas de Tierra Firme*, ed. José Ramírez, 2 vols. (Mexico City: J. M. Andrade y F. Escalante, 1867). See furthermore Yanna Yannakakis, *The Art of Being In-Between: Native Intermediaries, Indian Identity, and Local Rule in Colonial Oaxaca* (Durham, NC: Duke University Press, 2008), 3–11 and 220–27.

19. While her exact impact is hard to measure, her value to Cortés becomes already evident in his letters to King Charles. See Cortés, *Cartas*, 104; see also Juan Miralles Ostos, *La Malinche: Raíz de México*, 2nd ed. (Mexico City: Tusquets, 2004), 14; Camilla Townsend,

Malintzin's Choices: An Indian Woman in the Conquest of Mexico (Albuquerque: University of New Mexico Press, 2006), 40–41; and Lori Diel's chapter in this volume.

20. Letter of Cortés to King Charles, October 30, 1520, edited in Cortés, *Cartas*, 77–182, here 165–67; on the role of food, see Janet Long, ed., *Conquista y comida: Consecuencias del encuentro de dos mundos* (Mexico City: Universidad Nacional Autónoma de México, 1996).

21. E.g., from the Spanish settlement of Villa de la Victoria in Tabasco, the hungry Spaniards attacked neighboring villages and plundered their corn stocks but regarded this as perilous and unsustainable. AGI, Justicia, 1005, n. 3, r. 1, fols. 45r–46v, Lawsuit Francisco de Montejo, 1532–33.

22. Oudijk and Restall, *Conquista*, 74–79.

23. AGI, Indiferente, 427, L. 29, fols. 67r–93v, Ordenanzas de descubrimiento y población, July 13, 1573, edited either scattered around in Antonio de León Pinelo, *Recopilación de las Indias*, ed. Ismael Sánchez Bella (Mexico City: Escuela Libre de Derecho, 1992); or en bloc but with errors in the transcription in Diego de Encinas, *Cedulario indiano: Recopilado 1596*, ed. Alfonso García Gallo, 4 vols. (Madrid: Ediciones Cultura Hispánica, 1945), 4: 232–46.

24. AGI, Patronato, 193, r. 26, fols. 1r–6v, Requerimiento de repartimiento de indios Venezuela, 1534.

25. "Que si de aquí adelante ellos pacíficamente quisieren darse a su servicio que los españoles no ternán con ellos batallas ni guerras, antes mucha conformidad e paz, e serán en ayudarles contra sus enemigos, e todas las otras cosas que a vos os pareciere que les deben decir para los atraer a vuestro propósito." AGI, Patronato, 15, r. 11, fol. 4v, cited after José Luis Martínez, ed., *Documentos cortesianos: 1518–1528 Secciones I a III*, 3 vols. (Mexico City: Fondo de Cultura Económica, 1990), 1: 51; and AGI, Patronato, 193, r. 26, fols. 1r–6v, Requerimiento de repartimiento de indios Venezuela, 1534, 312–13.

26. On the ally between the Spanish and Tlaxcaltecah, see Andrea Martínez Baracs, *Un gobierno de indios. Tlaxcala, 1519–1750* (Mexico City: Fondo de Cultura Económica, 2008), 37–67.

27. See the classic studies by Robert Chamberlain, "Castilian Backgrounds of the Repartimiento-Encomienda," *Contributions to American Anthropology and History* 5, no. 25 (1939): 19–66; and Hilda Grassotti, "Para la historia del botín y de las parias en León y Castilla," *Cuadernos de Historia de España* 39–40 (1964): 43–132.

28. Erin Stone, *Captives of Conquest: Slavery in the Early Modern Spanish Caribbean* (Philadelphia: University of Pennsylvania Press, 2021), 63–70.

29. Peter Villella, "Indian Lords, Hispanic Gentlemen: The Salazars of Colonial Tlaxcala," *Americas* 69, no. 1 (2012): 1–36; of the vast literature on the encomienda, see José Miranda, *El tributo indígena en la Nueva España durante el siglo XVI*, 4th ed. (Mexico City: El Colegio de México, Centro de Estudios Históricos, 2005); and Lesley B. Simpson, *The Encomienda: The Beginning of Spanish Mexico*, 3rd ed. (Berkeley: University of California

Press, 2008). On the Mesoamerican habits, see Ross Hassig, *Aztec Warfare: Imperial Expansion and Political Control* (Norman: University of Oklahoma Press, 1988); and chaps. 20–21 of bk. 8 of Bernardino Sahagún, *Historia general de las cosas de Nueva España*, ed. Juan Carlos Temprano, 2 vols. (Madrid: Linkgua, 2001), 682–87; and Bodleian Library Oxford, Ms. Arch. Selden A. 1, fol. 64r.

30. Archivo General de la Nación, Hospital de Jesús 4a, L. 19(2), Ordenanzas de buen gobierno, March 20, 1524, edited in Martínez, *Documentos cortesianos*, 1: 277–83. For my argument that this shift of the responsibility of rewarding the conquistadors was crucial for the establishment of colonial structures, see Huber, *Beute und Conquista*, 301–26.

31. AGI, Patronato, 54, n. 6, r. 1, fols. 2r–3r, IMS Francisco de Granada, 1529.

32. *Las siete partidas del sabio rey don Alonso el nono, nuevamente glosadas por el licenciado Gregorio López del Consejo Real de Indias de su Majestad*, 3 vols. (Madrid 1972; orig. printed ca. 1265) (henceforth Partidas), 2: título 25, ley 2.

33. For an in-depth analysis of this phenomenon, see Huber, *Beute und Conquista*, 57–68 and 301–57; or with a focus on Castile, see Victoria Sandoval Parra, *Manera de galardón: Merced pecuniaria y extranjería en el siglo XVII* (Mexico City: Fondo Cultura Económica, 2014), 76–91.

34. António Hespanha, "Les autres raisons de la politique: L'économie de la grâce," in *Recherche sur l'histoire de l'État dans le monde ibérique (15e–20e siècle)*, ed. Jean-Frédéric Schaub (Paris: Presses de l'École normale supérieure, 1993), 81–84.

35. AGI, Patronato, 54, n. 6, r. 1, fols. 2v–3r, IMS Francisco de Granada, 1529.

36. AGI, México, 1088, L. 1bis, fols. 170r–172r, Real provisión Francisco de Granada, 1532.

37. "Soy de los primeros vezinos e moradores de esta çibdad e que he mi casa en ella e la tengo poblada de los primeros." AGI, Patronato, 54, n. 6, r. 1, fol. 2v, IMS Francisco de Granada, 1529.

38. Real Provisión, October 22, 1523, edited in Martínez, *Documentos cortesianos*, 1: 272–74.

39. Huber, *Beute und Conquista*, 214–25.

40. "Podria traer ynconviniente la yda de hernando cortes porque todos los spañoles se yran con el al nuevo descubrimiento y se despoblara la tierra pero que se le haria agravio en detenerle estando a punto para hazer su viaje [*al margen*: fiat.] Paresçe que no deve ser detenido sino que vaya." AGI, Indiferente, 737, n. 5, fols. 1r–2v, Consultas Consejo de Indias, 1529.

41. Letter Jerónimo López to Charles V, 10 February 1534, edited in *Epistolario de Nueva España: 1505–1818*, ed. Francisco Paso y Troncoso, 16 vols. (Mexico City: Porrúa, 1939–42), 3: 132–35.

42. AGI, Patronato, 54, n. 6, r. 1, fol. 2v, IMS Francisco de Granada, 1529; Partidas vol. 2, título 26, ley 1–9. For an example of judicial dispute about Cortés's first allotment, see AGI, Justicia, 220, n. 1, fols. 3v–525v, Juicio de residencia Cortés, 1526.

43. "Tengo e [h]e tenido armas e cavallo e [h]e ayudado a sustener lo ganado en servi*ci*o de su mag*estad* hasta agora e q*ue* dende q*ue* entre en esta nueva españa con cortes el capitan q*ue* fue e govern*ad*or nunca e salido desta t*ie*rra." AGI, Patronato, 54, n. 6, r. 1, fol. 3r, IMS Francisco de Granada, 1529.

44. "Syenpre me [h]e llegado al servi*ci*o de su mag*estad* e q*ue* no e hecho cosa contra su servi*ci*o porq*ue* me ayan castigado ni de otra m*a*nera." AGI, Patronato, 54, n. 6, r. 1, fol. 3r, IMS Francisco de Granada, 1529.

45. "Ni podremos sustentarnos e*n* la perpetuaçion de la tierra para dexar en ella n*ues*tros hijos a v*ue*stra m*a*gestad vmillmente suplicamos [. . .] mandarnos dar m*er*çed conviniente para n*ues*tro sustento y perpetuaçion pa*r*a q*ue* en v*ue*stro real serviçio podamos sustentar e perpetuar la tierra q*ue* con tantos trabajos ganamos." AGI, Patronato, 184, r. 36, fol. 1r–v, Petition from Conquistadores de México, 1544.

46. "Yo [Juan Garrido] fui el primero senbro [sic] y otras cosas por razón de lo qual e por aver hecho esta espirencia vino gran bien a esta tierra." Witness Alonso Martín de Jerez confirmed that "este testigo le vido senbrar dos granos de trigo en una huerta . . . e que de los dichos dos granos de trigo se cojo ciento e sesenta espigas donde fue prencipio que se senbrase trigo." Juan González Ponce de León stated that he saw him sow two grains of wheat "de donde ay todo quanto trigo que hay en esta nueva españa." Cited after Hugh Thomas, *Who's Who of the Conquistadors* (London: Cassell, 2000), 60–61; for more on Garrido, see Restall, "Black Conquistadors."

47. "Su Majestad debría mandar proveer de aquí un par de navíos que fuesen allá para traer a estas partes planta e simiente del Especiería, pues todas estas islas y tierras [de Nueva España] son aptas para ello, la cual extendería por todas estas tierras, y deshacerse hía todo el trato de Levante y Portugal, y quedaría en Castilla, y todas estas tierras se ennoblecerían y poblarían mucho más, y Su Majestad podría haber dello muy grandes rentas, ganando bula de Su Santidad de los diezmos della, y imponiendo otro diezmo por sus derechos, más lo que había de los almojarifazgos de lo que allá fuese." AGI, Patronato, 184, r. 6, fols. 1r–7r, cited in Martínez, *Documentos cortesianos*, 1: 397–98.

48. "Enviando buenos pilotos y personas que sepan de planta y simiente; y aun para los armar y enviar, aquí habría quien lo hiciese si Su Majestad no lo quisiese hacer a su costa, con que les dejasen rescatar y traer especiería en ellos; pero lo mejor era hacello los oficiales de Su Majestad. Y también, señores, mandando Su Majestad descobrir las dichas islas y tierras en la Mar del Sur, se ennoblecería esta Nueva España, enviando Su Majestad aquí, como le han suplicado, todo género de planta y simientes, pues lo lleva la tierra en mucha abundancia." AGI, Patronato, 184, r. 6, fols. 1r–7r, cited in Martínez, *Documentos cortesianos*, 1: 398. For botany in the Spanish empire in general, see Antonio Barrera-Osorio, *Experiencing Nature: The Spanish American Empire and the Early Scientific Revolution* (Austin: University of Texas Press, 2006); and Omri Bassewitsch Frenkel, "Transplantation of Asian Spices

in the Spanish Empire 1518–1640: Entrepreneurship, Empiricism, and the Crown" (PhD diss., McGill University, Montreal, 2017).

49. E.g., Archivo General de Notarías de México (henceforth AGNM) 1, vol. 52, ficha 45, fols. 85r–87v, Compañía Lorenzo Genovés, Pedro de Maya, and Pedro Rodríguez de Carmona 1525; or AGNM, 1, vol. 54, ficha 253, fol. 209r–v, Tenure García de Llerena for Pedro García Moreno 1528. This archive would be a good point of departure for examining, e.g., the importance of pig farms, the introduction of cattle or sugar mills, etc. More generally, ecological influences *on* and the role of animals *in* the *Conquista* and early colonial phase—beyond the aspects of horses or dogs and the "Columbian exchange"—offer still a field for further research.

50. See, e.g., José Miranda, *La función económica del encomendero en los orígenes del régimen colonial (Nueva España, 1525–1531)*, 2nd ed. (Mexico City: Universidad Nacional Autónoma, 1965); Esteban Mira Caballos, *El indio antillano: Repartimiento, encomienda y esclavitud (1492–1542)* (Seville: Múñoz Moya, 1997); and Simpson, *Encomienda*.

51. Cf. note 36.

52. AGI, Patronato, 56, n. 2, r. 1, fol. 4r, IMS Francisco Téllez et al., 1541.

53. AGI, Patronato, 56, n. 2, r. 1, fols. 3v–4r, IMS Francisco Téllez et al., 1541.

54. On early colonial negotiations, see Lara Sembolini, *La construcción de la autoridad virreinal en Nueva España, 1535–1595* (Mexico City: Colegio de México, 2014); and Martin Nesvig, *Promiscuous Power: An Unorthodox History of New Spain* (Austin: University of Texas Press, 2018); on the important role of local rulers, see Ethelia Ruiz Medrano, *Reshaping New Spain: Government and Private Interests in the Colonial Bureaucracy, 1531–1550* (Boulder: University Press of Colorado, 2006); for the lords of Tetzcoco, see Bradley Benton, *The Lords of Tetzcoco: The Transformation of Indigenous Rule in Postconquest Central Mexico* (New York: Cambridge University Press, 2017).

55. Letter reserved for Charles V of 15 October 1524, edited in Martínez, *Documentos cortesianos*, 1: 285–95, here 289–90; Real Academia de la Historia, Madrid, 2/Ms caja 5, n. 57, Cortés's statement on repartimiento, 1526.

56. "Porque el bien de todos estos reinos tan anchos é espaciosos está en que estén poblados de indios, y faltando estos falta todo." Letter of January 22, 1518, edited in Martin Fernández de Navarrete, ed., *Colección de documentos inéditos para la historia de España*, 113 vols. (Madrid: Imprenta de la Viuda de Calero, 1842–95), 2: 347–75, here 348.

57. AGI, Patronato, 277, n. 4, r. 142, fols. 1r–4r, Real Provisión, September 18, 1538; see also AGI, México, 203, n. 32, fols. 1r–24v, IMS Gutierre de Badajoz et al., 1537.

58. For the common practice of sending indios to work in mines, see the data on temporary companies (compañías) in the Archivo General de Notarías de México. E.g., AGNM, 1, vol. 52, ficha 17, fols. 17r–18r.

59. See Hildeberto Martínez, *Codiciaban la tierra: El despojo agrario en los señoríos de Tecamachalco y Quecholac (Puebla, 1520–1650)* (Mexico City: Centro de Investigaciones y Estudios Superiores en Antropología Social, 1994), 137–48.

60. Cf., e.g., Archivo General de la Nación, Mexico City, Hospital de Jesús, vol. 414, leg. 235, exp. 8, Accounts of Cortés's sugar production, 1542; Jonas Schirrmacher, *Die Politik der Sklaverei: Praxis und Konflikt in Kastilien und Spanisch-Amerika im 16. Jahrhundert* (Paderborn, Germany: Ferdinand Schöningh, 2018), 209–91.

61. Schirrmacher, *Politik der Sklaverei*, 292–349.

62. On the casuistic application of the colonial laws, see Victor Tau Anzoátegui, *Casuismo y sistema: Indagación histórica sobre el espíritu del Derecho Indiano* (Buenos Aires: Instituto de Investigaciones de Historia del Derecho, 1992); and on the Crown's policy of flexibility, see Arndt Brendecke, *The Empirical Empire: Spanish Colonial Rule and the Politics of Knowledge* (Berlin: De Gruyter, 2016), esp. 235–78.

63. Cf. note 23.

64. For further details, see Huber, *Beute und Conquista*, 301–57.

65. See Serge Gruzinski, *La colonisation de l'imaginaire: Sociétés indigènes et occidentalisation dans le Mexique espagnol XVIe–XVIIIe siècle* (Paris: Gallimard, 1988), 6–10.

66. E.g., "Asimismo he por bien que [*a Cortés*] se le haga merçed de las tierras de labrança y pensiones que sup*l*ico en la nueva españa con que se ponga la clausula que sea sin perjuizio de terçero." AGI, Indiferente, 737, n. 1, fols. 1r–4v, here fol. 3v, Consulta del Consejo de Indias, 1529.

67. The classic work is Michel-Rolph Trouillot, *Silencing the Past: Power and the Production of History* (Boston: Beacon, 1995). For more recent studies, see Ann Laura Stoler, *Along the Archival Grain: Epistemic Anxieties and Colonial Common Sense* (Princeton, NJ: Princeton University Press, 2009); Nancy van Deusen, "Indigenous Slavery's Archive in Seventeenth-Century Chile," *Hispanic American Historical Review* 101, no. 1 (2021): 1–33; or Jorge Cañizares-Esguerra and Adrian Masters, *The Radical Spanish Empire: Petitions and the Creation of the New World* (Cambridge, MA: Harvard University Press, 2021).

68. AGI, Patronato, 54, n. 6, r. 1, fols. 1r–9v, IMS Francisco de Granada, 1529.

3

The *Conquista* of Mexico Today

Hyperactive Memory, National Identity, and Symbolic Violence

JUSTYNA OLKO

It is as if Hernando Cortés and his soldiers had conquered Mexico only yesterday. At any given moment the Conquest looms more immediate than the forays of Pancho Villa. The attack upon the Great Teocalli, the Noche Triste, and the Destruction of Tenochtitlan did not take place early in the sixteenth century, but just last year.
—José Clemente Orozco, *An Autobiography* (2011)

We have one attitude toward the dead Indians, a very different one toward the living. The dead Indians excite our admiration, stimulate a stream of tourists; the living Indians make us blush with shame, give a hollow ring to our fine words of progress and democracy.
—Fernando Benítez, *Los indios de México* (1967)

Today, August 13, a day of mourning, as our teacher Carlos Pellicer would say, we recall the fall of the Great Tenochtitlan and we offer forgiveness to the victims of the catastrophe caused by the Spanish military occupation of Mesoamerica and the rest of the territory of today's Mexican Republic.
—Andrés Manuel López Obrador, August 13, 2021

To see, we must set aside the dark glass, and see as we are seen, ideas for what they are, history what we make.... If we see history as it is, we see our places in it, what

we might change, and how we might do better. We halt our thoughtless journey from inevitability to eternity, and exit the road to unfreedom.
—Timothy Snyder, *The Road to Unfreedom: Russia, Europe, America* (2018)

REMOTE PAST AND CONTEMPORARY HISTORY

The multiplicity of stories of the *Conquista* of Mexico reflecting different perspectives, goals, and even ontologies are retrievable from the complex historical records and narratives created and re-created, modified and transforming from the very first moments of contact between the Indigenous people and the Europeans. While historians are well aware of this diversity of voices and viewpoints, it is difficult to resist the impression that the official—and no doubt most popular and widely shared—story of the Spanish *Conquista* in contemporary Mexico and beyond is surprisingly uncomplicated. And yet, despite the over 500 years that separate us from these historical events, it is not about a remote and objectivized story that does not have any real impact on the present social reality. The profound source of this connection is not just the solemn and spectacular celebrations of different anniversaries, beginning with the commemoration of 500 years since the "discovery of America" in 1992 and ending in the most recent anniversary of 500 years since the fall of Tenochtitlan in 2021, even if these public spectacles and associated media content no doubt highlight the relevance of these historical developments for the present. By focusing on symbolic events detached from the multiplicity of perspectives represented by their protagonists and from their long-term aftermath, anniversary celebrations have obscured answers to the question of why this remote past matters so much and how it really connects to the present. When addressing the complex issue of the *Conquista* of Mexico today, it would indeed be difficult to provide a more salient example that illustrates the fundamental statement made in 1961 by Edward Carr in his book *What Is History?*, namely, that "all history is 'contemporary history.'"[1] The *Conquista* of Mexico does not merely occupy a prominent and powerful space in historical research. More important, it both shapes and has been shaped by social reality in at least two powerful ways. One is through the contemporary interpretations, renderings, understandings, uses, and misuses of the past that inform both "public knowledge" and academic discourses. The second exerts an even more profound impact on people's lives as it involves the present outcomes of long-term historical processes. Perhaps less obviously, I wish to argue that the two processes reinforce and sustain each other; and, paradoxically, that they carry the potential for challenging the social reality of stigma, discrimination, and symbolic violence.

PARTICIPANTS AND NARRATIVES OF THE *CONQUISTA*

I would like to mark explicit distance from the Spanish *Conquista* for several reasons. During the last two decades or so, historians working with Indigenous sources from Mesoamerica have repeatedly shown the inadequacy of this concept. The fact that the historical circumstances reached well beyond the Spanish-Mexica conflict was extensively documented and discussed in an important vein of "New conquest history" exploring the role of Indigenous actors in these events. This revisionist history reintroducing the important group of Indigenous agents, or *indios conquistadores*, on the historical scene, was both in line with the Spanish concept of military alliance and the Indigenous tradition of war making and interethnic collaboration, even if their ontological frameworks differed on many levels.[2] This line of scholarship, however, has been followed by another important "interpretative turn," the explicit manifestation of which was an ethnohistory workshop in 2019 organized by John F. Schwaller and titled "The Spanish-Mexica War at 500." The conceptual switch from conquest to war implies in fact a paradigm change. During the 2019 workshop, I proposed to add yet another dimension to this conflict of profound historical consequences: the Tenochtitlan-Tlaxcallan war. It is widely recognized that political, social, and ethnic loyalty in Mesoamerica was primarily owed to the local *altepetl*, or Indigenous states. The localized sense of identity made interethnic tensions and conflicting interests especially salient during the Spanish invasion. It is enough to recall the disparate Mexica and Tlatelolca narratives of the defense of Tenochtitlan, with the latter even accusing the former of cowardice and poor military performance.[3] Under the circumstances provoked by the European intruders, most of the local altepetl continued to view and explain the situation through their own traditional lens, securing their assets and often attempting to profit from the conflict. Later on, active military participation as Spanish allies—based or not on fact—became a recurrent political argument and rhetorical assertion in negotiations with the crown. The Tlaxcaltecah were not unique actors on this scene, though they were perhaps among the most visible and definitely the most remembered in Mexican history.

As the Mexicah and their allies consolidated their expanding empire in the second half of the fifteenth century, they clashed with the strong regional state of Tlaxcallan. The Mexicah, inhabitants of Tenochtitlan, and the Tlaxcaltecah, a people who established their own multiethnic state, shared much of their origins and cultural traditions. Both derived their ancestry from the quasi-mythical Chichimecs, who had arrived from the north and established their states through war and conquest, subjugating local agrarian populations in the areas they settled, often including other ethnic groups, such as the Otomi, in their expanding states.

They spoke closely related variants of Nahuatl, which is evident in their rich corpora of colonial texts in this language. Many historical myths have emerged around the Mexica-Tlaxcalteca conflict, beginning with the *xochiyaoyotl*, or flowery war, that according to early colonial sources, was a predetermined battle aimed not at conquest and killing but at capturing prisoners for ritual sacrifice. Scholars still argue whether it was indeed a mechanism for acquiring captives for sacrifice, a training arena for young warriors, a passionate sport, or a real confrontation in which the Mexicah hid their defeats under political rhetoric. Notably, it was only the Mexicah, not the Tlaxcaltecah, who called them "flowery wars."[4] And according to early colonial accounts, the death toll was heavy on both sides, thus unmasking the imperial "disinformation strategy" concerning what was in fact a harsh and recurring war of conquest and defense.

If the permanent resistance and sustained military conflict between the Mexicah and the Tlaxcaltecah was real, and there is no reason to believe it was not, we should rethink the military, psychological, political, and social impact of the Tlaxcalteca participation as Spanish allies in the war against Tenochtitlan in 1519–21. Of course, the Tlaxcaltecah had visited Tenochtitlan before, but according to the written sources, these were secret visits of elites during state festivals, hidden from the general population. And it was the participation of the Tlaxcaltecah in this war that became one of the key moments that determined their place in Mexican history—much different from any other Indigenous group in Mexico—even if, needless to add, they were just one of the many local states that decided to side with Spaniards. Some pro-Tlaxcallan historians claim that the military leader Xicotencatl used all possible resources to stop the invaders. Only after failing did he resort to different tactics and begin negotiations.[5] And the decision of the Tlaxcaltecah to offer peace to the newcomers was not determined by suspicions about their possible supernatural origin; it could have been directly spurred by the actions of Tenochtitlan. In fact, the determination was probably made in view of the appearance of Moteuczoma's messengers in Tlaxcallan territory, suing for peace and offering tribute in the Spanish defensive camp.[6] Tlaxcalteca rulers decided to offer their friendship before it was too late and a possible Mexica-Spanish alliance could be assembled against them. As a result, later in 1519 the Tlaxcaltecah were received along with the Spaniards in imperial Tenochtitlan. Thus, the Mexicah were forced to not only peacefully receive but also maintain thousands of the enemies of Tlaxcallan along with Cortés.

It is not surprising, then, that the Mexica and Tlaxcalteca discourses of the *Conquista* were markedly different and remain so to this day, the former narrative having been appropriated and reelaborated by the Mexican state. Unlike so many other groups in Central Mexico and beyond, the Mexicah did not claim the merit of having collaborated with the invaders; rather, they conveyed a heroic vision of resistance, bravery, and extreme suffering that reflects their construction of historical memory in the first decades after the war. Influential examples of these narratives are the accounts written in Nahuatl and contained in Book 12 of the *Florentine Codex* as well as the *Anales de Tlatelolco*. However, these reports also make us aware of other interethnic conflicts during the invasion and in the decades that followed it, revealing the historical reality as much more complex than the way that it is reconstructed and retold in contemporary discourses.

OPPRESSION, CONTINUITY, AND RESILIENCE: MISSING CENTURIES IN MEXICAN NATIONAL HISTORY

Despite differing experiences and roles in the Spanish invasion, the fate of the Native altepetl under Spanish rule was in many ways similar, no matter the extent of royal privileges, which were never sufficient enough to stop the many forms of violence, increasing exploitation, socioeconomic disadvantage, and discrimination. Violent measures aimed at the eradication of preconquest beliefs and practices in the early colonial period deeply affected numerous aspects of social and ritual life: they had broad repercussions and were remembered by the Nahuas as the time of "terror" and were accompanied by a sense of cultural trauma.[7] These adverse circumstances were exacerbated by climatic anomalies, recurring series of epidemics, demographic and economic changes, and new forms of migration.[8] An inherent aspect of the long-term resilience of Indigenous people securing their ethnic, sociopolitical, and cultural survival was that they internalized key elements of Spanish culture, economy, and the legal system in order to resist colonialism.[9] Indigenous people learned how to use the existing regulations for their own benefit, especially drawing on the privileges resulting from their adscription to the Indigenous group (*indios*). However, the colonial circumstances also set in motion processes of prolonged change that proved disruptive to many aspects of life and culture. In the later colonial period, continuing epidemics and climatic anomalies as well as increased pressure form Spanish settlers and landholders, often encroaching on Native communities, became major challenges.

It was in the colonial period when the *Conquista*, or rather its aftermath, including the establishment of the Spanish administration, became an important part of the engaged memory of the altepetl. Even though it was transformed by more recent colonial history and cross-cultural contact, it remained a story of resilience and defense of lands and autonomy.[10] When viewed through Indigenous sources, colonial history is not just a record of oppression and violence but also a record of collective agency, manifest most likely in all of the spatiotemporal dimensions of life in New Spain. This history of resilience of the Indigenous people, documented and perpetuated in the historical record created by the Native people in their own languages, has become a fertile ground for scholarly research in the last several decades; surprisingly enough, it has only found a very pale and highly incomplete reflection in the educational programs of the Mexican state and even less so in the Indigenous communities struggling to preserve their ethnic identity and integrity in much the same ways as their ancestors in colonial times.

The public visibility of Indigenous history during the "dark ages" of Spanish rule is also limited or virtually absent. A notable exception is the rich section of colonial history in the Museo de la Memoria in Tlaxcala, which includes direct testimonies from Indigenous alphabetic and pictorial manuscripts from the region that are contextualized in complex narratives covering many aspects of past ways of local life. The most striking example of this absence is the Museo Nacional de Antropología in the Mexican capital, which attests to the unbridgeable gap between the glorious civilizations of the pre-Columbian era and the impoverished and marginalized contemporary cultures of Mexico, separated by the shameful hiatus of the colonial era. And this, in fact, has strong ideological underpinnings in the modern history of the Mexican state, which produced, among other visible *manifestos* of its celebrated national past, the Museo Nacional de Antropología. The creation and development of this institution coincide with the emergence and evolution of the independent Mexican state, with the origins of the museum going back to 1825; a significant increase in support and investment for archaeological explorations came during the regime of José de la Cruz Porfirio Díaz and its glorification of the splendid "Aztec" history, so violently and irreversibly interrupted by the arrival of the Spaniards. No wonder "scholars found it more profitable to confine their attention to Indians who had been dead for a number of centuries."[11]

A NATIONAL RECONNECTION WITH THE AZTECS: A FICTITIOUS "HISTORICAL TURN" FOR THE INDIGENOUS PEOPLE

The situation for the Indigenous people experienced a profound and even more adverse change during the first century of Mexican independence; in fact, it threatened the very basis of their ethnolinguistic and cultural existence. The position of Native towns and their sociopolitical autonomy became heavily undermined. During the colonial period, they operated as dynamic and self-governed corporate organizations with fundamental economic, political, religious, and educational functions. However, while the general and enduring strategy of the new state oscillated between extermination and assimilation, one of its fundamental aims was to weaken the links of the Indigenous people to specific communities and integrate them in the market of global labor.[12] Following the loss of communal land as a result of the reform of the Ley Lerdo of 1856, many of their inhabitants turned to work as hired workforce in haciendas and ranchos, rural estates, as well as in plantations, mines, and factories to a much greater degree than was the case in the colonial period.

The adverse situation of local communities was closely linked to the abolition of the colonial category of indios, along with its rights, privileges, and some important administrative and organizational principles at the community level. The Congreso Constituyente of 1822 introduced the broad category of "citizens," excluding any ethnic identifications, as a necessary step in the creation of a modern and unified nation. Liberal thinkers of that time believed that the Indigenous people needed to be fully "fused" with the general society and that the indios did not exist anymore,[13] doomed to disappear as a major obstacle to progress. Thus, for example, the liberal politician and ideologist José María Luis Mora described Indigenous people as "stubbornly addicted to their opinions, uses, and customs and it is never possible to make them change it; and this inflexible obstinacy is an insurmountable obstacle to the progress they could make."[14] Moreover, "in their actual condition . . . they will never be able to reach the degree of enlightenment, civilization, and culture of the Europeans nor sustain themselves on equal terms with them in a society of which both of them would be part."[15] Accordingly, the contemporary evolutionists, "as they regarded the Indian from the glorious height of European cultural superiority, tended to think of him as a being who had lost out in the struggle for existence, as a living fossil, as a datum to be studied, measured, described, and assigned to his lowly place in the grand evolutionary structure."[16] After 1855, the strong focus of liberal historians fell on the glories of pre-Hispanic Mexico, which was fundamental in building the sense of national identity, pride, and self-confidence. The regime of Porfirio Díaz continued the efforts of "upgrading" the poor indios to mestizo status so that they could march jointly on the road of progress, while "scientifically" justifying the appropriation of Native lands and accusing the resisting community members of communism and "violations of public order."[17]

Paradoxically, the word *indio* did not disappear but became a highly derogatory term denoting the lowest social group—despite its official nonexistence!—identified with despised ethnic origin, backwardness, poverty, and lack of education. Thus, right from the onset of the Mexican state, the long-term project of nation building did not envision any space for Native communities and speakers of Indigenous languages. Spanish became absolutely dominant in the political and administrative spheres, while communities speaking heritage languages were gradually reduced to secluded hamlets whose inhabitants lived marginalized. Moreover, despite the liberal declarations of the Mexican state, the typical rural schools organized in the nineteenth century were characterized by ethnic and racial segregation.

The legal equality of the Mexican republic notwithstanding, pupils were divided according to the officially abolished colonial categories of *castas*. Thus, in one part of the room *niños de razón* ("children of reason," derived from the colonial category of *gente de razón*, "people of reason") were seated; in another were separated Indigenous children who were only instructed orally in the *doctrina* and were not taught to read—only in special cases the most "gifted" among them could be moved to the group de razón.[18]

Thus, whereas in the national mythology of the Mexican state the idealized and remote pre-Hispanic people provided the nation's glorious foundations, an unbridgeable gap was created between the "historical Indian" whose prestigious past deserved to be recalled and extolled, and the real, modern Indian belonging to the marginalized and derided part of society.[19] Contemporary Indigenous people were conceived as relics in urgent need of salvation that could only be achieved through their accelerated assimilation into the national mestizo culture: "the redemption of the Indian through his disappearance."[20] Paradoxically, then, the official *indigenismo* ideology extolled the Aztec nobility and other members of other long-dead pre-Hispanic cultures, whose great artworks were admired as items of national heritage in museums and whose monumental pyramids became "national icons."[21] Symptomatically, in the second half of the nineteenth century university courses in such languages as Nahuatl, Otomi, or Purepecha no longer served as the linguistic preparation of clergy destined to work in Native communities as they were transformed into the studies of "antiquities," reserved for erudite persons and scholars.[22] On the one hand, this policy change reflects the "petrification" of Indigenous languages and cultures in their idealized and remote historical forms. On the other, it was both grounded in and justified by the denial of abstract and rational thinking among Indigenous people, who purportedly were not able to "conceive the abstract ideas of space, time, divisibility, necessary bases for mathematics, which, in its turn, is the base of all science."[23]

Similar views were shared by the founder of Mexican archaeology and anthropology, Manuel Gamio, an important member of the *indigenismo* movement. In his famous book *Forjando patria: Pro-nacionalismo* (1916), he advocated for the assimilation of Indigenous people and for removing the barriers toward full *mestizaje* necessary for the creation of a homogenous Mexican nation.[24] Thus, he saw the complete incorporation of Native communities into mainstream society as a necessary condition for modernization, including the achievement of "scientific progress" characteristic of European civilization.[25] In Gamio's own words,

> However brilliant and surprisingly developed pre-Hispanic civilization was for its time, the traces of it that we see today seem anachronistic, inappropriate, and

impractical.... Indian herbalists that possess the secret of a vast medicinal pharmacopeia would have justly been considered medical notables in the past, but our modern doctor disdains them and accuses them of being untrained poisoners.[26]

Therefore, although the "imposition of European civilization has failed because we do not know the reasons for the Indians' resistance," "we should ... collaborate in the evolutionary fusion of this culture with the culture of the race that has been dominant until now."[27]

Pervasive ethnic discrimination did not wane in the following decades. Despite the omnipresent socialist rhetoric and the redistribution of land to the "rural poor," the 1910–20 Mexican Revolution did not abolish social stratification. In a post-revolutionary redefinition, the former indios became peasants (*campesinos*), likewise associated with the lowest social status, lack of education, and poverty. In contrast, the true citizens of the Mexican state became represented by mestizos, not by Indigenous people.[28] Indeed, some reforms oriented toward Indigenous people were brought about during the presidency of Lázaro Cárdenas in the 1930s, with the distribution of huge quantities of land to the campesinos, the construction of schools and roads, and the creation of a Departamento de Asuntos Indígenas. Unchanged along the political paradigms of liberal and conservative governments was that "whereas the condition of the living Indians improved little, if at all, Mexican government and society continued to pay homage to their dead ancestors."[29] The strong sense of historical national identity has not given much value and recognition to the contemporary descendants of the glorified Indigenous founders of the modern Mexican state.

HYPERACTIVE MEMORY, ETHNOCIDE, AND SYMBOLIC VIOLENCE

In his influential *México profundo: Una civilización negada* (1987),[30] Guillermo Bonfil Batalla convincingly argues that an authentic "deep Mexico" rooted in Indigenous cultures is in opposition to an "imaginary Mexico" based on foreign, first European then North American, imports and inspirations. Thus, "de-Indianization" has been a long historical process in which Native people were forced to reject their own ethnic identity; this loss is not the result of biological mixing (*mestizaje biológico*) but rather the effect of ethnocide disrupting cultural continuity: "This ... process, de-Indianization, has been called mestizaje, but it was—it is—ethnocide."[31] Whereas it has been argued that after 1950 the profound transition marking the long-term assimilation process broke from stratification rooted in colonial-period ethnic relations toward class stratification along national lines,[32] mestizaje still remains an important concept, especially in the context of hyperactive historical memory,[33] reflected in the exuberant celebrations of anniversaries of 1492, 1519, and 1521.

In his widely quoted speech delivered at the celebrations of the 500th anniversary of the fall of Mexico-Tenochtitlan, Mexican president Andrés Manuel López Obrador reportedly asked for the forgiveness of the victims of the *Conquista*. However, while this is what the public definitely wanted to hear, it is not what the president actually said:

> Today, August 13, a day of mourning, as our teacher Carlos Pellicer would say, we recall the fall of the Great Tenochtitlan and *we offer forgiveness* [emphasis: J.O.] to the victims of the catastrophe caused by the Spanish military occupation of Mesoamerica and the rest of the territory of today's Mexican Republic.[34]

In view of this rather shocking statement, one may ponder if the use of the expression *ofrecemos perdón* (we offer forgiveness) instead of *pedimos perdón* (we ask for forgiveness) was indeed the intended message or an unintended error of appalling magnitude that went unnoticed by the presidential speechwriters. More shocking perhaps is the thoughtless delivery—with neither the slightest stutter nor hesitancy—of this offensive message to the descendants of the Indigenous victims of the Spanish *Conquista* and its calamitous and devastating aftermath. This mistake is in fact symbolic of the long-term attitude of the Mexican state toward Native people, an attitude extoling the splendid pre-Hispanic roots of Mexico but failing to protect the rights of Indigenous people today. No single statement in the speech of López Obrador refers to the responsibility of the Mexican state for the continuing legacy of colonialism, oppression, marginalization, discrimination, and stigmatization of the living descendants of the Indigenous protagonists of the violent events of 1521 and other Native American people.

In view of the generous offer of forgiveness and the omission of the role of the Mexican state in this complex, continuing historical process, perhaps less shocking is the presidential assessment of the state of historical research on the *Conquista*: "It is not easy to make an objective analysis of the process of military occupation and Spanish colonization of our country," because Spanish accounts and their justificatory rhetoric overshadow Indigenous sources that are posterior with regard to the events in question. Thus, despite years of fruitful historical research on Indigenous memory and perspectives on the Spanish invasion and colonization, the official discourse maintains the ambiguity of the zone of the "irretrievable unknown" and the powerlessness of historical narratives, denying the proper space of Indigenous history as not only equal but also capable of challenging dominant and simplifying historical paradigms. Moreover, the president also referred to the still-controversial—at least at the level of popular public debates and opinions—issue of the Indigenous participants in the *Conquista* and the possible justification of the latter as an alleged act of liberation from the tyranny of the Aztec empire. As he attempted to give the rationale for the participation of different Indigenous groups as allies of Spaniards as well as the argument that the Spaniards did not "conquer" any flourishing empire but rather a "decadent" state[35] (again, largely ignoring the existing historical research on the topic), he also criticized a "promonarchist writer" (Marcelo Gullo Omodeo), who compared the "anthropophagous tyranny" of the Aztecs to the tyranny of the "Nazis."[36] The president distanced himself from such an abhorrent comparison, so much abused today by Russia in its invasion of Ukraine in what constitutes a repetition of the darkest pages in European history. However, this part of the presidential discourse provokes a great sense of ambivalence—and the disturbing sense of an absence of deeper historical understanding—regarding the nature of the Aztec empire, the "tyranny" of its leader, and the motivations of the Indigenous polities involved in the dramatic events initiated by the landing of the Spaniards in 1519.[37]

The presidential speech was delivered in the heart of the former Mexico-Tenochtitlan, in the Plaza del Zócalo, where the mockup of the Huei Teocalli, the Great Temple, was constructed just to the side of the actual ruins of the temple destroyed by the siege in 1521 and the construction of the colonial city. It was accompanied by the traditional dances of *concheros* clad in exuberant feathered attire alluding to the pre-Hispanic insignia of their remote ancestors. It seems irresistible for historians viewing this splendid performance to wonder, to what extent did this participation differ from the colonial *fiestas reales* organized by the authorities of New Spain, featuring the dances and other performances of Indigenous subjects in their traditional attire? And at the very same time, not very far from the Zócalo, in front of the Palacio de Bellas Artes, were the Triquis from Tierra Blanca Copala, a rural community in Oaxaca and victims of forced displacement, who returned to the streets of the capital after a failed attempt to return to their land.[38]

Indigenous languages are rarely, if ever, heard during official state celebrations. Perhaps the most emotional experience for me was to discover that there, in the center of the former Aztec empire, in the center of Tenochtitlan, one can indeed hear languages of the Indigenous people spoken. These are the voices of artisans from different Indigenous communities selling their craftsmanship to tourists in the Zócalo on one side of the cathedral. But they are not always spoken aloud, as the sellers know too well the experience of mocking and stigma to which they are exposed when speaking their heritage languages. It has always taken me some time to convince the artisans to respond and continue the conversation in Nahuatl when I addressed them in their language. The conversations initially provoked distrust. Some of my interlocutors were even curious to know if I was a Jehovah's Witness trying to convert them, a common experience in local communities (and indeed, Jehovah's Witnesses are quite exceptional at learning the Indigenous languages of people they try to proselytize). In this very center of the former Mexico-Tenochtitlan, I have also seen Indigenous artisans chased by the police as they protested against the Mexican state and demanded a safe space to sell their merchandise to make their living.

The commemoration of the 500th anniversary of the fall of Tenochtitlan was not limited to state-sponsored and state-orchestrated celebrations. Some communities performed peaceful "acts of resistance": for example, the members of the Congreso Nacional Indígena in Oaxaca protested against the policies of the Mexican state toward Native people, especially with regard to their land rights. Also in Oaxaca, the people from San Pablo Cuatro Venados demonstrated against numerous mining concessions that put their land, environment, and sacred spaces in danger. These current threats continue to be considered projects of "modernization" and "development" obstructed by Indigenous communities, a recurring concept since the foundation of the Mexican state. On the other side of the Atlantic, the Mayas Zapatistas, representatives of other Indigenous communities and activists from across Europe organized a demonstration, "No Nos Conquistaron," and marched through symbolic places in Madrid, including the Plaza Colón, demanding decolonization and social justice. Thus,

> five hundred years after the fall of México Tenochtitlan the descendants of the Mexicas offered their dances in the Zócalo. The Mayas Zapatistas went through Madrid with an anticapitalist message. Other communities demanded justice but there were still some who were not even aware [of what was happening]. This is the chronicle of an extraordinary day, the 13th of August of 2021.[39]

The anniversary was accompanied by heated social media disputes and battles, from accusations of cruelty and cannibalism directed toward the Mexicah, to voices of Indigenous activists commenting on the absurdity of the imperative to "get past the conquest" when fundamental issues of social justice, Native rights, and pervasive racism still need to be effectively addressed and tackled.

Awareness of this fundamental problem of course greatly predates the commemorations of the fall of Tenochtitlan: "It would be incorrect to think in terms of the past about the oppression and structural inequality that the inhabitants of the lands today called America suffered, because the circumstances of disadvantage form part of the social climate of contemporaneous Mexico."[40] However, recognition of the ongoing circumstances of deep disadvantage is somehow miraculously disentangled from the responsibility of the Mexican state and its long-term policies operating for the last 200 years and credited to the "late effects" of the colonial era. Another constant is the absence of actual Indigenous voices and agency, reduced, at best, to a symbolic, often folkloric presence at historical commemorations. This omission mirrors, in fact, the modern Mexican state's denial of Indigenous peoples' self-definition both in social reality and in more formal or symbolic ways. This denial is evident in the national censuses and other administrative records as well as in anthropological research, all common tools of symbolic and epistemological violence. The latter may manifest itself in numerous ways: imposed rigid demographic and ethnic categories, fears of stigma and shame upon revealing adscription to the despised social category,[41] the "invisibility" of specific ethnic groups in state records,[42] and the lack of property rights in research results generated with Indigenous participation by means of extractive field methods directed toward local "informants" and their knowledge.[43]

It should be stated very clearly and without any space for ambiguity that the Indigenous people of the Americas continue to be subject to colonial relationships that originated in the time of the *Conquista* and were further extended and perpetuated after the creation of the nation-states—for example, with regard to linguistic rights and control over land and resources vital for local communities. The so-called *políticas indigenistas* of Latin American governments have been in fact oriented toward the destruction of Indigenous cultures, imposing control over them in order to consolidate existing social structures.[44] Two of the most ardent problems are pervasive racism and ethnic discrimination. Although it can be argued that racially (genetically and phenotypically) Mexico is overwhelmingly Indigenous, the ideals of physical appearance are strongly European, reinforced through television and graphic advertising. Accordingly, a light complexion—along with certain desired cultural characteristics—provides an advantage in upward mobility, while darker skin color is perceived as a mark of lower-class origin.[45] I witnessed a very painful experience with regard to the racist legacy of colonialism during a conversation held in Nahuatl in the summer of 2019 with the elderly grandmother of an Indigenous friend of mine in his home community in Sierra Norte de Puebla. When asked about the memory of Spaniards and outsiders in her community, the first thing she quietly said was "gente de razón." Hearing these words left us initially in a state of profound shock, before we realized that this still must have been a common appellative for non-Indigenous people in the time of her youth.

Indigenous communities continue to pay a high price for their ongoing marginalization, discrimination, and historical victimization. Sustained racism against Native people has been a key factor contributing to vulnerability and health inequity among Aboriginal populations.[46] Perceived ethnic and ethnolinguistic discrimination and related posttraumatic stress disorder as well as different aspects of acculturation stress are associated with poorer self-rated health and higher levels of depression among Nahua communities today, regardless of the levels of their cultural assimilation.⁴⁷ Our survey, carried out during the COVID-19 pandemic and directed toward Indigenous people of all ethnic groups in Mexico, revealed some specific forms of discrimination, including unequal access to health care and to information. Of Indigenous participants, 25.5 percent stated that they were discriminated against with regard to access to healthcare during the pandemic, while 44.4 percent were convinced that they did not receive adequate information about the coronavirus.⁴⁸ Indeed, data published by the Mexican Secretaría de Salud show that the mortality rate of users of Indigenous languages who were positively tested for COVID-19 was 16.87 percent, whereas that of the remaining part of the society was only 9.04 percent.⁴⁹ It is clear that the pandemic has made salient and exacerbated the existing inequalities and vulnerability of Indigenous populations. In fact, according to official data from the Encuesta Nacional de Ingresos y Gastos de los Hogares, seven out of ten speakers of Indigenous languages in Mexico live in poverty, twice as much as those who exclusively speak Spanish (74.9% vs. 39.4%), while in the case of extreme poverty the difference becomes more dramatic: 35.6 percent versus 5.6 percent.⁵⁰ According to the most recent state census of 2020, there are over 7 million speakers of Indigenous languages over three years of age in Mexico, and almost 12 million people living in households with at least one speaker of an Indigenous language.⁵¹ These numbers, perhaps more visibly than anything else, speak not only to the scale of economic disadvantage but also to the strength of Indigenous resilience and cultural survival after centuries of colonization and 200 years of assimilationist policies at the hands of the Mexican state.

Therefore, while it is important to acknowledge the historical traumatization of Indigenous people, reinforced by ongoing structural discrimination and marginalization, it is also fundamental not to reduce Native populations to the mere status of victims. The fact that they are victims of the long-term processes of oppression and violations of human rights as well as the colonial and postcolonial violence to which they are subject in their daily existence should not obscure their active presence throughout history.⁵² Native agency can be best understood in the historical continuum extending from the first moments of contact with the European intruders to the present day, and it should be viewed through the lens of the actions and testimonies of Indigenous people themselves.

GOOD AND BAD ANCESTORS, OR THE STORY OF THE TLAXCALTECAH AND MEXICAH

When I first started my fieldwork in Tlaxcala some years ago, I could not immediately understand why so many of my interlocutors were reluctant to talk about their homeland's past, and particularly about the *Conquista* of Mexico. I was aware,

Figure 3.1. *Tlaxcala resistió el sitio mexica / Tlaxcala se fundamenta en el extranjero* (Tlaxcala resisted the Mexica siege / Tlaxcala is grounded in the foreign). Museo de la Memoria, Tlaxcala. Documentary exhibition: "Tlaxcala colonización y mestizaje: Memorias en papel a 500 años del Encuentro de dos Culturas." Photo by Justyna Olko.

of course, of the pervasive historical discourse situating the Tlaxcaltecah on the "wrong side of history," but I was not aware that this history, 500 years later, is still an essential part of their social reality. In 2019, during the 500-year anniversary of the landing of Cortés and the beginning of the Spanish-Tlaxcalteca alliance, the Museo de la Memoria in Tlaxcala housed an excellent exhibition that presented the local view of these historical events. One of the pieces of artwork at the exhibit explicitly, in its simplicity, referred to the opposing and irreconcilable visions that form part of Tlaxcallan memory and historical identity today: resisting the Mexicah and depending on the foreigners, or *malinchismo* (figure 3.1). Just next to it, another artistic creation tried to establish distance from the historical stigma by comparing the *Conquista* to an invasion from outer space (figure 3.2), which, in the ontology of the Mesoamerican people back then, it indeed was.[53] But artistic confrontations with the past-in-the-present are not enough to leave the shadows of history, which are much darker for the Tlaxcaltecah than for any other group in Mexico today.

Figure 3.2. *La llegada de Hernán Cortés a Tlaxcala o la invención de México* (Jorge Bordello) (The arrival of Hernán Cortés at Tlaxcala or the invention of Mexico). Museo de la Memoria, Tlaxcala. Documentary exhibition: "Tlaxcala colonización y mestizaje: Memorias en papel a 500 años del Encuentro de dos Culturas." Photo by Justyna Olko.

Indeed, their campaigns as allies of the Spaniards secured them numerous rights and privileges and established their reputation as loyal servants of the crown, which in the sixteenth century provided the people of Tlaxcallan with important legal means, including viceregal orders, to protect their land and natural resources.

However, they were not immune to colonial abuse and violence and were not able to prevent the Spanish intrusion into their lands and towns.[54] Fighting for land and resources against non-Indigenous landowners until Mexican Independence, they did not differ much from other Indigenous *repúblicas de indios*. This changed in the first decades after 1821 that saw the spread of the notion of the Tlaxcaltecah as traitors of the newly founded nation, based on the idea that as allies of the Spaniards they had committed treason against the "Mexican state." So as it happens, the official Mexican historical discourse identified an early version of the Mexican state with the Aztec empire. This equivalence, based on a rather bewildering historical manipulation, made the Tlaxcaltecah *traidores a la patria*, and this notion was in fact fundamental for the construction of Mexican nationalism. As expressed by Benito Juárez, "Mexico, populated by countless warrior nations and defended by nature itself, received the law of a handful of adventurers because the vile Tlaxcaltecah preferred a groveling revenge to national honor, and offered their fatal alliance to the invader of Castile."[55] Thus, after Independence the Mexicah became the glorified symbol of a heroic past and resistance, while the Tlaxcaltecah were assigned the status of universal traitors. As publicly announced in 1823: "On the ruins of this infamous town a monument should be erected that says: This was treacherous Tlaxcala which sold its country to foreigners; it no longer exists so that it will never again commit a similar parricide."[56]

The Tlaxcalteca perspective and its own story did not make their way into this national vision of the past and were barely heard until the second half of the twentieth century. It was then when a famous Tlaxcalteca artist, Desiderio Hernández Xochitiotzin, began to create monumental wall paintings in the municipal palace of his hometown. Often believed to have been inspired by the famous murals of Diego Rivera in Mexico City glorifying the Mexica role in the *Conquista*, they convey a vivid image of the hostilities between the Mexicah and the Tlaxcaltecah and the violent wars waged by Tenochtitlan on its independent neighbor. In the scene of the siege of Tenochtitlan, the warriors from Tlaxcallan are shown fighting side by side with the Spaniards, and the political message is complemented by the civilizing mission of populating the wild Chichimec lands in the north, at the request of the Spanish crown. Another key theme, mestizaje, makes its presence through the pregnant figure of Malintzin, and the union of local women and Spaniards, as well as the baptism of Tlaxcalteca lords, converting Tlaxcallan into the "cradle of mestizaje." In the words of Desiderio Hernández Xochitiotzin,

> Mexico is a typically mestizo country as was Tlaxcala since the sixteenth century! ... Constantly, since the beginning of the nineteenth century, the myth was sustained that the Tlaxcaltecah were traitors of Mexico! When Mexico did not yet exist? This

stigma against us, the Tlaxcaltecah, this black legend that constantly troubles us and that is due to the lack of information and knowledge of our national history. The Tlaxcaltecah were not traitors, they were patriots who bravely defended their land, their nation, from Tenochca imperialism, misnamed Aztec![57]

But it was precisely at this time, in the second half of the past century, when acculturation and mestizaje, so fundamental for the emergence of the Tlaxcalteca voice in the national discourse, took on a much darker face. It was the time of the accelerated hispanization of Indigenous towns and especially of Indigenous children, replete with many forms of violence.[58] The educational policy launched at the beginning of the second half of the twentieth century introduced instruction exclusively in Spanish with the goal of "civilizing" Nahuatl-speaking children by transitioning them quickly and efficiently to the national language, often employing violent corporal and psychological punishment. Parents, many of them monolingual in Nahuatl, were strongly advised by teachers to communicate with their children only in Spanish in order to shield them from suffering and offer them an opportunity for a better, educated life. This strict recommendation to abandon the heritage language was often paired with instructions regarding the hygiene and health of their children.[59] Thus, local attempts to challenge Mexican nationalism and "rehabilitate the image" of Tlaxcala in the official discourse did not involve any form of reevaluation of the state's resilient, surviving Indigenous component: the Indigenous people, their culture, and their still-spoken Nahuatl language. The change was quick and widespread. The heritage language and many elements of Indigenous culture began to be associated with shame and backwardness.[60] Many speakers went silent and learned to communicate exclusively in Spanish. Sometimes their own children did not even know that Spanish was not their parents' native language. Several years ago, while doing fieldwork with immigrants from Tlaxcala in the United States, I had an opportunity to meet an elderly woman from San Francisco Tetlanohcan in Tlaxcala who was visiting her children and grandchildren. I addressed her in Nahuatl, and we spoke. Her children were deeply shocked, and her daughter started to cry. She said that she had never heard her mother speak Nahuatl. Facing historical stigmatization and choosing the path of full mestizaje, modernization, and progress—offered by the Mexican state and supported by the authorities of Tlaxcala—have come with a harsh price and a sense of loss.

While Indigenous children have been subjected to assimilation in local schools in Tlaxcala, those who leave the state in order to continue their education have had to face the historical stigma. The negative attitudes toward the Tlaxcaltecah have no doubt been strengthened and perpetuated by nationalistic historical narratives that made their way into the textbooks read and memorized by both Indigenous and non-Indigenous Mexican children. In 2019, 500 years after the beginning of this story, when I talked to university students and community members in Tlaxcala in several focus group and individual interviews, there were very few who would deny having had a similar experience. Some had heard it as children and had found it very difficult to understand the accusation. Some recall feeling anger and a sense of injustice that they associate with this stigmatizing experience. The stigma was so profound that some even denied their own Tlaxcalteca identity when living or traveling outside Tlaxcala. This happened often to those who had tried to get a job in another state or enter a school, for example in the neighboring state of Puebla, because they were treated with distrust. Protecting oneself from stigma could even lead a person to go as far as registering temporary residence outside the state in order to avoid problems when applying for a job or entering a university.

The scale of this phenomenon was documented during our online survey carried out among the residents of Tlaxcala in 2020, during the first phase of the pandemic. Of the people completing the survey,[61] 75.3 percent confirmed that they had been called a traitor (24.4% rarely, 19.8% sometimes, 31.1% often and very often; $N = 1,260$). Of the respondents, 94.7 percent admitted having heard people say that persons from Tlaxcala were traitors (11.4% rarely, 21% sometimes, often and very often 62.3%; $N = 1,276$). The statistics are startling, but even more moving are the words of people from Tlaxcala who have experience studying, traveling, or working in other Mexican states:

> It is a chain, and they instill it in other people, their grandchildren, and they all consider the state of Tlaxcala a traitor. You go to Mexico and they tell you, "The Tlaxcaltecah are very treacherous, don't trust them, they are very treacherous." That is why many of our age are ashamed to say that they are from Tlaxcala because they always classify you as treacherous, you are a traitor, *pata rajada* ("bare-footed Indian") or other things that they tell you. And many who seek to study in other places, are afraid to admit "I'm from Tlaxcala" when they start bullying you for the same reason. You do not have the ability to stand out, that is, it's like they classify you as inferior. Many people who go to other regions sometimes are afraid, for example when they look for work, they prefer to get an ID with a local address or proofs of residence. Why do you classify me as pata rajada, as a traitor, when you don't really know anything about our culture? So you call me a traitor or pata rajada, but actually at the end of the day we are the cradle of the nation, from here you originate. You feel anger, they tell you that so as to offend you. . . . They tell you that in front of everyone, gosh, and if you don't really know how things happened, then you keep your head down, right? One even begins to cry because of helplessness. There are children who are very weak emotionally and who start to cry and complain to the teacher.[62]

Likewise, in the words of Ethel Xochitiotzin Pérez, the Tlaxcalteca poet and teacher of Nahuatl, "Nohuiuhqui ompa itech in ciudad de Mexico ce tonal oniccac, 'Ompa ye huitz non traidor, non traidora.' Amo cualli timomachiliah, neh nicmachilia, amo, amo nechnequih, amo nechtlazohtlah" (Also there in the city of Mexico one day I heard, 'Here comes that guy who's a traitor, that girl who's a traitor.' We do not feel good about it. I feel that they do not like me, they do not respect me).

If one agrees that the *Conquista* forms part of the hyperactive national memory of Mexico today, then the stigmatization of the present inhabitants of Tlaxcala is perhaps its most disturbing and painful component, originating in the nationalistic historical ideologies developed in the nineteenth and twentieth centuries but still shared and reproduced by broad sectors of Mexican society.

PAST AND PRESENT

"The most powerful meanings of the past come out of the dialogue between the past and the present, out of the ways the past can be used to answer pressing current-day questions about relationships, identity, immortality, and agency."[63] As convincingly argued by an outstanding American historian, Ross Rosenzweig, the past should become a vehicle for social justice. But what if it is the vehicle of stigma, oppression, and violence? What if it obscures rather than unveils pressing problems of social reality and injustice? As the case of the Mexican historical memory of the *Conquista* shows, this may happen even if that historical legacy has been converted into a source of national pride and identity. I believe, however, that for the Tlaxcaltecah and other Indigenous groups in Mexico the past can also become a source of empowerment and self-esteem, of pride and motivation to act. As the past reinforces the sense of connection and belonging, stimulating discussions about Indigenous views of the history and forms of Indigenous agency and resilience, it may provide the inspiration to transform reality, making the past relevant for the present in ways other than those offered by the discourses controlled and perpetuated by the state. And it may additionally serve to inform current governmental policies by uncovering the long-lasting mechanisms of oppression, violence, marginalization, and discrimination.

Turning again to the words of Ethel Xochitiotzin, "Neh niquihtoa tlan nechiliah, tlen quimi nitraidora, neh amo nechcocoa, tlica porque neh nicmati aquin tehhuan, neh nicmati aquin oyec tocohcolhuan, neh nicmati aquin notatahhuan" (I say that if they tell me that I'm a kind of traitor, it does not hurt me because I know who we are, I know who my ancestors were, I know who my parents are). Indigenous people in today's Mexico not only have a past: they also have a History.

* * *

As I write this essay, the words "conquest" and "invasion" have become part of our present again. With the Russian invasion of Ukraine launched in February of 2022,[64] the never-to-be-repeated history begins to unveil itself right in front of our eyes, crushing our faith in the historical progress and reviving the painful legacy of colonialism accompanied by so many forms of violence and atrocities of war. Like many other countries in the world, including Mexico, Ukraine is a post-colonial state. And while we are witnesses daily as the Russian "empire enforces objectification on the periphery and amnesia at the center,"[65] I recall the words that the Mexican president Andrés Manuel López Obrador, pronounced in the heart of the former capital of the Aztec empire on August 13, 2021, exactly 500 years after, following a long siege, the city surrendered to the invaders:

> Let us all make the commitment not to repeat, not to again commit the same mistakes and horrors. Let us put an end to these anachronisms, these atrocities, and let us say "Never again" to an invasion, an occupation, or a conquest, even if it is undertaken in the name of faith, peace, civilization, democracy, freedom, or even more grotesquely, in the name of human rights.[66]

Historical memory is a human right that reminds us of our joint belonging despite the seemingly unique and localized trajectories of the past. "To break the spell of inevitability, we must see ourselves as we are, not on some exceptional path, but in history alongside others."[67] Despite its painful history, however, the government of Mexico has sided with those few countries who have refused to impose sanctions and condemn the Russian invasion, choosing a place on the dark side of history, under its own long shadow of both external and internal colonialism.

NOTES

Acknowledgment: I would like to thank Joanna Maryniak and John Sullivan for their valuable comments and suggestions. I am particularly grateful to the members of the Tlaxcalan community who decided to share their painful experiences with me. Research reported in this paper was developed within Project 2018/29/B/HS3/02782 funded by the National Science Center in Poland.

Epigraphs: José Clemente Orozco, *An Autobiography*, trans. Robert C. Stephenson, introduction John P. Leeper (Austin: University of Texas Press, 1962), 107; Fernando Benítez, *Los indios de México*, trans. Benjamin Keen, *The Aztec Image in Western Thought* (New Brunswick, NJ: Rutgers University Press, 1971), 467 (orig. page 47); Andrés Manuel López Obrador, August 13, 2021, accessed March 21, 2022, https://lopezobrador.org.mx/2021/08/13/discurso-del-presidente-andres-manuel-lopez-obrador-en-los-500-anos-de-resistencia-indigena

-1521-mexico-tenochtitlan/; Timothy Snyder, *The Road to Unfreedom: Russia, Europe, America* (New York: Tim Duggan Books, 2018), 279–81.

1. Edward Hallett Carr, *What Is History?* (London: Macmillan / Penguin Books, 1984), 21.
2. Laura E. Matthew and Michel R. Oudijk, *Indian Conquistadors: Indigenous Allies in the Conquest of Mesoamerica* (Norman: University of Oklahoma Press, 2007); Matthew Restall, *When Montezuma Met Cortés: The True Story of the Meeting That Changed History* (New York: Ecco Press, 2018).
3. *Anales de Tlatelolco: Los manuscritos 22 y 23bis de la Bibliothèque de France*, trans. Susanne Klaus (Markt Schwaben, Germany: Anton Saurwein, 1999); Matthew Restall, Lisa Sousa, and Kevin Terraciano, *Mesoamerican Voices: Native-Language Writings from Colonial Mexico, Oaxaca, Yucatan, and Guatemala* (Cambridge: Cambridge University Press, 2005), 24, 42–43.
4. Frederic Hicks, "'Flowery War' in Aztec History," *American Ethnologist* 6, no. 1 (1979): 87–92, here 90; Barry L. Isaac, "The Aztec 'Flowery War': A Geopolitical Explanation," *Journal of Anthropological Research* 39, no. 4 (1983): 415–32.
5. Andrea Martínez Baracs, *Un gobierno de indios: Tlaxcala, 1519–1750* (Mexico City: Fondo de Cultura Económica, 2008), 38.
6. Ryszard Tomicki, *Ludzie i bogowie: Indianie meksykańscy wobec Hiszpanów we wczesnej fazie konkwisty* (Wrocław: Wydawnictwo Polskiej Akademii Nauk, 1990), 90; Baracs, *Gobernio de indios*.
7. Justyna Olko and Agnieszka Brylak, "Defending Local Autonomy and Facing Cultural Trauma: A Nahua Order against Idolatry: Tlaxcala 1543," *Hispanic American Historical Review* 98, no. 4 (2018): 573–604.
8. Bradley Skopyk, *Colonial Cataclysms: Climate, Landscape, and Memory in Mexico's Little Ice Age* (Tucson: University of Arizona Press, 2020).
9. E.g., see James Lockhart, *The Nahuas after the Conquest: A Social and Cultural History of the Indians of Central Mexico, Sixteenth through Eighteenth Centuries* (Stanford, CA: Stanford University Press, 1992); Susan Kellogg, *Law and the Transformation of Aztec Culture: 1500–1700* (Norman: University of Oklahoma Press, 2005).
10. E.g., see Stephanie Wood, *Transcending Conquest: Nahua Views of Spanish Colonial Mexico* (Norman: University of Oklahoma Press, 2003).
11. Keen, *Aztec Image*, 416.
12. Zarina Estrada Fernández and Aarón Grageda Bustamante, "Colonización y política del lenguaje: El norte de México," in *Historia sociolingüística de México*, vol. 1, ed. Rebeca Barriga Villanueva and Pedro Martín Butragueño (Mexico City: Colegio de México, 2010), 545–603, here 580; Frida Villavicencio Zarza, *Lenguas indígenas en el México decimonónico: Ecos, pregones y contrapuntos* (Mexico City: Centro de Investigaciones y Estudios Superiores en Antropología Social, 2013), 86–87.

13. Shirley Brice Heath, *Telling Tongues: Language Policy in Mexico, Colony to Nation* (New York: Teachers College Press, 1972), 64; María Ana Luna González, "La política lingüística en México entre Independencia y Revolución (1810–1910)," in *Actas del Congreso de la Asociación Internacional de Hispanistas* (Rome: Bagatto Libri, 2012), 91–101, here 94.

14. "Tenazmente adicto a sus opiniones, usos y costumbres, jamás se consigue hacerlo variar; y esta inflexible terquedad es un obstáculo insuperable a los progresos que podría hacer," José María Luis Mora, *México y sus revoluciones* (Mexico City: Fondo de Cultura Económica, 1986), 63–65; see also Eva Sanz Jara, "Indio y nación: La imagen del indígena en los escritos de intelectuales y políticos nacidos en el siglo XIX de las repúblicas latinoamericanas. Primeras aproximaciones: José María Luis Mora y Faustino Domingo Sarmiento," in *El pensamiento liberal atlántico, 1770–1880: Fiscalidad, recursos, naturales, integración social y política exterior desde una perspectiva comparada*, ed. Maria Eugenia Claps Arenas and Pedro Pérez Herrero (Alcalá, Spain: Instituto de Estudios Latinoamericanos—Universidad de Alcalá, 2011), 158–87.

15. Mora, *México*, 64–65: "Es verdad que en su estado actual . . . no podrán llegar nunca al grado de ilustración, civilización y cultura de los Europeos, ni sostenerse bajo el pie de igualdad con ellos en una sociedad de que unos y otros hagan parte."

16. Keen, *Aztec Image*, 380–81.

17. Keen, *Aztec Image*, 412–16.

18. Villavicencio Zarza, *Lenguas indígenas*, 94.

19. Villavicencio Zarza, *Lenguas indígenas*, 81–82.

20. Guillermo Bonfil Batalla, *México profundo: Una civilización negada* (Mexico City: Secretaria de Educación Pública—CIESAS, 1987), 115.

21. Hugo H. Nutini and Barry L. Isaac, *Social Stratification in Central Mexico* (Austin: University of Texas Press, 2009), 57.

22. Villavicencio Zarza, *Lenguas indígenas*, 768.

23. Porfirio Parra, "La Ciencia en México," in *México: Su evolución social. Síntesis de la historia política . . . bajo la dirección del Lic. Din Justo Sierra*, no. 22 (1902): 417–66, here 424: "Consignar las ideas abstractas de espacio, de tiempo, de divisibilidad, bases necesarias de la matemática, que a su vez es base de toda ciencia."

24. David A. Brading, "Manuel Gamio and Official Indigenismo in Mexico," *Bulletin of Latin American Research* 7, no. 1 (1988): 75–89.

25. Fernando Armstrong-Fumero, "Translator's Introduction: Manuel Gamio and Forjando Patria. Anthropology in Times of Revolution," in *Forjando patria: Pro-nacionalismo*, ed. Manuel Gamio (Boulder: University Press of Colorado, 2010), 10–16.

26. Manuel Gamio, *Forjando patria: Pro-nacionalismo*, trans. Fernando Armstrong-Fumero (Boulder: University Press of Colorado, 2010), 97–98.

27. Gamio, *Forjando patria: Pro-nacionalismo*, 39, 158.

28. Nutini and Isaac, *Social Stratification*, 52.

29. Keen, *Aztec Image*, 466.

30. Bonfil Batalla, *México profundo*.

31. Bonfil Batalla, *México profundo*, 52: "Este último proceso, a la desindianización, se le ha llamado mestizaje; pero fue -es- etnocidio."

32. Nutini and Isaac, *Social Stratification*, 171.

33. My inspiration to use this term came from Skopyk's brilliant analysis of what he calls "hyperactive memory" and "amnesia" in late colonial Tlaxcala (Skopyk, *Colonial Cataclysms*, 169, 200). However, I use this expression with a slightly different meaning, referring to the "overpresence" and exorbitant burden of historical memory and related discourses, attitudes, and prejudice in contemporary social reality.

34. "Hoy 13 de agosto, fecha funeral, como diría el maestro Carlos Pellicer, recordamos la caída de la Gran Tenochtitlan y ofrecemos perdón a las víctimas de la catástrofe originada por la ocupación militar española de Mesoamérica y del resto del territorio de la actual República mexicana," accessed March 21, 2022, https://lopezobrador.org.mx/2021/08/13/discurso-del-presidente-andres-manuel-lopez-obrador-en-los-500-anos-de-resistencia-indigena-1521-mexico-tenochtitlan/.

35. "A la llegada de los españoles era evidente la decadencia del poderío de Moctezuma y de sus aliados."

36. "Por ejemplo, hace unos días, un escritor promonárquico de nuestro continente, que no son pocos, por cierto, afirmaba que España no conquistó América, sino que España liberó América, pues 'Hernán Cortés—cito textualmente—aglutinó a 110 naciones mexicanas que vivían oprimidas por la tiranía antropófaga de los aztecas y que lucharon con él'. Agrega que 'pedir perdón por liberar a los mexicanos de los aztecas es como pedir perdón por haber derrotado a los nazis.'"

37. E.g., "La idea dominante, por mucho tiempo, hasta nuestros días de que Moctezuma era un tirano puede ser cierta."

38. Daniela Pastrana, Daliri Oropeza, and Arturo Contreras, "No nos conquistaron: Nunca nos fuimos," accessed March 21, 2022, https://piedepagina.mx/no-nos-conquistaron-nunca-nos-fuimos/.

39. "Quinientos años después de la caída de México Tenochtitlán, los descendientes mexicas ofrendaron sus danzas en el Zócalo. Mayas zapatistas recorrieron Madrid con un mensaje anticapitalista. Otros pueblos reclamaron justicia y unos más ni se enteraron. Esta es la crónica del extraordinario 13 de agosto de 2021." Daniela Pastrana, Daliri Oropeza and Arturo Contreras, "No nos conquistaron. Nunca nos fuimos," accessed March 21, 2022, https://piedepagina.mx/no-nos-conquistaron-nunca-nos-fuimos/.

40. David Olvera López, "La invasión de América: Desentrañar la opresión y racismo históricos. Secretaria de Cultura: Blog," accessed March 21, 2022: https://www.gob.mx/cultura/es/articulos/la-invasion-de-america-desentranar-la-opresion-y-racismo-historicos?idiom=es. "Sería incorrecto pensar en términos de pasado la opresión y desigualdad estructural que padecieron los habitantes de las tierras que hoy llamamos América,

pues dichas circunstancias de desventaja forman parte del clima social del México contemporáneo," accessed on March 21, 2022, https://www.gob.mx/cultura/es/articulos/la-invasion-de-america-desentranar-la-opresion-y-racismo-historicos?idiom=es.

41. E.g., David Robichaux, "Identidades cambiantes: 'Indios' y 'mestizos' en el suroeste de Tlaxcala," *Relaciones* 104, no. 26 (2005): 58–104; Nutini and Isaac, *Social Stratification*; Justyna Olko, "Language Attitudes and Educational Opportunities: Challenging a History of Oppression and Assimilation among Indigenous Communities in Mexico," *Dutkansearvvi dieđalaš áigečála / Journal of the Sámi Language and Culture Research Association* 1 (2019): 1–38.

42. See, e.g., Rubio Badán, "Indigenous Data in the Covid-19 Pandemic: Straddling Erasure, Terrorism, and Sovereignty," 2014, accessed May 6, 2022, https://items.ssrc.org/covid-19-and-the-social-sciences/disaster-studies/indigenous-data-in-the-covid-19-pandemic-straddling-erasure-terrorism-and-sovereignty/; https://eldiariofederal.com.ar/2019/09/16/la-invisibilidad-estadistica-una-de-las-formas-de-racismo-oculto-institucional/.

43. E.g., Justyna Olko, "Acting in and through the Heritage Language: Collaborative Strategies for Research, Empowerment and Reconnecting with the Past," *Collaborative Anthropologies* 11, no. 1 (2018): 48–88.

44. Liliana Tamagno, "Pueblos indígenas: Racismo, genocidio y represión," *Corpus* 1, no. 2 (2011): 1–9, here 2–3, accessed April 30, 2019, http://journals.openedition.org/corpus archivos/1164.

45. Nutini and Isaac, *Social Stratification*, 53–54.

46. Ann Larson et al., "It's Enough to Make You Sick: The Impact of Racism on the Health of Aboriginal Australians," *Australian and New Zealand Journal of Public Health* 31, no. 4 (2007): 322–29; D. R. Williams and S. A. Mohammed, "Discrimination and Racial Disparities in Health: Evidence and Needed Research," *Journal of Behavioral Medicine* 32, no. 1 (2008): 20–47; Anna M. Ziersch et al., "Responding to Racism: Insights on How Racism Can Damage Health from an Urban Study of Australian Aboriginal People," *Social Science and Medicine* 73, no. 7 (2011): 1045–53; Ricci Harris et al., "The Pervasive Effects of Racism: Experiences of Racial Discrimination in New Zealand over Time and Associations with Multiple Health Domains," *Social Science and Medicine* 74, no. 3 (2012): 408–15; Yin Paradies et al., "Racism as a Determinant of Health: A Systematic Review and Meta-Analysis," *PLOS ONE* 10, no. 9 (2015): e0138511.

47. Justyna Olko et al., "The Spiral of Disadvantage: Ethnolinguistic Discrimination, Acculturation Stress and Health in Nahua Indigenous Communities in Mexico," *American Journal of Biological Anthropology* 181, no. 3 (2023): 364–78.

48. Justyna Olko, Joanna Maryniak, and Bartłomiej Chromik, "Facing Vulnerability and Mobilizing Resilience: The Impact of the COVID-19 Pandemic on Speakers of Indigenous Languages in Mexico and Their Protective Behaviours," in *COVID-19 and a World of Ad Hoc Geographies*, ed. S. D. Brunn and D. Gilbreath (London: Springer Nature, 2022), 1393–1410.

49. "Datos Abiertos Dirección General de Epidemiología," Dirección General de Epidemiología, accessed March 29, 2021, http://datosabiertos.salud.gob.mx/gobmx/salud/datos_abiertos/datos_abiertos_covid19.zip.

50. http://estadistica.inmujeres.gob.mx/formas/tarjetas/Poblacion_indigena.pdf, accessed March 21, 2022.

51. https://www.inegi.org.mx/contenidos/programas/ccpv/2020/doc/censo2020_principales_resultados_ejecutiva_eum.pdf, accessed March 21, 2022.

52. Tamagno, *Pueblos indígenas*, 6.

53. Tomicki, *Ludzie i bogowie*.

54. Charles Gibson, *Tlaxcala in the Sixteenth Century* (Stanford, CA: Stanford University Press, 1967); Baracs, *Gobierno de indios*; Skopyk, *Colonial Cataclysms*; Olko, "Ethnolinguistic Discrimination."

55. "México, poblada de mil naciones guerreras y por la misma naturaleza defendida, recibió la ley de un puñado de aventureros; porque los viles tlaxcaltecas prefirieron una rastrera venganza al honor nacional, y prestaron su funesta alianza al invasor de Castilla." Benito Juárez, "Discurso patriótico pronunciado por Juárez en la ciudad de Oaxaca el 16 de septiembre de 1840," in *Miscelánea*, ed. Ángel Pola (Mexico City: A. Pola, 1906).

56. "Sobre los escombros de tan infame pueblo, debe levantarse un monumento que diga: Aquí fue la traidora Tlaxcala que vendió su patria al extranjero y que ya no existe, para que no vuelva a cometer semejante parricidio." "Bosquejo estadístico de la celebre ciudad de Tlaxcala y su territorio," *El Sol*, December 8, 1823.

57. Desiderio Hernández Xochitiotzin, "Escenificación de la salida de 400 familias de Tlaxcala," in *Memoria: Coloquio de teatro de Tlaxcala* (Tlaxcala: Gobierno del Estado de Tlaxcala, 1996): 47: "¡México es un país típicamente mestizo y Tlaxcala lo ha sido desde el siglo XVI! . . . Constantemente, desde principios del siglo XIX se patrocinó el mito ¡de que los tlaxcaltecas fueron traidores a México! ¿Cúando México aún no existía? Este estigma en contra de nosotros, los tlaxcaltecas, esta leyenda negra que nos molesta constantemente y que se debe a la falta de información y conocimiento de nuestra historia nacional. Los tlaxcaltecas no fueron traidores, ¡fueron patriotas que defendieron con gran valor a su tierra, a su nación, del imperialismo tenochca, mal llamado azteca!"

58. Robichaux, "Identidades cambiantes"; Nutini and Isaac, *Social Stratification*.

59. Jane H. Hill and Kenneth C. Hill, *Speaking Mexicano: Dynamics of Syncretic Language in Central Mexico* (Tucson: University of Arizona Press, 1986).

60. Refugio Nava Nava, "Retención y revitalización del náhuatl a través del arte," in *Integral Strategies for Language Revitalization*, ed. Justyna Olko, Tomasz Wicherkiewicz, and Robert Borges (Warsaw: Faculty of "Artes Liberales," University of Warsaw, 2016), 269–94; Jacqueline Messing, "Multiple Ideologies and Competing Discourses: Language Shift in Tlaxcala, Mexico," *Language in Society* 36, no. 4 (2007): 557–77.

61. In total, 2,366 people completed the survey, but the numbers differed depending on a specific question. Therefore, I give the exact number of respondents of the two questions mentioned in the text (*N*).

62. "Es una cadenita y ellos se lo inculcan a otras personas a sus nietos y todos tienen al estado de Tlaxcala por traidor. Vas a México [y te] platican, 'Los tlaxcaltecas son bien traicioneros, no confíes en ellos, son bien traicioneros.' Por eso a muchos de nuestra edad les da pena decir que son de Tlaxcala porque siempre te catalogan así como que, traicionero, eres traidor, este pata rajada o equis cosas que te dicen. Y muchos que buscan estudiar en otros lados, les da miedo comentar 'soy de Tlaxcala' cuando por lo mismo te empiezan a hacer bulíng. No tienes la capacidad para sobresalir, o sea, como que te catalogan en lo más bajo. Mucha gente que sale a otras regiones pues a veces les da miedo, por ejemplo cuando buscan trabajo mejor prefieren conseguir credenciales o cartas de radicación. ¿Por qué me catalogas como pata rajada, como traicionero, cuando en realidad no conoces nada de nuestra cultura? Entonces si me dices traicionero o pata rajada, porque en realidad a final de cuenta nosotros somos cuna de la nación, nosotros desde acá tú inicias. Siente uno coraje, te lo dicen así como en forma de ofenderte..., te lo dicen así en frente de todos, híjole y si no sabe uno en realidad como pasaron las cosas pues agacha uno la cabeza, ¿no? Uno se pone hasta llorar por la impotencia. Hay niños que son muy, emocionalmente soy muy débiles y empiezan a llorar y se quejan con el maestro." Interview with a man from an Indigenous community in Tlaxcala, working as a taxi driver, August 2019.

63. Roy Rosenzweig, "Everyone a Historian," in *The Presence of the Past: Popular Uses of History in American Life*, ed. Roy Rosenzweig and David Thelen (New York: Columbia University Press, 1998), 177–89, here 178.

64. The war started in fact in 2014, with the annexation of Crimea by Russia.

65. Timothy Snyder, "The War in Ukraine Is a Colonial War." *New Yorker*, April 22, 2022, accessed January 2, 2023, https://www.newyorker.com/news/essay/the-war-in-ukraine-is-a-colonial-war.

66. "Ojalá todos hagamos el compromiso de la no repetición, de no repetir los mismos errores y horrores. Pongamos fin a esos anacronismos, a esas atrocidades y digamos nunca más una invasión, una ocupación o una conquista aunque se emprenda en nombre de la fe, de la paz, de la civilización, de la democracia, de la libertad o, más grotesco aún, en nombre de los derechos humanos," accessed March 21, 2022, https://lopezobrador.org.mx/2021/08/13/discurso-del-presidente-andres-manuel-lopez-obrador-en-los-500-anos-de-resistencia-indigena-1521-mexico-tenochtitlan/.

67. Snyder, *The Road to Unfreedom: Russia, Europe, America* (New York: Tim Duggan Books, 2018), 278. The full quote is "To break the spell of inevitability, we must see ourselves as we are, not on some exceptional path, but in history alongside others. To avoid the temptation of eternity, we must address our own particular problems, beginning with inequality, with timely public policy."

Part II

Narratives and Memories

4

The Last Journey of Cuauhtemoc

Models for the Anales de Tlatelolco's *Version of Cuauhtemoc's Death*

JULIA MADAJCZAK

The Mexicah's lost war with the Spanish empire has a few iconic hallmarks. The mysterious death of Moteuczoma; the Spaniards' escape from the city-trap during Noche Triste; August 13, 1521, capturing of Tenochtitlan's last independent ruler, Cuauhtemoc; and, eventually, his execution in far-away Yucatan. All of these events received exceptional attention in historical sources, from which they filtered to more recent pieces and even popular culture, where they still resonate with the audience. Arguably, for the sixteenth-century Tenochcah, Cuauhtemoc's death impacted their existence as a community the most. Cuauhtemoc was the last dynastic ruler (*tlahtoani*) of Tenochtitlan elected without either Don Hernando Cortés's or the later colonial regime's influence. His death symbolically marked the end of the Mexica hegemony and, on a smaller scale, the *altepetl*, or city-state, of Tenochtitlan because an autonomous state could not exist without its tlahtoani. In the decades following Cuauhtemoc's execution, the Tenochcah dedicated much space in their codices and annals to describe this event. Simultaneously, Spaniards wrote their versions of history, while other Central Mexican altepetl incorporated and reinterpreted Cuauhtemoc's death within their local traditions. Paradoxically, the resulting corpus allows us to establish only a handful of historical facts. Sources differ with respect to several important details, beginning with the date, hour, and place of the execution, through the reasons for it and legal procedures preceding the punishment, the method used by the executioners, the identity of Cuauhtemoc's traitor (if a text mentions one) and his motivations, to the exact number and identity of the people killed alongside Cuauhtemoc.[1] Many of these texts and graphic representations tell us more about the ideologies, personal interests, or the political views of their authors than about the final hours of the Tenochca tlahtoani.

Among the clamor of voices, one account stands out for its length, attention to details, and unorthodox take on the topic: a story included in the *Anales de Tlatelolco*. Labeled somewhat misleadingly, the *Anales* is a heterogeneous collection of five documents, of which the actual annals form only a fragment. Two manuscripts, held by the Bibliothèque nationale de France, tend to form the basis for modern publications of this source. *Ms. 22*, written on the amate paper by at least three different hands, dates to the sixteenth century and never included the story on Cuauhtemoc's death. The account only appears in the later *Ms. 22bis* produced on European paper by a single scribe, who copied most of *Ms. 22*, adding new content and excluding some of its passages. He inserted a portion of the text containing information about Cuauhtemoc between folios 3r and 3v of the sixteenth-century Document 1.[2] His addition goes right between the lists of Tlatelolco and Tenochtitlan rulers. It includes an account of Cuauhtemoc's execution followed by a curious adventure of the Tlatelolca lords—Don Martín Ecatl and Don Pedro Temilotl—who traveled to Spain hidden in Cortés's ship. The account ends with Ecatl returning to New Spain and receiving a grant of the altepetl Tziuhcohuac.[3]

Ms. 22bis's take on Cuauhtemoc's death is so "ahistorical" and full of surprising elements absent from other sources that scholars have long learned not to trust it. Kevin Terraciano deemed it "a complex mix of facts and fantasies,"[4] while María Castañeda de la Paz remarked that it must have derived from some "vague memories and rumors."[5] This chapter will scrutinize some of these "fantasies" in an attempt to demonstrate that *Ms. 22bis*'s story on the execution of Cuauhtemoc has more structure than it, perhaps, shows on the surface. The essay will not focus on determining historical facts connected to Cuauhtemoc's death, for example, pondering the question of whether the Tenochca ruler indeed conspired against the Spaniards.[6] Instead, it will dive into the relations between some of the sources available to today's readers, tracing the narrative tropes and motives of *Ms. 22bis* to early and mid-colonial Nahua tradition. This work aims to clarify how various, often puzzling, details found their way into the *Anales de Tlatelolco* corpus and where we can look for their origins. It searches through Nahua tales, symbols, and metaphors woven into the *Anales*' fantastic story on Cuauhtemoc's final moments.

THE DEATH OF CUAUHTEMOC IN THE *ANALES DE TLATELOLCO*

The *Ms. 22bis* of the *Anales de Tlatelolco* presents Cuauhtemoc as the tlahtoani of Tlatelolco since the year 10 Reed (1515). It narrates that when the Spanish-Tlatelolca war was over, Don Hernando Cortés set off to the coast, from where he planned to depart to Spain, accompanied by a retinue of Native lords. Among them were Cuauhtemoc, Coanacoch (tlahtoani of Tetzcoco), Tetlepanquetzal (tlahtoani of Tlacopan), and a pitiful figure named Mexicatl, who was trying to usurp the power in Tenochtitlan. Mexicatl, one of the protagonists of this dramatic story, was a dwarf with deformed legs[7] (*huel cozoololtic,* "he had very round calves"). During the trip to the coast, Cuauhtemoc would refuse to sleep in the same hut as Mexicatl, and other rulers did not want to socialize with the usurper either. Mexicatl's frustration and humiliation reached their peak when the party stopped for a rest in Acallan—the last leg of their journey before boarding the ship. Acallan was an altepetl loyal to Tlatelolco, so Cuauhtemoc courteously sent emissaries to its authorities, and they, in return, invited him for a feast. The Acalteca went out of their way to host their hegemon. They dressed him in exquisite garments and adornments and offered him eight baskets of the costliest jewelry. All the Native lords accompanied Cuauhtemoc to bathe in his splendor, eat, and dance to the beat of drums. All but Mexicatl. Uninvited, he had to stay in his humble hut, listen to the sounds of the party, and look from a distance at the quetzal feathers ruffling above the heads of the crowd. Excluded from the circle of the glamourous elites, he turned to vengeance. The opportunity soon presented itself in the shape of Cortés's consort and interpreter, Malintzin, stopping at the door to the hut for a casual small talk. Not wasting his time, Mexicatl revealed to her Cuauhtemoc's supposed plan to attack the Spaniards, and she hastily ran to Cortés with the news.[8]

Now the events picked up speed. Cortés's men arrested Cuauhtemoc and the other lords during a meal. They tied up the *tlahtohqueh* of Tlatelolco, Tetzcoco, and Tlacopan "as if they were dogs" (*yuhqui chichitzitzin*) and brought them to the execution site. As *Ms. 22bis* dryly states, "All three went to die in Hueymollan on a *pochotl* tree" (ynmeyxtintzitzin ompa momiquillito y Hueymolla pochotitech), hanged without a trial.[9] However, Mexicatl's treason did not bring him the prestige he desired. Malintzin communicated to him that although Cortés had been planning to take him to Spain, now he had changed his mind. She ordered the usurper to return to Tenochtitlan and wait for them there. With this faint promise of future collaboration, Mexicatl returned home. His false accusation earned him a new nickname: the Tlatelolcah called him Cotztemexi (from *cotztetl,* "calf," and *mexi*[*co*]: "Calf-Mexicatl").[10] They aimed at humiliating the traitor, ensuring that he would forever be remembered for his physical difference.

GENRE AND AUTHORSHIP OF THE ACCOUNT

The unusual take on the death of Cuauhtemoc by *Ms. 22bis* drifts far away from those few historical facts that we can establish from other sources. Cuauhtemoc died during Cortés's trip to Honduras, not Spain. Acallan, described by Cortés as a province near Puerto de Términos (Yucatan),[11] and inhabited by Chontal Maya, could hardly have been Tlatelolco's domain. No little person had ever held a significant position in Tenochtitlan.[12] Finally, according to Castañeda de la Paz,[13] Malintzin could not have witnessed Cuauhtemoc's execution, because she did not take part in Cortés's journey to Honduras; neither did she accompany the conquistador to Spain.[14] The dating of *Ms. 22bis* from the late seventeenth to the early eighteenth century may explain its twisted perspective but only to some degree. As Terraciano observed,[15] its genre better elucidates the multiple deviations from historical facts. Terraciano's analysis of the stories of Cuauhtemoc's death and the adventure of Don Martín Ecatl led him to believe that their narration displays numerous traits of the so-called primordial titles. Dubbed "frauds" by early scholars, primordial titles arose in the late colonial period from the Indigenous communities that sought to assert land rights and reinforce their local identities.[16] The genre tends to present history from a local, sometimes even familial, perspective, reinterpreting it in a way characteristic of the oral tradition, which compresses extensive periods, organizing them around a few key events or characters. The titles do not eschew transforming the available tradition to better serve the community's purpose. Terraciano proposed that *Ms. 22bis*'s account of Cuauhtemoc's death represents just such a particular way of recording the local memory of this event.[17] He observed that its author(s) worked from an anti-Tenochca perspective, typical of the Tlatelolcah.[18] Finally, after some earlier scholars he convincingly proposed that either Ecatl or his descendants contributed to *Ms. 22bis*'s additions to the *Anales de Tlatelolco*.[19]

Further insight into the matter of *Ms. 22bis*'s authorship came from the research by Castañeda de la Paz on the professional activities of Don Diego García de Mendoza Moctezuma.[20] Active around 1700, this famous forger of documents was responsible for fabricating multiple primordial titles, including Techialoyan codices. He also worked for the Indigenous authorities of Tlatelolco,[21] producing, as Castañeda de la Paz reveals, a title known as the *Ordenanza de Cuauhtemoc*, which they used in land litigations in 1704 and 1709. The scholar proposes that Don Diego García manufactured contracted titles using scraps of early colonial tradition extracted from old documents the communities provided him. Since the *Ordenanza* and the *Anales de Tlatelolco* share some passages and multiple details, Castañeda de la Paz suggests that García had the *Anales* in his hands and copied them, producing *Ms. 22bis*. He did not use a hypothetical, now lost, version of the *Anales de Tlatelolco*, which contained all the additions absent in *Ms. 22*, as Prem and Dyckerhoff thought.[22] In the scenario sketched by Castañeda de la Paz,[23] García would supplement the manuscript with the stories found in different documents.

To sum up state of the art, the *Anales de Tlatelolco*'s account on the death of Cuauhtemoc must be an early eighteenth-century—rather than faithfully copied sixteenth-century—text, which falls within the framework of primordial titles. It was written down by Don Diego García, who was contracted by the authorities of Tlatelolco, but calling García the account's author would be too far fetched. As suggested by Terraciano, the narrative shows the influence of Don Martín Ecatl's family. However, it is impossible to know whether this was García's only source. The famous forger might have compiled his text from several documents, oral accounts, or a mix of various media. Likewise, until his source(s) reached him around 1700, they may have already gone through significant reshaping or editing. The authorship of Cuauhtemoc's death story was most probably a collective endeavor, stretched in time and gradually built up by numerous generations of the Tlatelolca tradition keepers.

HISTORICAL BACKGROUND OF CUAUHTEMOC'S DEATH

Tlatelolco was the closest neighbor of Tenochtitlan, located on the same island and, like the latter, inhabited by the Mexicah.[24] It was also Tenochtitlan's mortal enemy, crushed by the Tenochcah in the 1473 war, which ended with the symbolic death of the Tlatelolca tlahtoani, Moquihuix, falling off the city's main pyramid.[25] Moquihuix's final flight was, at the same time, the end of Tlatelolco's *tlahtohcayotl* (dynastic rulership) and independence. The Tenochcah replaced their neighbor's ruling position with an office of *cuauhtlahtoani*, who, although connected to the traditional dynasty, responded to the tlahtoani of Tenochtitlan via an imposed majordomo. Castañeda de la Paz believes that ever since Moquihuix's defeat, the policy of the Tenochca rulers was to integrate Tlatelolco within the complex altepetl of Tenochtitlan.[26] When the last Tlatelolca cuauhtlahtoani, Itzcuauhtli, died in 1520, and the deaths of Moteuczoma and his successor Cuitlahua left Tenochtitlan without a tlahtoani, Cuauhtemoc assumed control over both polities. His ancestry earned him acceptance from the Tlatelolcah.[27] A lost graphic document (*pintura*) elaborated by Don Alonso Jiménez of Colhuacan and converted into alphabetic writing by the annalist Chimalpahin claimed that Cuauhtemoc's mother, Tecapan, was a daughter of Epcoatl, who came from the Tlatelolca ruling dynasty.[28] According to Don Fernando de Alva Ixtlilxochitl,[29] Cuauhtemoc's ancestry was even more fit for the Tlatelolca rulership because Tecapan was a daughter of the miserable Moquihuix—the last autonomous tlahtoani of this polity. Whatever Cuauhtemoc's qualifications to the authority over the Tlatelolca part of the island, he did not enjoy it for a long time. After the surrender of the Mexica in 1521, Cortés appointed Temilotl as the first Tlatelolca tlahtoani since 1473, and Temilotl was still on duty during the trip to Honduras, in which he took part.[30]

The 1521 defeat of Tenochtitlan provided the Tlatelolcah with a kind of sour moral victory because it was their part of the island that, in the last phase of the siege, hosted the Tenochca elites fighting fiercely against the Spaniards until the very end. This pride, as well as unquenchable animosity toward Tenochtitlan, shows throughout the *Anales de Tlatelolco*. In Cuauhtemoc's death story, it manifests itself in a reinterpretation of the alliance of Tenochtitlan, Tetzcoco, and Tlacopan that dominated today's Central Mexico before the Spanish invasion. The hated Tenochtitlan was converted into a pathetic polity governed by a crippled and vengeful creature, while Tlatelolco replaced it as the most potent altepetl of the region. As for Cuauhtemoc, he was as distant from Tenochtitlan as he could be, portrayed as a tlahtoani of Tlatelolco since 1515. The tradition of his longtime rule in the latter polity must have existed before the elaboration of *Ms. 22bis* because both Alva Ixtlilxochitl and Fray Diego Durán claim that Cuauhtemoc was *señor* in Tlatelolco prior to his election for the tlahtoani of Tenochtitlan.[31] However, *Ms. 22bis* went even further, eliminating Itzcuauhtli and Temilotl from the Tlatelolca rulers. Castañeda de la Paz suggests that this narrative choice may have drawn from the collective memory,[32] in which, at the time of shaping the story, Cuauhtemoc was the most outstanding character associated with the first decade of the Spanish presence in the formerly Mexica lands. Still, the author(s) of *Ms. 22bis* did not forget about the existence of Temilotl or his participation in the expedition. Rather than acknowledging his position as a tlahtoani, they ascribed to him a hardly enviable role of Ecatl's companion who panicked on board the ship and threw himself into the open sea, paddling hopelessly toward an invisible shore. Were these writers or storytellers somewhat biased against Temilotl's lineage? If so, they skillfully took care of several things in one move. By making Cuauhtemoc the sole Tlatelolca tlahtoani of the 1520s decade, they ridiculed Temilotl and the Tenochcah; they suggested that Tlatelolco enjoyed a rightful tlahtoani before the Spanish invasion, and they pushed their altepetl to the forefront of Cuauhtemoc's death story.

Another shift from the generally accepted facts occurs in the execution's circumstances. *Ms. 22bis* conflates two journeys of Cortés: to Honduras and Spain. The former was a long and arduous trip begun in 1524 to punish the rebel Cristóbal de Olid, who had set off for an exploratory expedition to Honduras but, on the way, allegedly betrayed Cortés's interests. The party, which initially included Cuauhtemoc and a throng of Indigenous elites and warriors, returned to Tenochtitlan in 1526 with significant losses.[33] Cuauhtemoc died halfway through this journey, executed by order of Cortés in Yucatan at the beginning of 1525.[34] The fatal decision to go after Olid resulted in Cortés's steady loss of power, influence, and wealth over the next several years. Eventually, in 1528, he departed to Spain to pursue his agenda at the royal court. He came back in 1530 as the Marqués del Valle de Oaxaca,[35] bringing back some of the Indigenous noblemen who had accompanied him overseas. Among them were members of the Tenochca ruling lineage and the son of Tenochtitlan's interim ruler, Motelchiuh,[36] but no testimony would corroborate Ecatl's or Temilotl's travel to Spain.[37]

The memory of Nahua elite members crossing the Atlantic Ocean in the company of Cortés could inspire the story on Temilotl and Ecatl. Nonetheless, it does not explain why, in the minds of the mid-colonial Tlatelolcah, the 1525 Yucatan incident merged with the 1528 boarding of the ship in Veracruz. The key to this mysterious association lies in the name "Acallan," or "The Place of Boats." In a recently published case study, Katarzyna Szoblik explores how Nahua cultural memory shaped stories of a seemingly historical nature.[38] She discusses a warrior named Tlacahuepan, who made his appearance in various points of the Mexica history, always playing his archetypical role of an almost suicidal sacrificial victim—a role established in the primordial era of the fall of Tollan. Songs of the *Cantares mexicanos* commemorate the heroic death of the most recent Tlacahuepan—a brother of Moteuczoma Xocoyotl—in the war of Huexotzinco just years before the arrival of the Spaniards. Szoblik concludes that rather than seeking "historical truth,"[39] the Nahua tradition operated within the paradigm of circular time, in which some events repeated over and over again, mirroring their archetypes from the primordial era. We will see this phenomenon in *Ms. 22bis*'s account of Cuauhtemoc's execution. By sheer coincidence, the place of Cuauhtemoc's death, Acallan, shared its name with a port from which the ancient ruler of Tollan, Topiltzin Quetzalcoatl, set off to the Otherworld. This random homonymy allowed the author(s) of *Ms. 22bis*'s tale to interpret Cuauhtemoc's tragic end as a repetition of Topiltzin Quetzalcoatl's last journey.

NARRATIVE TROPES IN CUAUHTEMOC'S DEATH STORY
ACALLAN

Topiltzin Quetzalcoatl is probably the best-known character of Nahua literature and one of the pre-contact Nahuas' essential cultural heroes and deities.[40] He brings together an infinite number of themes and cultural references, from initiating the shift of the cosmic eras and creating humankind, through shaping the Central Valley's sacred landscape and becoming the morning star (Venus), to providing a model for a priest and a tlahtoani, and more. One of the recurrent themes in Topiltzin Quetzalcoatl's biography is his last journey or escape from the city of Tollan. The *Anales de Cuauhtitlan* describes Topiltzin as Tollan's ruler, who brought his altepetl to exuberant prosperity. However, a malicious intervention of his adversary Tezcatlipoca forced him to leave Tollan. Quetzalcoatl started his journey by lying for four days in a stone chest. He then summoned his pages, and the party set off to "Tlillan Tlapallan Tlatlayan" (The Place of Black and Red, the Place of Cremation). When they reached the coast, Quetzalcoatl adorned himself and stepped onto a funeral pyre. The ashes of his burned body rose to the sky and transformed into various precious tropical birds, with Quetzalcoatl's heart turning into Venus—a star that appears to the east, immediately preceding the sunrise.[41] In the condensed version included in *The Legend of the Suns*, which mixes the adventures of the young Quetzalcoatl with the solemn journey of his final days,[42] Topiltzin reaches the coastal region, called Acallan, after a series of conquests. In Acallan, he "crosses over the water" (*panoa*) to Tlapallan, where he gets sick, dies, and eventually gets cremated.[43] A song from the *Cantares mexicanos* records a similar tradition,[44] in which Nacxitl Topiltzin "goes to his destruction" in Tlapallan, passing through Poyauhtecatitlan and then crossing over the water (*quiyapanahuiya*) in Acallan.[45]

Densely packed with symbolic and esoteric references, Topiltzin Quetzalcoatl's journey was (among other mutually nonexclusive interpretations) a passage from the realm of the humans to the Otherworld. His destination, Tlapallan, was located across the sea, in the eastern part of the sky, also known as *tonatiuh ichan*, or the Home of the Sun[46]—an afterworld for the warriors killed in battle and women who died at their first childbirth.[47] According to the *Histoyre du Mechique*—a sixteenth-century French translation of a 1546 account in Spanish[48]—it was also the place of the origin of music. The god of the air (another aspect of Quetzalcoatl) reached it, stepping on the backs of sea creatures.[49] Sources complete the picture of the supernatural itinerary joining the human earth with the eastern Otherworld via ocean by mentioning several primordial groups that came from the places of origin located beyond the sea and landed along the Gulf Coast: in the Huasteca region, near Veracruz, or the Yucatan's Potonchan.[50] Chimalpahin recorded the tradition of the Nonohualca Teotlixca Tlacochcalca Tecpantlaca, who departed precisely from Tlapallan, described, throughout his account, with the terms Huehue, Nonohualco, or Chicomoztoc.[51] On their way, they crossed "the ocean, the heavenly river" (*huey teohuatl, ylhuicaatoyatl*). Nahuatl terms used for the sea—*ilhuicaatl*, "heavenly water," or *amictlan*, "watery land of the dead"—reflected a belief that the ocean consisted of the same substance as the sky, and, like the sky, it formed part of the Otherworld.[52] An afterworld governed by the rain deities, Tlalocan—another place represented in the story of Topiltzin Quetzalcoatl—was also sometimes located in the eastern section of the sky.[53] In the *Cantares mexicanos*, the name "Poyauhtecatitlan," "Place of the Poyauhtlan people," alludes to the children sacrificed to Tlaloc, who dwelled in the Home of the Sun.[54] Poyauhtlan was the name of mountains and temples understood as Tlalocan's replicas.[55] Likewise, the crowd of exotic birds rising to the sky from Topiltzin's funeral pyre symbolized Tlaloc's realm.[56]

The Nahuas conceptualized the Gulf Coast as the threshold to the Home of the Sun,[57] and Acallan—the otherworldly haven—could have been located anywhere along its line. When interpreting a painted manuscript, the Spanish author of the *Historia de los mexicanos por sus pinturas* observed that Quetzalcoatl (here named Ce Acatl) departed "toward Honduras," to "a place which today is also called Tlapallan."[58] From the moment Topiltzin Quetzalcoatl had reached the Gulf Coast, he found himself in a liminal space of mutually permeating otherworldly regions (Tlalocan, sea-sky) that led him in the direction of the rising Sun. In a way, he was going back home. Michel Graulich proposed that the ulcerated god Nanahuatl, who had thrown himself into a bonfire to become the Sun, was an aspect of Quetzalcoatl.[59] Graulich interpreted Quetzalcoatl's "solarized" biography as the passage of the Sun, which first rises young and fierce, moving across the sky and making conquests, to reach the peak of its power at midday. For Quetzalcoatl, this time was when he settled in Tollan, turning the city into the capital of the mighty empire. Pass midday, the Sun loses his vigor and heads toward the land of the dead, just like Quetzalcoatl, who acquired some characteristics of the monstrous Tlaloc before his passage to the Otherworld. For the Nahuas, there was nothing inappropriate in that the descending Sun-Quetzalcoatl traveled in the eastern rather than western direction. According to the *Historia de los mexicanos por sus pinturas*, the Sun only goes as far as midday, at which point he turns back and returns to the east, leaving only his light to linger until the end of the day.[60]

I suggest that the tradition recorded in the *Anales de Tlatelolco*'s *Ms. 22bis* associated the dying Cuauhtemoc with the Sun, who retreats to the eastern Otherworld. Such an association was possible because, similarly to Quetzalcoatl, the Mexica tlahtohqueh were viewed as representations or embodiments (*ixiptla*) of the Sun. Many Nahua texts compare the altepetl deprived of its ruler to the world that lies in the darkness awaiting the sunrise—or the ascension of a new tlahtoani.[61] Parallel to Quetzalcoatl's biography, Graulich applied the solar model to the entire list of the Tenochca rulers.[62] According to his interpretation, Moteuczoma Ilhuicamina was the tlahtoani at the zenith, his power reflected in his miraculous birth modeled on the births of Quetzalcoatl or Huitzilopochtli. From this perspective, Cuauhtemoc would be the setting Sun, an identification stressed by his name—"He Descended Like an Eagle"—which refers to a solar bird, the eagle.[63] In the cyclical approach to history practiced by the Mexica, he could be the perfect candidate to repeat Quetzalcoatl's cross-ocean travel toward the east at the time of his death. The fact that Cuauhtemoc's end occurred in a place called "Acallan" could have resonated with the Topiltzin Quetzalcoatl archetype of the Nahua oral tradition.

Possibly, the author(s) of the *Anales de Tlatelolco*'s *Ms. 22bis* were not the first one(s) who saw the extraordinary implications of Cuauhtemoc's death in Acallan.

Alva Ixtlilxochitl remarks: "Some authors write that the death of Cuauhtemoc occurred in Itzancámac but the natives and the paintings, songs, and stories of this land that I follow, declare it, as it is told above. And be that as it may, they died in the lands of the province of Acalan."[64] Both names mentioned by the Tetzcoca chronicler—Acallan and Itzancámac—come from Cortés's letters;[65] the latter refers to a town in which the party was staying when the events leading to Cuauhtemoc's death started to unfold. Thus, when pinpointing the execution's location, all the posterior writers could choose between two valid names: the town or the province. Spanish chroniclers opted for the former: Francisco López de Gómara,[66] Antonio de Herrera y Tordesillas,[67] and Fray Juan de Torquemada[68] all placed Cuauhtemoc's death in Itzancámac (or Yzancanac). However, Nahua "paintings, songs, and stories" collected by Alva Ixtlilxochitl, as well as some Indigenous sources that have survived to this day, preferred the name "Acallan."[69] Although Nahua texts (including the *Anales de Tlatelolco*) also tend to use the name "Hueymollan" to describe the larger region in which the execution took place,[70] their preference of "Acallan" over "Itzancámac" is significant. While the name "Itzancámac" meant nothing to the Nahuas, "Acallan" possibly allowed them to inscribe the death of Cuauhtemoc into the sacred cycle of repeating events, spiraling back to the primordial era of Tollan.

The author(s) of *Ms. 22bis*'s account may have been drawing from Nahua tradition keepers' collective feeling that the fate of Cuauhtemoc resembled that of Topiltzin Quetzalcoatl. They reinforced Cuauhtemoc's otherworldly destination by reinterpreting the expedition to Honduras as the first leg of Cortés's trip to Spain. Now Cuauhtemoc was traveling to the coast, where the ships set off to sail across the sea-sky to Europe. With this, more than in other known colonial Nahua texts, in the *Anales de Tlatelolco*, Yucatan's Acallan became a threshold to the Home of the Sun. With the archetype in place, the story of Cuauhtemoc's death could now adopt more elements from the tradition regarding Topiltzin Quetzalcoatl's last moments. One of them, which also built on the cultural connotations of the Nahua rulers, was the motif of the silk-cotton tree, known as the ceiba, or, in Nahuatl, *pochotl*.

The Ceiba

Along with the *Anales de Tlatelolco*, multiple Nahua sources specify, either alphabetically or graphically, that Cuauhtemoc was hanged on a pochotl—a silk cotton tree.[71] In contrast, Spanish sources, including Cortés's letters, do not mention what served as the gallows for the miserable tlahtoani.[72] This difference between the two corpora is particularly salient in the work by Torquemada,[73] who critically compares the accounts of López de Gómara and Herrera y Tordesillas with an anonymous "Tetzcocan history written in the Mexican language." As a result, Torquemada gives two versions of the execution: in the Spanish one, Cuauhtemoc and other rulers are just hanged (*se ahorcaron*), while in the Nahua one, Cortés hangs them during the night on a pochotl tree ("fuelos ahorcando aquella noche de un árbol que llaman pochotl"). The exact time of the execution is yet another detail treated differently by Spanish and Nahua sources. Cortés does not specify it, but he claims that he arrested Cuauhtemoc and the other rulers at dawn and interrogated them before hanging, from which we can calculate that the killing occurred sometime during the day.[74] Later Spanish writers do not express any interest in the time of the execution. In contrast, several Nahua sources insist that it took place during the night. In *Ms. 22bis*, the Spaniards arrest the rulers after the evening meal;[75] Alva Ixtlilxochitl claims that they started to hang them one by one three hours before dawn;[76] and the Tetzcocan account cited by Torquemada reports that by sunrise, the rulers were already dead ("amanecieron todos estos tres reyes colgados").[77]

Some scholars have interpreted the image conveyed by Nahua sources of Cuauhtemoc's body hanging from a ceiba (Spanish for pochotl) in the darkness as a criticism toward Cortés's decision to execute the tlahtoani. Discussing Torquemada's account, Patrick Lesbre commented that a nighttime execution meant an illegal sentence.[78] Juan José Batalla Rosado proposed several possible reasons for hanging Cuauhtemoc on a tree,[79] among them haste and Cortés's intention to degrade the Mexica tlahtoani. Batalla Rosado observed that in sixteenth-century Spain, the law required executions by hanging to be performed on a structure composed of two vertical poles joined on top with a horizontal beam, although, in reality, trees often provided as good gallows—particularly for lower-class convicts. However, a review of the graphic representations of hanging from Central Mexican codices made by the scholar has rendered a surprising result: only Cuauhtemoc is dangling from a tree among the crowd of miserable hanged men populating their pages. Why single him out like that? Furthermore, why, among all the botanical richness of Yucatan, do Nahua sources invariably identify this tree as a pochotl/ceiba?

When seen from the Nahua rather than the Spanish point of view, introducing the ceiba as Cuauhtemoc's gallows may have had an effect opposite to that proposed by Batalla Rosado. In his analysis of *Ms. 22bis*'s account, Terraciano suggested that its mention of the ceiba was not accidental.[80] According to Castañeda de la Paz, in this and other Nahua texts, the ceiba may have added dignity to the scene because it was a tree recognized as sacred across Mesoamerica.[81] More specifically, it had a strong association with dynastic rulership. The metaphor *pochotl ahuehuetl*, which juxtaposed two types of tall and imposing trees—a ceiba and a swamp cypress—referred to a tlahtoani in his capacity of people's protector.[82] The ceiba had additional fiery connotations, which made it a perfect companion of Sun-Cuauhtemoc's final moments.[83] Likewise, dawn, when it was still dark, could refer to a solar symbolism of the dying tlahtoani. For the Nahuas, rather than concealing the illegal execution, the darkness may have symbolized the ruler-less world, waiting for the "sunrise." In line with the Topiltzin Quetzalcoatl's paradigm, the perfect moment for a royal death would be at the time of the Morning Star's appearance, at early dawn, a few hours before the solar disk emerges from behind the horizon. In a scene of the Azcapotzalco tlahtoani Tezozomoc's death and funeral, the sixteenth-century *Codex Xolotl* uses calendric symbolism to compare Tezozomoc to the setting Sun; among others, it points explicitly to dawn as the time of his passing.[84] Similarly, the nighttime schedule of Cuauhtemoc's execution combined perfectly with the royal symbolism of the ceiba, building an ideal scene for a dying tlahtoani.

The significance of the ceiba for the narrative of both the *Anales de Tlatelolco* and earlier Nahua texts does not end with this tree's connection to royal power. As in the case of Acallan, the presence of the pochotl in many variants of Cuauhtemoc's death story may also owe to its liminal properties. In a model proposed by Alfredo López Austin for Mesoamerican cultures, the ceiba was a cosmic tree, which grew from the body of the "earth crocodile" to hold up the sky.[85] It integrated four cosmic trees that stood at the earth's limits and allowed for a constant flow of opposing forces between the sky, the earth, and the underworld.[86] Although it seems that López Austin's identification of the cosmic tree with a ceiba derives mainly from Mayan texts and artifacts, traces of the ceiba's cosmic connotations also appear in other Mesoamerican cultures. Some pre-contact painted books of the Puebla-Tlaxcala region, known as the Borgia Group codices, include ceiba trees with trunks modeled as bodies of crocodiles.[87] In early-colonial Nahua culture, which directly influenced the alphabetic texts about Cuauhtemoc's death, the pochotl seemed to have been one of the many possible entrances to the Otherworld. Interestingly, the clues that allow for this conclusion come from the stories on the last journey of Topiltzin Quetzalcoatl.

According to the *Florentine Codex*, on his way to the coast, Topiltzin shaped the landscape through which he passed, leaving marks, building structures, setting up rocks, and naming places.[88] His route led through lands that did exist, and sixteenth-century Nahuas could probably take a visitor on a tour around the region and show them memorial sites of Topiltzin's journey. Simultaneously, though, some details suggest that these lands were a liminal space that overlapped an actual geographical region in the same way as the seacoast discussed above. Michel Graulich observes that the *Florentine Codex*'s Topiltzin followed the road through the land of the dead, Mictlan, combatting obstacles known from Nahua cosmological accounts, like a great river or a pass between two snow-covered mountains.[89] He also moved in view of the Tlalocan-replicating mountain of Poyauhtecatl, and he once descended underground to erect a house "in a place called Mictlan." The episode with a ceiba occurred right before the latter feat: Topiltzin "shot a ceiba (as if it were an arrow). He shot it to the effect that it has passed through another ceiba (forming a cross)."[90] Graulich uses a matching episode in the *Histoyre du Mechique* to interpret this puzzling account.[91] This source says that Quetzalcoatl, on the run from his adversary Tezcatlipoca, "went to a desert and shot an arrow at a tree, and he entered inside the hole [made by] the arrow, and thus he died."[92] Graulich speculates that Quetzalcoatl entered inside the ceiba to either hide from Tezcatlipoca or rejuvenate. He corroborates this interpretation with the data from Armenian and African cultures. However, there is an explanation for this adventure that does not require reaching to regions so distant from Mesoamerica.

In a way characteristic of oral tradition's redundancy,[93] the *Florentine Codex* and other sources multiplied symbolic references to the focal themes of the journey: royal death and world creation. Traveling in the primordial era of Tollan, Topiltzin set precedence for the former and contributed to the latter by shaping the landscape and converting himself into the Morning Star. His ceiba adventure responds to both themes. On the one hand, it is yet another sign—along with the mountain Poyauhtecatl, the Mictlan house, and the seashore—of the otherworldly character of the lands Topiltzin passed through. At the same time, it establishes a landmark—a weirdly shaped pochotl tree—that, in the sixteenth century, perhaps really existed in the region associated with Topiltzin's journey. Descriptions of land boundaries from primordial titles suggest that Nahua communities of the late colonial period still considered the pochotl and ahuehuetl trees important landmarks and recognized their sacred connotations.[94]

The versions of Topiltzin Quetzalcoatl's last journey recorded in the *Florentine Codex* and the *Histoyre du Mechique* suggest that, like Acallan, the ceiba was a threshold to the Otherworld. One could enter inside it and die. Simultaneously, it was a metaphor for a ruler and connector between various dimensions of the cosmos. All these connotations explain why Nahua tradition—songs, Chimalpahin's annals, the *Codex Vaticanus A*, and other sources—"hanged" Cuauhtemoc precisely on a ceiba. It was not a detail meant to stress his humiliation or the execution's illegality. Instead, it was a logical way to end the life of a Mesoamerican ruler,[95] and the authors of the *Anales de Tlaltelolco*'s story recognized that too. Cuauhtemoc passing away at night, on a ceiba, at the seacoast emanated strong royal and solar symbolism while repeating the primordial model set by Topiltzin Quetzalcoatl.

Cotztemexi the "Dwarf"

The last salient detail of *Ms. 22bis*'s narrative that seems to have arisen from early colonial or even pre-contact tradition concerning rulers' deaths is Cuauhtemoc's traitor's identity. Cortés claims that the person who revealed to him the supposed conspiracy was an "honored citizen" of Tenochtitlan named Mexicalcingo and later baptized as Cristóbal.[96] Among the posterior Spanish authors, López de Gómara took from Cortés both names without questioning them,[97] while Herrera y Tordesillas changed "Mexicalcingo" to "Mexicalzin."[98] Finally, Torquemada and Alva Ixtlilxochitl,[99] both better acquainted with Nahuatl, correctly identified "Mexicaltzinco" as a toponym and named Cortés's informant "Mexicaltzincatl" or "a person from Mexicaltzinco." This version originating from an eyewitness and the leading force behind the execution contrasts with the information given by some Nahua sources. The Tenochca chronicler Don Hernando de Alvarado Tezozomoc,[100] the copyist and coauthor of his *Crónica mexicayotl*, Chimalpahin,[101] and Fernando de Alva Ixtlilxochitl call the traitor Cotztemexi or Coztemexi.[102] Chimalpahin could have taken this name straight from Alvarado Tezozomoc, mainly because they both suggest that Cotztemexi was involved with the Tlatelolca (and, according to the latter author, the Michhuaque).[103] Nevertheless, Alva Ixtlilxochitl must have used a different source because in his *Compendio histórico del reino de Texcoco*, along with citing Cortés-derived data (Cristóbal from Mexicaltzinco), he names the traitor "Coztemexi from Itztapalapan."[104] The variation as to the traitor's home altepetl suggests that Alvarado Tezozomoc was not responsible for inventing the name "Cotztemexi." Instead, it must have formed part of a more widespread, cross-altepetl tradition, still vivid in the early seventeenth century, when Alva Ixtlilxochitl worked on his *Compendio*. The same tradition found its way into *Ms. 22bis* of the *Anales de Tlatelolco*.

In striking contrast to Cortés's "honored citizen," *Ms. 22bis* presents Cotztemexi as an evil dwarf of deformed legs and a usurper of the Tenochca rulership. These contrasting descriptions mirror the feelings of both Cortés and the Nahua heirs of Cuauhtemoc's political legacy toward this figure. However, the Nahua resentment toward Cuauhtemoc's traitor goes back to a period much earlier than the time of putting together *Ms. 22bis*. Translating or paraphrasing from an Acolhua source, Torquemada calls him a "villain and a commoner."[105] Lesbre interprets these epithets as, on the one hand, an attempt to reinforce the dignity of the executed rulers by contrasting them with a low-class denouncer and, on the other hand, an early-colonial critique of ennobled commoners.[106] Castañeda de la Paz explores another path, proposing that Bernal Díaz del Castillo's account may have inspired Torquemada's mention.[107] Díaz del Castillo claimed that the denouncers were "two big Mexican caciques named Tapia and Juan Velázquez."[108] They easily identify with Don Andrés de Tapia Motelchiuh and Juan Velázquez Tlacotzin, both made by Cortés interim rulers (*cuauhtlahtohqueh*) of Tenochtitlan after Cuauhtemoc's death. From a reconstructed biography of Motelchiuh, Rossend Rovira Morgado concluded that Díaz del Castillo's identification of the traitors is the most likely of all the existing versions.[109] Although he did not write it openly, Rovira Morgado suggests that the ambitious Motelchiuh contributed to Cuauhtemoc's execution and then murdered his accomplice, Tlacotzin, to gain power over Tenochtitlan. Several sources that insert details connected to Motelchiuh (whose name roughly translates to "The Hated One"[110]) in their descriptions of the Yucatan execution seem to justify this intuition. Alvarado Tezozomoc[111] and, after him, Chimalpahin,[112] identify the traitor as a Tlatelolcatl—and Motelchiuh was from Tlatelolco;[113] the former adds that the Michhuaque collaborated with the Tlatelolcah in preparing the false accusation—and in 1528, Motelchiuh was involved in the negotiations with the Michhuaque's ruler, a Tarascan *cazonci*;[114] Torquemada's mention of the "commoner Indian" may allude to the fact that Motelchiuh was born a commoner and only earned his noble status later in life;[115] finally, a sixteenth-century Nahua chronicler, Cristóbal del Castillo,[116] makes a puzzling claim that Cuauhtemoc died in "Huei Molan Xalixco," but it was Motelchiuh who met his end during the Jalisco war.[117]

The *Ms. 22bis* of the *Anales de Tlatelolco*, which strategically avoids affiliating the traitor as a Tlatelolcatl, still includes some random details taken from Motelchiuh's biography. In its compressed time frame, Don Martín Ecatl takes the place of Don Hernando de Tapia, Motelchiuh's son, traveling in 1528 to Spain and returning several years later; upon his return, Ecatl receives the grant of the altepetl Tziuhcohuac, which belonged to the family of Motelchiuh;[118] last but not least, *Ms. 22bis* presents Cotztemexi as a usurper, and we know that Motelchiuh did not have the dynastic rights to rule in Tenochtitlan.[119] While the surviving, highly biased sources make it difficult to find out the truth about Motelchiuh's (and Tlacotzin's) involvement in Cuauhtemoc's death, they show signs of an early-colonial tradition that associated the figure of the traitor with Tenochtitlan's interim rulers. The *Historia de los mexicanos por sus pinturas* indirectly confirms the existence of rumors about Tlacotzin's appetite for power by clearly defending his image as the protector of the legitimate rulership in Tenochtitlan.[120] I believe that the tales about Motelchiuh's and Tlacotzin's Machiavellian conspiracy could inspire Díaz del Castillo's account. Although like Cortés, Díaz del Castillo was an eyewitness to Cuauhtemoc's execution, he wrote decades after the events, which made him vulnerable to filling the gaps in his memory with anything other than direct recollections. The same tradition—which over the years perhaps condensed two denouncers into one Motelchiuh-like, "Hated," person—may have also fueled the Acolhua source used by Torquemada. Many decades later, an evolved version of this tradition, with details vaguely connected to Motelchiuh, was still around, and Don Diego García eternalized it in his *Ms. 22bis*.

A possible association of Cuauhtemoc's traitor with Motelchiuh and, perhaps, also Tlacotzin explains why *Ms. 22bis* would paint this figure as a usurper of the Tenochca rulership. It is, however, still unclear why its author(s) chose to turn him into a little person. Alva Ixtlilxochitl's *Sumaria relación de todas las cosas que han sucedido en la Nueva España* contains the first hint toward understanding this detail—a story of a tragic death of Tayauh. Tayauh was a son of the powerful Azcapotzalca tlahtoani Tezozomoc and, according to Alva Ixtlilxochitl, his rightful successor. Unfortunately for Tayauh, his brother Maxtla, upon Tezozomoc's death, rushed to usurp the power in Azcapotzalco. Seeking a remedy for this injustice, the bitter Tayauh went to Tenochtitlan and, together with the tlahtoani Chimalpopoca, coined a sophisticated plot to kill Maxtla during a festive opening of his new palace. Everything would have gone perfectly well for Tayauh were it not for a sneaky dwarf, Tlatolton, or Telón, Maxtla's servant. He heard all the details of Tayauh's conspiracy from his hiding place and did not hesitate to share them with Maxtla. The usurper calmly waited for the palace to be finished, and then, during the inauguration banquet, he murdered Tayauh in the same way his miserable brother had planned for him.[121] The structure of this story strikingly resembles the version of Cuauhtemoc's death presented by *Ms. 22bis*: an evil dwarf denounces the ousted ruler (Cuauhtemoc/Tayauh) to the usurper (Cortés/Maxtla), which results in the execution of the betrayed ruler.

Ms. 22bis's author(s) did not use Alva Ixtlilxochitl's text to inspire their story directly. Instead, they may have recurred to a ruler's-death-by-dwarf's-treason topos; as suggested by Alva Ixtlilxochitl's work, it could have been part of the Nahua tradition from the turn of the sixteenth and seventeenth centuries, or even earlier. Alva Ixtlilxochitl based his *Sumaria relación* on an informed interpretation of the *Codex Xolotl*, which he often supplemented with other oral and written sources. The *Codex*'s leaf 8,[122] which includes the story of Tayauh, does not represent the traitor as a little person. This information may have come from one of the now lost accounts by Don Alonso Axayaca written circa 1560–70.[123] Alvarado Tezozomoc, our earliest existing source for the name "Cotztemexi," born circa 1523,[124] was also active around this time. I mention this detail because the name "Cotztemexi," "Calf-Mexicatl," may allude to something distinctive about the calves of the traitor—perhaps a leg disability. Speculating even further, the name "Cotztemexi" may signal that already in the mid-sixteenth century, Nahua authors liked to give the role of a denouncer or a traitor to people whose bodies differed from the accepted norm. One hundred fifty years later, the *Anales de Tlatelolco*'s *Ms. 22bis* elaborated on the name "Cotztemexi," deriving from it the epithet *cozooloztic*, "he of the round calves," which indicated a physical difference of the traitor. His dwarfism reinforced the "disfiguration" feature and, perhaps, also fit the mold set by other stories of treacherous dwarves circulating in New Spain. Still, there were even more reasons to make Cotztemexi a little person, and here is where Topiltzin Quetzalcoatl once again enters the scene.

The pre-contact Nahua society considered people with unusual physical features—such as dwarfism, having a hump, or albinism—able to cross the borders between the world of humans and the Otherworld. Multiple Nahua tales mention these people traveling to the lands beyond, such as Tlalocan or Cincalco. Because of their liminal character, little people and people with hunched backs often accompanied Nahua rulers during their last journeys.[125] A Tlaxcalteca chronicler, Diego Muñoz Camargo,[126] describes how a large procession escorted the lavishly adorned body of a deceased Nahua ruler to the funeral pyre, where his servants cast themselves into the flames in a desire to follow their master. These servants of little stature and hunched backs were always kept by the rulers for personal service, palace entertainment, delicate missions, or sacrifice.[127] Muñoz Camargo makes it clear just a few lines further, where he explains that some royal burials did not involve cremation, in which case "the maidens and servants, and dwarves, and hunchbacks, and other things that this ruler loved very much" were buried alive alongside his body.[128] The Tenochcah practiced similar customs.[129] The funeral of the tlahtoani Axayacatl included a mass sacrifice of his physically different minions, whose hearts became offerings to Huitzilopochtli.[130] The liminal servants also played their roles of psychopomps in the story of Topiltzin Quetzalcoatl's final journey to the House of the Sun. The version recorded by the *Florentine Codex* describes how they all froze in the mountains, following their master through the Mictlan-like landscape.[131] These liminal characters in Topiltzin's retinue add to various other elements that build a primordial model for the Nahua tlahtoani's death and funerary rites. Among them was keeping the deceased ruler in the palace for four days before the cremation,[132] a burial by fire, or a comparison of the dying ruler to the setting sun. The figure of a little person is thus yet another motif—along with Acallan and the ceiba—associated with the passage to the afterlife, specifically, of Topiltzin Quetzalcoatl's royal imitators.

Although the *Anales de Tlatelolco*'s Cotztemexi is not a classic Nahua psychopomp who escorts his beloved master to the land of the dead, his dwarfism may owe to inspiration with a model of a dying tlahtoani. This hypothesis builds particularly on the presence of other elements connected to this model in *Ms. 22bis*'s story: Acallan, death at dawn, and the ceiba. For an individual or collective author submerged in the Nahua tradition, a little person may have been a perfectly logical narrative choice for someone who contributed to Cuauhtemoc's execution. He embodied the figures of a denouncer, a servant (which stressed his inferior status), and an assistant to the ruler-Sun's last journey. With the setting of Cuauhtemoc's execution in the context of Cortés's trip to Spain, Cotztemexi the dwarf—at the last moment banned from boarding the ship—may have also been a distant echo of the little people who indeed accompanied Cortés to Europe in 1528.[133]

CONCLUSION

The author(s) of the tale that Don Diego García wrote down circa 1700 composing *Ms. 22bis* did not treat Cuauhtemoc's death as historical in modern Western terms. Although separated by decades or even centuries from the Nahua historiographical tradition, which modeled ever-repeating events after the primordial Toltec set of themes, the late colonial storytellers thought along the same lines. They made the most of oral and, perhaps, also written, accounts passed down by Central Mexican communities to create a compelling narrative of a dying ruler-Sun. The version of Cuauhtemoc's death in the *Anales de Tlatelolco* bears traces of mid-colonial, early-colonial, and even pre-contact tradition. It pivots around two fundamental motives: the execution of Cuauhtemoc in Yucatan and the journey of Topiltzin Quetzalcoatl to the Home of the Sun. This narrative framework then grows by incorporating other matching elements from Nahua stories, such as a motif of a treacherous dwarf and rumors about the involvement of Motelchiuh and Tlacotzin in Cuauhtemoc's execution, or royal connotations of the ceiba tree. The mix also includes what we would call "historical facts": along with some details connected to the Yucatan incident, they entail knowledge of the 1528 trip to Spain or memory of the Nahua rulers' funerary rites.

As it occurs with the reading of primordial titles, the mixture of facts and narrative tropes in *Ms. 22bis* is heterogeneous only in the eyes of modern Westerners. The late-colonial Tlatelolcah must have viewed it as a perfectly consistent story, which added a cosmic dimension to the last moments of the semi-legendary Cuauhtemoc. The seed of this story germinated in the early sixteenth century, when Nahua authors focused on facts significant to them but ignored by the Spanish writers (Acallan); or reworked the narrative, adding details that matched their logic of the events (the ceiba, death at dawn). By the time the tale on Cuauhtemoc's execution expanded, evolved, and reached *Ms. 22bis*, the Tlatelolcah may have lost a deep understanding of its pre-contact nuances and connotations. They may have recognized some details (like the ceiba) as sacred symbols that belonged to ancient rulership and not much more. However, the fact that they passed this piece of their tradition to Don Diego García proves that they still kept their collective memory of the general significance of the cultural elements that composed the story on Cuauhtemoc's death. They still actively used this story to bolster their interests and cultivate pride in their ancestry. Far from being an old grandma's tale, it juxtaposed two critical founding moments in Central Mexican history: the fall of Tollan and the end of Mexicah's power. Through preserving their tradition, the Tlatelolcah did what they could to be remembered as the leading agent in this cosmic circle of eras.

NOTES

Acknowledgment: This research received funding from the National Science Center of Poland, project No. UMO-2019/33/B/HS3/00528. I would like to thank Agnieszka Brylak, Katarzyna Mikulska, and Katarzyna Szoblik for consulting my ideas and sharing their expertise and bibliographical resources with me. Any errors in this chapter are my own.

1. Jorge Gurría Lacroix, *Historiografía sobre la muerte de Cuauhtémoc* (Mexico City: Universidad Nacional Autónoma de México, 1976), 68–69.
2. Hanns J. Prem and Ursula Dyckerhoff, "Los Anales de Tlatelolco: Una colección heterogénea," *Estudios de Cultura Náhuatl* 27 (1997): 181–85, 203.
3. Rafael Tena, ed., *Anales de Tlatelolco* (Mexico City: Conaculta, 2004), 29–39.
4. Kevin Terraciano, "Narrativas de Tlatelolco sobre la Conquista de México," *Estudios de Cultura Náhuatl* 47 (2014): 211–235, here 219.
5. María Castañeda de la Paz, "Fragmentos de la Conquista a través de los relatos del siglo XVI," in *Los relatos del encuentro, México, siglo XVI*, ed. Christian Duverger (Guanajuato: Universidad de Guanajuato and Centro de Estudios Cervantinos, 2019), 151–92, here 171. Castañeda de la Paz maintains this view in her contribution to this volume. See her chapter for a competitive approach to *Ms. 22bis*'s account of Cuauhtemoc's death. Despite different conclusions as to the process of the account's composition, Castañeda de la Paz and I still coincide in many detailed observations.
6. Eduardo Matos Moctezuma, "La muerte de Cuauhtémoc: ¿Conspiración o pretexto?," *Arqueología Mexicana* 111 (2011): 37–41. For a historical perspective on different accounts of Cuauhtemoc's death and a critical review of the most important sources, see Castañeda de la Paz, this volume.
7. Throughout the chapter, I use terms such as "dwarf" or "deformation" to reflect the negative associations of these concepts in some Nahuatl and Spanish narratives that I analyze. These terms are as equivalent as possible to the original non-English terminology of the period. The last section of the chapter discusses this topic in more detail.
8. Tena, *Anales de Tlatelolco*, 28–33.
9. Tena, *Anales de Tlatelolco*, 34.
10. Tena, *Anales de Tlatelolco*, 34–35.
11. Hernán Cortés, *Cartas y relaciones de Hernán Cortés al Emperador Carlos V*, ed. Pascual de Gayangos (Alicante, Spain: Biblioteca Virtual Miguel de Cervantes, 2019 [orig. pub. 1866]), 419, accessed December 27, 2021, http://www.cervantesvirtual.com/obra/cartas-y-relaciones-de-hernan-cortes-al-emperador-carlos-v-974782/.

12. Kevin Terraciano, "Narrativas," 223.
13. Castañeda de la Paz, "Fragmentos," 162.
14. Gurría Lacroix, *Historiografía*, 21.
15. Terraciano, "Narrativas," 222.
16. Robert Haskett, "Primordial Titles," in *Sources and Methods for the Study of Postconquest Mesoamerican Ethnohistory*, ed. James Lockhart, Lisa Sousa, and Stephanie Wood (Provisional Version hosted by the Wired Humanities Project at the University of Oregon).
17. Terraciano, "Narrativas," 222.
18. Terraciano, "Narrativas," 227.
19. Gurría Lacroix, *Historiografía*, 20–21; Prem and Dyckerhoff, "Anales de Tlatelolco," 185–86; Terraciano, "Narrativas," 222.
20. María Castañeda de la Paz, *Verdades y mentiras en torno a don Diego de Mendoza Austria Moctezuma* (Mexico City: Universidad Nacional Autónoma de México, Universidad Intercultural del Estado de Hidalgo, El Colegio Mexiquense, 2017), 177–80.
21. Stephanie Wood, "Don Diego García de Mendoza Moctezuma: A *Techialoyan* Mastermind?," *Estudios de Cultura Náhuatl* 19 (1989): 245–68, 256.
22. Prem and Dyckerhoff, "Anales de Tlatelolco," 204.
23. Castañeda de la Paz, *Verdades*, 180; Castañeda de la Paz, "Fragmentos," 183.
24. I use the term "Mexicah" in reference to the ethnic group dominant in both Tenochtitlan and Tlatelolco. The inhabitants of these altepetl are the "Tenochcah" and the "Tlatelolcah," respectively. I also sometimes use the term "Nahuas" to refer to Nahuatl-speaking people who included the Mexicah and many other ethnic groups of today's Mexico.
25. For the symbolism of Moquihuix's death, see Emily Umberger, "The Metaphorical Underpinnings of Aztec History: The Case of the 1473 Civil War," *Ancient Mesoamerica* 18 (2007): 11–29; and Oswaldo Chinchilla Mazariegos, "La muerte de Moquíhuix: Los mitos cosmogónicos mesoamericanos y la historia azteca," *Estudios de Cultura Náhuatl* 42 (2011): 77–108.
26. Castañeda de la Paz, *Verdades*, 29–30.
27. Terraciano, "Narrativas," 226.
28. Domingo Francisco de San Antón Muñón Quauhtlehuanitzin Chimalpahin, *Codex Chimalpahin*, 2 vols., ed. and trans. Arthur J. O. Anderson and Susan Schroeder (Norman: University of Oklahoma Press, 1997), 2: 79.
29. Fernando de Alva Ixtlilxochitl, *Historia de la nación chichimeca*, ed. Germán Vázquez Chamorro (Madrid: Dastin, 2000), 232.
30. Bernardino de Sahagún, *Florentine Codex: General History of the Things of New Spain*, 12 vols, ed. and trans. Charles E. Dibble and Arthur J. O. Anderson (Santa Fe, NM: The School of American Research and the University of Utah, 1950–82), 8: 7–8; Castañeda de la Paz, "Fragmentos," 171.

31. On Alva Ixtlilxochitl's claim, see Alva Ixtlilxochitl, *Historia*, 293. On Fray Diego Durán's claim, see Diego Durán, *Historia de las Indias de la Nueva España e Islas de la Tierra Firme*, 2 vols., ed. Ángel María Garibay Kintana (Mexico City: Porrúa, 2006), 2: 556.

However, it was not the only available tradition. The *Historia de los mexicanos por sus pinturas*, an extract of Fray Andrés de Olmos's extensive work—Rafael Tena, ed., *Mitos e historias de los antiguos nahuas* (Mexico City: Conaculta, 2002), 16—of which at least parts derive from a Tenochca source, claims that Cuauhtemoc became ruler of Tlatelolco in 1523. The *Historia* does not record Cuauhtemoc's death, although it mentions Cortés's expedition to Honduras. Tena, *Mitos*, 79.

32. Castañeda de la Paz, "Fragmentos," 171–72.

33. Hugh Thomas, *Conquest: Montezuma, Cortés, and the Fall of Old Mexico* (London: Simon and Schuster, 1993), 596.

34. Cortés, *Cartas*, 419; Francisco López de Gómara, *Historia de la conquista de México*, ed. Jorge Gurría Lacroix and Mirla Alcibíades (Caracas: Fundación Biblioteca Ayacucho, 2007), 336.

35. G. Micheal Riley, *Fernando Cortés and the Marquesado in Morelos, 1522–1547: A Case Study in the Socioeconomic Development of Sixteenth-Century Mexico* (Albuquerque: University of New Mexico Press, 1973), 22–26; Thomas, *Conquest*, 597.

36. Rossend Rovira Morgado, "De valeroso *quauhpilli* a denostado *quauhtlahtoani* entre los tenochcas: Radiografía histórica de don Andrés de Tapia Motelchiuhtzin," *Estudios de Cultura Náhuatl* 45 (2013): 157–95, here 164–65.

37. Castañeda de la Paz, "Fragmentos," 175.

38. Katarzyna Szoblik, "Traces of Aztec Cultural Memory in Sixteenth-Century Songs and Chronicles: The Case of Tlacahuepan," *Americas* 77, no. 4 (2020): 513–37.

39. Szoblik, "Traces of Aztec Cultural Memory in Sixteenth-Century Songs and Chronicles," 527, 535.

40. Henry B. Nicholson, *Topiltzin Quetzalcoatl: The Once and Future Lord of the Toltecs* (Boulder: University Press of Colorado, 2001) holds an extensive compendium of all the versions of Topiltzin Quetzalcoatl's biography.

41. John Bierhorst, trans., *History and Mythology of the Aztecs: The Codex Chimalpopoca* (Tucson: University of Arizona Press, 1998), 30–36; John Bierhorst, ed., *Codex Chimalpopoca: The Text in Nahuatl with a Glossary and Grammatical Notes* (Tucson: University of Arizona Press, 2011), 12.

42. Michel Graulich, "Los reyes de Tollan," *Revista Española de Antropología Americana* 32 (2002): 87–114, here 99.

43. Bierhorst, *History and Mythology*, 155; Bierhorst, *Codex Chimalpopoca*, 95.

44. John Bierhorst, ed. and trans., *Cantares Mexicanos: Songs of the Aztecs* (Stanford, CA: Stanford University Press, 1985), 218–19. My interpretation slightly differs from the translation proposed by Bierhorst.

45. I thank Katarzyna Szoblik for bringing this song to my attention.

46. Hernando de Alvarado Tezozomoc, *Crónica mexicana*, ed. Gonzalo Díaz Migoyo and Germán Vázquez Chamorro (Madrid: Dastin, 2001), 464; Domingo Francisco de San Antón Muñón Quauhtlehuanitzin Chimalpahin, *Memorial breve acerca de la fundación de la ciudad de Culhuacan*, ed. and trans. Víctor M. Castillo F. (Mexico City: Universidad Nacional Autónoma de México, 1991), 118; Ryszard Tomicki, *Ludzie i bogowie: Indianie meksykańscy wobec Hiszpanów we wczesnej fazie konkwisty* (Wrocław, Poland: Zakład Narodowy im. Ossolińskich, 1990), 106–7, 118.

47. Sahagún, *Florentine Codex*, 6: 162.

48. Tena, *Mitos*, 117–18.

49. Tena, *Mitos*, 156–57.

50. Sahagún, *Florentine Codex*, 10: 185; Alva Ixtlilxochitl, *Historia*, 62; Tomicki, *Ludzie*, 103–4.

51. Chimalpahin, *Memorial*, 118; Domingo Francisco de San Antón Muñón Quauhtlehuanitzin Chimalpahin, *Séptima relación de las Différentes histoires originales*, ed. and trans. Josefina García Quintana (Mexico City: Universidad Nacional Autónoma de México, 2003), 8, 18, 20.

52. Alonso de Molina, *Vocabulario en lengua castellana y mexicana y mexicana y castellana*, 2 vols. (Mexico City: Editorial Porrúa, 1977); 1: 82r; Sahagún, *Florentine Codex*, 11: 247; Tomicki, *Ludzie*, 100–101.

53. Katarzyna Mikulska, "Los cielos, los rumbos y los números: Aportes sobre la visión nahua del universo," in *Cielos e inframundos: Una revisión de las cosmologías mesoamericanas*, ed. Ana Díaz (Mexico City: Universidad Nacional Autónoma de México, 2015), 109–74, here 123, 144, 148.

54. Elena Mazzetto, *Lieux de culte et parcours cérémoniels dans les fêtes des vingtaines à Mexico-Tenochtitlan* (Oxford: Archaeopress, 2014), 123; Mikulska, "Cielos," 114.

55. Sahagún, *Florentine Codex*, 2: 208; Bierhorst, *History and Mythology*, 86; Elena Mazzetto, "Las *ayauhcalli* en el ciclo de las veintenas del año solar," *Cultura Náhuatl* 48 (2014): 139, 167.

56. Justyna Olko and Julia Madajczak, "An Animating Principle in Confrontation with Christianity? De(re)constructing the Nahua 'Soul,'" *Ancient Mesoamerica* 30, no. 1 (2019): 78–79.

57. Bierhorst, *Cantares*, 20; Szoblik, "Traces," 518–19.

58. "Hazia Honduras, en un lugar que oy día también se llama Tlapalla," Tena, *Mitos*, 42.

59. Graulich, "Los reyes de Tollan," 92–97.

60. Tena, *Mitos*, 30–31, 81.

61. Bierhorst, *Codex Chimalpopoca*, 42; Sahagún, *Florentine Codex*, 6: 17; Juan de Tovar, *Historia y creencias de los indios de México*, ed. José J. Fuente del Pilar (Madrid: Miraguano Ediciones, 2001), 131.

62. Michel Graulich, *Quetzalcóatl y el espejismo de Tollan* (Antwerp, Belgium: Instituut voor Amerikanistiek, 1988), 199–201.

63. I thank Agnieszka Brylak for bringing the question of Cuauhtemoc's name to my attention. Susan Gillespie observes that the key characters of both the beginning and the end of Tenochtitlan have eagle-related names that correspond perfectly with their historic roles: Cuauhtlequetzqui, "Eagle that rises," and Cuauhtemoc, "He Descended Like an Eagle," respectively. Susan Gillespie, *The Aztec Kings: The Construction of Rulership in Mexica History* (Tucson: University of Arizona Press, 1989), 199–200.

64. Fernando de Alva Ixtlilxochitl, *Obras históricas*, vol. 1, ed. Edmundo O'Gorman (Mexico City: Universidad Nacional Autónoma de México, 1975), 505: "Algunos autores escriben que la muerte de Quauhtémoc fue en Itzancámac: Pero los naturales y las pinturas, cantos y historias de esta tierra, a quien yo sigo, lo dicen según está referido atrás, y sea como fuese, ellos murieron en tierras de la provincia de Acalan." All translations from Spanish, French, and Nahuatl are mine.

65. Cortés, *Cartas*, 419.

66. López de Gómara, *Historia de la conquista*, 336.

67. Antonio de Herrera y Tordesillas, *Historia general de los hechos de los castellanos en las islas y tierra firme del mar oceano: Decada terzera* (Madrid: Imprenta Real, por Juan Flamenco, 1601–15), 287, accessed December 28, 2021, http://www.memoriachilena.gob.cl/602/w3-article-8394.html.

68. Juan de Torquemada, *Monarquía indiana*, 6 vols. (Mexico City: Universidad Nacional Autónoma de México, 1975), 2: 317, accessed December 28, 2021, https://historicas.unam.mx/publicaciones/publicadigital/monarquia/index.html.

69. Bierhorst, *Cantares*, 278–79; Domingo Francisco de San Antón Muñón Quauhtlehuanitzin Chimalpahin, *Codex Chimalpahin*, 2 vols., ed. and trans. Arthur J. O. Anderson and Susan Schroeder (Norman and London: University of Oklahoma Press, 1997), 2: 38–39.

70. Cristóbal del Castillo, *Historia de la venida de los mexicanos y de otros pueblos e historia de la conquista*, ed. and trans. Federico Navarrete Linares (Mexico City: Consejo Nacional para la Cultura y las Artes, 2001), 162–63, accessed December 28, 2021, https://www.rae.es/sites/default/files/Aparato_de_variantes_Historia_verdadera_de_la_conquista_de_la_Nueva_Espana.pdf; Chimalpahin, *Codex Chimalpahin*, 1: 168–9, 2: 38–39; Chimalpahin, *Séptima relación*, 214–16; Domingo Francisco de San Antón Muñón Quauhtlehuanitzin Chimalpahin, *Annals of His Time*, ed. and trans. James Lockhart, Susan Schroeder, and Doris Namala (Stanford, CA: Stanford University Press, 2006), 134–35; "Codex Aubin," in *Geschichte der Azteken*, ed. and trans. Walter Lehmann and Gerdt Kutscher (Berlin: Gebr. Mann Verlag), 1–60, here 34; Lori Boornazian Diel, *The Tira de Tepechpan: Negotiating Place under Aztec and Spanish Rule* (Austin: University of Texas Press, 2008), 134.

71. Bierhorst, *Cantares*, 278–79; Chimalpahin, *Codex Chimalpahin*, 1: 168–69, 2: 38–39; Chimalpahin, *Séptima relación*, 214–16; Chimalpahin, *Annals*, 134–35; Torquemada,

Monarquía indiana, 2: 316; Ferdinand Anders and Maarten Jansen, *Religión, costumbres e historia de los antiguos mexicanos: Libro explicativo del llamado Códice Vaticano A* (Mexico City: Fondo de Cultura Económica, 1996), 360.

72. Cortés, *Cartas*, 420–21; López de Gómara, *Historia*, 335–36; Bernal Díaz del Castillo, *Historia verdadera de la conquista de la Nueva España: Aparato de variantes*, ed. Guillermo Serés (Madrid: Real Academia Española, 2014), 783–84, accessed December 28, 2021, https://www.rae.es/sites/default/files/Aparato_de_variantes_Historia_verdadera_de_la_conquista_de_la_Nueva_Espana.pdf; Durán, *Historia de las Indias*, 2: 574–75; Herrera y Tordesillas, *Historia general*, 286–87; Torquemada, *Monarquía indiana*, 2: 315–16; Alonso de Zorita, *Relación de la Nueva España*, ed. Ethelia Ruiz Medrano and José Mariano Leyva (Mexico City: Conaculta, 1999), 604–5.

73. Torquemada, *Monarquía indiana*, 2: 315–17.

74. Cortés, *Cartas*, 421.

75. Tena, *Anales de Tlatelolco*, 33–34.

76. Alva Ixtlilxochitl, *Obras históricas*, 503.

77. Torquemada, *Monarquía indiana*, 2: 317.

78. Patrick Lesbre, *La construcción del pasado indígena de Tezcoco de Nezahualcóyotl a Alva Ixtlilxóchitl*, trans. Mario Zamudio Vega (Mexico City: INAH, El Colegio de Michoacán, 2016), 261.

79. Juan José Batalla Rosado, "La pena de muerte durante la colonia—siglo XVI—a partir del análisis de las imágenes de los códices mesoamericanos," *Revista Española de Antropología Americana* 25 (1995): 71–110.

80. Terraciano, "Narrativas," 223.

81. Castañeda de la Paz, "Fragmentos," 167, 182.

82. Mercedes Montes de Oca, *Los difrasismos en el náhuatl de los siglos XVI y XVII* (Mexico City: Universidad Nacional Autónoma de México, 2013), 124–38.

83. Alfredo López Austin, *Tamoanchan y Tlalocan* (Mexico City: Fondo de Cultura Económica, 2000), 151.

84. Julia Madajczak, "Assassinations in the *Codex Xolotl*: Who Really Are the Bad Guys?," in *Deciphering the Codex Xolotl: Nahuatl Writing, Mesoamerican History*, ed. Benjamin Johnson and Gordon Whittaker (Denver: University Press of Colorado, forthcoming).

85. Alfredo López Austin, "Difrasismos, cosmovisión e iconografía," *Revista Española de Antropología Americana* vol. extraordinario 1 (2003): 143–60, here 151.

86. López Austin, *Tamoanchan*, 19–20, 225.

87. Katarzyna Mikulska, *El lenguaje enmascarado: Un acercamiento a las representaciones gráficas de deidades nahuas* (Mexico City: Universidad Nacional Autónoma de México, 2008), 2: 140.

88. Sahagún, *Florentine Codex*, 3: 31–36.

89. Graulich, *Quetzalcóatl*, 221–24.

90. "Quimjn pochotl injc qujmjn çan no ie in pochotl hitic nalquixticac" (Sahagún, *Florentine Codex*, 3: 35).

91. Graulich, *Quetzalcóatl*, 226–27.

92. "Le quel se voiant tant persecute de ce Tezcatlipuca, s'en fuit en un desert, et tirat ung coup de flech a ung arbre, et se mit dedans le partuis de la fleche et ainsi mourut." Tena, *Mitos*, 162–63.

93. Walter J. Ong, *Orality and Literacy: The Technologizing of the Word* (New York: Routledge, 2005), 39–40.

94. Haskett, "Primordial Titles," 7.

95. Significantly, the Chontal Maya of Acallan also remembered Cuauhtemoc dying on a ceiba. However, in their interpretation, rather than hanging him, it served to expose his cut-off head (Gurría Lacroix, *Historiografía*, 51; Batalla Rosado, "La pena de muerte," 77).

96. Cortés, *Cartas*, 420.

97. López de Gómara, *Historia de la conquista*, 335.

98. Herrera y Tordesillas, *Historia general*, 2: 287.

99. Torquemada, *Monarquía indiana*, 2: 315; Alva Ixtlilxochitl, *Obras históricas*, 502.

100. Chimalpahin, *Codex Chimalpahin*, 1: 168–69.

101. Chimalpahin, *Codex Chimalpahin*, 2: 38–39; Chimalpahin, *Séptima relación*, 216–17.

102. Alva Ixtlilxochitl, *Obras históricas*, 502.

103. Castañeda de la Paz, "Fragmentos," 162.

104. "Llamó después Cortés secretamente a un indio llamado Coztemexi, que después se llamó Cristóbal, natural de Iztapalapan o según algunos de Mexicalcinco." Alva Ixtlilxochitl, *Obras históricas*, 502.

105. Torquemada, *Monarquía indiana*, 2: 316.

106. Lesbre, *Construcción*, 262.

107. Castañeda de la Paz, "Fragmentos," 168.

108. Díaz del Castillo, *Historia verdadera*, 783.

109. Rovira Morgado, "Valeroso *quauhpilli*," 183–84.

110. I thank Agnieszka Brylak for pointing out to me that, like the name of Cotztemexi, Motelchiuh's name can suggest the attitude that the fellow Mexicah had toward him.

111. Chimalpahin, *Codex Chimalpahin*, 1: 168–69.

112. Chimalpahin, *Codex Chimalpahin*, 2: 39–39; Chimalpahin, *Séptima relación*, 216–17.

113. Rovira Morgado, "Valeroso *quauhpilli*," 167.

114. Rovira Morgado, "Valeroso *quauhpilli*," 186.

115. Rovira Morgado, "Valeroso *quauhpilli*," 166.

116. Castillo, *Historia de la venida*, 162–63.

117. Rovira Morgado, "Valeroso *quauhpilli*," 186.

118. Rovira Morgado, "Valeroso *quauhpilli*," 164, 177.

119. Castañeda de la Paz, "Fragmentos," 168.

120. It informs the reader that in 1522, Tlacotzin banished the Tetzcocan prince Ixtlilxochitl from Tenochtitlan, acting against the will of Cortés, who wanted Ixtlilxochitl to rule there. Next year, Cuauhtemoc gave a war call, and the people responded by reporting to Tlacotzin, who modestly told them that he was not the ruler. It looks like this information came from informants interested in defending Tlacotzin's reputation. See Tena, *Mitos*, 79.

121. Alva Ixtlilxochitl, *Obras históricas*, 354–55.

122. *Códice Xolotl*, accessed December 20, 2021, https://www.amoxcalli.org.mx/laminas.php?id=001-010&act=sig&ord_lamina=001-010_16.

123. Lesbre, *Construcción*, 90.

124. Germán Vázquez Chamorro and Gonzalo Díaz Migoyo, "Introducción," in *Crónica mexicana* by Hernando de Alvarado Tezozomoc, ed. Germán Vázquez Chamorro and Gonzalo Díaz Migoyo (Madrid: Dastin, 2001), 5–51, here 30–31.

125. José Contel and Katarzyna Mikulska, "'Mas nosotros que somos dioses nunca morimos'. Ensayo sobre *tlamacazqui*: ¿Dios, sacerdote, o que otro demonio?," in *De dioses y hombres: Creencias y rituales mesoamericanos y sus supervivencias, Encuentros 2010*, vol. 5, ed. Idem (Warsaw: University of Warsaw; Toulouse: University of Toulouse, 2010), 23–65, here 51–52.

126. Diego Muñoz Camargo, *Descripción de la ciudad y provincia de Tlaxcala*, ed. René Acuña (San Luis Potosí: Biblioteca Tlaxcalteca, 2000), 200.

127. Elena Mazzetto, "Diversión y funciones simbólicas de los enanos y jorobados en la sociedad mexica," *Memoria Americana: Cuadernos de Etnohistoria* 29, no. 1 (2021): 27–53.

128. "Y allí se enterraban vivos, con ellos, doncellas y criados, y enanos y corcobados, y otras cosas que el tal s[eñ]or mucho amaba." Muñoz Camargo, *Descripción de la ciudad*, 200.

129. Mazzetto, "Diversión y funciones," 40–42.

130. Tezozomoc, *Crónica mexicana*, 245–46.

131. Sahagún, *Florentine Codex*, 3: 35; Graulich, *Quetzalcóatl*, 223.

132. Bartolomé de Las Casas, *Apologética historia sumaria* (Digital book: Fundación El Libro Total), vol. 2, bk. 3, ch. CCXXVII, accessed December 28, 2021, https://www.ellibrototal.com/ltotal/?t=1&d=4072_4167_1_1_4072; Durán, *Historia de las Indias*, 1: 55–56; Graulich, *Quetzalcóatl*, 222.

133. Mazzetto, "Diversión y funciones," 37.

5

Zacarías de Santiago

A Tlaxcalteca Conquistador in the Evolution of Nahua Historical Memories

ROBERT HASKETT

The fame of heroes owes little to the extent of their conquests and all to the success of the tributes paid to them.
—JEAN GENET, *PROVERBICALS*

INTRODUCTION

The illustrious Don Zacarías de Santiago was remembered in the eighteenth century as a ruling-class Tlaxcalan "conquistador" from the *cabecera* (head town) of Tepeticpac.[1] He came to be associated with Hernando Cortés and the alliance forged with the Spaniards during the struggle to defeat the Tenochca empire. He greeted Cortés and helped win honors and rewards from his new allies for his own and other communities in the region. His regal image was inscribed on several pictorial manuscripts, one of them called the *Mapa de Tepetomatitlan*, where he stands dressed as an early sixteenth-century Nahua lord.[2] In other words, he was an Indigenous conquistador par excellence.

Well, not exactly. There is no doubt that Don Zacarías was a real person with lordly status in sixteenth-century Tlaxcala, but he was not actually this kind of Nahua conquistador. He turns out to have been in the same league as other Indigenous lords remembered later as having been on the scene when the Spaniards arrived in Mexico for the first time. Don Toribio Cortés, a long-serving *gobernador* of Tlahuica Cuernavaca, who held power in the later decades of the sixteenth century, was nonetheless remembered a hundred years later in that *villa*'s primordial titles as the local hero who welcomed and allied with Cortés, facilitating as well the implantation of the Catholic faith. Don Zacarías is similar in another way to Acxotecatl, lord of the Tlaxcalan *altepetl* (city-province) of Atlihuetzian, best known now for murdering his son Cristóbal (now San Cristóbal), one of the so-called Boy Martyrs. Yet well into the seventeenth century there was an alternate, sanitized memory of Acxotecatl among some of the region's surviving Nahua nobility that omitted the gory, inconvenient details of his dark deeds. This alternate biography boasted of his prowess as an ally of Cortés who received from that grateful leader an image of the Virgin Mary, known eventually as La Conquistadora. Even today there is a statue of Acxotecatl on the edge of his hometown's main square that lacks any information about the murder of his son, despite that a lurid painting of the martyr's death in 1527 by his father's hand can be found in the nearby church.[3]

Acxotecatl had indeed allied with the Spaniards during their conflict with the Mexica, so the "valiant ally" image was not completely false, just incomplete. And like Don Toribio of Cuernavaca, Don Zacarías didn't flourish politically in Tlaxcala until the second half of the first colonial century. Though he is not known to have murdered anyone, Don Zacarías was certainly an ally of Spain, and even met and conversed with Philip II. Yet his "conquests" had to do with winning concessions from that monarch within the context of his repeated exercise of high-level sociopolitical authority in Tlaxcala, not because he welcomed and aided Cortés during the struggle to defeat and control the Mexicas and their allies. In its own way, then, memories of Don Zacarías's triumphs turn out to be an indication of how Nahuas were looking to the past in ways that justified their situations and goals in the later-colonial present.

Over the last several decades, scholars have complicated the traditional binary rendition of the so-called *Conquista* by moving beyond the iconic figures of Cortés and Moteuczoma and the famous war chronicles created by the likes of Bernal Díaz de Castillo and the authors of Book 12 in the *Florentine Codex*. It turns out that there are many competing versions of what happened during and after the fall of Tenochtitlan and the identities of significant actors in these events. As the Nahua memory of events connected with the Spanish victory evolved, Don Zacarías was converted into the "incarnation of the *altepetl*," to use historian James Lockhart's terms.[4] Don Zacarías became so famous, at least in his regional context, he was "adopted" in various *lienzos*, *títulos*, and *mercedes* (pictorial manuscripts, titles to land, grants) created by or for other Indigenous communities trying to make sense of the beginnings of their journey through the "colonial" centuries. How and why all of this happened to Don Zacarías (and other, similar people)—that is, the processes by which he became a stunning icon of Nahua agency in the allied struggle against the Triple Alliance—can help us understand how memories of the conflict that raged beginning in 1519 underlay the formation of proud, self-governing Catholic altepetl in the postwar era and beyond.

THE HEROIC "CONQUISTADOR" DON ZACARÍAS DE SANTIAGO

As he was remembered in a number of later-colonial manuscripts, Tlaxcala's Don Zacarías de Santiago was a prominent ruling-class figure who somehow achieved fame as a valiant Indigenous conquistador. In this guise he appears in two copies of documents purporting to date from 1525 and 1546, one set presented in or around March 9, 1774, another version probably dating from the earlier eighteenth century. The text of the 1774 set claims that it was a copy presented to "El General don Joachín Moreno, Alcalde maior y Capitan a Guerra," by a group of town officers of the Huexotzinco-area pueblo of San Simón Atzitzintlan (near Calpan)—*fiscal* (chief ecclesiastical officer) Dionisio Pérez, *teniente fiscal* (assistant ecclesiastical officer) Nicolás Pérez, *alguacil mayor* (head constable) Pasqual de la Encarnación, and "other *naturales* of the pueblo"—because the original was "very old and worm eaten."[5] The centerpiece of both sets is a grant issued in the name of Hernando Cortés on November 13, 1525, to Atzitzintlan.[6] "Don Hernando Cortés, Capitan General y Presidente en esta Nueba España y Governador de esta Provincia, por su Magestad" refers to his travails on the march into Mexico, notes how the "Yndios Casiques y Principales" of Calpan and other communities such as San Simón Atzitzintlan provided the arriving Spaniards with *tlamemes*. All of these porters put themselves "at grave risk of their lives against our enemies" in campaigns in the Huexotzinco and Calpan area, service that would be remembered for all time. In response to a request from Don Antonio de Galicia, cacique and governor of the city of Huexotzinco, Cortés recognized the legitimate tenure of the people and community of San Simón to lands they had occupied since they were gentiles (presuming they were now Catholics, apparently), signing off on this grant along with a notary named Alonso Valiente and a witness called "el Doctor Duenos."[7]

Two other documents associated with Atzitzintlan are dated in Tlaxcala, one on November 20, 1525, the second on the twenty-fourth of the same month. Both mention Tlaxcala's heroic governor, Don Zacarías de Santiago as presiding over the confirmation of Cortés's grant on November 20, 1525, in the presence of the "principales y muchos naturales del Pueblo de San Simon Achichintlan [*sic*]." A walking survey of the pueblo's lands encrusted with pageantry was conducted by at least some of the assembled Nahua notables and witnesses.[8] The leaders of the group carried two standards, one blue, one white. *Clarines* (a kind of trumpet) blared while participants threw stones and uprooted plants, symbolizing possession. Historic events are remembered as the survey party advanced: a *congregación*, the distribution of posts to town officers, the construction and decoration of the church, among other things. Since Don Zacarías actively participated in all of these events, he "signed" at the end of every document having to do with them. The whole thing was purportedly later verified on June 6, 1546, by Viceroy Antonio de Mendoza and then endorsed again by the leaders of Tlaxcala around the same time, with Don Zacarías still listed as that altepetl's governor.[9]

However, the Atzitzintlan merced and the other "1525" documents associated with it have a number of questionable elements. It is hard to believe that Atzitzintlan, or any of the other communities mentioned in the text, already had saints' names at this time. Nor that they would have had substantial churches such as the one supposedly built in the center of San Simón Atzitzintlan (though humbler chapels of various kinds could have been present).[10] The claim that Atzitzintlan had been congregated around 1525 with another town referred to as "San Gregorio" seems anachronistic, at best. And of course Cortés could not have been in central Mexico in November of that year to draw up such a grant, when he was forcing his way cross-country to Honduras to confront what he thought was a mutiny of Spaniards there.[11]

Moreover, it is highly doubtful that in 1525 men bearing the title gobernador and who had completely Spanish-style names ruled any of the communities named in the merced, or that they already presided over full rosters of Iberian-style town councils. Huexotzinco did not gain the status of *ciudad* (city) or own a coat of arms until 1553. While the process of establishing quasi-Iberian cabildos in New Spain began in 1532, there is no evidence that the altepetl had a full-blown roster of officials with the titles *gobernador, alcalde, regidor, mayordomo, fiscal, alguacil,* and *escribano* until 1543.[12] An early gobernador was Juan Xuárez Quecehuatl, his "Christian" name the same as that of the first *guardián* of the altepetl's recently founded Franciscan *convento*. Other sixteenth-century gobernadores were Pedro de Suezo (ca. 1551, originally from Tetzcoco), Juan de Almonte (1572, 1574), and Don Juan Martín de Hojacastro (1575). No one with the surname "Galicia" seems to have held the office in Huexotzinco during the sixteenth century, however.[13] For the moment, the identity of "Don Antonio de Galicia," and why he was inserted into various late-colonial texts, remains a mystery.[14]

THE "REAL" DON ZACARÍAS DE SANTIAGO

As he appears in the 1525 Cortés merced, Don Zacarías can actually be described (in our way of thinking) as a mixture of fiction and fact. He was a real person but could not have been a ruler and Indigenous conquistador in the 1520s. Tlaxcala did not have its first gobernador until 1534. His name was Diego Tlilquiyahuatzin of the Tlaxcalan cabecera of Ocotelulco, a cousin of the famous *tlatoani* (ruler) Maxixcatzin the Elder. Governors continued to have mixed Spanish and Nahuatl names into the later sixteenth century, though fully "Spanish" names had become more and more common by that time. One of the latter was Tepeticpac's Don Zacarías de Santiago, who served as Tlaxcala's governor not in 1525 or 1546 but rather from 1581–82, then again in 1589–90, and for one additional year in 1594.[15]

Among his official functions as a member of the cabildo or as its gobernador, Don Zacarías was involved in various kinds of financial processes. As governor in 1581, he oversaw the appointment of two men, Francisco Martínez de Placencia and Don Diego Téllez (a former governor), to collect the altepetl's tribute. Once again governor in 1590, Don Zacarías led the cabildo in a rental agreement with Alonso Durán for some land apparently held by the city in the Pago de Minchaque.[16]

Don Zacarías appears to have had a penchant for economic dealing. He seems to have been the landlord of some houses available for rent, and also had other kinds of property interests. In August 1573, a short notice indicates that disgruntled Indigenous house renters named Doña Pascuala de Santiago and her husband, Juan de Siena, were suing Don Zacarías in this connection. In 1578 he joined Alonso Xuárez and Alejandro de Zamora in a land rental deal involving a large property called Apiaco.[17] Glimpses of the ways in which Don Zacarías acquired his property are found in a short bill of sale dated July 5, 1581, in which an *indio* named Pedro Tochi was somehow persuaded to "donate" a lot with some houses to the governor. Near the end of his life, in 1596, Don Zacarías was still buying land, at that time in partnership with Don Juan de Ribas, a deal requiring the services of the interpreter Diego Muñoz Camargo.[18] Whether or not Don Zacarías used his political clout in some way (as in the case of the Tochi "donation") to buy, sell, and rent is open to question.

As far as his enduring memory as an important political figure is concerned, the pinnacle of his career was undoubtedly his diplomatic representation of Tlaxcala as a member of the delegation of lords from its four main cabeceras sent to Spain in 1584–85 (along with Antonio de Guevara, Pedro de Torres, Diego Reyes Téllez, and Diego Muñoz Camargo).[19] As remembered in entry for 1584, 1 Flint-knife year of the *Anales de Tlaxcala*, Don Zacarías departed for Spain with "don Antonio Téllez de Guevara; don Pedro de Torres; Diego Téllez; and Diego Mayor, child of don Diego Téllez." The next year, "1585, 2 House year," was when "the rulers who had gone to Spain came back."[20] According to Charles Gibson, this delegation was especially noteworthy because it was awarded fifteen of "the most famous of Tlaxcalan privileges, including several of those later incorporated in the *Recopilación* [*de leyes*]."[21] The king seems to have been impressed by the delegation's reminder that Cortés had promised the Tlaxcalteca special privileges when they joined the Spanish cause and that subsequently the people of the province had given great service to the Catholic Church. As one scholar puts it, this latter argument "gave them the upper hand since piety was akin to loyalty" in the mind of Philip II.[22]

The important privileges bestowed in response by the king included an enhanced civic title and status, the endorsement of the altepetl's territorial limits, and relief from all forms of tribute payment. Don Zacarías was granted a coat of arms, as were Diego Reyes de Téllez and Pedro de Torres (Antonio de Guevara had already received this honor in 1563).[23] Don Zacarías's crest—typically displaying both European and Indigenous-style devices—was conferred on this "cacique e yndio principal" in a royal grant drawn up in Barcelona on May 20, 1585, in recognition of his and his late father Alejandro de Santiago's loyalty to the crown and, in the father's case, fealty to Charles V.[24] Alejandro de Santiago had represented the cabecera of Tepeticpac in the capacities of alcalde and regidor between 1547 and his death in 1556.[25]

Not all of Don Zacarías's activities would have been seen as entirely in keeping with his later reputation as a champion of the people. In 1585 he was among several nobles of Tlaxcala who "testified that the native population was dispersed in the forests and ravines thus causing inconvenient lapses in proper religious indoctrination," and were falling into idleness. The group spoke in favor of congregating the people so that they, as well as the crown and the church, could better access their labor and supervise their piety.[26] While undoubtedly a potential source of resentment among affected people, this and presumably other more negative memories for other actions taken by Don Zacarías as governor seem to have faded away by the time texts and pictorials featuring Don Zacarías as a heroic figure were created. For instance, his trip to Spain was remembered in very positive terms in the seventeenth-century work of the royal chronicler Gil González Dávila's *Teatro eclesiástico* of 1649, who records negotiations "in the name of the *República de Puebla* [by] the very noble *caballeros* Don Antonio de Guevara, Don Diego Téllez, Don Pedro Torres, and Don Zacarías de Santiago, *indios principales*," who met with Philip II. Since these Indigenous nobles were mainly representing the interests of Tlaxcala, not the "República de Puebla," there is already some slippage of memory here.[27]

Don Zacarías was well known to the late seventeenth-century Tlaxcalan annalist and historian Don Juan Buenaventura Zapata y Mendoza, who remembered that in "1581 Cali xihui yn iquac governador Don Çacarias de Santiago" (1581 House year, was when Don Zacarías de Santiago was governor), and "1582 Tochtli xihuitl [*sic*] yquac gobernador Don Çacarias de Santiago" (1582 Rabbit year, was when Don Zacarías de Santiago was governor).[28] The annalist records that Don Zacarías was also governor in 1589 (another "house" year), 1590 (another "rabbit" year), and 1594 (yet another "rabbit" year).[29] Zapata y Mendoza recorded as well that Don

Zacarías served as alcalde of Atlancatepec, Tlaxcala, in the "house" year of 1593, not long before he returned to the governorship for a yearlong term, acting once again as alcalde in the "flint" year of 1596, and was one of the "alcaldes de provincia" in the "house" year of 1597.[30] He seems to have been among the Tlaxcalan lords who greeted the newly arriving viceroy Don Luis de Velasco at Atlancatepec, accompanying the viceregal party as far as Huamantla (though the language of this entry for 1590 is somewhat ambiguous on this point).[31] More emphatically, Zapata y Mendoza reports that he died on October 12 of the following "rabbit" year, 1598.[32]

Of course, in another way Don Zacarías has never died. In this he appears to be similar to a Cuernavacan hero in later-colonial Nahuatl town history and land boundary text (a genre called *títulos primordiales*) Don Toribio Cortés, that real, long-serving governor of that altepetl of the later sixteenth century who was relocated temporally speaking to the formative years of the community's emergence as a "colonial" municipal entity.[33] Don Toribio seemed to have been remembered as an important figure in Cuernavaca's history because of his association with significant later sixteenth-century events connected with the operation of town government and with the fortunes of a political faction under his leadership. Similarly, Don Zacarías may have gained even wider fame in the Tlaxcala area thanks to his participation in notable happenings in that privileged altepetl's political history, leading to his adoption as a "local" cultural hero by a number of different peoples and places. His association with tribute relief must have loomed large in Tlaxcala and the broader Puebla-Tlaxcala region. Much later, there were several men whose names incorporated his—Mariano Zacarías de Santiago Gallegos, Pedro Nolasco Zacarías de Santiago y Gallegos, and José Antonio Zacarías de Santiago y Gallegos (a notary)—active on Tlaxcala's town council between 1787 and 1803.[34] Thus, some memory of his and the other 1580s Tlaxcalan ambassadors' stress on early support for Cortés and for the Catholic faith could have led to his erroneous association with the first decade of the Spanish presence in Mexico. If so, this may be why he was "borrowed" by the creators of the Atzitzintlan manuscript and, possibly, remembered by the people of that community.

PICTURING A HERO

This was not the only appropriation of Don Zacarías as a heroic figure, however. The *Mapa de Tepetomatitlan*, described as stylistically "heavily Europeanized," features a coat of arms that may have been intended to represent one of Tlaxcala's four cabeceras or possibly Don Zacarías's crest won on his trip to Spain. This *Mapa* is accompanied by a Spanish-language grant having to do with "lands held by Alonso Sarmiento, Gusman Paderes [*sic*, actually one person], and Zacarias de Santiago [*sic*]."³⁵ The *Mapa* bears a Nahuatl text on its reverse side, describing the pictorial as "this painted map patent of nobility..." (inin Pinturia [*sic*] mapa executoria...). If this was the intent of the coat of arms image, the *Mapa* not only memorialized Don Zacarías's honor obtained from the king in Castile but connected him with the legitimacy of the altepetl of San Matías Tepetomatitlan.³⁶

What can we make of this set of manuscripts? The *Mapa* has been thought to come from around 1556, the apparent date of the Spanish grant recognizing Don Zacarías's stature and political authority as an altepetl founder.³⁷ Pictorially, the *Mapa* features footprints indicating roads in a "pre-contact" way (though the roads are not outlined). Don Zacarías de Santiago is shown standing a bit above and to the left of a crowned coat of arms with what looks like a stork in its center that is holding a staff with a faded red, forked pennant attached. Don Zacarías wears a pre-contact-style embroidered cape and Indigenous-style clothing, and is holding a representation of a traditional *macuahuitl* (sword). There are two churches depicted on the *Mapa*, a small one in the lower right corner glossed as San Juan Tetetl, and a larger one in the upper middle labeled San Matías Tepetomatitlan. A mountain in the upper left of the pictorial has been identified as a representation of Matlalcueye (aka Mt. Malinche); it does not resemble a traditional place glyph-style mountain, however.³⁸

The Spanish-language grant associated with the *Mapa* and said to have been issued in Philip II's name definitely recognizes Don Zacarías as a worthy Indigenous conquistador. The king proclaimed that

> In regards to the esteem of my loyal vassals of that noble city of Tlaxcala, we would command that you uphold them and see them as conquerors and supporters of my crown... the legitimate descendants Don Alonso Sarmiento Guzman Paderes [*sic*, Paredes] and Don Zacarías de Santiago are due 500 coins (*sueldos*) as so ordered from Spain to my kingdoms and territories.

The monarch gave "'you, Don Alonso Sarmiento Guzman Paderes and Don Zacarías de Santiago, the right that you ask to found towns where you would please near the principal town of Xotelulco.'"³⁹ The Nahuatl-language text has to do with the grant of lands, the recognition of Tepetomatitlan as a cabecera, and the endorsement (or creation) of a governing cabildo bestowed by the king and announced to the people of this community by Don Zacarías. The Nahuatl text serves in a similar role to that in the supposed 1525 manuscripts from Atzitzintlan: in Tepetomatitlan he is receiving, transmitting, and personifying the king's largess for that community.⁴⁰ He becomes Tepetomatitlan's "town founder," at least in its post-contact, Catholic guise.

But while the *Mapa* and other associated texts have been accepted as a mid-sixteenth-century creation by the Lilly Library, or perhaps somewhat later than that in the same century according to another study, this cannot be.⁴¹ Don Zacarías did not obtain official recognition of a coat of arms until his trip to Spain in the 1580s, long after the manuscript was supposedly created. He was not a major figure in Tlaxcalan-area politics in 1556, either, so that it is highly unlikely that King Philip II would single him out for special attention along with Don Alonso Sarmiento Guzmán Paredes in a grant recognizing these figures and their altepetl's exceptional contributions as Indigenous conquistadors. It is also not clear what kind of civic status Tepetomatitlan actually enjoyed in the colonial era, or when (and if) it became an independent altepetl and/or a cabecera. As of this writing, the earliest reference to this place discovered in an archival document is dated 1692, when at least two presumed Indigenous men of the community, Juan Martín and Juan Luis, were involved in a lawsuit having to do with land tenure.⁴² Several other cases of a similar nature date from between 1709 and 1797. Even so, its municipal status in the eighteenth century remains unclear; in 1709 it is referred to as a pueblo, but in 1714–15 it is called a barrio, while it is again glossed as a pueblo in later-eighteenth-century records.⁴³ Whatever this means, it is possible that the *Mapa* and the texts accompanying it were created during one of these later colonial land disputes.

In fact, Don Alonso Sarmiento Guzmán Paredes's purported descendants were engaged in a protracted lawsuit during this same period, which might help date and explain references to him in the *Mapa*, if not his association with Don Zacarías. Beginning in the late 1650s and extending into the eighteenth century, people who claimed an ancestral link to Don Alonso were engaged in a struggle to defend their self-declared status as the legitimate holders of a *cacicazgo* (lordly estate) in the Tlaxcala area. One of these alleged descendants, Doña Leonor Hernández (or Fernández) Luna, was referred to as Don Alonso's only granddaughter and heir, entitling her and her descendants to the "privilegios de nobleza, y cacicazgo que poesyeron los Sarmientos de Guzman." Don Alonso is described as having been married "in the Holy Mother Church to Doña Luisa Xiuhtonateotzin, legitimate sister of the great Xicotencatl, late lord of the cabecera of Tizatlan [Tlaxcala]," presumably Xocotencatl the Elder (d. 1522).⁴⁴ If he had indeed wed Xicotencatl's sister, Don Alonso could well have been decades older than Don Zacarías, despite the fact that the *Mapa de Tepetomatitlan* had relocated the latter as a contemporary in the mid-sixteenth century.⁴⁵

That is, if Don Alonso had ever actually existed. According to Doña Leonor, her grandfather was recognized by Philip II "of glorious memory" for his "many and loyal services" in New Spain with a grant of a coat of arms, conferred in Madrid on August 16, 1563. This may or may not have been true. There was a Don Alonso Sarmiento y Guzmán in Tlaxcala, whose crest is described in Guillermo Fernández de Recas's classic *Cacicazgos y nobiliario indígena de la Nueva España*.⁴⁶ Recas's summary and quoted sections of text underline some confusion about what Don Alonso's name actually was: Don Alonso Sarmiento y Guzmán; Don Alonso Guzmán; or Don Alonso de Guzmán Sarmiento, the latter of whom was "the same who His Majesty granted an escudo de armas and other privileges, which his legitimate descendants have used."[47] More recently, María Castañeda de la Paz pictured and described this crest in an article dealing with coats of arms claimed by Tlaxcalan noble families. Don Alonso's *escudo*—preserved in a colorful eighteenth-century rendering—was one of four purportedly granted to a quartet of men who claimed descent from ancestors who aided Hernando Cortés during the war with Tenochtitlan. In Don Alonso's case, the illustrious ancestor is his father, Don Martín Trueba, whose exploits outlined in a *cédula* (royal order) granted by Philip II emphasize his important role in the defeat of the Mexica and on the frontier in Jalisco and among the "Chuchumecas" [*sic*, Chichimecas], deeds that were posthumously rewarded in the person of his son.[48]

But what sort of political stature (if any) did Don Alonso enjoy in Tlaxcala? There is no one with this exact name mentioned in the *Tlaxcalan Actas* during the period of time that he might have been active in the altepetl's government.[49] While records seeming to come from Don Alonso's purported lifetime have yet to appear, there were people living in sixteenth-century Tlaxcala with the Sarmiento and Paredes names. A man named Gaspar Sarmiento Paredes was related to a prominent Indigenous figure named Don Diego de Paredes (an *alcalde ordinario* [town councilor] in 1553 and Tlaxcala's governor from 1554 to 1555). Don Diego died in 1573 or earlier, and in 1574 his widow was trying to sell an *estancia de ganado menor* (small livestock ranch) called Alexeloya that her husband had acquired via a merced in 1563, a grant that had been confirmed once again in 1571.[50] Gaspar Sarmiento Paredes himself passed away by 1577.[51] The Guzmán name is also found among the altepetl's political leaders, since a Don Diego de Guzmán served as an alcalde ordinario alongside Don Diego de Paredes in 1553.[52] However, no records found in a published guide to the Archivo General del Estado de Tlaxcala, nor in various studies of town government and society in Tlaxcala's first colonial century, reveal the activities of a Don Alonso Sarmiento Guzmán Paredes. These records also lack any reference to his father, Don Martín Trueba.[53] What, exactly, Don Alonso's "loyal services" rewarded by the king in 1563 might have been is not spelled out by his granddaughter—those of Don Martín may have been meant—but these records put Don Alonso on the same footing as Don Zacarías as far as winning rights and privileges from Philip II is concerned. The idea that Don Alonso had wed Xicotencatl's daughter obviously was firmly established in family lore by the second half of the seventeenth century and may have been more widely believed among the Indigenous (and even non-Indigenous) population.

Leaving aside the puzzle of Don Alonso's apparent fame, the *Mapa* and accompanying texts abound in other clues that they were all created much later than 1556.[54] The Spanish loan *executoria* (judgment) has not been attested in Nahuatl until 1577, when it is used in the sense of official proof of ownership.[55] But the presence of the loan *Mapa* has yet to be found earlier than 1722, though a *pintura* does appear in some later sixteenth-century manuscripts, and an *armas*, for coat of arms, is seen in the late sixteenth century, as well.[56] So while it is clear that some of the Spanish loanwords were in at least limited use in central Mexico in the late sixteenth century (but not in 1556 as far as is known), the most prominent one used to describe the pictorial—*Mapa*—has not been securely identified in a Nahuatl text until the eighteenth century. Added to this, the Nahuatl orthography suggests that it was created during what James Lockhart has identified as the era of Stage 3 Nahuatl, putting it in the late seventeenth century at the earliest: this text is full of the use of *s* rather than *z* or *ç*, something that is typical of Stage 3 manuscripts. According to James Lockhart, "by the eighteenth century, '*s*' was the norm and anything else an exception."[57] In other words, a document written in or around 1556—early Stage 2 Nahuatl—would not have *s* instead of either of these other letters.

As far as the large coat of arms near the center of the *Mapa* is concerned, it may or may not represent Tepetomatitlan. But it does not seem to be one associated with Tepeticpac, Don Zacarías's home altepetl, or the escudo granted to him by Philip II. A set of anonymous eighteenth-century works of art depicting the four "kings" of contact-era Tlaxcala feature crest-like emblems as well, such as the portrait of Don Gonzalo Tlahuexolotzin of Tepeticpac, shown flanked by a column surmounted by a coat of arms. This crest features a feathered device but not a bird. It seems that whoever painted the scene in the *Mapa de Tepetomatitlan* had a less-than-secure grasp on Don Zacarías's emblematic associations with Tlaxcalan cabeceras if that was the intent.[58]

Taken as a whole, historical and linguistic evidence strongly suggests that the pictorial *Mapa* and its accompanying Nahuatl text held in the Lilly Library most likely were created in the late seventeenth or eighteenth centuries.[59] Grants of land and coats of arms made by the king to a noble named Don Alonso Sarmiento Guzmán Paredes as well as Don Zacarías on August 24, 1556, feature people who either would not have been prominent enough at that time to warrant such recognition or, in the case of Don Alonso, very well may not have existed. Moreover, the Spanish text seems to have little to do with Tepetomatitlan and a great deal to do with Tlaxcala and its seemingly legendary nobility. Whatever the case, neither Don Alonso nor Don Zacarías were lords of Tepetomatitlan but rather significant figures from Tlaxcala enjoying what seems to have been wider fame in the region. Both Don Zacarías and Don Alonso were invoked in later-colonial litigation records or suits having to do with community landholding and corporate status, so it is quite possible that this litigation revived their fame in some way among those who crafted things like the *Mapa de Tepetomatitlan* as they sought illustrious ancestors who underwrote their community's purported legitimacy as a landholding corporate entity.

In the end, Don Zacarías had a much better documented career than Don Alonso. As a result, he seems to have had a much stronger and more enduring role in the historical memory of people living in what are now the states of Tlaxcala and Puebla. His stature as a local hero propelled him into another pictorial manuscript, the *Lienzo de San Simón Tlatlauhquitepec* (a town north of Tlaxcala near Xaltocan), which bears a gloss with the date "año de 1734."[60] The *Lienzo* purports to show boundaries established in and around San Simón, includes Spanish-language glosses describing them and giving the dates of their establishment, shows the church of San Simón, and shows houses and properties of other local figures. While the legend at the bottom of the pictorial is badly damaged, it explains that it is a

> Mapa del Pueblo de San Simon en donde [c]onstan sus [—] linden y [como] se lindaron sus Antesedentes los que fueron a conquistar chichimecos d.n Simon cacamatzi Don Diego tlapati ano de 1595 otro li[nd]ero puc[-]s [-] nuestro [—] el añ[o] de 616 y consta por titulos tener ya tres posesiones la primera el año de 1734 la gumda [*sic*; la segunda] el año de 173[-].[61]

All of this underlines the legitimacy of San Simón's status as a semiautonomous landholding municipality and its loyalty to the viceregal state. The "map" names several different places besides San Simón—a road going toward Atlihuetzian, a barrio called Atzaqualco—but not Tlatlauhquitepec (the community which now holds the Lienzo in its local archive).

Why the Nahuatl place-name is not written on the *Lienzo* remains a puzzle, but the manuscript obviously has to do with the Tlaxcala region and had some sort of link or links to the cabecera of Tepeticpac. It depicts nobles who were rulers of the province of Tlaxcala and some information about one of their embassies to Castile. Pictorially, it features four European-looking Tlaxcalan town officers glossed as "los Caballeros que fueron a españa de la cabesera de tepticpac Don Pablo de Galicia Don Alonzo Gomes Don Antonio mano de Plata Don Lucas Garcia" ("the nobles who went to Spain from the cabecera of Tepeticpac," etc.). They are flanked on each side by coats of arms, one of them that of León and Castile. Don Pablo de Galicia is dressed in a very European style, with light brown hair and a full beard, a representation shared with the other three nobles in his group; they all look very European, rather than Indigenous.[62] On the other side of this device are four more notables—Don Luys, Don Juan Catla, Don Francisco, and Don Juliano; while the text describing their role is badly damaged, they seem to have been linked with the arrival of the viceroy in Tlaxcala in some way.[63] There is a third, elaborate coat of arms depicted above Don Francisco and Don Juliano, with "el caballero Don Sacarias de Santiago" standing alone to this crest's right on the upper edge of the manuscript. There are other figures on the document, what appear to be two friars in the badly damaged upper center of the *Lienzo*, the "Gobernador Don Valeriano Quetzalcoltzin," the "Licenciado Don Juan Días," and "El Marqués," among them.

As in the case of Don Pablo de Galicia and his compatriots, most of the Indigenous figures wear either completely or partly "Spanish" outfits, including Iberian-style hats, resembling "El Marqués" in this way. They are in other words wholly creatures of the colonial era. However, Don Zacarías is more like the figure seen on the *Mapa de Tepetomatitlan*, in that while he has on what appears to be a Spanish-style tunic and knee pants, his lower legs are bare and he is shod with traditional *cactli*-style sandals rather than Spanish shoes. His cloak seems reminiscent of a Nahua regal "rich cape, silver in color and bordered in gold" bearing some Indigenous-style decoration. The cape is held together by a brooch adorned with the emblem of the military order of Santiago, to which he did indeed belong. His hair seems to mimic Iberian modes, but he is hatless.[64] An even more "Indigenous" kind of figure is found in the *Lienzo*'s upper left corner, "El Rey Pabo [*sic*] Nombrado Tlahuexolitzi" (probably Tlehuexolotzin, one of the four lords who allied with Cortés, ruler of Tepeticpac). He is dressed as a warrior in what seems to have been intended as fully Indigenous garb, complete with a royal diadem headdress, a macuahuitl, and a feathered shield bearing the device of what seems to be a turkey (*huexolotl* means "turkey").

The crest next to Don Zacarías appears to be a simplified version of the crest he received from Philip II in 1585. The original conferred in Barcelona on May 20, 1585, was divided into four quarters, one featuring a blue bird with green wingtips in flight on a field of red. The second quarter showed a hill surmounted with a castle, with a stream and flowers below, while the third quarter had a yellow-feathered shield on a white field. The fourth displayed a habit and cross of the Order of Santiago. The whole was surmounted by a helmet, with the Latin motto "Quia Fecit Mihi Magna Qui Potens Est, Et Sanctum Nomen Ejus" (He has done great things for me, and holy is His name), an apparent reference to God rather than Don Zacarías. The eighteenth-century depiction seems to have been streamlined, with the first quarter showing a shield and emblems of the Order of Santiago in a blue field, the second a building with an open door on a hill associated with a river and yellow flowers on a silver field (appearing to be more in keeping with a pre-contact-style place glyph than what is found in the original), a third quarter with a blue bird in flight, and a fourth field with another shield. The motto associated with this crest is "qua fecit magna. qui potens est, et sanctun, no eyvs" (which roughly translated is "he has made a great slaughter. He is powerful and holy"), with the "he" perhaps a bit more ambiguous given Don Zacarías's posthumous elevation to the status of Nahua conquistador.[65]

Tlehuexolotzin obviously stands for Tepeticpac's immemorial legitimacy as well as the alliance with Cortés, or in other words his and his people's status as Indigenous conquistadors, while the more "hispanized" Indigenous figures connote the altepetl's mastery of and legitimacy in the "colonial" scheme of things. But what of Don Zacarías? Since it is known from other sources that he was part of a delegation to Spain in the mid-1580s, it could be argued that there is an implication in the manuscript that he had some kind of association with the four lords glossed as having done the same. However, they were actually all members of a previous delegation that departed in 1562 and, despite the Tepeticpac-centric cant of the *Lienzo*, they were not all from that cabecera: Don Pablo de Galicia was from Tizatlan, Alonso Gómez from Quiahuitztlan, Antonio Mano de Plata (i.e., Antonio del Pedroso) from Ocotelulco, and Lucas García from Tepeticpac.[66] Don Zacarías himself is not placed on the *Lienzo* in close association with these four figures but is separated from them by a fair distance and is not glossed as having visited Spain himself. He and Tlehuexolotzin flank the important scenes at the top of the manuscript, acting as transitional figures from the past whose stature underwrites Tepeticpac's colonial legitimacy, as do the several coats of arms associated with the human figures in this part of the *Mapa*. Just as Tlehuexolotzin represents the dawning of the Spanish era and Tlaxcala's first embrace of it, Don Zacarías can be seen as a transitional figure, part "Indian," part "acculturated Nahua," who led his people during an equally crucial era of change and evolution, someone who deepened Tlaxcalan mastery of the new age that came to fruition in the time of the lords who traveled to and from Iberia. This is despite the fact that Don Zacarías's career postdated that of Don Pablo de Galicia and the others, so the transition seemingly displayed on the *Lienzo* is flipped; Don Pablo was active politically closer in time to Tlehuexolotzin than was Don Zacarías, but when this particular manuscript was painted the lore associating Don Zacarías with Hernando Cortés in 1525 must have been very well established.

A few of the characters found in the *Lienzo*, including Don Zacarías, appear in yet another eighteenth-century pictorial, the *Pintura de San Lucas Tecopilco. Año 1714*, which also refers to a place called Santa Bárbara.[67] He appears seated at a table with four other people: a woman named Doña Berónica [*sic*, Verónica], Don Pedro Galicia, Don Pablo de Castilla, and Don Felix Mexia. Doña Veronica and Don Pablo hold cups, his with "steam" coming out, possibly indicating hot chocolate. But Don Zacarías is the central figure of the group, dressed as a colonial-era Indigenous lord and holding an alphabetic document while leaning slightly toward Doña Verónica. That manuscript is undoubtedly the one mentioned in a Nahuatl text written below this rather cozy tableau. As translated by noted scholar and Nahuatlato Luis Reyes García, this text claims to be a Nahuatl translation made on Monday, April 22, 1714, of a cédula that "the *principales* named Don Zacarías de Santiago and Don Pablo de Castilla y Galicia brought from Castile." This would have been a key document in Tecopilco's colonial formation, with the king (unnamed) recognizing the town as a cabecera in light of their military aid "when this new realm was won." For this reason too, "they received the sweet words of our great ruler, his majesty . . . that the Spaniards cannot establish themselves where you have your lands . . . [and] the [Spanish] officials will not enter," or in other words a guarantee of local political autonomy. The king also granted the community a coat of arms, a device featured on the manuscript, as well. This shield ensured that the community's nobles not only "will always be known as *principales*" but also will be the town's "strength and defense."⁶⁸

The statement that the coat of arms would protect the town and its leaders is very similar to the powers associated with coats of arms found in Cuernavaca-area primordial titles, many of which feature drawings of such devices as well as explanations about their real and symbolic importance. For instance, the authors of so-called *Códice municipal de Cuernavaca* asserted that

> this is how or ruler the King granted it to us, so that we made this coat-of-arms, which is to become our empowerment and protection . . . Our great ruler Cortés and our great ruler the king granted us this coat-of-arms, with which we will be protected, and which will become our empowerment.⁶⁹

Assuming that the Nahuatl text on the *Pintura* was newly written in or around 1714 and not, as is claimed, a translated copy or paraphrase of an earlier Spanish-language royal cédula, it would indeed date from the same period when the primordial titles were being created, or in other words from the later seventeenth and eighteenth centuries.⁷⁰ This was a time when communities like Tepetomatitlan, Tlatlauhquitepec, Tecopilco, and Cuernavaca were facing the increasing encroachments of non-Indigenous peoples and a concomitant threat to the integrity of their corporate landholdings. This was also a time when the urgency of displaying symbols of royal protection and recognition—such as coats of arms, mercedes, and cédulas—was spreading.

It is important to note that whereas the tableau of the notables sitting around the table features a Don Pablo de Castilla and Don Pedro Galicia as separate people, in the Nahuatl text there is only one man with both these surnames, Don

Pablo de Castilla y Galicia. This apparent confusion about these figures suggests a date of production long after the supposed events depicted in the *Pintura* would have taken place. As well, while Don Zacarías and Don Pablo de Galicia had indeed both been members of Tlaxcalan delegations who traveled to Spain, it should be remembered that they had not been in the same group: Don Pablo among the 1562 embassy, and Don Zacarías visiting Philip II between 1583 and 1585. As in the *Lienzo de Tlatlauhquitepec*, the association of these two men who had not actually acted together, and the confusion over the identities of Don Pablo/Pedro, display a marked telescoping of time and memory that supports the idea that the *Pintura* had been created in its entirety in the early eighteenth century and was not some sort of copy of earlier manuscripts.

While Don Zacarías, Don Pablo, and Don Pedro represent the lords who brought the cédula from Spain to Tecopilco, the other two people in the pictorial, Doña Verónica and Don Felix Mexia, may be intended as noble representatives of that pueblo itself. There is no explanation in the document about Doña Verónica, aside from her physical nearness to Don Zacarías at the center of the tableau, nor is Don Felix, who is behind Don Pedro Galicia, mentioned in the Nahuatl text. Perhaps the two represent the classic "founding couple" found in so many pictorial manuscripts produced in colonial New Spain.

WHO WAS DON PABLO DE GALICIA?

Like Don Zacarías, Don Pablo was a very real sixteenth-century political figure in Tlaxcala. By 1560 this "very noble lord Pablo Galicia, *alcalde ordinario*" of the cabecera of Tizatlan was adjudicating a dispute between Juan Jiménez, a "noble and citizen" of Ocotelulco, and a man named Miguel Petztetl, who had allegedly invaded some land belonging to Jiménez and began cultivating it. According to a Nahuatl-language record of this case, "The lord *alcalde* listened to it carefully. He issued orders to Juan Jiménez. He said to him, 'Bring two or three people as witnesses, those who know that it is really your field.'" After the witnesses arrived, took an oath with hands on a cross and then kissed it,

> the lord *alcalde* said to them, "In the name of God and in the name of Holy Mary, may you speak the truth in everything that you will be asked. If you do not speak the truth, the devil will take you to hell; if you speak the truth, then Our Lord God will have mercy on you."

In the end, based on the testimony of the witnesses provided by the plaintiff (who asserted that Don Jiménez had inherited the land from his father), Pablo [de] Galicia ruled in favor of Juan Jiménez and barred Miguel Petztetl from the agricultural field in question, even though no witness testimony seems to have been presented on the latter's behalf. This ruling is perhaps no surprise, since Jiménez turns out to have been not only a fellow noble but also another *alcalde ordinario* who was often in office at the same time as Don Pablo de Galicia.[71]

Don Pablo de Galicia served as the altepetl's governor between 1561 and 1962 and was indeed part of the 1562 delegation that traveled to Spain. He was again Tlaxcala's governor in 1585–86, making sense of his association with Don Zacarías in later colonial records.[72] He died on Friday, October 10, 1586, apparently still in office.[73] During his first term as governor, he had supervised a dispute about the "possession of an *estancia* at Acacingo," which was allegedly a "detriment to the *naturales* of that place."[74] The annalist Juan Buenaventura Zapata y Mendoza recorded that while Don Pablo was governor a new mill was constructed at a place called Atenpan and that he was also in office when a delegation of people traveled to Mexico City to buy a crucifix for "el templo" at the cost of 100 pesos.[75]

Don Pablo had been active politically in Tlaxcala earlier than this, having been an alcalde in 1547, and was among those alcaldes discussing the acquisition of a new "church altarpiece or great painting" ahead of an expected viceregal visit in 1550, and as alcalde in 1560 was connected with the fashioning of a new city clock.[76] He had served as regidor at the time of the well-known cabildo deliberations of March 1553 about the ill effects of cochineal production on the local population, economy, and social structure. Once the council had decided to limit an individual to no more than "ten plantings of cactus," and ruled that "the women who gather dye in the marketplace are to gather dye no more," he was sent with four other council members to Mexico City to get final viceregal approval for these laws.[77] A Pablo de Galicia appears as the only man with a fully Spanish name in the *Padrón de nobles de Ocotelolco* (rather than Tizatlan), an entry dated from between 1555 and 1556.[78] A "Pablo de Garizia [*sic*, Galicia]," or "Don Pablo de Garizia" appears several times in the Nahuatl-language records of a 1567 land dispute; he, or perhaps they, are said to hold property abutting the parcel in dispute. Galicia is only referred to once with the honorific "Don" in this record, opening the possibility of more than one landholder by this name in the area.[79] But there was also a Don Pedro de Galicia, an "indio principal," active as a landlord renting houses to a man named Pedro González in 1580 and 1581, and there are other indications that he had been involved in some landlord-like role in house construction in earlier decades, possibly when he was governor in the early 1560s.[80]

Whether or not these Pablos were all the same man as the governor Don Pablo de Galicia remains unclear. Confusion over his first name—Pedro or Pablo—in the *Pintura de San Lucas Tecopilco* could be a melding of two different principales with the same surname who lived during the later sixteenth century. And there may actually have been several Pablo de Galicias in Tlaxcala who were active politically and economically at approximately the same time too; the records are not always precise as to cabecera affiliation, but it would not be unusual for a single, composite "Don Pablo de Galicia" to emerge in later-colonial records as people looked back in time to celebrate the exploits of local heroes and altepetl champions. For instance, two different Cuernavacan nobles named "Don Toribio Cortes"—one the testator of the 1550s, the other flourishing politically and socially in the late sixteenth century—were fused into one heroic "town founder" in the villa's primordial titles.[81]

As far as the existence of a Pedro or Pablo de Castilla is concerned, there were at least two men with this surname active in sixteenth-century Tlaxcala, though neither was called "Pablo" or "Pedro": Don Julián Atempan of Tizatlan assumed the name "de Castilla" in 1564 (he served repeatedly as regidor and alcalde from 1549 to 1570), and Juan del Castillo, sometimes written as "del Castilla," was a regidor of Tepeticpac in 1564 and 1566.[82] Nonetheless, an eighteenth-century copy of a royal cédula granting Don Pablo de Castilla a coat of arms (rendered in full color and described in the text) is part of a set of four such records that also feature Don Alonso Sarmiento de Guzmán. "Don Pablo de Castilla" seems to have become equated with Don Pablo de Galicia as far as this crest is concerned, since it is known that Galicia did meet with and get a grant of a shield from the king in 1563.

However the existing cédula refers to the recipient as "Don Pablo de Castilla" and describes him as a "principal de la provincia de Tlaxcala," son of the "very loyal" Don Francisco Aquiyaualcatlechutel [sic], probably a corruption of Aquiyauhtecuhtli.[83] Don Francisco is said to have aided Cortés by being "one of the first to receive" Hernando Cortés "with much love," to have assisted in the defeat of the Aztecs, and to have fought for the crown in Jalisco and against the "Chuchumecas" [sic, Chichimecas].[84] "Francisco Aquiyahuatl" is a plausible name for a recently baptized lord during and immediately after the Spanish invasion.[85] In fact, a noble with this name (though lacking the honorific "Don") is found among the *pipiltin* (nobles) of the Tizatlan cabecera.[86]

While it is not entirely clear that a paternal figure named Aguiyauhtecuhtli (or some variation thereof) really existed, his association with Don Pablo de Castilla is graphically depicted in the *Genealogía de Don Francisco Aquiyauacateuhtli*, an eighteenth-century manuscript featuring two male figures, Don Francisco seated on a pre-contact-style woven *icpalli* ("throne"), and below him a standing "Don Pablo de Castilla," dressed as a pre-contact warrior holding a stylized macuahuitl, Luis Reyes argues that the manuscript was copied (or made) around 1776. A note appended to it remarks that "the authorities of Atlihuetzian" had jailed a man named Gaspar Miguel, who was accused of "fabricating" documents, and feared that his peddling of these would cause conflicts among various pueblos, ruling that one associated with the "*Barrio* of Calapan" was "false" (the implication was that the genealogy was also created by Gaspar Miguel, it seems).[87]

Whether or not the figures in the late-colonial pictorial are the same father Aquiyahuatl and son Pablo is not clear, nor is the apparent confusion of the surname "Castilla" with "Galicia" in the cédula. But as far as a Tlaxcalan lord called Pedro or Pablo with the surname Castilla is concerned, none of the sixteenth-century Indigenous governors of Tlaxcala have this cognomen, nor does this name appear in the mid-sixteenth-century *padrones*.[88] By the later colonial era, references to Don Pablo de Castilla, Don Pedro [de] Galicia, and Don Pablo de Castilla y Galicia may indeed have referred to the gobernador Don Pablo de Galicia who went to Spain in 1562 and who received a grant of a coat of arms from Philip II on August 16, 1563. As such, he had become prominent in the same way as Don Zacarías de Santiago, a member of Tlaxcala's political elite who had personally conversed with the king.

At any rate, as Don Pablo de Galicia the gobernador was not only appropriated in apocryphal pictorial manuscripts but is also featured in the supposed testament of Don Juan Oselotl Chalchiuhtecutli of San Bartasal Tochpan, a pueblo or barrio seemingly somewhere in the Tlaxcala region. This fully alphabetic Nahuatl will was allegedly drawn up on May 14, 1523, on behalf of Don Juan as well as the nobles and community of Tochpan more generally speaking. In it, the testator claims that he is legitimately passing on lands he was given by Don Pablo de Galicia as well as a Don Lucas Maxixcatzin. His heirs were his sons (or perhaps grandsons), Pedro Tlahuelahualol and Bartasal Chalchiuhteccuitli, whose perpetual right to the property was confirmed by Tlaxcala's then gobernador Blas Osorio and cabildo in 1569. Not only are these two men to hold the land "always" but so are "all those of the pueblo who are named in the testament."

While Tlaxcala did have a governor named Blas Osorio in 1569, the idea that Don Pablo de Galicia would have been a fully baptized, adult Tlaxcaltec lord in 1523 is outlandish, to say the least.[89] The Nahuatl-language testament and the 1569 cabildo deliberations are found among records of a much later land dispute running from 1702 to 1713 pitting "Los naturales del Pueblo [de] San Balthazar Tospan" against people who had allegedly usurped the properties in question.[90] The entire set of records is in the same obviously eighteenth-century hand, including the testament and cabildo texts, which are written on paper with official stamps from 1712 to 1713 on them. Charitably speaking, it might be possible that these were copies of much earlier documents from the sixteenth century, but there is too much evidence undermining this idea for the records to hold up to careful scrutiny.

While this is not the place to go into a full-blown analysis of the texts and the case in which they appear, several damning elements suggest that the Nahuatl texts, at least, were fabricated around the time the lawsuit was being pursued. Most obviously, it would have been incredible if an entirely alphabetic Nahuatl testament had been crafted in 1523, years before any other text of this kind is known to have existed. While Nahuatl-language wills did begin to appear somewhat later in the sixteenth century—and for Nahuas, at least, a "model" will text was eventually created by Fray Alonso de Molina in 1569—the full-blown alphabetic genre certainly did not exist two years after the fall of Tenochtitlan.[91] Among other orthographic quirks, the existing copy, as well as the 1569 text, betray their later-colonial production by the ubiquitous presence of *s* instead of *c*, *ç*, or *z*.

Not only is Don Pablo placed far out of his time, but his co-donor Don Lucas Maxixcatzin is an altogether problematic character. He does indeed sport one of the most famous surnames in invasion and colonial-era Tlaxcalan history. However, a Maxixcatzin family tree dating from 1562 features the tlatoani Maxixcatzin (ruling when the Spaniards arrived on the scene and who may or may not have been baptized as "Lorenzo"), two sons—Don Lorenzo, Don Francisco—several daughters, and a relative called Don Diego Tlilquiyahuatzin (who became Tlaxcala's first governor in 1534) but no one named "Lucas." A will written for Don Juan Maxixcatzin, tlatoani of Ocotelulco (1546–62), in April 1562 is bristling with the names of heirs, contemporary cabildo officers, and nobles, but again no one named Don Lucas Maxixcatzin. The ruling line continued, eventually passing into the Pimentel family, with whom the Maxixcatzins seem to have intermarried; for example, Don Luis Pimentel Maxixcatzin was active in 1626 and 1627 as a "permanent" regidor and tlatoani for his cabecera.[92] But as of this writing, no one with the first name "Lucas" has been located in available sixteenth-century records having to do with that ruling-class family, the cabecera of Ocotelulco, or Don Pablo de Galicia.

On the other hand, the supposed 1569 Nahuatl text of Don Juan Oselotl's will does have at least some town officers named in it who were active in that year, including the governor Blas Osorio and the notary Tadeo de Nisa [*sic*], but they were figures who were probably as well known in Tlaxcala as Don Pablo de Galicia and the Maxixcatzin family; Niza is thought to have written a history of the Tlaxcalan alliance with Cortés in 1548 that, according to Charles Gibson, was "in reality authenticated by thirty Tlaxcalan principals."[93] Nonetheless, questions surrounding the existence of a Don Lucas de Maxixcatzin remain, as does the puzzle of the status and location of Tochpan, not mentioned in any of the sixteenth-century works consulted for this chapter, nor does Diego Muñoz Camargo refer to it in his *Historia*. The annalist Juan Buenaventura Zapata y Mendoza alludes to people going to "the land of the Totonaca, in the east," including Tochpan (probably modern-day Tuxpan de Rodríguez, Veracruz State) and three other places, in his opening "Origen de la nación tlaxcalteca," but this place-name appears nowhere else in the work.[94]

Don Juan Oselotl's testament appears to be what Stephanie Wood has identified as a "will-título," a later-colonial document (perhaps concocted by locals, possibly by a for-profit workshop) concerned with land, its extent, sometimes with a smattering of local history, and featuring one or more notables from the past like Don Pablo de Galicia whose presence legitimizes the whole thing.[95] Looking carefully at the text, it is soon clear that rather than a document leaving various properties and goods to heirs, informing *albeceas* (executors) about what sort of burial and bequests to the church should be made, and how to fund such things—standard components in almost every will—the current text deals with only a single property, conveniently the same land that was later involved in the early eighteenth-century lawsuit. In the testament, detailed boundary descriptions reminiscent of the primordial title genre are found too. But if somehow this 1523 will is genuine despite all the other red flags associated with it, why would Don Juan Oselotl fail to mention any fancy family heirlooms he was bequeathing to his heirs, as was very common in the wills of Indigenous elites? Why does he not only leave the land in question to descendants of his family line but also to his community and everyone named in his testament, most of whom were supposedly local town officers?

Much of this line of questioning calls to mind a testament associated with sixteenth-century Cuernavacan noble and former governor, Don Toribio Cortés, who died around 1559, as well as another dated to 1640 concerning the humble Juan Bautista. Most of Don Toribio's surviving Nahuatl testament is orthodox, except, that is, for a codicil that seems to have been added to a recopied sixteenth-century original later in the colonial era. As in Don Juan Oselotl's will, this codicil focuses only on properties that are characterized as lands of the altepetl whose tenure is supposedly being underwritten in the document. Juan Bautista's will appears to be that of a poor commoner with very little property of any sort, except for a lengthy inserted text pertaining to community lands that seem to have nothing to do with the testator; this intrusive text was almost certainly added to an unassuming Nahuatl original at some later date during a protracted eighteenth-century lawsuit pitting Cuernavaca's Indigenous cabildo against the owner of the nearby sugar estate of Santa Ana Amanalco.[96] It was not uncommon for testaments to be submitted as proof of legitimate land tenure as the colonial period lengthened. James Lockhart has written that "one consequently finds Nahuas using wills not only against competing heirs but to establish property rights against outside claims."[97] A disclaimer attached to Don Juan Oselotl's will that "this will was lost and appeared in the time of a son of these lords who inherited" hints that whoever created it was giving themselves an excuse for any anomalies that might have been detected, hinting this Nahuatl text was created for a very specific purpose: the protection of a particular plot of land that was in jeopardy of being lost in the eighteenth-century lawsuit.

FAKE OR FORTUNE?

Documents such as the *Mapa de Tepetomatitlan*, the *Lienzo de Tlatlauhquitepec*, and the *Pintura de San Lucas Tecopilco* are all related to a specific colonial altepetl. Yet, in each case whoever created these manuscripts borrowed well-known, regional figures in Don Zacarías, Don Pablo de Galicia, and the others to endorse their own municipal legitimacy.[98] Somehow, it seems, the fact that the Tlaxcalan lord and governor Don Zacarías had received a coat of arms, had become a member of the exalted Order of Santiago, and later had come erroneously to be associated with the arrival of Cortés in the region and the defeat of the Aztecs "rubbed off" on these lesser pueblos at a time when they must have been struggling to preserve their autonomy in the face of the expanding non-Indigenous population in the Puebla-Tlaxcala region. Don Pablo de Galicia, another ruling-class lord who preceded Don Zacarías as an important political figure in the altepetl, seems to have had a similar pedigree in terms of regional historical memory. His apparent appearance in late records as Don Pablo de Castilla could have been the result of the confusion of Galicia's trip to Castilla in the 1560s, but somehow the very real Tlaxcalan noble Don Pablo de Galicia had become associated with the Castilla surname and a parent named Aquiyauhtecuhtli too.

Don Alonso Sarmiento de Guzmán and Don Pedro or Pablo de Castilla may or may not have ever existed. They may have been partly or even wholly invented figures serving to underpin claims by later colonial Indigenous elites or would-be elites trying to assert or protect their privileges. There are certainly questions to be asked about the royal cédulas purporting to show Philip II granting them coats of arms in recognition of ancestors' and their own support of the crown's interests. The Don Pablo de Castilla text is suspiciously similar to the one found in the supposed cédula granting Don Alonso Sarmiento a coat of arms on the strength of his father's support for Cortés: both fathers served in the defeat of México-Tenochtitlan, in Jalisco, and on the Chichimec frontier in Jalisco. This relationship is not entirely implausible, yet no heroic military ally with the name Aquiyauhtecuhtli can be found in such sources as Diego Muñoz Camargo's *Historia*, nor in the surviving copies of the *Tlaxcalan Actas*.[99] And it was Don Pablo de Galicia, the Tlaxcalan gobernador who went to Spain in the 1560s, not a "Don Pablo de Castilla." Granted, some of this is negative evidence, but it does suggest that a certain amount of caution should be exercised when dealing with the 1563 cédula of Don Pablo de Castilla and Don Alonso de Sarmiento.

As Michel Oudijk has argued in a study of falsified coats of arms from what is now the state of Mexico, fabricated ancestors linked to significant events, families, and communities that had "consequences for the local historical memory ... could be converted into 'true'" individuals.[100] This type of linking is quite possibly what happened to Don Pablo de Galicia and certainly true of Don Zacarías, who by the eighteenth century had become a "true" endorser of the corporate legitimacy of a number of pueblos in the Tlaxcala region with which he may or may not have had anything to do with when he was alive.

The possible implications of the similarities found in the texts of the Sarmiento and Castilla cédulas, the anomalous nature of such things as the Spanish-language Atzitzintlan manuscripts that were supposed to date from 1525 and 1546 but clearly did not—as well as the *Mapa*, *Lienzo*, and *Pintura* (along with the primordial-title-like Nahuatl texts associated with them) depicting Don Zacarías de Santiago—were sometimes, if not always, recognized by eighteenth-century Spanish authorities. More recently, possibly contrived "sixteenth-century" manuscripts asserting the sovereignty of Indigenous towns and the legitimacy of their leading families have become embroiled in scholarly debates over their authenticity. Were they the product of local authors or contrivances generated by *talleres* (workshops) taking advantage of a later-colonial market consisting of pueblos, *sujetos*, or barrios desperate to produce written proof of their immemorial possession of a legitimate land base and ruling class? Records associated with Don Zacarías seem to conform to a model described by Stephanie Wood: "Documents [that] not only have shared themes, but at the same time contain elements specific to each community." Wood, who has studied workshops connected with falsified Spanish-language land grants, the Techialoyan codices, and other types of supposedly autochthonous Indigenous manuscripts, believes a fair number of such workshops were in operation during the colonial era and beyond.[101]

The appearance of community-specific elements can indeed be found in a number of Nahuatl-language títulos primordiales from the Cuernavaca region that can be linked to the interests of several different political factions of that *villa*. For instance, titles featuring the local hero Don Toribio Cortés seem to be related to the activities of his later seventeenth-century political heirs who were at odds with one or two local partisan factions who had their own sixteenth-century heroic town founders. The titles related to these groups share a certain amount of overarching thematic content, as well as verifiable local lore and details, standardization suggesting that one or more talleres was at work. But if so, whoever ran them took the trouble to inject altepetl-related information—perhaps gleaned from interviewing members of Cuernavaca's political elites—along with more generic content.[102]

It seems likely, then, that the prose and pictorial records highlighting the heroic figure of Don Zacarías de Santiago were the result of various kinds of collaborations between locals and outsiders seeking to profit from the increasingly pressured land tenure situation of the later colonial era.[103] Though he had not actually been on the scene as a leading political character in the first half of the sixteenth century, Don

Zacarías had been an influential member of Tlaxcala's political elite. It would not be overly surprising if some of the later-colonial manuscripts featuring him as a sort of primordial founding character (in the post-contact sense) were linked in some way to altepetl- or regional-level political factionalism and alignments.[104]

San Simón Atzitzintlan's set of Spanish-language records purporting to date from 1525 and 1546 provides additional evidence for the activities of a taller. The general language and many specific elements of the Atzitzintlan 1525 Cortés records are nearly identical to two other sets of questionable Spanish-language cédulas in which the conquistador granted privileges to the Nahua communities of Tenango Tepopula, and San Pedro y San Pablo in 1525.[105] These two sets of cédulas and mercedes stress the recognition and benefits the towns received from Cortés and the crown because of their services in the Spanish-led campaigns against the Empire of the Triple Alliance. Typically, their eager embrace of Christianity was another mark of their worthiness and service to the Iberian Catholic enterprise in New Spain. The mercedes feature the same statements about hardships, allied service at the risk of life and limb, and the enduring memory of such sacrifices. Yet the purported sixteenth-century mercedes of these towns are not exactly carbon copies, either, but rather variations of the same basic texts that have been customized in a number of ways. The rewards received by San Nicolás y San Pedro are due to the importance of its allied combat troops, while as in the case of Atzitzintlan, Tenango Tepopula was honored for its provision of tlamemes for the Spaniards: on November 3, 1525, "Don Ernan Cortes, Capitan General of New Spain and Governor of its provinces" praised the "Indian caciques and principales of the pueblo of San Juan Tenanco Tepopula," who welcomed him and later supplied him with tlamemes for his expedition to pacify "Aguastepeque and Cuaunahuac" (rather than in the Huexotzinco and Calpan regions, as found in the similar Atzitzintlan manuscript). Cortés lauded them for their willingness to put their lives on the line at grave risk from the "Mexicanos."[106] Land boundaries are traced in all of these sets of documents, but they are unique to each community, suggesting local input focused on properties that may have been at risk by the later eighteenth century. As such, there must have been a sort of "Ur text" used for all three communities (perhaps a copy of an authentic contact-era manuscript) that was amenable to revisions that could reward any community in central New Spain for its supposed alliance with Hernando Cortés.

As far as boasts about the worth of tlameme service being recognized and rewarded by Cortés are concerned, the pattern here seems similar to one identified in the Zapoteca Sierras of Oaxaca by historian Yanna Yannakakis. There, Nahuas who had been involved in the invasion of that region by allied Spanish and Indigenous forces eventually settled in the Analco barrio of Spanish Villa Alta. In the early eighteenth century, petitioners from Analco asked representatives of the colonial government for recognition as *indios conquistadores* and the privileges that went with it. Yet between 1519 and 1521 the ancestors of these petitioners had served the Spaniards as *naborías*, or in other words in a role of "dependent servitude" much like the *tlamemes* of Tenango Tepopula.[107] Later colonial representatives of Analco, Tenango Tepopula, and Atzitzintlan were all trying to distance themselves from a menial, if logistically essential status that had made them much less illustrious than those who fought in battle alongside Spaniards. In the sixteenth century, being a naboría had the flavor of being subjugated or even forced to participate involuntarily.[108] According to Yannakakis, when in 1709 Analco's petitioners identified themselves as naborías, they were doing so at a time when "urban life [had] facilitated an upward trajectory for naborías from dependent servitude to purported cultural and social superiority over other indigenous groups." She believes that the usage adopted by Analco "represented a strategy of anachronism . . . as memory of the conquest faded" so that "claims of service to the Crown during the glorious years of the conquest—evoked by the term *naboría*—must have had particular resonance."[109]

CONCLUDING THOUGHTS

Whether or not a workshop or workshops created all of the supposedly sixteenth-century manuscripts featuring Don Zacarías de Santiago as a powerful man on the scene when Cortés arrived in central Mexico, these manuscripts should not be dismissed as valueless fakes. Stephanie Wood has argued that these kinds of materials should be seen as vehicles providing "unique insights" into the ways in which "the phenomena of Spanish colonization . . . affected the people at the level of small communities."[110] During his lifetime Don Zacarías de Santiago was confronted with the need to make decisions about what was best for him and for his community. He chose to embrace his own privilege as a ruling-class Nahua and to pursue a sociopolitical career under the paternalistic umbrella of the Spanish system. He was not a rebel. Instead, he was a collaborator or, perhaps better, a partner—though not an abjectly compliant one—of the royal government and its representatives.

Nonetheless, as the colonial era lengthened any rough edges that may have been attached to the memory of this man were rounded off as he was relocated in time and place to be on the scene when Cortés and the Spaniards arrived. He was borrowed by pueblos in the region as a sort of ancestor who, as a conduit of legitimacy, oversaw the recognition of these places as true landholding communities. Somehow, this man who met king Philip II, who helped solidify Tlaxcala's civic stature, won it exemptions from tribute, and gained a coat of arms and entry into the exalted Order of Santiago ended up becoming larger than life, freed from temporal and even spatial anchors as the colonial era progressed. Whether or not Don Zacarías de Santiago really had anything to do with San Simón Atzitzintlan, Tepetomatitlan, Tlatlauhquitepec, or San Lucas Tecopilco was beside the point by the later colonial era. His stunning pictorial presence standing next to a depiction of a coat of arms, and in association with local churches and landmarks, was the essential thing. Upbeat language and imagery connected with Don Zacarías celebrate the benefits brought by the advent of Spanish overlordship and religion, land grants, and coats of arms, just as they do with other figures who came to be associated with him in this timeless way: Don Pedro de Galicia and the more historically amorphous figures of Don Pedro (or Pablo) de Castillo/a and Don Alonso Sarmiento Paredes de Guzmán.

But Don Zacarías and those linked to him are not depicted as conquered peoples. Even if Don Zacarías neither used a weapon in anger during the first Mexican War nor was on the scene to endorse Hernando Cortés's supposed actions in 1525, he fought to master and to benefit from the new order on behalf of his people. This carried him to Spain into the court of Philip II and eventually from there into the memories of those who later regarded him as a legitimating hero of an earlier age. His stature, the preexisting political autonomy he and his people enjoyed, and the legitimacy of corporate land tenure was recognized and confirmed—not created for the first time—thanks to everyone's voluntary and enthusiastic service to the crown and the Catholic Church. Far from suggesting "conquered" people, the combined arrival of Cortés, the king, and the archbishop were moments of corporate invigoration. In this way, Don Zacarías battled for them from the grave as a latter-day noble champion.

NOTES

Epigraph: Jean Genet, *Proverbicals*, accessed May 11, 2023, https://proverbicals.com/fame. Jean Genet (1910–86) was a French novelist, poet, essayist, playwright, and political activist. See also David Bradby and Clare Finburgh, *Jean Genet* (Abingdon, UK: Routledge, 2012).

1. Laura E. Matthew and Michel R. Oudijk, eds., *Indian Conquistadors: Indigenous Allies in the Conquest of Mesoamerica* (Norman: University of Oklahoma Press, 2007). See also José Luis Pérez Flores, "Indígenas guerreros de la Nueva España del siglo XVI: La representación de sí mismos como conquistadores," *Fronteras de la Historia* 18, no. 1 (2013): 15–43.

2. Tony Hessenthaler, "The Tlaxcalans: Pleading for What Was Promised," in *Constructing the Medieval and Early Modern across Disciplines*, ed. Karen Christianson (Chicago: The Newberry Library, 2011), 119–34, here 128, fig. 2.

3. Robert Haskett, *Visions of Paradise: Primordial Titles and Mesoamerican History in Cuernavaca* (Norman: University of Oklahoma Press, 2005).

4. James Lockhart, *The Nahuas after the Conquest: A Social and Cultural History of the Indians of Central Mexico, Sixteenth through Eighteenth Centuries* (Stanford, CA: Stanford University Press, 1992), 415.

5. Archivo General de la Nación, Mexico (henceforth AGN), Tierras, vol. 2709, exp. 1, fol. 59r; the Spanish-language boundary description was supposedly based on a *pintura* not found in the *expediente*.

6. AGN, Tierras, vol. 2709, exp. 1, fols. 60r–62v (1774 version); AGN, Tierras, vol. 2708, exp. 3, 6 fols. (earlier version).

7. The name Galicia is not mentioned in the famous letter written to the king from Huexotzinco. James Lockhart and Enrique Otte, eds., *Letters and People of the Spanish Indies* (Cambridge: Cambridge University Press, 1976), 163–72.

8. AGN, Tierras, vol. 2709, exp. 1, fols. 62v–66r (1774 version), 2r–5r (earlier version). The documents are "signed" by Don Zacarías and several other high nobles: Don Miguel Sainos, Don Lucas Osorio, and Don Antonio de Galicia.

9. AGN, Tierras, vol. 2709, exp. 1, fol. 67r (1774 version), fols. 4r–5r (earlier version).

10. Today San Simón Atzitzintlan is part of the San Salvador el Verde municipality, situated west of the autopista México-Puebla.

11. See AGN, Tierras, vol. 2709, exp. 1, fol. 61v.

12. Robert Haskett, *Indigenous Rulers: An Ethnohistory of Town Government in Colonial Cuernavaca* (Albuquerque: University of New Mexico Press, 1991), chap. 4, discusses the duties and functions of these and other town officers. While the exact status and function of such positions could vary over time and from place to place, on a basic level they were similar all over central New Spain: *gobernador* (sometimes called a *gobernador jues*), chief political officer, often someone of lordly status; *alcalde*, town councilor; *regidor*, lower-status town councilor; *mayordomo*, steward; *escribano*, notary.

13. Brito Guadarrama, *Códice Chavero de Huejotzingo*, accessed May 11, 2023, https://books.google.com/books?id=YDd7DwAAQBAJ&pg=PT606&dq=codice+guillermo+tovar+de+huejotzingo&hl=en&sa=X&ved=0ahUKEwjAwNXZuqjgAhWlwMQHHdm0DsQQ6AEIMTAB#v=onepage&q=gobernador&f=false.

14. *Matrícula de Huexotzinco* (n.p.: s.n, 1560), accessed May 11, 2023, https://www.wdl.org/en/item/15282/view/1/1/, fol. 685, "Don Francisco Vázquez" is *gobernador* of San Juan Huexotzinco; no official is named Don Antonio de Galicia.

15. Charles Gibson, *Tlaxcala in the Sixteenth Century* (Stanford, CA: Stanford University Press, 1952), 105, 107, 219–23, and 226–27.

16. Archivo General del Estado de Tlaxcala (henceforth AGET), Registro de Instrumentos Públicos (RIP), libro 4, fol. 334r–v, 1581; AGET, RIP libro 8, fol. 106, 1590.

17. AGET, RIP, Libro 1, fol. 255v, 1573; AGET RIP libro 3, fol. 107, 1578.

18. AGET, RIP, Libro 4, fols. 305–6, 1581; AGET RIP libro 11, fol. 75, 1596.

19. For the lasting fame of his participation in this delegation, see Ángel María Garibay and Felipe Teixidor, *Diccionario Porrúa de historia, biografía y geografía* (Mexico City: Porrúa, 1964), 1944.

20. Camilla Townsend, ed. and trans., *Here in This Year: Seventeenth-Century Nahuatl Annals of the Tlaxcala-Puebla Valley* (Stanford, CA: Stanford University Press, 2010), 170–71. See also Juan Buenaventura Zapata y Mendoza, *Historia cronológica de la Noble Ciudad de Tlaxcala*, trans. Luis Reyes García and Andrea Martínez Baracs (Tlaxcala: Universidad Autónoma de Tlaxcala, Secretaría de Extensión Universitaria y Difusión Cultural, 1995), 174–75. An appendix in Diego Muñoz Camargo, *Historia de Tlaxcala (MS. 210 de la Biblioteca Nacional de París)*, ed. Luis Reyes García, with the collaboration of Javier Lira Toledo (Tlaxcala: Gobierno del Estado de Tlaxcala; Centro de Investigaciones y Estudios Superiores en Antropología Social, Universidad Autónoma de Tlaxcala, 1998), 319–32, shows Don Zacarías as governor and alcalde between 1580 and 1596; a record dated December 14, 1596, notes that Don Zacarías and Don Juan de Ribas received a license to sell land, with Muñoz Camargo as interpreter.

21. Gibson, *Tlaxcala*, 167. See also Jovita Barber, "Empire, Indians, and the Negotiation for the Status of City in Tlaxcala, 1521–1550," in *Negotiation within Domination: New Spain's Indian Pueblos Confront the Spanish State*, ed. Ethelia Ruiz Medrano and Susan Kellogg (Louisville: University Press of Colorado, 2021), 19–44.

22. Alejandra Jaramillo, "Litigious Paupers: Natives and Colonial Demands in Tlaxcala, 1545–1800" (PhD diss., University of Houston, 2014), 75.

23. Gibson, *Tlaxcala*, 232–33. See also Ana Díaz Serrano, "La República de Tlaxcala ante el Rey de España durante el siglo XVI," *Historia Mexicana* 61, no. 3 (2012): 1049–107, 1091–99; and José Luis de Rojas, "Boletos sencillos y pasajes redondos: Indígenas y mestizos americanos que visitaron España," *Revista de Indias* 69, no. 246 (2009): 185–206, here 194.

24. José Casas y Sánchez, *Armorial de nobles indígenas de Nueva España: Escudos de armas otorgados por los monarcas españoles a nobles indígenas (caciques y principales) (1534–1588)* (n.p.: Academia Mexicana de Genealogía y Heráldica, ca. 2015), accessed May 11, 2023, https://aristo.hypotheses.org/files/2015/10/Jos%C3%A9-Casas-y-S%C3%A1nchez.-Armorial-de-los-nobles-indigenas-de-Nueva-Espa%C3%B1a.pdf, 165–67; the Latin motto on the crest was "Quia Fecit Mihi Magna Qui Potens Est, Et Sanctum Nomen Ejus" (translated by the author as "Porque Grandes Cosas Me Ha Hecho El Poderoso, y Santo Es Su Nombre"). See also Mario Jaramillo, *Nobleza precolombina: Visión hispánica y expresión emblemática* (Madrid: Sanz y Torres, 2021), 158–62; *The Tlaxcalan Actas: A Compendium of the Records of the Cabildo of Tlaxcala (1545–1627)*, trans. and ed. James Lockhart, Frances Berdan, and Arthur J. O. Anderson (Salt Lake City: University of Utah Press, 1986), 138 (note that Alejandro de Santiago's Nahuatl surname was Tlapialtzintli).

25. *Tlaxcalan Actas*, 138. He was regidor in 1547, 1550, 1552, 1554, and 1556, dying while still in office on April 27, 1556. He was alcalde in 1548.

26. Jaramillo, "Litigious Paupers," 111.

27. Gil González Davila, *Teatro eclesiástico de la primitive iglesia de las indias occidentales, vidas de sus arzobispos, obispos y cosas memorables de sus sedes* (Madrid: Diego Díaz de la Carrera, 1649), 92.

28. Zapata y Mendoza, *Historia cronológica*, 172–75.

29. Zapata y Mendoza, *Historia cronológica*, 178–79, 186–87. For Don Zacarías's role as governor, see also *Anales de Tlaxcala* 1581, 1582, 1589, 1590, and 1594 in Townsend, *Year*, 170–73.

30. Zapata y Mendoza, *Historia cronológica*, 186–91.

31. Zapata y Mendoza, *Historia cronológica*, 178–79. See also Eric Taladoire, *De América a Europa: Cuando los indígenas descubrieron el Viejo Mundo (1493–1892)* (Mexico City: Fondo de Cultura Económica, 2017), 52–56.

32. Zapata y Mendoza, *Historia cronológica*, 192–93. See also José Luis de Rojas, "Boletos sencillos," *Revista de Indias* 69, no. 246 (2009): 185–206, here 194.

33. See Haskett, *Visions of Paradise*, 236–49.

34. Enriqueta Vila Vilar and María Justina Sarabia Viejo, eds., *Cartas de cabildos hispanoamericanos: Audiencia de México (siglos XVIII y XIX)* (Seville: Escuela de Estudios Hispano-Americanos; Consejo Superior de Investigaciones Científicas; Excma. Diputación Provincial de Sevilla, 1990), 448–52.

35. Indiana University Lily Library—see Gordon Brotherston, in collaboration with Galen Brokaw et al., *Footprints through Time: Mexican Pictorial Manuscripts at the Lilly Library* (Bloomington: Lilly Library, Indiana University, 1997), 28, 80. See also John F. Schwaller, *A Guide to Nahuatl Language Manuscripts Held in United States Repositories* (Berkeley, CA: Academy of American Franciscan History, 2001), 86, item 62. The Spanish-language document sounds similar to the one featuring Don Zacarías and Don Juan de Ribas obtaining a license to sell land.

36. Schwaller, *Guide to Nahuatl*, 74. The odd word "Pinturia" may be a transcription error for "pintura"; "pintura mapa" could be a typical Nahuatl *difrasismo*, two loanwords meaning essentially the same thing.

37. See Hessenthaler, "Tlaxcalans," 119–34.

38. Brotherston et al., in *Footprints through Time*, 31, pl. 3, identified as a *tepetl* (mountain) glyph studded with ocote pines, a logograph for "Ocotelulco," but if so, it is certainly not rendered in a traditional way. The authors identify the crest as Ocotelulco's coat of arms, but, if so, it pertains to a Tlaxcalan cabecera, not to Don Zacarías or Tepetomatitlan. See also Nazario A. Sánchez Mastranzo, "Los Códices de Tlaxcala," Tlaxcala: INAH, PDF article, author's files, 127–52, here 141–45; and Hessenthaler, "Tlaxcalans," 119–34.

39. Hessenthaler, "Tlaxcalans," 123–24; Hessenthaler believes that the reference is to Ocotelulco but notes that Don Zacarías was from Tepeticpac, not Ocotelulco.

40. Provisional translation by the present author; for an earlier rendition, see Sánchez Mastranzo, "Los Códices de Tlaxcala." A poor-quality digital reproduction is found in Hessenthaler, "Tlaxcalans," 132.

41. See Hessenthaler, "Tlaxcalans," 120.

42. AGN, Indios, vol. 31, exp, 125, fol. 86v.

43. See AGN, Indios, vol. 37, exp. 132, fol. 1311r–v, 1709; AGN, Tierras, vol. 1436, exps. 3 and 7, 1714–97; and AGN, Padrones, vol. 22, fol. 281r–v, and vol. 48, fol. 234r (the "pueblo" is paired with a "barrio" called Teopahcaltitlan, 1790s).

44. AGN, Tierras, vol. 1275, exp. 7, fols. 2v, 7v. The expediente includes the January 24, 1628, Nahuatl-language will of Doña Leonor's mother, Doña Juana Hernández.

45. AGN, Tierras, vol. 1275, exp. 7, fol. 50r. Verification of this marital alliance requires more genealogical work than is practical at present. However, Pedro de Alvarado is known to have wed a daughter, "Luisa," of Xicotencatl the Elder. Is Doña Leonor referring to Xicotencatl the Younger, who died an alleged traitor in 1521, or the ever-loyal Xicotencatl the Elder, who died in 1522? Would Don Alonso really have had a fully Spanish name in the 1520s when he supposedly married into the Xocotencatl family? Could he really have been grandfather to a woman living in the mid-seventeenth century?

46. Guillermo S. Fernández de Recas, *Cacicazgos y nobiliario indígena de la Nueva España* (Mexico City: Universidad Nacional Autónoma de México, 1961), 187–89.

47. Fernández de Recas, *Cacicazgos y nobiliario indígena de la Nueva España*, 188.

48. María Castañeda de la Paz, "Los Escudos de Armas de Tlaxcala: Un recorrido por su rico repertorio heráldico," in *Los escudos de armas indígenas de la colonia al México independiente*, ed. María Castañeda de la Paz and Hans Roskamp (Zamora: El Colegio de Michoacán; Mexico City: Universidad Nacional Autónoma de México, Instituto de Investigaciones Antropológicas, 2013), 71–107, here 98, 101, fig. 37, 103–5. The text of the cédula and a line drawing of the crest are found in Casas y Sánchez, *Armorial de nobles indígenas*, 121–25.

49. See Lockhart et al., *Tlaxcalan Actas*; and Eustaquio Celestino Solís, Armando Valencia R., and Constantino Medina Lima, eds., *Actas de Cabildo de Tlaxcala, 1547–1567* (Tlaxcala: Instituto Tlaxcalteca de la Cultura; Mexico City: Archivo General de la Nación, Centro de Investigaciones y Estudios Superiores de Antropología Social [CIESAS], 1984).

50. Archivo Histórico del Estado de Tlaxcala (henceforth AHET), Fondo Colonia, caja 90, exp. 3.

51. Rosaura Hernández Rodríguez, *Catálogo de documentos del siglo XVI del Archivo General del Estado de Tlaxcala*, vol. 1 (Tlaxcala: Gobierno del Estado de Tlaxcala; Mexico City: Archivo General de la Nación, 1988), 77 (1573), 262 (1577). See Gibson, *Tlaxcala*, "Appendix VI: Indian Governors of Tlaxcala," for Diego de Paredes's term as governor.

52. Matthew Restall, Lisa Sousa, and Kevin Terraciano, eds., *Mesoamerican Voices: Native-Language Writings from Colonial Mexico, Oaxaca, Yucatan, and Guatemala* (New York: Cambridge University Press, 2005), 131.

53. E.g., Teresa Rojas Rabiela, ed., in collaboration with Marina Anguiano, Matilde Chapa, and Amelia Camacho, *Padrones de Tlaxcala del siglo XVI y Padrón de nobles de Ocotelolco* (Mexico City: Centro de Investigaciones y Estudios Superiores en Antropología Social [CIESAS], Casa Chata, 1987) does not include anyone with the Sarmiento surname, nor a noble with the name of Trueba.

54. See Brotherston with Galen Brokaw et al., *Footprints through Time*, 80–81.

55. See the online *Nahuatl Dictionary* (Stephanie Wood, ed., *Online Nahuatl Dictionary* [Eugene: Wired Humanities Projects, College of Education, University of Oregon, 2000–present], accessed May 11, 2023, https://nahuatl.uoregon.edu/); and Luis Reyes García et al., eds., *Documentos nauas de la Ciudad de México del siglo XVI* (Mexico City: Archivo General de la Nación, CIESAS, 1996), 170.

56. See Wood, *Nahuatl Dictionary* for this kind of information. See also Rocio Cortés, "El Nahuatlato Alvarado y el Tlalamatl Huauhquilpan": Mecanismos de la memoria colectiva de una comunidad indígena (New York: Hispanic Seminary of Medieval Studies, 2011), 30 (mapa); Luis Reyes García, ed., *¿Como te confundes? ¿Acaso no somos conquistados? Anales de Juan Bautista* (Mexico City: CIESAS, Biblioteca Lorenzo Boturini, Insigne y Nacional Basílica de Guadalupe, 2001), 146–47 (pintura); Reyes García et al., *Documentos nauas*, 170; Don Domingo de San Antón Muñón Chimalpahin Quauhtlehuanitzin, *Annals of His Time*, trans. and ed. James Lockhart, Susan Schroeder, and Doris Namala (Stanford, CA: Stanford University Press, 2006), 208–9; and Zapata y Mendoza, *Historia cronológica*, 248–49 (armas).

57. James Lockhart, *Nahuatl as Written: Lessons in Older Written Nahuatl, with Copious Examples and Texts* (Stanford, CA: Stanford University Press; Los Angeles: UCLA Latin American Center Publications, 2001), 115.

58. Hessenthaler, "Tlaxcalans," 126; and for a discussion of portraits of the four lords and Tlaxcalan crests, see Castañeda de la Paz, "Escudos de Armas," particularly 75–81 and 98–104. This author emphasizes the presence of eagles on such devices.

59. It is possible that this is a copy of an earlier document, but mistakes about Don Zacarías's activities and stature cast doubt on that interpretation.

60. The original, held in the municipal archive, is unavailable. See Raúl Macuil Martínez, "La memoria histórica de San Simón Tlatlauhquitepec en un lienzo del siglo XVIII," in *La memoria histórica de los pueblos subordinados*, ed. Wright Carr et al., accessed 2009, http://www.eumed.net/libros-gratis/2011f/1119/memoria_historica_de_san_simon_tlatlauhquitepec.html. Tepetomatitlan is not too far to the southeast of Tlatlauhquitepec, though a direct relationship between the two pictorials cannot be established at this time.

61. Given the poor state of the text, it is obviously somewhat difficult to translate it with complete accuracy. The gist of the information is that this "Map of the town of San Simón" links its boundary limits and historic events and people, such as those ancestors "who went to conquer the Chichimecos in 1595, Don Simón Cacamatzin, Don Diego tlapati." Another

event, difficult to determine, took place in 1616. There seems to be an assertion that their titles of possession had been confirmed at least three times, the first one in 1734. This sort of text is fairly typical of late-colonial "histories," pictorial or alphabetic, that project people and events back in time as a way to provide historic legitimacy for a community's land tenure and its ruling class. For instance, mentioning ancestors who fought against the Chichimecas, by implication in the service of the Spanish crown, on the northern frontier implies that some of the lands claimed by the community were granted, or at least recognized, by the authorities in thanks for their military alliance.

62. See Macuil Martínez, "La memoria histórica de San Simón Tlatlauhquitepec en un lienzo del siglo XVIII," 105, 314 (image 2:9), and in Gómez García, *Anales nahuas*.

63. This may refer to a tradition according to which Don Zacarías and others met Viceroy Velasco while on his way from Veracruz to Mexico City.

64. Observation by the present author, and Macuil Martínez, "Memoria histórica."

65. Macuil Martínez, "Memoria histórica."

66. Macuil Martínez, "Memoria histórica," believes that the manuscript stresses the importance of the cabecera by glossing all of the figures as locals. For details about the fifth delegation, see Gibson, *Tlaxcala*, 166; for Don Pablo de Galicia's participation in 1562, see Rojas, "Boletos sencillos," 194.

67. San Lucas Tecopilco is in the Tlaxcala region just off the Calpulapan-Apizaco highway and northwest of Tlaxcala city. See "Enciclopedia de los Municipios y Delegaciones de México: Estado de Tlaxcala, San Lucas Tecopilco," accessed May 11, 2023, http://www.inafed.gob.mx/work/enciclopedia/EMM29tlaxcala/municipios/29055a.html, and "San Lucas Tecopilco (Tlaxcala)," accessed May 11, 2023, https://en.mexico.pueblosamerica.com/i/san-lucas-tecopilco/. As of this writing, I have been unable to identify "Santa Bárbara" nor its relationship to San Lucas.

68. Luis Reyes García, ed., *La escritura pictográfica en Tlaxcala: Dos mil años de experiencia mesoamericana* (Tlaxcala: Universidad de Tlaxcala, Secretaría de Extensión Universitaria y Difusión Cultural; Mexico City: CIESAS, 1993), 204 (discussion and translation), image XVI, 255 (reproduction).

69. William L. Clements Library, University of Michigan, Cuernavaca Papers (CLCP), fols. 110r, 139v (translation by the present author). See also Haskett, *Visions of Paradise*, 219–36.

70. Two copies of the Cuernavacan title exist, one heavily damaged version probably from the last decades of the seventeenth century, and a cleaner version done in a seemingly eighteenth-century hand.

71. Agnieszka Brylak, "Lawsuit Brought by Juan Jiménez, Ocotelolco, Tlaxcala, Mexico, 1560," in *Dialogue with Europe, Dialogue with the Past: Colonial Nahua and Quechua Elites in their Own Words*, ed. Justyna Olko, John Sullivan, and Jan Szemiński (Boulder: University Press of Colorado, 2018), 85–88. All translations by Brylak; for another transcription

and translation, see AHET Fondo Colonia, caja 1, exp. 22, fols. 1r–v, in *Catálogo de documentos escritos en Náhuatl, siglo XVI*, vol. 1 (Tlaxcala: Archivo Histórico del Estado de Tlaxcala, Gobierno del Estado de Tlaxcala, Fideicomiso Colegio de Historia de Tlaxcala, 2013), 3–7. Galicia and Jiménez were both alcaldes in 1551, 1558, and 1560; *Tlaxcalan Actas*, 129, 131.

72. See Gibson, *Tlaxcala*, "Appendix VI, Indian Governors of Tlaxcala," entries for 1585 and 1586.

73. Zapata y Mendoza, *Historia cronológica*, 174–77.

74. AHET Fondo Colonia, caja 32, exp. 4, May 19, 1561.

75. Zapata y Mendoza, *Historia cronológica*, 160–61.

76. For Pablo de Galicia's 1547 election as alcalde, see "Municipal Council Records, Tlaxcala, 1547," in *Beyond the Codices: The Nahua View of Colonial Mexico*, trans. and ed. Arthur J. O. Anderson, Frances Berdan, and James Lockhart (Berkeley: University of California Press, 1976), 126–27. For his participation in cabildo deliberations about a new altarpiece, see Cheryl E. Martin and Mark Wasserman, eds., *Readings on Latin America and Its People*, vol. 1 (New York: Prentice Hall, 2011), 42. For his association with the new clock, see Zapata y Mendoza, *Historia cronológica*, 160–61. His name lacks the honorific "Don" in all of these instances. For Pablo de Galicia as alcalde in 1550, see Andrea Martínez Baracs, *Un gobierno de indios: Tlaxcala, 1519–1750* (Mexico City: Fondo de Cultura Económica; Tlaxcala: Fideicomiso Colegio de Historia de Tlaxcala, CIESAS, 2008), 156.

77. Restall et al., *Mesoamerican Voices*, 90–99. Other members of the Mexico City delegation were Alonso Gómez, alcalde; Antonio del Pedroso, regidor; Pedro Díaz, regidor; and Fabián Rodríguez, cabildo notary. For another reproduction, see Lynne Miles-Morillo and Stephen Morillo, *Sources for Frameworks of World History: Networks, Hierarchies, Culture*, vol. 2: *Since 1350* (New York: Oxford University Press, 2014), 21–23.

78. Rojas, *Padrones de Tlaxcala*, 318 (fol. 7v in the original), roster of the *Teccalli ychan Tlacaztalli*. Other nobles listed with Pablo de Galicia: Antonio Luiz Tlaol, Diego Chihuatzacual, Juan Chilmani Tlemacuentzin, and Mateo Mixcohuatl. The only two "dons" are Don Juan Maxixcatzin, of Cuitlizco Teccalli ychan Mxixcatzin (fol. 1r, page 309), and Don Domingo de Angulo, of Tlatempal Teccalli ychan Tlamacazcatecuitli (fol. 5v, page 316).

79. AHET, Fondo Colonial, caja 4, exp. 2, fols. 2r, 26r–v, 29r "Juan Peres y consortes contra Ana Xipal," in *Catálogo de documentos escritos en Náhuatl*, 49, 132–33, 136, 147.

80. AGET, RIP, libro 3, fols. 490v–491v (1580), libro 4, fols. 320v–321v (1581). See also Martínez Baracs, *Un gobierno de indios*, 151.

81. See Haskett, *Visions of Paradise*, 241–45.

82. Lockhart et al., *Tlaxcalan Actas*, 134 for Don Julian Atempan de Castilla, and 135 for Don Juan del Castillo or Castilla. See also Zapata y Mendoza, *Historia cronológica*, 168–71: Don Julian de Castilla as alcalde in 1567 and 1570.

83. Casas y Sánchez, *Armorial de nobles indígenas*, 82–85; quotes from 84. See also Jaramillo, *Nobleza precolombina*, 158.

84. Casas y Sánchez, *Armorial de nobles indígenas*, 84.

85. Castañeda de la Paz, "Escudos de Armas," 101, fig. 3.7, 105–6.

86. Rojas et al., *Padrones de Tlaxcala*, "Padrón de Tizatlan," 157, fol. 40r.

87. Reyes García, *Escritura pictográfica*, 206 (discussion), image XIX, 259 (reproduction). Reyes cites AGN, Tierras, vol. 914, exp. 2, lawsuit pitting the *naturales* of San Dionisio Yauhquemecan and its barrio of Calapan against Santa María Atlihuetzian over land. San Dionisio is located to the north and slightly east of Tlaxcala city. See Peter Gerhard, *A Guide to the Historical Geography of New Spain*, rev ed. (Norman: University of Oklahoma Press, 1993), 325.

88. A man named Pedro Lorenzo de Castilla served in the area as its *gobernador de la provincia* from 1592 to 1595. But he was a Spaniard. His title was sometimes used instead of the more familiar *corregidor* or *alcalde mayor* for a regional magistrate. See Gibson, *Tlaxcala*, 218, and "Appendix VI, Indian Governors of Tlaxcala."

89. According to *The Tlaxcalan Actas*, Blas Osorio of Tizatlan was gobernador in 1547 (128), alcalde in 1549 (128), alcalde in 1552 (129), alcalde in 1554 (130), alcalde in 1556 (130), alcalde in 1559 (131), alcalde in 1561 (132), alcalde in 1563 (132), alcalde in 1566 (133), regidor and fiscal in 1551 (137), and alcalde in 1568 (151).

90. AGN, Tierras, vol. 299, exp. 5. For a transcription and translation, see Teresa Rojas Rabiela, Elsa Leticia Rea Lopez, and Constantino Medina Lima, eds., *Vidas y bienes olvidados: Testamentos indígenas novohispanos*, vol. 2 (Mexico City: CIESAS, 1999), 66–69.

91. Perhaps Don Juan's will was created in 1569, but other things work against this solution. For Molina's model testament, see Lockhart, *Nahuas after the Conquest*, "Appendix B: Molina's Model Testament," 468–74. See also Rojas Rabiela et al., *Vidas y bienes olvidados*, 2: 20–27.

92. AGN, Tierras, vol. 20, 1a. Pte., exp. 1, fols. 46r–48v (Nahuatl testament); fols. 49r–53r (Spanish translation); fol. 63v (Maxixcatzin family genealogy). See also Rojas Rabiela et al., *Vidas y bienes olvidados*, 2: 37–38, 53 (genealogy), 124–29 (transcription of the testament); and *Tlaxcalan Actas*, 136 (Don Juan Maxixcatzin), 137 (Don Luis Pimentel Maxixcatzin). For both these men, see also Zapata y Mendoza, *Historia cronológica*, 158–59, 238–39. Fernández de Recas, *Cacicazgos*, 173–83, presents a digest of the "Cacicazgo de Tlaxcala, Galvez, Cores y Ramos" featuring a branch of the Maxixcatzin family, but there is no one named Don Lucas Maxixcatzin. According to Muñoz Camargo, the elder Maxixcatzin was baptized as Lorenzo, but other sources list him as Juan. See Luis Weckmann, *The Medieval Heritage of Mexico* (New York: Fordham University Press, 1992), 137; Bernal Díaz del Castillo, *Historia de la conquista de Nueva España*, ed. Joaquín Ramírez Cabañas (Mexico City: Porrúa, 1976), 247–53; Bernal Díaz del Castillo, *True History of the Conquest of New Spain*, 346; and Francisco Xavier Clavijero, *Historia antigua de México* (Mexico City: Grupo Editorial Exodo, 2011), 378. After the elder died in 1520 he was succeeded by his son, Lorenzo, who held the ruling position until his death in Spain sometime between 1528 and 1530, upon

which he was succeeded by Don Francisco Maxixcatzin, who died in 1546: Gibson, *Tlaxcala*, 89–91, 97.

93. Gibson, *Tlaxcala*, 146, notes that parts of this lost text were preserved in Ixtlilxochitl's historical work. See also *Tlaxcalan Actas*: Niza as regidor in 1551 (129), regidor in 1553 (130), regidor in 1555 (130), regidor in 1557 (131), regidor in 1559 (131), regidor in 1561 (132), escribano in 1562–66 (at least), and *elector* for Tepeticpac (137).

94. Zapata y Mendoza, *Historia cronológica*, 90–91, entry 22.

95. Stephanie Wood, "Testaments and Títulos: Conflict and Coincidence of Cacique and Community Interests in Central Mexico," in *Dead Giveaways: Indigenous Testaments of Colonial Mesoamerica and the Andes*, ed. Susan Kellogg and Matthew Restall (Salt Lake City: University of Utah Press, 1998), 85–111, here 85.

96. Robert Haskett, "Passing On: The Cuernavaca Testaments of Don Juan Ximénez, His Daughter Doña María Ximénez, Don Toribio Cortés, and Juan Bautista," *Estudios de Cultura Nahuatl* 55 (2018): 117–25.

97. James Lockhart, *Of Things of the Indies: Essays Old and New in Early Latin American History* (Stanford, CA: Stanford University Press, 1999), 109.

98. Whether or not the two pictorials were created by the same hand is for the moment impossible to determine with any accuracy.

99. See cédula texts in Casas y Sánchez, *Armorial de nobles indígenas*.

100. Michel Oudijk, "Falsificaciones de escudos de armas indígenas en el Estado de México (Siglo XVIII)," in *Escudos de Armas indígenas*, ed. Castañeda de la Paz and Roskamp (Zamora, Mexico.: El Colegio de Michoacán; Mexico City: Universidad Nacional Autónoma de México, Instituto de Investigaciones Antropológicas, 2013), 169–94, here 186–87.

101. Stephanie Wood, "La producción de manuscritos en talleres y el bienestar de los pueblos" (unpublished article, author's files), 29–30.

102. See Haskett, *Visions of Paradise*.

103. Haskett, *Visions of Paradise*; see also María de los Ángeles Romero Frizzi, "The Transformation of Historical Memory as Revealed in Two Zapotec Primordial Titles," in *Mesoamerican Memory: Enduring Systems of Remembrance*, ed. Amos Megged and Stephanie Wood (Norman: University of Oklahoma Press, 2012), 91–111, here 104.

104. A thorough study of political alignments in Tlaxcala has not been possible at the time of this writing.

105. Robert Haskett, "Escudos de papel: La ideología de los escudos de armas en los títulos primordiales del México colonial," in *Escudos de armas indígenas*, ed. Castañeda de la Paz and Hans Roskamp (Zamora, Mexico: El Colegio de Michoacán; Mexico City: Universidad Nacional Autónoma de México, Instituto de Investigaciones Antropológicas, 2013), 195–227.

106. Latin American Library, Tulane University, Vicegeral and Ecclesiastical Manuscript Collection (VEMC), leg. 64, exp. 30, fols. 2v–3v; see also Haskett, "Escudos de Papel."

107. Yanna Yannakakis, "Allies or Servants? The Journey of Indian Conquistadors in the *Lienzo de Analco*," *Ethnohistory* 58, no. 4 (2011): 653–82, here 654. Though the term *naboría* is not found in the Tenango Tepopula records, acting as a porter was a typical role for these types of indigenous allies (656).

108. Yannakakis, "Allies or Servants?," 656 ("the term *naboría* referred to former Indian slaves, refugees who had been subjugated by the Spanish invaders").

109. Yannakakis, "Allies or Servants?," 657.

110. Stephanie Wood, "El problema de la historicidad de los *Títulos* y los códices *Techialoyan*," in *De tlacuilos y escribanos*, ed. Xavier Noguez and Stephanie Wood (Zamora: El Colegio de Michoacán; Zinacantepec, Mexico: El Colegio Mexiquense, 1998), 167–221, 205.

6

How to Read Native Accounts of the *Conquista* of Mexico

MARÍA CASTAÑEDA DE LA PAZ

There was only one *Conquista* of Mexico but many and diverging stories about it. In general, the Spanish chronicles written by the conquistadors, eyewitnesses of the events, do not contradict each other nor the Indigenous chronicles that were written later. Rather, they complement each other, since the Indigenous sources gave answers to issues that the Spaniards were unable to grasp or conceive, though we should not forget, of course, the bias that exists in both. Hernán Cortés, Bernal Díaz del Castillo, and Francisco de Aguilar, for example, do not seem to have noticed the presence of religious dignitaries among the diplomatic retinues that Moteuczoma sent them with the purpose that, through incantations and spells, the conquerors would fall ill, die, or leave. This matter is mentioned in the Indigenous sources.[1] The same happens with the story that the Spaniards heard about a lord who brought several people to the center of Mexico and left with the promise of returning someday. It was the Native chroniclers who, at the time of writing their accounts, took it for granted that this story referred to Quetzalcoatl and his people (the Toltecs), since he was well known among them.[2]

Therefore, and as Romero Frizzi pointed out some years ago, when analyzing these sources, it is important to take into consideration that each of them was written with a specific purpose, at different times and circumstances, by people with different backgrounds and ideologies.[3] Wankel has also recently discussed this approach in a very accurate way.[4] An account written at almost the same time as the events, like a diary and like some parts of Cortés's *Letters*, is not the same as a letter written by an Indigenous nobleman years later, even if he was with Cortés in the battles and both of them addressed their writings to the monarch.

Cortés wrote his *Letters* after violating the orders of the governor of Cuba, Diego Velázquez, and going out to conquer without authorization. According to Romero Frizzi, Cortés was anxious not only because of the possible consequences of his disobedience but also because Velázquez and other conquistadors tried to obtain Crown's support to stop Cortés and to deprive him of his achievements.[5] Therefore, we must see the *Letters* as the instrument through which the conquistador could praise himself so that King Charles would believe in Cortés's ability and loyalty and, consequently, that the latter was the right person to lead the conquering enterprise.[6]

The purpose of a chronicle is to record the events of the past, with the distinction that its author is free to make assessments and interpretations of those events. Logically, this liberty to interpret and adapt the events caused other authors, when consulting this chronicle, to take these personal opinions as truths. The letters and reports of merits and services (*informaciones de méritos y servicios*) of the Indigenous nobility were written much later than Cortés's letters, by elites familiar with the colonial system. Their objective was to recover privileges of the past or gain new ones. To achieve this, the nobles knew that they had to support their rights on two fundamental premises: their participation in the *Conquista* and their true Christian conversion, for which they did not hesitate to distort some uncomfortable issues of the past. This is also evident in the Indigenous chronicles, whose authors took advantage of their writing to present themselves as loyal allies of the king and legitimate heirs of the new colonial order. For all the reasons stated, it is important that when analyzing the sources we detect patterns and keep in mind who wrote the document, when it was written, for what purpose it was written, and to whom it was addressed. This way we can understand why the chronicles may relate the same story so differently, what causes the omission or inclusion of certain figures or historical events, and the presence of anachronisms or the alteration of some events, among other issues. The purpose of this essay is precisely this: to critically analyze a selection of texts written about the *Conquista* of Mexico, not only to reconstruct as faithfully as possible some events of the past but also to show why and how those events were altered and reinterpreted.

"NOCHE TRISTE": THE NEED TO DISRUPT AND ALTER HISTORY

As we know, the so-called Noche Triste refers to the culmination of the uprising that took place against the Spanish presence in Tenochtitlan and forced the conquistadors to flee and abandon the city, leaving behind numerous casualties.[7] The rebellion was brewing because Cortés began to treat Moteuczoma disrespectfully to the point of publicly humiliating him without him putting up any resistance.[8] These acts included when (a) Cortés exhibited him in the public square in shackles to prevent violent reactions to the burning of a certain Cuauhpopoca, who was believed guilty of killing some Spaniards on the coast by order of Moteuczoma;[9] (b) Moteuczoma was taken up to the roof of the palace to calm the enraged mob after Pedro de Alvarado had ordered the massacre at the Templo Mayor; and (c) Cortés returned and refused to talk to Moteuczoma, suspecting him of being responsible for the previous events, which led his people to revolt. In a very heated atmosphere, Moteuczoma was forced to go up again to the roof to calm his people, although in this occasion the Spaniards had to protect him with their shields before the enraged mob. In spite of that, apparently a stone hit him in the head, and a few days later he died from the wound.[10] The one who led the rebellion was Cuitlahua, Moteuczoma's brother and chief of his army.[11]

With Moteuczoma dead, the Spaniards felt totally unprotected, so they decided to leave Tenochtitlan as soon as possible. The sources agree that they fled along the Tlacopan (today Tacuba) causeway, named after the city of the same name located at the other end (see map in figure 6.1). Though Cortés did not expect that, upon arriving there, the Tlacopanecah would attack him.[12]

Sometime later, and in the months prior to the final siege of the island of Mexico, Tlacopan was occupied by Cortés due to its privileged location. As the conquistador wrote, he settled with his men in some large houses to keep a close watch on the Mexicah. Meanwhile, his Indigenous allies looted and burned the city, as punishment for the attack suffered in the Noche Triste.[13] On the island, the Mexicah were preparing for the Spanish counterattack, when Cuitlahua died of smallpox. Tenochcah and Tlatelolcah then chose Cuauhtemoc as their lord. The other two members of the Triple Alliance, Tetlepanquetzal of Tlacopan and Coanacoch of Tetzcoco, entrenched themselves with him. We all know what followed: they ended up surrendering, and, despite the bloody battles, the leaders of the Triple Alliance survived.

Once the colonial system was established, some rulers of the towns in the Valley of Mexico began to write and send letters or reports to the king in search of privileges. As pointed out earlier, the arguments for the attainment of these privileges were grounded on two fundamental premises: the participation of their fathers, brothers, or themselves in the *Conquista* and their true Christian conversion.[14] Hence, the richness of these letters lies in the record of very particular deeds, which the Spaniards either did not notice or willingly ignored. This happened in the case of Quauhpopoca of Coyoacan, who played an outstanding role in the Noche Triste. Namely, he was the architect of the escape of the Spaniards, whom he led across the Tlacopan causeway. At least this is what his son Don Juan de Guzmán Itztlolinque

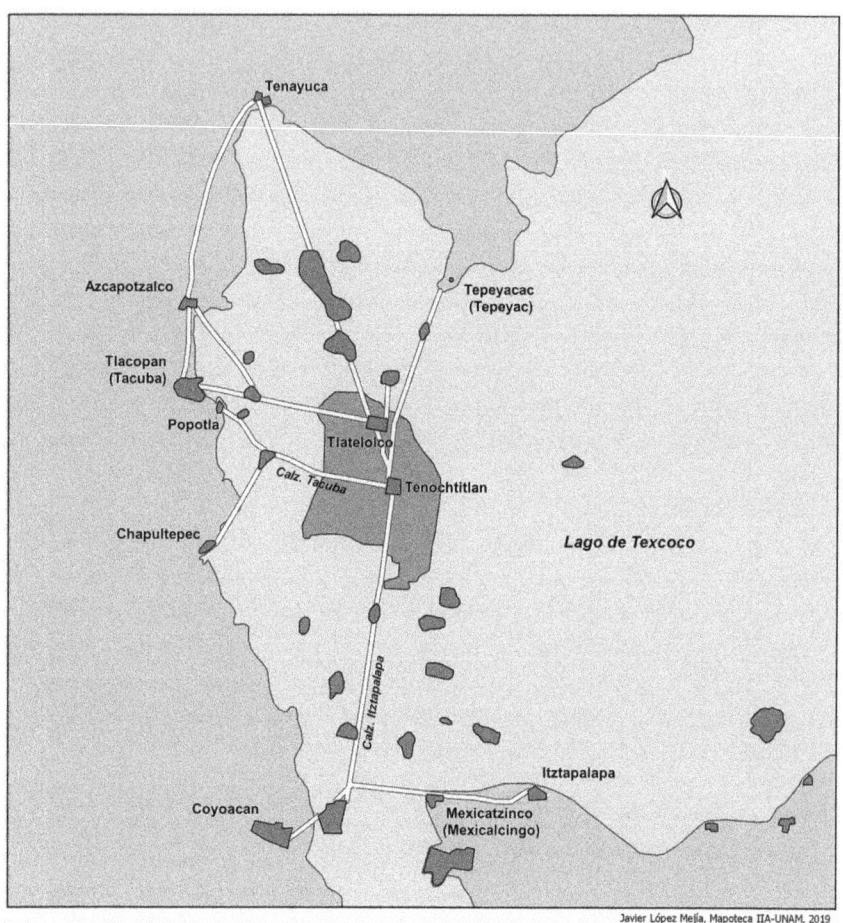

Figure 6.1. Map of the island of Mexico with its causeways and the towns with which it was connected on the mainland. Map based on that of Luis González Aparicio (1973).

stressed in question four of the latter's report of merits and services to Charles V in 1536.[15] What all the witnesses in this report agreed on was that during this flight, Quauhpopoca had asked to go ahead to check the state of the bridges and repair them. However, on crossing the first of the bridges, the Tenochcah attacked and Quauhpopoca stayed in the rearguard to cover the Spaniards' exit, giving his life for them.[16] We will never know how it really took place, but the purpose of the question was undoubtedly to establish Don Juan de Guzmán Itztlolinque's conviction that without Quauhpopoca all the Spaniards would have died and Tenochtitlan would never have been won.

One has to bear in mind that despite their richness, the letters and reports went through a process of purification. In pursuit of privileges, the Indigenous nobility came to gradually erase some uncomfortable matters of the past and distort others. The cacique-governor of Tlacopan/Tacuba, Don Antonio Cortés Totoquihuaztli, for example, did this in the letters he wrote to Philip II between 1552 and 1561.

In his first letter, Don Antonio referred to the time of Tetlepanquetzal, his ancestor, who fought alongside Cuauhtemoc in the defense of Tenochtitlan and Tlatelolco.[17] For obvious reasons Don Antonio never revealed his identity,[18] and less so when he was talking about the Noche Triste. In this regard he wrote to the king that without the Tlacopanecah not only more than half of the Spaniards but all of them would have died. Allegedly, instead of killing Spaniards the Tlacopanecah welcomed and fed them in Tlacopan, consequently suffering the revenge of the Mexicah. As mentioned earlier, this is not true and Cortés thus took reprisals, allowing the Indigenous allies to loot and burn the town of Tlacopan.

It is likely that for this reason the letter did not have the desired effect and Don Antonio had to write a second missive, only a few months later.[19] He then changed his strategy and went even further back in time to 1519, when his father Totoquihuaztli was the ruler of Tlacopan. On this occasion, his claim to the monarch was that Cortés and his father met in Tlacopan, where the latter supposedly hosted the conquistador and his men. However, there is no evidence of such a meeting, nor that Cortés stayed in Tlacopan, since he entered Tenochtitlan from the south by the Itztapalapa causeway (see map). Through this alteration, Don Antonio altered history in order to address one of the two weighty arguments for claiming privileges: the active participation of his progenitor in the *Conquista* of Mexico.

Don Antonio pointed out that his father put himself at the service of Cortés and the monarch, refusing to fight against the Spanish, as did Moteuczoma's allies. Conversely, we know very well that Totoquihuaztli was one of Moteuczoma's allies and that the latter never confronted Cortés because he chose the diplomatic route and not the confrontational one, unlike Cuauhtemoc of Tenochtitlan and Tetlepanquetzal of Tlacopan. It is highly improbable that Totoquihuaztli offered Cortés an alliance so that both could get rid of their respective enemies. It is even more doubtful that the lord of Tlacopan had the authority to forbid Moteuczoma to wage war against the Spaniards. Tlacopan, the third member of the Triple Alliance, lacked the power to give orders to the lord of Tenochtitlan:

> To this I will add that the said my father many times forbade Muntecuhçoma, tlatoani of Mexico, to wage war against the Spaniards. However, disregarding my father's warning, he waged war against them. And thus, when the Spaniards fled from Mexico and passed through my town, *as he [=Totoquihuaztli] had already been their*

friend, he again gave them what they needed to eat and freed them from the extreme hunger that consumed them.[20]

Ten years later, in 1561, Don Antonio continued to insist on his help to the Spaniards during the Noche Triste. In his third letter,[21] he addressed the second of the arguments with which the Indigenous nobility underpinned their right to certain privileges: the conversion to Christianity. Don Antonio quoted the following as his father's speech:

> Come happily with your army and know that we are ready to serve you and the one in whose name you come. *The God you worship, I will worship with all my people. Here you have the house of my gods, destroy it*, enter and whatever you find there and like, take it and use it.[22]

It is implausible that this happened, but the Tlacopan case is a clear example of how the Indigenous nobility had enough knowledge of historical facts to manipulate them to their convenience. The Crown was aware of this, which is why many years had to pass before it finally gave in and granted the longed-for favor.

THE DEATH OF CUAUHTEMOC: THE HISTORICAL ARRANGEMENTS[23]

A few years after the capture of Tenochtitlan, on October 12, 1524, Cortés began one of the longest and hardest conquering campaigns, from which he returned by ship on April 25, 1526, to enter the capital of New Spain sometime in May.[24] On this *entrada* to Honduras and Guatemala, better known as the expedition of the Hibueras, the Spanish conquistador took with him the most select of the Indigenous nobility of central Mexico. Among them were the *tlahtoque* of the Triple Alliance who had survived the final siege in Tlatelolco; namely, Cuauhtemoc of Tenochtitlan, Coanacoch of Tetzcoco, and Tetlepanquetzal of Tlacopan—who were accompanied by their retinue of principals.[25]

All the sources that recall this expedition agree on the existence of a plot by the leaders of the Triple Alliance against the Spaniards along the way. Some researchers are nonetheless reluctant to speak of conspiracy and argue that the plot was nothing more than an invention by Cortés to get rid of these uncomfortable leaders and dismantle the power they wielded in central Mexico.[26] But let us see what the sources say. According to Cortés, a certain Mexicalcingo (see table 6.1), later called Cristóbal, was the one who secretly warned him at night of the scheme, in which a Tlatelolcatl also participated.[27] However, everything points to the fact that Mexicalcingo was not his real name but his place of origin: a small locality in the south of the Valley of Mexico known as Mexicatzinco (today Mexicalcingo, see map). After receiving the information, Cortés interrogated several lords separately and ordered only Cuauhtemoc and Tetlepanquetzal to be hanged, considering them the instigators of the plan that the others had only heard about without wanting to participate. He says nothing about Coanacoch of Tetzcoco.²⁸

Díaz del Castillo's account varies significantly from the previous one. According to him, Cortés was warned by two "great Mexican caciques," that is, two Tenochcah,²⁹ called Tapia and Juan Velázquez, who would later be known as Juan Velázquez Tlacotzin and Don Andrés de Tapia Motelchiuhtzin (see table 6.1).³⁰ Cortés then questioned several other principals about the plan. Among them was Cuauhtemoc, who acknowledged that he had heard of it but defended himself by saying that it had not been his idea and that he did not know if the others agreed with it, or if it would ever be carried out. Tetlepanquetzal then said that he would rather die with Cuauhtemoc than slowly on the way, from the hunger they were all suffering. "And without further proof, Cortés ordered Guatemuz and the lord of Tacuba, who was his cousin, to be hanged."³¹ Before, the friars had encouraged them and commended them to God to later "confess them," always through Doña Marina, La Malinche. He did not say anything about baptizing nor about Coanacoch, and as far as we know, La Malinche was never in Spain.

Those who did speak of baptism were Tezozomoc and Chimalpahin, both of whom wrote their chronicles at the beginning of the seventeenth century.³² According to Tezozomoc, those who slandered Cuauhtemoc and the other lords were the Tlatelolcah and the Michhuacah. This accusation most likely stemmed from the contempt that the Tenochca chronicler felt for the Tlatelolcah, as he stated at the beginning of his work.³³ Now one could assume that Tezozomoc also distained the Michhuacah, a people that Tenochtitlan was never able to conquer despite its arduous attempts.

According to Tezozomoc, the informer was a Tlatelolcatl called Cotztemexi, whose name could be translated as "the Mexi(catl) of the calves,"³⁴ though I do not know where he got this information. Later, Cortés had Cuauhtemoc and Tetlepanquetzal baptized, together with Tlacotzin, giving them the name of Don Fernando Cuauhtemoctzin, Don Pedro Tetlepanquetzatzin, and Don Juan Velázquez Tlacotzin, before hanging the first two from a *pochote* (ceiba for the Spaniards), fortuitously a sacred Mesoamerican tree.³⁵ Chimalpahin had access to the *Crónica mexicayotl* of Tezozomoc; that is why their accounts are so similar.³⁶ In the work of the Chalca chronicler, the slanderer is again the Tlatelolcatl Cotztemexi, but Chimalpahin added one more person, Don Pedro Coanacoch of Tetzcoco, among those hanged from the pochote (see table 6.1).³⁷ Since the Chalca chronicler notes that Cuauhtemoc died in the Christian manner (*christianoyotica momiquilli*), with a cross between his hands, the others probably did so too; hence he provided the same first names as Tezozomoc.³⁸ A copying error occurred when,

TABLE 6.1. Comparative table of events in Hibueras[a]

Subject	Cortés	Bernal Díaz	Tezozomoc	Chimalpahin	Torquemada	Ixtlilxochitl	Anales de Tlatelolco
Traitor	Tlatelolca + Mexicalcingo = Cristóbal	Tapia + Juan Velázquez[b] (mexicanos)	Tlatelolca = Cotztemexi ("the Mexi[catl] of the calves") + Michoacano	Tlatelolca = Cotztemexi	a) Mexicatzincatl = Cristóbal b) a commoner mexicano (Tapia or Tlacotzin?)	Cotztemexi = Cristóbal (Mexicalcingo or Itztapalapa)	Mexicatl = Mexicatl Cotzoolóltic (tenochca)
Events	*Hangs 2 in Acallan: Cuauhtemoc Tetlepanquetzal *Mexicalcingo showed him a piece of paper containing those involved. *Cortés concludes that both were the instigators of the plan. The others only heard of it. *He interrogated them all separately.	*Hangs 2 in Acallan: Cuauhtemoc Tetlepanquetzal *Cuauhtemoc said to have heard of the plan but not to have designed it. *He interrogated them.	*Hang 2 in Hueymollan: Cuauhtemoc Tetlepanquetzal	*Hang 3 in Hueymollan: Cuauhtemoc Tetlepanquetzal Coanacoch.	*Hang 3 in Hueymollan: Cuauhtemoc Tetlepanquetzal Coanacoch others. *Mexicatzincatl showed him a piece of paper containing those involved. *Coanacoch speaks of a "joke." Cuauhtemoc asked not to speak about it anymore, as no one would believe that it was true.	*Hang 3 in Acallan:[c] Cuauhtemoc Tetlepanquetzal Coanacoch.[d] *Cortés asked Cotztemexi to draw those who were present in the talks. *Several men joke about it. *He calls them separately to hang them.	*Hang 3 in Hueymollan:[e] Cuauhtemoc Tetlepanquetzal Coanacoch. *Cuauhtemoc and the others are at a celebration at Acallan. He only complained about his fate, then he was brought to Castilla.[f]

		Pochote	Pochote	Pochote		Pochote
Tree	—				—	
Friars	—	They confess to them.	They baptize them.	They baptize them.	—	—
Other		Doña Marina (Malinche) in Hibueras				Doña Marina (Malinche) in Hibueras

a. It contains two historical versions. Italics are used for the one by Francisco López de Gómara (based on Cortés). Both versions coincide regarding the hanging.
b. It refers to Andrés de Tapia Motelchiuhtzin and Don Juan Velázquez Tlacotzin.
c. Ixtlilxochitl writes that according to certain authors, even though not those he was following, Cuauhtemoc was killed in "Itzancánac" (Ixtlilxochitl, 1975, I: 505).
d. They take him down and he dies afterward due to his wounds.
e. Everything takes place in Acallan, which here appears to be a place and not a province, although it is made explicit that they were hanged in Hueymollan.
f. It is when Coztemexi said that Cuauhtemoc had gone with his arms, and that the three members of the Triple Alliance had talked about eliminating the Spanish.

while speaking of the death of the Tenochca *tlahtoani*, Chimalpahin referred to him as Hernando de *Alvarado* Cuauhtemoc and not as Fernando Cortés Cuauhtemoc. He confused his name and surname with that of the Tenochca chronicler Don Hernando de Alvarado Tezozomoc.[39]

Torquemada followed two versions for this part of history, as he himself acknowledged: that of (a) Francisco López de Gómara and Antonio de Herrera and (b) a chronicle of Tetzcoco written in Nahuatl.[40] Gómara was Cortés's secretary and confessor and wrote his *History of the Conquest* based on the accounts that the conquistador and other persons provided him, since he never crossed the Atlantic. Nevertheless, his work was so successful that Herrera used it as the basis for his *Décadas*, in the seventeenth century. Gómara's link with Cortés explains why we find Cortés's version in Torquemada's work when indicating that the one who denounced the instigators of the plan to kill the Spaniards was an Indio called "Mexicatzincatl," who later adopted the name of Cristóbal. However, in this case, there were *ten* names of the accused on the paper that the latter allegedly showed Cortés. According to Torquemada, Cortés interrogated them separately. All stated that the instigators of the plot were the three members of the Triple Alliance and that although they were pleased with it, they did not consent to it. Now, Cortés was very precise in pointing out that he only hanged Cuauhtemoc and Tetlepanquetzal, but Torquemada—like Chimalpahin—did not care and included Coanacoch of Tetzcoco. This leaves a hint that Cortés also hanged other lords whose names he omitted. What Torquemada did mention is that Cortés hanged them almost immediately after the sentence was passed.[41]

Later, Torquemada brought up the anonymous history written in Nahuatl, which he considered more accurate than the previous ones. Its Acolhua origin explains why its protagonist is Coanacoch of Tetzcoco. According to this version, Cortés's sentence was triggered by Coanacoch's harangue about taking revenge on the Spaniards, in which the orator stated that his adhesion to the new faith prevented him from such a scheme. Cuauhtemoc asked him to stop the speech, since it would "not be understood and they [the Spanish] may think we mean this."[42] That is precisely what happened: It is said that "a Mexican Indio, villain and commoner" heard them and told Cortés the story. The latter believed him and hung them that same night from a pochote or ceiba tree; it was during Carnival, in the year 1525. Along with them were five others, whose names Torquemada omitted as well.[43]

Patrick Lesbre, who analyzed the text in detail, saw in it the recurrent adherence of Tetzcoco and its lords to the new faith, which was so present in Ixtlilxochitl's work. Lesbre also observed a "vague intention" of revenge in qualifying the plan as a "mockery" (as stated in the text). Later Acolhua historiography clung to this argument, reiterating that it was all a misinterpretation of the facts.[44] On this point, however, I am not so sure whether it was this Acolhua chronicle that gave rise to it, or whether it was Torquemada himself who authorized himself to express his following opinion about Cuauhtemoc's end: "If I were asked the cause of his death, I would say that it was this; and Cortes did not want him to go frightened and [was] solicitous of him and the other kings that he had in his company, and I do not think it was for wanting to raise these sad Indios with the land."[45]

It remains to be said that in the Acolhua story, Cuauhtemoc also came to the fore. In this case, he did so to prevent Coanacoch from continuing with his "mockery," so that the Spaniards would not believe it was true (see table 6.1). Moreover, the informer, whose name is omitted, is described as a "Mexicano" commoner. This is striking, since it invites one to think about the name referred to by Díaz del Castillo: Tapia or Juan Velázquez, who, as already mentioned, despite having acceded to the throne of Tenochtitlan, lacked the legitimate rights for it.[46]

Another Indigenous chronicler who dealt with the passage of the Hibueras was the already briefly mentioned Alva Ixtlilxochitl, Native of Tetzcoco. His work was also written in the seventeenth century, from various sources, correcting errors or inaccuracies that he observed, reinterpreting some data, and even inventing others.[47] Like Tezozomoc, Ixtlilxochitl also pointed out that the slanderer was Cotztemexi, although he ignored the Tlatelolca origin that the Tenochca chronicler had assigned him. Ixtlilxochitl, rather, followed Cortés and drew his own conclusions, stating that Cotztemexi "was later called Cristóbal, a Native of Iztapalapan or, according to some, of Mexicalcinco."[48] That is, he substituted Mexicalcingo (Cortés) for Cotztemexi (Tezozomoc) because he surely realized that "Mexicaltzingo" was not an anthroponym but the name of a locality (see table 6.1). Therefore, and in the absence of another proper name, he opted for the one Tezozomoc had provided. I do not know where he got the link with Itztapalapa, although both places lay very close to each other (see figure 6.1).

According to Lesbre, Ixtlilxochitl was the first to openly state that the members of the Triple Alliance were victims of a slander and even allowed himself to judge Cortés's sentence. Lesbre points out that Ixtlilxochitl did so based on what was intuited in Torquemada's anonymous account of Acolhua origin.[49] However, I think what really contributed to the chronicler taking this step was the friar's own opinion that I mentioned earlier. This probably invited Ixtlilxochitl to rework the anonymous account, so that a brief conversation was converted into a very relaxed one, with jokes included, in which other lords participated, beyond Coanacoch and Cuauhtemoc. These jokes, as Lesbre remarks, came to replace the mockeries that were mentioned in Torquemada's text, rendering them more innocent.[50]

Ixtlilxochitl stated that the Spanish conquistador was suspicious of that conversation, and, since it was in Nahuatl, he asked Cotztemexi what it was about. The subsequent information is ambivalent: on the one hand, Cotztemexi supposedly betrayed the lords by lying and informing Cortés about the plans of a supposed plot, the reason why Cortés had them hanged; on the other hand, Cortés was accused of inventing what Cotztemexi told him.[51] Because Ixtlilxochitl followed Torquemada's anonymous chronicle, we know that like the Spanish friar, Ixtlilxochitl also said that the sentence was executed on Carnestolendas (Carnival), in 1525.[52] Now, if Ixtlilxochitl knew Cortés's letters, it is possible that in order to adjust his account to them, where the death of Coanacoch was omitted, the chronicler of Tetzcoco narrated that the latter did not die hanging from the tree. Instead, his brother had taken him down from it, still alive. Nonetheless, Coanacoch died a few days later from the wounds caused by the cord in his throat. Ixtlilxochitl later added that this brother, furious at the sentence, wanted to rise up against the Spaniards, but after Cortés had shown the brother the evidence justifying the former's decision, Cortés appeased him.[53] The Texcoca chronicler's objective was to extol the role of that brother,[54] in order to obtain a series of privileges in the society of that time. Thus, Ixtlilxochitl emphasized the brother's appeasement: allegedly the latter was moved by his new faith and knew that if he went to war with the Spaniards, "everything would be lost, and the evangelical law would not advance."[55] This statement was part of a discourse around the acceptance of Tetzcoco and its lords to the new faith that, as Lesbre pointed out, was always present in the work of the Acolhua chronicler.[56]

What really happened then? The eyewitness accounts of the events are undoubtedly the starting point; nevertheless, Cortés and Díaz del Castillo gave sometimes quite different information, eventually leaving some out. For example, neither of them said that Cortés had Coanacoch hanged. Since it is a fact that the latter did not return from the Hibueras, most likely the troops, who witnessed those events, articulated his story in their accounts and nourished the Indigenous chroniclers. Additionally, Cortés did not say whether he baptized the lords he sentenced. Díaz del Castillo only spoke of a spiritual assistance when dying. This, it seems, Tezozomoc and Chimalpahin used to claim that the lords died baptized. For the nobles who had converted to the new religion, this matter ended up being very important. Moreover, Tezozomoc and Chimalpahin were keen to stress that they were not hanged from just any tree but from a pochote. This gave a certain dignity to the scene.[57]

As for the plot, there is no reason to doubt it. Only Ixtlilxochitl, in the seventeenth century, tells us about the innocent and even jocular conversation of its protagonists, blaming a third party for being the one who entangled Cortés. What I do not understand is the resistance of some historians to accept a plot's existence when, given the circumstances, the most natural thing is that the leaders of the Triple Alliance saw the convenience of putting an end to the Spaniards. The presence of traitors and even the fact that Cortés took advantage of these circumstances would also be logical.

What nobody denies is the central role of the informer. Even though his identity escapes us, he undoubtedly is one of those men who saw in betrayal a way to stand out in the new society that was emerging at that time. Cortés spoke of a Tlatelolcatl and of another who came from Mexicaltzingo. Bernal Díaz del Castillo, who wrote in the second half of the sixteenth century, identified the traitors as the Mexican (or Tenochca) caciques Andrés de Tapia Motelchiuhtzin and Juan Velázquez Tlacotzin. Meanwhile, Tezozomoc seems to have resorted to Cortés's account to focus on the Tlatelolca informer, probably because of his aversion against his neighbors. In any case, Tezozomoc mentioned that the informer's name was Cotztemexi, but we do not know where he got that name. Torquemada's reference is striking because it seems to be inspired by that of Bernal Díaz del Castillo. However, the former no longer referred to two caciques but to a Mexica commoner who could be Juan Velázquez Tlacotzin or Don Andrés de Tapia Motelchiuhtzin. In that case he lowered him in rank (he called him "plebeian"), most likely because in the seventeenth century it was well known that none of them had legitimate rights to take the title of governor of the Tenochcah. The first to ascend to that position after the death of Cuauhtemoc was Tlacotzin. He still never came to rule Tenochtitlan because he died on the way back from the Hibueras and was succeeded by Motelchiuhtzin. However, it is important to note that for the Indigenous chroniclers, none received the title of tlahtoani but rather *cuauhtlahtoani*. With this inferior rank, the chroniclers stressed their lack of legitimacy for the rank to which the Spaniards elevated them, after the disorders that the *Conquista* provoked.[58]

THE TLATELOLCA SOURCES. BETWEEN RUMOR AND NEWS

The *Anales de Tlatelolco* represent a compilation of sources of diverse origin.[59] They are difficult to date due to their narrative structure, which is sometimes associated with the early colonial period. There are two copies of the *Anales de Tlatelolco: Ms. 22*, on amate paper, and *Ms. 22bis*, on European paper.[60] No consensus exists about dating those copies, but it is a fact that they were not produced in 1528, as stated in the introduction of document V of *Ms. 22bis*. Lockhart assigned the date of 1545 to *Ms. 22* but placed *Ms. 22bis* to the seventeenth or eighteenth century.[61] For his part, Klaus concluded that if *Ms. 22* was from the sixteenth century, *Ms. 22bis* must be from the eighteenth century, while Tena dated *Ms. 22* to 1560 and *Ms. 22bis* to 1620.[62]

All three authors agree that *Ms. 22bis* was a late copy. The person who added the year 1528 to document V of *Ms. 22bis* (missing in document V of *Ms. 22*) must have done so in the late seventeenth or early eighteenth century. He must have realized that the account included in document V came from Fray Andrés de Olmos, who had arrived in Tlatelolco that year.[63] Differences can be explained by the copying process: these sources of different origin were exposed to historical reinterpretations, additions, and errors inherent to later editing or, even, to inconsistencies at the level of writing and internal organization. For all these reasons, in the *Anales de Tlatelolco*, we find narrative modes of the sixteenth century, with features typical of the primordial titles, as Kevin Terraciano has already noted.[64]

The same happens with the *Ordenanza de Cuauhtemoc*, another Tlatelolco document with which the *Anales* is intimately related. Precisely this was the reason for Perla Valle's musings regarding the *Ordenanza de Cuauhtemoc*. For after dating it to the sixteenth century throughout his work, at the end of it she went so far as to suggest that the *Ordenanza* might be a primordial title of the eighteenth century.[65] Today, however, we can confirm that the *Ordenanza*, made on amate paper and written in Nahuatl, was created for a lawsuit in 1704.[66] This evidence, in addition to the fact that *Ms. 22bis* was also produced in the late colonial period, is not fortuitous. Therefore, as I suggested a few years ago, everything points to the assumption that both documents were in the hands of a famous forger of the period.[67]

I am talking about Don Diego García, better known as Don Diego García de Mendoza Moctezuma, whom Wood identified as the artificer of the *techialoyan* codices, a subgenre within the primordial titles.[68] But there is more to it. As Wood demonstrated, through a trial to which he was subjected in 1705, it became known that Don Diego García had elaborated a series of titles for several communities so that they could defend some of their lands, in dispute with their neighbors. It does not seem fortuitous neither that Tlatelolco was among those communities, as Wood pointed out, nor, as we determined a few years ago, that the document that the Tlatelolcah used for this dispute was the *Ordenanza de Cuauhtemoc*.[69] Thus, it seems reasonable to think that the authorities of Tlatelolco, as did those of other towns, lent Don Diego several manuscripts with which to corroborate historically the rights of the Tlatelolcah to the lands in dispute.

Some alphabetical texts of the *Ordenanza* come therefore directly from the *Anales* and both sources share the names of many persons, although taken out of context, as Valle has already noted.[70] This happened, for example, with the Nahuatl chant of the *Anales de Tlatelolco*, which the author of the *Ordenanza* copied almost verbatim (see table 6.2). Nor is it accidental that Cuauhtemoc appears in both documents with the name "Xocóyotl Cuauhtemoctzin tlacateuctli," as Rafael Tena has pointed out.[71] A similar "game of names" was played with some of the figures (see table 6.3): while several of them act as founders of Tlatelolco in the *Ordenanza* (in the year 1335 approximately), in the *Anales* they act as the *cuauhtlahtoque* who ruled the city after 1473 (i.e., over a century later); and while five of them were witnesses of Cuauhtemoc in 1523 (*Ordenanza*), in the other source, they are the ones who defended Tlatelolco from the Spaniards (*Anales*). In other words, they were taken

TABLE 6.2. Song in the *Ordenanza de Cuauhtemoc* and in the *Anales de Tlatelolco*

Ordenanza de Cuauhtemoc	Anales de Tlatelolco
[10r] Y nima oca conilnami[que]	[11v] yn imicanpa
yn ixquich yn ipa mochiuh yn tlayouiliztlin yn Chapoltepec y Coluacan, ynic poliuque yn oualmochoquilique yn otla[oco]xque. Yn oquivalylnamique yn itlayouiliz yn ipa mochiuh yn ipa Çe Tochtli xiuitl, yn oya tleualaya choquiztli, yn [o]motlamachti y coluacatl omotlamachti tepanecatl.	yn ixquich ynpa omochiuh tlayhyouiliztli yn Chapoltepec yn Colhuaca. Yn Chapoltepec yn iuh poliuhque, ycuicatitech quilnamiqui yn intlayyouiliz; . . . ; yquac topa mochiva yeuaya, Ce yn Tochtonalli xiuin tlatquic yeuaya choquiztli yeuaya . . . nimexicatl yeuaia, omotlamachti y colhua omotlamachti yn tepanecatl yyo.
"Y nauhcapa uicaloque y mexican, y mochoquilitiu y Uitziliuitl teu[h]tli, y çepamitl ymac otecoc y Coluacan. Y tematitlaquizque y mexica ueuetque atlayaque, amoxtli quimoquetique [Ac] ocol[co],	Nauhcanpa uicalloque mexica; mochoquilitiuh tlacuchcatl Uiziliuitl, a ce panitl ymac tecoc yn Coluaca yyao yyan. Tematitlan quizque i mexica ueuetque atla yaque, amoxtli quimoquentique Acocolco.
y toli yn acatl ynic oyaca, ya y yeuayan! Yn quimamatiuitze yn inauatil yn tecnoca, quitlazque yn ixiuhchim[al] quetzalpamitl, ynic chimalcuecuepaloc yn Coluacan ynic atoliuhque. Yn timexica choquiztli y yeuaya, y çem[e] ti[a]mania yn [t] omaçeualuan pipil: 'Toteuhyouane, a yeuayan!, analoc y colin y chocan, y nica tictolinizque y ye timexica choquiztli, y yeu[aya]n!'.	Nica yn tolli acatl ycoyoca euaia quimamatiuitze inauatil. Tella uncan quitaque xiuhchimalli quetzalpayo ayo ouia. Yn chimalli cuecuepalloc y ye Tepantonco y yeuayya, ucaualloc Collivaca; yca tollinque ye timexica choquiztli euaya. Ye cematlmania momaceual ayyo pipilti totecuhua ayyeuaya, ocaualloc Collivaca; yca tollinque ye timexica choquiztli euaya. Ye cematlmania momaceual ayyo. [12r] Ao youalpa ye necalizpa uallolinque mexica ooo
Y Tiçapan y Coluaca y ualchimalpanoque y mexica ueuetque y tlacochpaneque ytlacuecuepa[l]chimaltican."	Tiçaapan Coluaca. Ualchimalpanoque y mesica i ueuetque tlacuchpanoque,
	[17r] Entonces Tecocoltzin, tlatoani de Acolhuacan, envió mensajeros para que vinieran a hablar con Topantemoctzin, tizociahuácatl de Tlatelolco, con el tezcacohuácatl Popocatzin, con el tlacatécatl Temillotzin, con el tlacochcálcatl Coyohuehuetzin, y con el tzihuatecpanécatl Matlalacatzin.
[12v] Xochitecatlteutli tlapanecatl Tepa[nt]emoctzin Temilotzin Yolotzin Tiaquinauacatzin Coyoueuetzin Totopilatzin	
[10r] Chichitzin Tlalteotzin Quiçemitouatzin Quetzalq[u] auhtzin Tlacochcalcatl Teyolococouatzi[n] Totoçac[a]tzin Moyoualito[u]atzin Ytziquauhtzin Yolotzin Acopilcatl Cal[pilc] atl Utziltecatl Quauhtecatl	[4] éstos son todos los señores que gobernaron la ciudad de Tlatelolco:[primero] se enseñoreó el tlacatécatl Chichitzin; cuando éste murió, se asentó el tlacatécatl Quicemitohuatzin; cuando éste murió, se asentó Tlacatécatl; cuando éste murió, se asentó el tlacatécatl Tlachochcálcatl; cuando éste murió, se asentó el tlacatécatl Totozacatzin; cuando éste murió, se asentó Tlacatécatl; cuando éste murió, se asentó Itzcuauhtzin; cuando éste murió, se asentó Tlacochcálcatl; cuando éste murió se asentó Teyolcocohuatzin, cuando éste murió, se asentó Tlacochcálcatl;

Source: Taken from Michel Oudijk and María Castañeda de la Paz, "El uso de fuentes históricas en pleitos de tierras: la Crónica X y la Ordenanza de Cuauhtémoc," *Tlalocan* 16 (2009): 255–80.

TABLE 6.3. Comparative table with the same characters in different contexts

Ordenanza Cuauhtemoc	Anales de Tlatelolco	Ordenanza Cuauhtemoc	Anales de Tlatelolco
(Founders of Tlatelolco)	*(Cuauhtlahtoque of Tlatelolco)*	*(Cuauhtemoc's companions)*	*(Defenders of Tlatelolco)*
Chichitzin	Chichitzin	Temilotzin	Temilotzin
Quicemitohuatzin	Quicemitohuatzin	Tepantemoctzin	Topantemoctzin
Totozacatzin	Totozacatzin	Yolotzin Tianquiznahuacatzin	
Itzcuauhtzin	Itzcuauhtzin	Coyohuehuetzin	Coyohuehuetzin
Teyolcocohuatzin	Teyolcocohuatzin	Totopilantzin	
Quetzalquauhtzin	*Tlacatecatl*		
Moyoualitouatzin	Tlacochcalcatl		
Yolotzin	*Tlacatecatl*		
Acopilcatl	Tlacochcalcatl		

Source: Based on María Castañeda de la Paz, *Conflictos*, 162.

out of context to place them in one place or another when composing a narrative.[72] As far as the expedition of the Hibueras is concerned, it is an anomalous account that was only recorded in *Ms. 22bis*. It is a late text, and therefore of great discursive richness, with abundant turns and Nahuatl expressions. Additionally, everything indicates that it was constructed from vague memories and some rumors, given its lack of historical precision in some cases and the sensationalism of its narration in others. Now, let us delve into its analysis.[73]

To begin with, the text states that when the Spaniards arrived, Cuauhtemoc had been ruling Tlatelolco for four years.[74] This is implausible because the sources are unanimous in declaring that the ruler at that time was Itzcuauhtzin, a character who accompanied Moteuczoma until his end and death.[75] What is certain is that after conquering the island of Mexico, Cortés appointed a lord for each of its parts: Cuauhtemoc ruled in Tenochtitlan, and Temilotzin in Tlatelolco.[76] The author of *Ms. 22bis*, however, eliminated Temilotzin from this passage and replaced him with Cuauhtemoc. He probably did so because in the second half of the seventeenth century Cuauhtemoc was the one who, in the collective memory of the Tlatelolcah, played the most heroic role in that part of the island.[77] Therefore, if Cuauhtemoc became lord of Tlatelolco, the author of *Ms. 22bis* had no choice but to look for a ruler for Tenochtitlan.

The chosen one was Mexicatl, "a dwarf with plump calves" (*cotzoololtic*),[78] who pretended to be a lord, "surrounded by his friends."[79] This Mexicatl was none other than Cortés's "Mexicaltzingo," who, when his name was cut off, remained as a Mexican (or Tenochca) and not as someone from Mexicaltzingo. However, the fact that the character also appears in this source with the name Mexicatl Cotzololtic ("the Mexicatl of the round calves") invites us to think that this was another way to invoke Tezozomoc's "Cotztemexi," whose name we translated as "the Mexi(catl) of the calves" (see table 6.1). In fact, later it will be said that this was the name he received as a liar, although the connotations of that nickname escape us.[80] It only remains for me to recall that if for the Tenochca chronicler the informer was a Tlatelolcatl, for the author of the *Anales de Tlatelolco* he was a Tenochcatl, or at least one who ruled in Tenochtitlan. In all the sources, including this latter one, he appears as the one who betrayed the members of the Triple Alliance.

According to the *Anales*, Cuauhtemoc and Mexicatl were taken to the Hibueras along with Tetlepanquetzal of Tlacopan and Coanacoch of Tetzcoco. When they arrived at Acallan, Cuauhtemoc did not stop repeating to his people and those of Acallan, who apparently were his vassals, that Cortés was going to take him to Castile to "greet the great emperor teul," from where he did not know if he would return.[81] The people of Acallan allegedly made him a great feast and danced all day and night. The lord of Tlacopan and the lord of Tetzcoco participated in it, but not Mexicatl, whom nobody had invited. It was then that Doña Marina passed by him and asked him what he was doing, since he was not with the others. Mexicatl took the opportunity to tell her about the attack that Cuauhtemoc was planning, since according to his version of events, he had visited those of Acallan and had heard Cuauhtemoc ask his companions if it would be too difficult to get rid of the Spaniards so as not to go to Castile. Afterward, and with a doubtful testimony, Mexicatl said: "That is why I grieve, [when thinking] that here you are going to die the captain Marquis and yourself."[82] Unsurprisingly, after these words, Malinche informed Cortés (the "Marquis"), and they went to capture Cuauhtemoc and the other two lords of the Triple Alliance in Acallan. They supposedly threw a rope around their necks as if they were dogs, to later hang them from a *pochote* in Hueymollan.[83] Consequently, the Tlatelolcah gave the liar Mexicatl the nickname of Cotztemexi, which is the one used by Tezozomoc in his *Crónica mexicayotl*.[84] It is odd that the Tlatelolcah gave him such a nickname, since, as mentioned above, according to Tezozomoc, the informer was a Tlatelolcatl and not a Tenochcatl, as the *Anales* say. And thus, bursts into the story Don Pedro Temilotzin, who upon seeing the scene hid with his *tlacatecatl*, Don Martín Ecatzin, in the ship that was going to Castile, as if it were there in Acallan.

As mentioned, Temilotzin was the lord whom Cortés invested as lord of Tlatelolco and who died in the Hibueras, which allowed Ecatzin to succeed him in the position.[85] The *Anales de Tlatelolco* narrate it differently: here, both snuck inside the ship, removed a plank, and hid in the place of the horses, until Doña Marina (la Malinche) found them after six or seven days of sailing. Then, they had to explain what they were doing there, and they answered that the fear produced by Cortés's sentence made them hide in the boat. Having heard the above, Cortés, through Malinche, replied: "Now we are going to Castile to visit the great emperor Teul; there you will be quartered or dragged, there you will die."[86] Shortly after, and for no apparent reason, Cortés named them lords. According to the story, the following happened:

> Temillotzin got up, and Ecatzin thought that perhaps he was going to urinate. He [Temillotzin] said to Ecatzin: "Lord Ecatzin, where are they taking us? Let us go to our home." Ecatzin replied, "What are you going to do, Temillotzin? Where can we go if the ship has been sailing for six days?" But Temillotzin would not listen to anyone trying to hold him back from going where he wanted to go; [and they all] saw how he threw himself into the water, how he kicked himself swimming toward the west. Malintzin shouted to him: "Where are you going, Temillotzin? Come back, come back!" [But] he did not listen to her, he left, and finally sank into the waters.[87]

What is very contradictory is that in another part of this work, as well as in Fray Bernardino de Sahagún's, Temilotzin stands out for his relevant role in the defense of Tlatelolco, while after its *Conquista* he is painted as a fearful and cowardly person.[88] As for Ecatzin, according to these *Anales*, he arrived in Castile and returned five years later to Tlatelolco, where he began to govern.[89] Considering all of preceding discussion, in my opinion, the account in *Ms. 22bis* is a fantasy story based on hearsay, though with a historical background: the expedition to the Hibueras and some of the journeys that the nobility of central Mexico undertook to the kingdom of Castile. While it is true that Temillotzin must have gone on the expedition to the Hibueras, it must be remembered that he did so as tlahtoani and died in it, at the time when Cortés must have named his tlacatecatl Ecatzin as his successor. Regarding a possible trip to Spain, there is no information that any of them went to visit the Court and much less that Doña Marina accompanied Cortés, neither to the Hibueras nor to Castile. These inclusions increase the incredibility of the story, clearly written by a person unfamiliar with the details of the Tlatelolca history.

CONCLUSIONS

Some of the fragments selected for this work have been used frequently to write about the *Conquista*, although, as shown in this chapter, they are all problematic, stemming from their authors' circumstances. Another noteworthy issue is that the accounts become more and more elaborate as time goes on. Enough time had passed to allow the authors to read different versions, compare them, listen to alternate oral accounts, and draw conclusions. Cortés, by contrast, wrote almost at the same time as the events. Díaz del Castillo, the other famous eyewitness, did not write his work until several decades later. His information does hence differ from Cortés's letters in some respects.

The Indigenous sources differ even more. The nobility knew that in order to recover some of their privileges and survive in New Spain's society, they had to fashion themselves as allies of the Spaniards and as true Christians. For that reason, in the letters and reports that the nobles addressed to the monarch, they took great care in both aspects. Certainly, they exaggerated and went so far as to erase some uncomfortable issues of the past, in the same way that Cortés could have done by extolling his "achievements" and making up for some of his "failures." Our job is to analyze the contexts in which these sources were written in order to know both sides of the process of the *Conquista*, and of New Spain's society.

The Indigenous chronicles were likewise crafted according to specific colonial contexts. At a time when the Indigenous nobility was in clear decline, some nobles became chroniclers, taking on the task of recording the events of the past, and, eager for information, they tapped into various written texts and oral accounts, which were analyzed and mixed to adapt their information to the new times. This is the case for Tezozomoc and Chimalpahin, whose works were written to praise their people's history for their people, which is why they were written in Nahuatl. In some cases, it is easy to determine which sources they were using to compose their narratives, as demonstrated with the passage about the expedition to the Hibueras. Some additions they made to their works can be detected without much complication, for example, the question of the baptism of the members of the Triple Alliance, which only became relevant by the time the chroniclers wrote their works. Another such example is the tree where they were hanged: by turning the unspecified tree into a sacred Mesoamerican pochote (or ceiba for the Spaniards), the chroniclers tried to add a certain dignity to the way in which the lords had died.

The similarity between the work of Tezozomoc and Chimalpahin is because the latter had access to the former's work, from which he copied passages and took data. Torquemada's case elucidates that this was the way of composing such texts. He himself pointed out that he was using an Acolhua chronicle in Nahuatl that was also used by Ixtlilxochitl, who—unlike Torquemada—transformed it to such a degree as to state that the members of the Triple Alliance had been victims of a plot and openly accused Cortés of manipulating the events to that end.

The *Anales de Tlatelolco* are a case apart but a very important one. They are a compilation of documents from the sixteenth century (*Ms. 22*) that was copied in the seventeenth century (*Ms. 22bis*) but also manipulated by the author to incorporate stories absent in the earlier version, such as the passage about the Hibueras. Since the author was the well-known forger Don Diego García de Mendoza Moctezuma, we can assume that he did not play accidentally but willingly with the historical data as he pleased to compose his story. To conclude, that is the way in which many of the narratives we are dealing with in our work were constructed. This process did not end in the colonial period but continued in the nineteenth century, when Mexican nationalism took up the figure of Cuauhtemoc.[90] Working on the *Conquista* is not a simple task, but I hope that this essay serves to shed light on how accounts of it were constructed and how they could alter their content.

NOTES

Translated from Spanish by Vitus Huber. A first version of this essay was published as "Fragmentos de la Conquista a través de los relatos del siglo XVI," in *Los relatos del encuentro, México, siglo XVI: XXIX Coloquio Cervantino Internacional*, ed. Christian Duverger (Mexico City: Fundación Cervantina de México; Guanajuato: Gobierno del Estado de Guanajuato, Universidad de Guanajuato y Centro de Estudios Cervantinos, 2019), 151–92. I thank Christian Duverger and the publishers for their permission to publish this new edition.

1. This is the case with Fray Bernardino de Sahagún, *Historia general de las cosas de Nueva España*, 3 vols. (Mexico City: Conaculta, 2000), 3: bk. 12, ch. VIII, 1175–76, who refers specifically to this type of retinue.

2. Neither Hernán Cortés, *Cartas de Relación* (Mexico City: Porrúa 1992), *Segunda carta de Relación*, 52, 64–65; nor Bernal Díaz del Castillo, *Historia verdadera de la conquista de la Nueva España* (Mexico City: Porrúa, 1992), ch. XXXVIII, 65 mentioned Quetzalcoatl when they heard of this story. The informants of Sahagún, *Historia general*, 3: bk. 12, ch. II, 1163, ch. III, 1165–66; and Fernando de Alva Ixtlilxochitl, *Obras históricas* (Mexico City: Instituto de Investigaciones Históricas, UNAM, 1975), 2: ch. LXXX, 200, whose works were written much later, did.

3. Romero Frizzi and María de los Ángeles, "Reflexionando una vez más: La etnohistoria y la época colonial," *Dimensión Antropológica* 1, no. 1 (1994): 37–56, here 43.

4. Lara Wankel, *Dimensiones sensoriales en los relatos españoles de la conquista de Tenochtitlan* (Mexico City: Instituto Humboldt, El Colegio del Estado de Hidalgo y Asociación Nacional de Archivos y Bibliotecas Privados, 2022), 20–33.

5. Frizzi and de los Ángeles, "Reflexionando," 46.

6. Frizzi and de los Ángeles, "Reflexionando," 46.

7. For this topic, see Cortés, *Cartas*, *Segunda carta*, 83–84; Díaz del Castillo, *Historia verdadera*, ch. CXXVIII: 254–62 and Sahagún, *Historia general*, 3: bk. 12, chs. XIX–XX, among others. On the occasion of several anniversaries, among them the *Conquista* of Mexico,

the government of Mexico City changed the name of "Noche Triste" to "Noche Victoriosa." See the newspaper Claudia Sheinbaum, "Cambian nombre del Árbol de la 'Noche Triste' a la 'Noche Victoriosa,'" *El Financiero*, July 27, 2021, https://www.elfinanciero.com.mx/cdmx/2021/07/27/cambian-nombre-del-arbol-de-la-noche-triste-a-la-noche-victoriosa/; and Pablo Ferri, "La noche triste de Hernán Cortés es ahora victoriosa," *El País*, March 11, 2021, both accessed May 8, 2023, https://elpais.com/mexico/2021-03-12/la-noche-triste-de-hernan-cortes-es-ahora-victoriosa.html. See also Eduardo Matos Moctezuma, "Reflexiones acerca de la conquista de Tenochtitlan y Tlatelolco," in *Tenochtitlan y Tlatelolco: A 500 años de su caída, Museo del Templo Mayor* (Mexico City: INAH, 2021), 45–54. What often gets omitted is that on this night, in addition to the Spaniards, a large number of Indigenous allies and members of the Tenochca nobility died. According to Ixtlilxochitl, *Obras históricas*, 2: ch. LXXXVIII, 230, in the attack in the Toltec ditch, later called the Salto de Alvarado, 450 Spaniards, 4,000 allied Indians, and 46 horses died. This toll on the Indigenous side is why I continue to refer to this historical episode as the Noche Triste.

8. On details of the transition of power from Moteuczoma, see Pastrana in this volume.

9. Cortés, *Cartas*, 55; and Díaz del Castillo, *Historia verdadera*, ch. XCV, 184. I have addressed the subject more extensively in María Castañeda de la Paz, *Conflictos y alianzas en tiempos de cambio: Azcapotzalco, Tlacopan, Tenochtitlan y Tlatelolco (siglos XII al XVI)* (Mexico City: Instituto de Investigaciones Antropológicas, UNAM, 2013), 337–43. For an iconographic analysis of Montezuma's prison, see Juan José Batalla Rosado, "Prisión y muerte de Moctezuma según los relatos en los códices mesoamericanos," *Revista Española de Antropología Americana* 26 (1996): 106–9. The author discusses the different images of Montezuma's representation and their problems.

10. In an interesting and important article, Michel Graulich, "La muerte de Motecuhzoma II Xocoyotzin," in *Orbis in Orbem: Liber amicorum John Everaert*, ed. Jan Parmentier and Sander Spanoghe (Gante, Belgium: Academia Press, 2001), 1–16, collected all the versions of Moteuczoma's death and observed that except for that of the eyewitnesses of the events, all were hopelessly contradictory. This fact seems to confirm that Moteuczoma died from the stone injury. On Moteuczoma vis-à-vis the Spanish, see also the work of Matthew Restall, *When Montezuma Met Cortés. The True Story of the Meeting That Changed History* (New York: Harper Collins, 2018); Michel Oudijk, "La Conquista como historia mesoamericana," in *Los relatos del Encuentro: México, siglo XVI, XXIX Coloquio Cervantino Internacional* (Mexico City: Museo Iconográfico del Quijote, Centro de Estudios Cervantino, Fundación Cervantina de México, 2019), 193–224; María Castañeda de la Paz, "Lealtades y desavenencias entre la nobleza indígena durante la conquista de Tenochtitlan," *Arqueología Mexicana*, special issue 163 (2020): 42–47; María Castañeda de la Paz, María Luque Talaván, and Miguel Luque Talaván, "Los Moctezuma y sus escudos de armas," in *Para que de ellos e de vos quede memoria: La heráldica indígena novohispana del centro de México* (Mexico, City: UNAM, Instituto de Investigaciones Jurídicas e Instituto de Investigaciones Antropológicas; Xalapa,

Mexico: Universidad Anáhuac, 2021), 111–19; Guilhem Olivier, "El regreso de Quetzalcóatl y la divinización de los españoles," in *1519: Los europeos en Mesoamérica*, ed. Ana Carolina Ibarra and Pedro Marañón Hernández (Mexico City: UNAM, Instituto de Investigaciones Históricas, Dirección General de Publicaciones y Fomento Editorial, 2021), 11–36; Miguel Pastrana Flores, "La entrega del poder de Motecuhzoma: Una propuesta crítica," *Estudios de Historia Novohispana*, 62 (2020): 111–44; Miguel Pastrana Flores, "El estado anímico de Motecuhzoma durante la Conquista en la obra sahaguntina," in *Tenochtitlan, la caída de un imperio: Acercamiento y reflexiones*, ed. Eduardo Matos Moctezuma, Miguel Pastrana Flores, and Patricia Ledesma (Mexico City: Secretaría de Cultura, INAH, 2021): 213–22.

11. Cortés, *Cartas, Tercera carta*, 110–11. For more on Cuitlahua, see Cortés, *Cartas, Tercera carta*, 110–11; *Segunda carta*, 51, 94; and Fray Juan de Torquemada, *Monarquía indiana*, 7 vols. (Mexico City: UNAM, Instituto de Investigaciones Históricas, 1975–83), bk. 4, ch. LXXX, 248, ch. XLV, 149–50, ch. XLVI, 150–51.

12. Cortés, *Cartas, Segunda carta*, 83–84, mentions this attack, and in more detail, Díaz del Castillo, *Historia verdadera*, ch. CXXVIII, 256–57.

13. Cortés, *Cartas, Tercera carta*, 118. On the moment of the attack, see the *Second Letter* (Cortés, *Cartas, Segunda carta*, 83–84). Since it was a large house, Ixtlilxochitl, *Obras históricas*, 1: ch. XCII, 247, ch. XCIV, 257, deduced later that it was the *tecpan*, or palace of the lord of Tlacopan. In the seventeenth century, Ixtlilxochitl, *Obras históricas*, 2: ch. LX, 157; and Torquemada, *Monarquía Indiana*, 4: ch. LXXXVI, 261, explained that the city was practically abandoned, when its lords went to help the Mexicah.

14. We see the same process in the Canary Islands and the Nasrid kingdom of Granada, antecedents of the *Conquista* of the Americas (Castañeda de la Paz and Luque Talaván, "Moctezuma," 26–33). On the king's obligation to reward his vassals, see Vitus Huber's contribution in this volume, and in more detail: Vitus Huber, "The Spiral of Spoils: Booty, Distributive Justice, and Empire Formation in the *Conquista* of New Spain," *Colonial Latin American Review* 31, no. 1 (2022): 133–57.

15. The report is edited in Emma Pérez Rocha and Rafael Tena, eds., *La nobleza indígena del centro de México después de la conquista* (Mexico City: Instituto Nacional de Antropología e Historia, 2000), 108–9. However, the responses of the witnesses were slightly different. One of them pointed out that it was Moteuczoma who asked Quauhpopoca to communicate to the Spaniards the disadvantages of leaving by the Coyoacan causeway. That is the Itztapalapa road but in the direction of Coyoacan. Another witness said that the indications were given by Quauhpopoca when he had seen Moteuczoma dead, although some others specified that the one who had asked how to get out of there was Cortés, at which point Quauhpopoca had answered and assumed his prominent role. Report edited in Pérez Rocha and Tena, eds., *La nobleza indígena del centro de México después de la conquista*, 111–13 and 118–20.

16. Edited in Pérez Rocha and Tena, eds., *La nobleza indígena del centro de México después de la conquista*, 114. However, Cortés, *Cartas, Segunda carta*, 83, pointed out that

when they reached the first bridge that the Mexicah had pulled up to prevent them from crossing, he was the one who replaced it with one that he had brought with him. He agrees that when they crossed it, they were attacked.

17. It is the one dated August 6, 1552. Edited in Pérez-Rocha and Tena, *Nobleza indígena*, 163–65.

18. The lord who ruled Tlacopan when the Spaniards arrived was Totoquihuaztli. His son Don Antonio Cortés ruled during the colonial period, but Tetlepanquetzal ruled during the *Conquista*, although it is unknown whether he was another son of Totoquihuaztli or his brother. Castañeda de la Paz, *Conflictos y alianzas*, 206–8.

19. It is the one dated December 1, 1552. Edited in Pérez-Rocha and Tena, *Nobleza indígena*, 167–78.

20. All quotes in this essay have been translated by V. H., all italics by M.C.P. "A esto agregaré que el dicho mi padre muchas veces prohibió a Muntecuhçoma, tlatoani de México, mover guerra a los españoles; sin embargo él, menospreciando el aviso de mi padre, les hizo la guerra, y así, cuando huyendo de México los españoles pasaron por este mi pueblo, *como ya desde antes [Totoquihuaztli] era su amigo*, nuevamente les dio lo necesario para comer y los libró del hambre extrema que los consumía." Quoted in Pérez-Rocha and Tena, *Nobleza indígena*, 176. Since Totoquihuaztli was on Moteuczoma's side, he presumably was in Tenochtitlan at that time. Then it would be Tetlepanquetzal who fought a hard battle against the Spaniards in Tlacopan, during the Noche Triste.

21. February 20, 1561. Edited in Pérez-Rocha and Tena, *Nobleza indígena*, 245–47.

22. "Ven enhorabuena con tu ejército, y sábete que nosotros estamos prestos a servirte a ti y a aquel en cuyo nombre vienes; *al Dios que tú adoras, adoraré yo con todo mi pueblo; aquí tienes el cu de mis dioses, destrúyelo*, entra y lo que allí encontrares y te agradare tómalo y úsalo." Quoted in Pérez-Rocha and Tena, *Nobleza indígena*, 176.

23. This section was the starting point for another article on various aspects of Cuauhtemoc's life: María Castañeda de la Paz, "Cuauhtemoc: Auge y caída de una leyenda," in *Tenochtitlan, la caída de un imperio: Acercamiento y reflexiones*, ed. Eduardo Matos Moctezuma, Miguel Pastrana Flores, and Patricia Ledesma (Mexico City: Secretaría de Cultura, INAH, 2021): 223–37. Moreover, see Madajczak's contribution to this volume, which focuses on this subject too.

24. Cortés, *Cartas, Quinta carta*, 221, 274–75. Throughout his *Fifth Letter*, Cortés narrated the news that the messengers brought him from Tenochtitlan, which is why he says he did not go into Nicaragua. Cortés, *Cartas, Quinta carta*, 272; see also Torquemada, *Monarquía indiana*, 5: chs. II–VIII, 335–55.

25. Among those that Cuauhtemoc carried were Huanitzin and Tehuetzquititzin, who many years later would come to govern in the cabildo of Tenochtitlan. The former did so in 1538, as Don Diego de Alvarado Huanitzin; the latter in 1554, when he appears as Don Diego de San Francisco Tehuetzquititzin. Castañeda de la Paz, *Conflictos y alianzas*, 241, 251–57.

On the presence of both in the Hibueras, see Domingo Francisco de San Antón Muñón Chimalpahin Cuauhtlehuanitzin, *Las ocho relaciones y el Memorial de Colhuacan*, ed. Rafael Tena, 2 vols. (Mexico City: Conaculta, 1998), *Séptima relación* 2: 169. This *entrada* was followed by others during the sixteenth century. Laura E. Matthew, "Los conquistadores 'mexicanos' de Centroamérica," in *De conquistados a conquistadores: La raíz indígena del reino de la Nueva España. Una mirada renovada*, ed. Alejandro Salafranca (Mexico City: FARO, 2022), 131–46; William R. Fowler, "Los conquistadores mexicanos y los primeros asentamientos urbanos españoles en Centroamérica," in *De conquistados a conquistadores: La raíz indígena del reino de la Nueva España. Una mirada renovada*, ed. Alejandro Salafranca (Mexico City: FARO, 2022), 147–67; Florine Asselbergs, "Pintar lo que no se ha contado: Quauhquechollan, una voz nahua se alza de nuevo," in *De conquistados a conquistadores: La raíz indígena del reino de la Nueva España. Una mirada renovada*, ed. Alejandro Salafranca (Mexico City: FARO, 2022), 209–24.

26. In fact, they do so following Torquemada and Ixtlilxochitl (seventeenth century), who are the first to take this position, as we will see later.

27. Cortés, *Cartas, Quinta carta*, 236–37.

28. Cortés, *Cartas, Quinta carta*, 236–37.

29. It is common in colonial sources to use the name "mexicanos" to refer to the Tenochcah, while the Tlatelolcah are usually "those of Santiago." That is, those of Santiago Tlatelolco. Juan Velázquez Tlacotzin was a member of the royal house of Tenochtitlan (Fernando Alvarado Tezozomoc, *Crónica mexicayotl*, trans. Adrián León [Mexico City: UNAM, Instituto de Investigaciones Históricas, 1992], 164), but he had no rights to access the throne and, much less, Andrés de Tapia Motelchiuhtzin (Castañeda de la Paz, *Conflictos y alianzas*, 191–97). Therefore, it is likely that Díaz del Castillo called them "caciques" for the positions they achieved, thanks to their stratagems in the period of the *Conquista*.

30. Díaz del Castillo, *Historia verdadera*, ch. CLXXVII, 469–70.

31. Díaz del Castillo, *Historia verdadera*, ch. CLXXVII, 470.

32. Tezozomoc, *Crónica mexicayotl*, 165; Chimalpahin, *Ocho relaciones, Séptima relación* II, 167.

33. Tezozomoc, *Crónica mexicayotl*, 5–6.

34. Tezozomoc, *Crónica mexicayotl*, 165.

35. The text does not use the word "baptize" but "to wet the head": "They wet their heads their names were made [*sic*]." Tezozomoc, *Crónica mexicayotl*, 165–66.

36. The oldest version we have of the *Crónica mexicayotl* is, paradoxically, the one handwritten by Chimalpahin, inserted in the so-called *Codex Chimalpahin*. For this matter, see Susan Schroeder, "'*Codex Chimalpahin*': *Society and Politics in Mexico Tenochtitlan, Tlatelolco, Texcoco, Culhuacan and other Nahua Altepetl y Central Mexico*," ed. Arthur J. O. Anderson and Susan Schroeder (Norman: University of Oklahoma Press, 1997), 1: 8–10; and María Castañeda de la Paz, "Los anales del 'Grupo de la Tira de la Peregrinación

o Códice X." Copias, duplicaciones y su uso por parte de los cronistas," *Tlalocan* 15 (2008): 188–93.

37. Chimalpahin, *Ocho relaciones*, 2: 167–69.
38. He added that a chain had them tied from the shackles on their feet to a ceiba tree (*pochote* in the Nahuatl text). Chimalpahin, *Ocho relaciones*, 2: 166.
39. Chimalpahin, *Ocho relaciones*, 2: 167.
40. Torquemada, *Monarquía indiana*, 4: ch. CV, 315–17.
41. Torquemada, *Monarquía indiana*, 4: ch. CV, 316.
42. Torquemada, *Monarquía indiana*, 4: ch. CV, 316.
43. On the day and hour that the sources shuffle, see Madajczak's chapter in this volume.
44. According to Lesbre, the fact that Cortés tried and hanged the members of the Triple Alliance before dawn was also synonymous with the illegality of his trial. Patrick Lesbre, *La construcción del pasado indígena de Tezcoco de Nezahualcóyotl a Alva Ixtlilxochitl*, trans. María Zamudio Vega (Mexico City: Secretaría de Cultura, Instituto Nacional de Antropología e Historia, CEMCA; Zamora: El Colegio de Michoacán, 2016), 260–61.
45. "Si a mi me preguntasen la causa de esta su muerte, diría que fue ésta; y no querer Cortés andar con él tan sobresaltado y cuidadoso con él y con los otros reyes que llevaba en su compañía y no pienso que fue quererse alzar estos tristes indios con la tierra." Torquemada, *Monarquía Indiana*, 4: ch. CV, 317.
46. See note 29.
47. Ixtlilxochitl, *Obras históricas*, 1: 501–5. For the sources from which he drew, see Lesbre, *Construcción*, 385–90; and Jongsoo Lee, *The Allure of Nezahualcoyotl: Pre-Hispanic History, Religion, and Nahua Poetics* (Albuquerque: University of New Mexico Press, 2008), 27–37. Lee did focus on the use of these sources to redraw the figure of Nezahualcoyotl.
48. Ixtlilxochitl, *Obras históricas*, 1: 502.
49. Ixtlilxochitl, *Obras históricas*, 1: 500, 503, 505; Lesbre, *Construcción*, 262–63.
50. Lesbre, *Construcción*, 267.
51. For a more detailed analysis of the facts surrounding this passage, see Lesbre, *Construcción*, 262–68.
52. Ixtlilxochitl, *Obras históricas*, 1: 503.
53. Ixtlilxochitl, *Obras históricas*, 501–4.
54. He is Ixtlilxochitl, with the same name as the chronicler and his ancestor.
55. Ixtlilxochitl, *Obras históricas*, 503.
56. Lesbre, *Construcción*, 260.
57. See Madajczak's chapter in this volume on further interpretations of the representation of the pochote or pochotl.
58. Castañeda de la Paz, *Conflictos y alianzas*, 191–97. In these circumstances, the son of Don Andrés de Tapia Motelchiuhtzin tried to gain a place in the colonial society of the time. He went to Spain to see the king, received a coat of arms and became a *nahuatlato*

(translator) of the Audiencia, although the chronicler Tezozomoc noted that he was the cause of the death of Don Martín Moteuczoma (son of Moteuczoma Xocoyotzin), whom he allegedly poisoned when he returned from Spain. Tezozomoc, *Crónica mexicayotl*, 151; Castañeda de la Paz, *Conflictos y alianzas*, 254.

59. Robert H. Barlow, "Resumen analítico de 'Unos anales históricos de la nación mexicana,'" in *Anales de Tlatelolco: Unos anales históricos de la nación mexicana y Códice Tlatelolco*, ed. Robert H. Barlow and Heinrich Berlin (Mexico City: Ediciones Rafael Porrúa, 1980): xvii–xxxiii, here ix; Hanns J. Prem and Ursula Dyckerhoff, "Los Anales de Tlatelolco: Una colección heterogénea," *Estudios de Cultura Náhuatl* 27 (1997): 181–84.

60. On each of the copies and their particularities, see the works of James Lockhart, ed., *We People Here: Nahuatl Accounts of the Conquest of Mexico* (Eugene, OR: Wipf and Stock, 1993), 37–43; Susanne Klaus, ed., *Anales de Tlatelolco: Los manuscritos 22 y 22bis de la Bibliothèque de France* (Munich: Anton Saurwein, 1999), 7–21; and Rafael Tena, ed., *Anales de Tlatelolco* (Mexico City: Conaculta, 2004), 11–18.

61. Lockhart, *People*, 37–43.

62. Klaus, *Anales de Tlatelolco*, 7; Tena, *Anales de Tlatelolco*, 14–15; Prem and Dyckerhoff, "Anales de Tlatelolco," 181–82, also thought so, because of the typeface used.

63. María Castañeda de la Paz and Michel R. Oudijk, eds., *Códice Mexicanus* (Mexico City: UNAM, Instituto de Investigaciones Antropológicas, Instituto de Investigaciones Filológicas y Coordinación de Humanidades, Colegio Mexiquense; Oaxaca de Juárez: Fundación Alfredo Harp Helú Oaxaca, 2019), 100–102.

64. Kevin Terraciano, "Narrativas de Tlatelolco sobre la conquista de México," *Estudios de Cultura Náhuatl* 47 (2014): 211–35, here 219.

65. Perla Valle, ed., *Ordenanza del Señor Cuauhtemoc* (Mexico City: Estudio de Perla Valle, Gobierno del Distrito Federal, 2000), 44, 133.

66. See Michel Oudijk and María Castañeda de la Paz, "El uso de fuentes históricas en pleitos de tierras: La Crónica X y la Ordenanza de Cuauhtémoc," *Tlalocan* 16 (2009): 255–80.

67. María Castañeda de la Paz, *Verdades y mentiras en torno a don Diego de Mendoza Austria Moctezuma* (Mexico City: UNAM, Instituto de Investigaciones Antropológicas, 2017), 177–80.

68. Stephanie Wood, "Don Diego García de Mendoza Moctezuma: A Techialoyan Mastermind?," *Estudios de Cultura Náhuatl* 19 (1989): 245–68. When a document ends with a certain character, it usually happens that he, his children, or grandchildren were the ones who sent it to be elaborated. That is why Terraciano suggested that Ecatzin or his descendants were the authors of this account of the *Anales de Tlatelolco*, as the story ends with him and his return to Tlatelolco, where he was to receive a series of privileges. Terraciano, "Narrativas," 222. In this case, however, the matter is more complex because of the arguments that I will present.

69. Wood, "Don Diego García," 246; Stephanie Wood, "El problema de la historicidad de Títulos y los códices del grupo *Techialoyan*," in *De tlacuilos y escribanos: Estudios sobre documentos indígenas coloniales del centro de México*, ed. Xavier Noguez and Stephanie Wood (Mexico City: El Colegio Mexiquense; El Colegio de Michoacan, 1998): 167–221, here 176; Oudijk and Castañeda de la Paz, "Fuentes históricas," 267–68.

70. Valle, *Ordenanza*, 45–46.

71. Tena, *Anales de Tlatelolco*, 29, no. 6. It is thus not fortuitous that this name appears only in *Ms. 22bis*, dated in the late colonial period, as does the *Ordenanza*.

72. Castañeda de la Paz, *Conflictos y alianzas*, 160–65.

73. Madajczak's contribution to this volume is mainly about this issue. While we both agree on several aspects, we also offer different interpretations of others.

74. Tena, *Anales de Tlatelolco*, 29.

75. As already noted, versions of Montezuma's death are discordant, although some say that Itzcuauhtzin died with him: Sahagún, *Códice Florentino*, 3 vols. (Mexico City: Archivo General de la Nación, 1979), bk. 12: ch. XXII, fols. 39v–40r; Chimalpahin, *Ocho relaciones*, *Séptima relación* 2: 155. On Itzcuauhtzin, see Barlow, "Resumen analítico," 128–29.

76. As Castañeda de la Paz, *Conflictos y alianzas*, 199–202, pointed out, the chosen one was Temilotzin, as Sahagún, *Historia general*, 2: bk. 7, ch. II, 727; and not Torquemada, *Monarquía indiana*, bk. 4, ch. CII, 311, who stated that it was Ahuelitoc (or Don Juan Ahuelitoc). A *Memorial de los Indios principales de la ciudad de México-Tlatelolco*, elaborated in 1537, corroborates that first it was Temilotl, then Ecatzin, and, after him, Ahuelitoc or Don Juan Mixcoatlaylotlac, as he was also known. Archivo General de Indias, Audiencia de México, vol. 95, exp. 37, fol. 267r.

77. However, it should be remembered that Cuauhtemoc was the son of a Tenochca father (Ahuitzotl) and a Tlatelolca mother (Tiyacapatzin). For this, see Ixtlilxochitl, *Obras históricas*, 2: ch. LXX, 177; and Torquemada, *Monarquía indiana*, bk. 4, ch. LXXX, 248.

78. Note that word "dwarf" is a more historically authentic translation than "little person." In the text the person also appears as "Mexícatl Cotzolóltic," although this second part of the name actually alludes to the physical description of the character, since, as we have already seen, *cotz-tli* is translated as "calf" (Fray Alonso de Molina, *Vocabulario en lengua castellana y mexicana* [1] *y mexicana y castellana* [2] [Mexico City: Porrúa, 2001], 2: fol. 24v) and *ololtic* as "round thing like a ball, or ball" (Alonso de Molina, *Vocabulario en lengua castellana y mexicana* [1] *y mexicana y castellana* [2] 2: fol. 76r). See also Terraciano, "Narrativas," 212.

79. Tena, *Anales de Tlatelolco*, 29. Indeed, the text highlighted his plebeian condition, as Torquemada highlighted that of Tapia or Motelchiuhtzin, for being people who reached a position that under normal circumstances they would never have reached. Terraciano, "Narrativas," 223, also warned about their low status, which is why he was struck by the respect with which Malinche and he treated each other (from the use of language).

80. Tena, *Anales de Tlatelolco*, 35.

81. Tena, *Anales de Tlatelolco*, 29, 31. As Cortés, *Cartas*, 236, *Quinta Relación* pointed out, Acallan was a province, while in the *Anales de Tlatelolco* it seems to allude to a town.

82. Tena, *Anales de Tlatelolco*, 33.

83. Tena, *Anales de Tlatelolco*, 33, 35.

84. Tena, *Anales de Tlatelolco*, 35; Tezozomoc, *Crónica mexicayotl*.

85. See note 76. On Ecatzin and Temilotzin in the sources, see Terraciano, "Narrativas," 219–22.

86. Tena, *Anales de Tlatelolco*, 37.

87. Tena, *Anales de Tlatelolco*, 37.

88. See Tena, *Anales de Tlatelolco*, 35–37, 109, 117–19. However, due to the similarity of the stories and the important role played there by Temilotzin, among other figures, it seems that the anonymous author of this part of the work was based on that of Sahagún, *Historia general*, 3: bk. 12, ch. XXXVIII, 1229. The same happens in Torquemada, *Monarquía indiana*, 2: bk. 4, ch. XCII, 283. It is not coincidental that all of them were written in Tlatelolco. On the prominent role of Temilotzin in Sahagún's work, see also Terraciano, "Narrativas," 220.

89. Tena, *Anales de Tlatelolco*, 39.

90. See Tomás Pérez Vejo, "El Gólgota mexicano: El suplicio de Cuauhtémoc," in *La conquista de la identidad: México y España, 1521–1910*, ed. Tomás Pérez Vejo and Alejandro Salafranca, with the collaboration of Jon Juaristi (Mexico City: Turner y Universidad Autónoma de Nuevo León, 2021), 213–25.

Part III

Power and Negotiations

7

Moteuczoma's Surrender of Power

A Critical Proposal

MIGUEL PASTRANA FLORES

THE PROBLEM

Among the various significant events in the process of the military conquest of Tenochtitlan by the forces of the Spanish-Indigenous alliance, the act of surrender and submission attributed to Moteuczoma Xocoyotzin, in favor of King Charles I of Spain, mediated by Hernando Cortés, stands out. This episode is well known among specialists, but it is convenient to recall it briefly as well as the main sources to have a clearer picture.

According to Cortés's *Second Letter*, Moteuczoma, in his position as *huey tlahtoani*, the title of "great mandatory" or "great ruler" given to the governor of Tenochtitlan, Tetzcoco, and Tlacopan, delivered three speeches on different occasions in which he expressed the same ideas, with minor variations, on the subject of our concern. The first happened during the Spaniards' arrival in Tenochtitlan; the second, at the very act of handing over the command; and the third, during the attempt to remove the sacred images of the Nahua gods in the *huey teocalli*, or Templo Mayor, of Tenochtitlan. Although the chronology of the *Conquista* is imprecise, it can generally be said that the arrival to Tenochtitlan was on November 8, 1519, while the surrender of power and the attempt to take away the images of the Templo Mayor occurred between January and April 1520. According to Cortés, the huey tlahtoani declared that the Mexicah were foreigners, who were brought from distant lands by a "great lord or king... whose vassals they all were,"[1] who returned to his place of origin while the Mexicah remained in the Central Valley. Later, the "great lord" reappeared with the intention of taking the Mexicah with him to their land of origin, but they refused and he withdrew again but not before announcing that he would return to reclaim his command.[2] According to Cortés, Moteuczoma identified this obscure "great lord" with Charles I, to whom Moteuczoma believed he owed obedience, and as soon as they came into direct contact, he turned over political command to Cortés.[3] Moreover, on the second occasion, when the main rulers of the Excan Tlahtoloyan, "the place of the triple seat of command," or Triple Alliance, were gathered, Moteuczoma handed over the power in favor of the king of Spain and exhorted them to obey Cortés. In the words of the latter, the Mexicatl said: "And I greatly beseech you, since to all it is well known, that thus as up until now you have held me and obeyed me as your lord, that from here forward, you might have and obey this great king since he is your natural lord, and in his place have this person as your captain."[4] Even the third of the texts mentioned, the one that refers to the attempt to remove the images of the Nahua gods, suggests that the Mexicah could be related to the Spanish, since it was said that both groups came from the same place. Additionally, the Mexicah had migrated from that place a long time ago; thus, they may have forgotten aspects of the original religion. Cortés wrote:

> They responded to me that they had already explained that they were not originally from this land; and that many ages before, their predecessors had come to it; and that they well believed that they could be in error regarding all that they had believed since so much time had passed since they left their origin; and that I, as one newly come, might know of these things that they were holding and believing better than they, that I might say and have them believe, which they will do since I have told them better.[5]

In this way, according to the captain from Extremadura, the *tlahtoani* of the Mexicah had agreed to surrender the political command, not only of Tenochtitlan but of the entire Excan Tlahtoloyan, in favor of the peninsular monarchy. For Cortés, it was undoubtedly an act of vassalage by Moteuczoma, which also implied a complete surrender, cession, or transfer of the sovereignty of the Mexica tlahtoani to the king of Spain, an act to which full formality and legal value were attributed, since Cortés assured the act was declared before a notary and with the signature of witnesses.[6] Later, however, he states that the documents disappeared during the retreat of the so-called Noche Triste.[7] As if that were not enough, according to Cortés, six days after the arrival in Tenochtitlan, he captivated the huey tlahtoani, who was confined in some of his royal chambers under close surveillance of the Spaniards.

The acceptance of both the factual reality and the legal value of this transfer of power soon became one of the most solid titles of Spanish dominion over the

American lands. This was especially the case for the nascent New Spain, which was conceived as founded on the ancient domains of the Excan Tlahtoloyan. Cortés also used this argument to justify the military campaign against Tenochtitlan after the "Noche Triste" as a "just war" that allegedly subdued "rebellious vassals."[8] Since then, many authors—such as Juan Ginés de Sepúlveda in the sixteenth century, William H. Prescott and Manuel Orozco y Berra in the nineteenth century, Carlos Pereyra, Juan Miralles, and Bernard Grunberg in the twentieth century, and Jaime Montell and Germán Vázquez in the twenty-first century—have accepted this episode as unquestionable truth and Cortés's words as faithful testimonials to the event.[9]

However, this passage of the political process of the *Conquista* of Tenochtitlan and the Cortesian text that refers to it have been the subject of extensive discussions. Since the sixteenth century, several scholars have questioned both the plausibility of the story and its veracity, as well as its factual accuracy and legality. Early authors such as Gonzalo de Oviedo and Bartolomé de Las Casas expressed many doubts about Cortés's words and actions in their works. For instance, the bishop of Chiapas said that it was "manifestly false that Moctezuma ceded jurisdiction to the Kings of Spain over what, by right of nations, belonged to him."[10] The controversy is still present in the works of Eulalia Guzmán, Víctor Frankl, John H. Elliott, Anthony Pagden, Susan Gillespie, and Matthew Restall, among others, who have distrusted the account of Cortés's *Letters* viewed from very diverse ideological and academic trenches, either qualifying them as apocryphal, literary invention, legal fiction, a lie, or malicious misrepresentation.[11] Others—such as Hugh Thomas, Michel Graulich, or Valeria Añón—while accepting a factual core in Cortés's account, warn that it is a tendentious or flatly manipulated text that certainly reflects Cortés's interpretation to justify his actions rather than the authentic words of the Mexica tlahoani.[12] Some other authors, such as Silvio Zavala, emphasize that the Tenochca sovereign and his fellow rulers of the Tlahtoloyan Excan were prisoners under constant coercion, so for this reason they were forced to obey Cortés's command.[13] Antonio de Solís argues that although Moteuczoma rendered vassalage to the king of Spain, in reality he did not intend to keep his word, since "one must believe that Motezuma, no matter how much he looked to the king of Spain as the legitimate successor of that empire, had no intention of fulfilling what he offered. His aim was to get rid of the Spaniards."[14] Even Francisco Martínez thinks that Moteuczoma may have suffered from what today is called Stockholm syndrome, identifying with the interests of his captors.[15]

In any case, various scholars have linked the analysis of Cortés's texts and the actions of their author to a broader legal and political context, thus establishing connections with the tradition of the *Siete partidas* of Alfonso X of Castile, with the theory of papal authority, with the idea of universal empire, with the

Requerimiento elaborated by Juan López de Palacios Rubios, or the concept of *translatio imperii*.[16] Undoubtedly, the controversy and the study of this topic will continue for a long time.

However, the problem can be studied not from a Spanish legal, political, documentary, or historiographical perspective but from what is known about the institutions, beliefs, and political practices of the ancient Nahuas. In other words, it is quite relevant to examine whether the alleged surrender, cession, transfer, or alienation of political command by Moteuczoma in favor of Charles I is in line with what is known about the political world of the ancient Nahuas and, in a complementary way, to ask what sense this alleged cession of command and sovereignty would have within the conceptions, practices, and institutions associated with political power in Nahua culture.

But before doing so, it is appropriate to make some brief observations on the sources of knowledge of the subject. Undoubtedly, the main source is the *Second Letter* of Hernán Cortés, dated October 30, 1520, and first published in 1522. It is the closest testimony in time, and, moreover, it is a text on which others are based.[17] After the *Second Letter*, the main references of Spanish tradition on the subject are the *History of the Conquest of Mexico* by Francisco López de Gómara, published in 1552, which closely follows Cortés's letters with only minor variations in the passages mentioned, and Bernal Díaz del Castillo's *True History of the Conquest of New Spain*, completed about 1568, which, although its author pretended to contradict and correct Gómara's work, in general follows it very closely without significant variations,[18] as observed by Ramón Iglesia and others.[19] Other important works are the *Crónica de la Nueva España* by Francisco Cervantes de Salazar, the first chronicler of Mexico City, who wrote during the lifetime of several conquistadors who were governors of the city and who were his informants; like Bernal, this humanist tried to correct Gómara but also followed him closely in the parts that interest us.[20] On the other hand, the works of conquistador-chroniclers and historians, such as the *Relación de méritos y servicios* by Bernardino Vázquez de Tapia, the "Relación de algunas cosas de las que acaecieron al Muy Ilustre Señor Don Hernando Cortés Marqués del Valle" by Andrés de Tapia, and the *Relación breve de la conquista de la Nueva España* by Fray Francisco de Aguilar, add little information to the discussion. Some merely state that Moteuczoma transferred his power, while others do not even mention the event.[21] There are also the testimonies collected during the trial of Cortés, which provide some interesting nuances, not so much about the transfer of power but about the events surrounding it.[22] Furthermore, the earliest print referring to the meeting between the tlahtoani and Cortés we know today, a German newsletter from late 1521 or early 1522, omits a submission of "Madozoma" but states that after telling his "advisors" that he had allowed the Spanish to enter

Tenochtitlan, he was deposed by the Indigenous and executed on his own request. His son then took command.[23]

In the historiography of the Indigenous tradition, clear and explicit passages on the transfer of power are conspicuous by their absence.[24] Thus, in the main Nahua codices from New Spain that deal with the period, there are no records, mentions, allusions, or simple implications on the subject of the transfer of power.[25] The event is not mentioned either in works as relevant as the *Lienzo de Tlaxcala*, the *Pinturas tlaxcaltecas de la conquista*, the *Codex Vaticanus A*, the *Codex Telleriano Remensis*, or the *Codex Azcatitlan*;[26] nor in less-known codices, such as the *Annals of Tula*, the *Codex en Cruz*, or the *Tira de Tepechpan*.[27] Also missing is the act of handing over power touched upon in the famous account of the conquest collected as Book XII in Fray Bernardino de Sahagún's *General History of the Things of New Spain*. Although it has been claimed that Moteuczoma's welcome speech to Cortés in this book implies some kind of submission to the captain general from Extremadura, this is not clear. The forms of greeting addressed to Cortés have remarkable similarities with those with which the triumphant warriors and Pochtecah were received in pre-Hispanic times.[28] In the corrected version of the text known as *The Conquest of New Spain, 1585 Revision*, according to Fray Bernardino, "certain mistakes were made, namely that some things were improperly included in the narrative of the conquest and others were improperly left out."[29] The greeting speech is omitted: perhaps it was one of those things "improperly left out." Moreover, it should be noted that this reception speech is not followed by any ceremony or ritual confirming the supposed transfer of command. Similarly, the Chalca chronicler Chimalpahin Cuauhtlehuanitzin, in the self-written copy with annotations and variants that he made of Gómara's work, does not add any comment or observation regarding the passages of the *Conquista* studied here. This could imply either that Chimalpahin agreed with this version, or that he had no additional information precisely because the Chalca historical tradition did not mention the subject.

There are two notable exceptions: the works of Fray Diego Durán and Fernando de Alva Ixtlilxóchitl. The former explicitly mentions the surrender of power of the tlahtoani in these terms: "Motecuhzoma submitted to him and surrendered to the service of His Majesty from that hour on."[30] However, some nuances might come to bear, because it is unclear whether in this part of his work the Dominican continues using the so-called *Chronicle X*, a text in Nahuatl of Mexica origins, as the main source. He obviously used a greater quantity and quality of Spanish sources, among them the testimony of his fellow friar Francisco de Aguilar, a former conquistador, who, in turn, follows Cortés's interpretation. Therefore, it is impossible to state whether the passage about the handing over of power corresponds to the Tenochca tradition of *Chronicle X* or to the Spanish version transmitted to him by Aguilar.[31]

Ixtlilxóchitl, for his part, only in the *Historia de la nación chichimeca*, of his five historical works, relates the surrender of power and mentions Moteuczoma's speech of vassalage.[32] Nonetheless, it should be noted that on this point the Tetzcocatl followed Gómara very closely without apparently adding elements of Acolhua origin.[33] On the other hand, in the *Compendio histórico del reino de Texcoco*, Don Fernando wrote just that Moteuczoma "offered to be a friend of the emperor."[34] This is ambiguous and therefore does not contribute to clarify the type of relationship established between the parties. Notwithstanding these deficiencies, all these works and other sources of Indigenous tradition, are fundamental to comprehending the social, conceptual, political, religious, and institutional contexts of the exercise of power among the ancient Nahuas at the moment of contact with the Mediterranean world.

FOUNDATIONS OF POLITICAL POWER IN THE NAHUA WORLD

It can be said that for the ancient Nahuas, political command and its practice were linked, in an organic and indissoluble manner, with multiple aspects of their society, beliefs, and culture. Among these aspects, the following can be recognized as the most relevant.

First,[35] political power found its source in the presence and power of superhuman beings. Indeed, for ancient Mesoamerican beliefs, power had a divine or sacred essence. It was seen as a divine transmission or gift. This belief was manifested in different texts about political command and implied the presence of various gods, not only Quetzalcoatl, as has been often said, but also Tezcatlipoca, Huitzilopochtli, Xiuhtecuhtli, Cihuacoatl, Tlaloc, and Xipe Totec, at least.[36] This body of work allowed Alfredo López Austin to affirm that the rulers were "delegates of the gods."[37]

Second, to exercise command, the tlahtoani was required to receive and concentrate, in his own body, a significant amount of sacred forces and soul entities. On this matter, the ancient Nahuas conceived the human body as able to be a receptacle for those forces and entities. This ability was common for every human being but was increased in the case of the ruler. Fray Diego Durán summarized this condition when he said that "it is not a fable to say that their lords were taken for gods because in reality they were adored as gods."[38] In that sense, there are abundant references to the concentration of sacred forces in the tlahtoani's body. For example, it was mentioned that his feet could not directly touch the ground, related to the idea that the nature of the sacred forces that inhabit his body forbade him to make direct contact with the mundane world. Likewise, the fact that no one could look directly into his eyes responds precisely to the idea that through his gaze the tlahtoani could transmit part of his strength and cause illness and even death to common people. This power can also be observed in the first meeting between Moteuczoma and Cortés that occurred on the road from Itztapalapa: the latter gets off his horse to embrace the tlahtoani but is stopped by two Nahua lords, who prevent physical contact that would be risky, possibly fatal, for the Spaniard, given Moteuczoma's sacred force. Cortés reported it this way: "And when we met, I dismounted and went to embrace him alone, and those two lords who were with him stopped me with their hands so I would not touch him."[39] Gómara captured part of the sacredness of the act when he wrote, "Cortés . . . went to embrace him as is our custom. Those who were at his [Moteuczoma's] arms stopped him [Cortés], so that he would not reach him, since it was a sin to touch him."[40] While Juan de Torquemada said it more clearly: "Those who carried him [Moteuczoma] by the arm stopped him [Cortés] because it seemed to them that it was a great sin for any man to touch him [Moteuczoma], because they considered him as something divine."[41] In a complementary way, the very action of touching the leader from Extremadura implies that direct physical contact with him was not considered dangerous for the Nahua dignitaries.[42]

Third, one needed to have the required lineage, to aspire to power; it was indispensable to belong to a prestigious lineage, mainly of Toltec roots, as modern historians have been pointing out since Alfredo Chavero.[43] Although it is generally correct that having such lineage was essential, it is also true that it was not enough. Lines of descent linked to other prominent figures were likewise relevant, such as Xolotl for the Acolhuah, or Tezozomoc from Azcapotzalco among the Tepanecah. In any case, it cannot be affirmed that the Spaniards were considered part of prestigious lineages. They were strangers and obviously ignorant of the Nahua protocol. Additionally, they had brought too few Spanish women with them to establish reciprocal matrimonial links with the Indigenous allies.

Fourth, as is widely known, the system for the succession in leadership among the Mexicah consisted of a system of collective deliberations and designation carried out by the *tlahtocan*. Under normal conditions, this "Council of Four" or "supreme council" was constituted by the huey tlahtoani, the *cihuacoatl*, and four great dignitaries called *tlachocalcatl, tlacatecatl, tlillancalqui*, and *ezhuahuacatl*. The *tlahtoque* of Tetzcoco and Tlacopan intervened in the designation of a new ruler as well and almost certainly also the rulers of other cities of the Central Valley, such as Itztapalapa and Ehecatepetl, along with the high priests of the huey teocalli of Tenochtitlan, the Tlaloc *tlamacazqui* and *Totec tlamacazqui*, as well as the lords of lords (*teuctlahtoque*), the *achcaucauhtin*, and the *yaotequihua*. Therefore, one can infer that as in the case of a change of huey tlahtoani, all these dignitaries had to participate in the process of designation. As far as it is possible to know, there are no signs of the participation of the tlahtoque in such a relevant occasion as the supposed cession of power of Moteuczoma in favor of Charles I or Cortés.[44] In addition, in the case of the designation of the tlahtoani, the decision of the tlahtoque was considered inspired by the deities. For that reason, it could be neither overruled nor appealed, because as the Sahaguntine texts say: "The kings and lords who elected you, signaling and ordering that through the inspiration of our lord god, whose election one cannot abrogate nor vary because it occurred through divine inspiration."[45]

Fifth, all the preceding indicates that the transmission of power required a strong ceremonial frame. This also implied a complex ritual, both for the management of the sacral forces that were concentrated in the ruler and for the public exercise of his diverse duties. This ceremonial facet was reflected in several of the fundamental functions and prerogatives of the ruler. In fact, among the ancient Nahuas, the tlahtoani was much more than the main political leader. He likewise served as high priest in the most important public ceremonies, as he presided over various rituals related to the renewal of the natural world and society. Furthermore, he was the highest judge within the Nahua legal system. Thus, death sentences had to be ratified by him. For all these reasons, he was seen as the head of the social body and the "heart of the city";[46] that is, he was considered the center of conscience and decision making of Tenochtitlan and the whole Mexica society.

On the other hand, it is clear that Nahua thought included mechanisms, conditions, and instances by which a ruler could lose power.[47] Due to its ritual, political, and social transcendence, this was always a collective decision. Only the highest authorities of the Excan Tlahtoloyan could order the execution of a tlahtoani and his lineage. Therefore, it can be inferred that, the tlahtocan, or Council of the Four, had an obligation to be involved in the possible death of the ruler. An "ancient speech" (*huehuetlahtolli*) collected by Fray Bernardino de Sahagún, for instance, speaks of the consequences of the bad performance of a tlahtoani.[48] In some cases it seems that the elder leaders of the housing units (*calpulltin*) of the common population could intervene, asking a higher authority, such as the Excan Tlahtoloyan, to execute a ruler and his lineage for failing to fulfill their obligations.[49]

All the factors presented necessarily implied the death of the current ruler and the participation of his entire lineage in order to designate a new ruler. As far as the sources of the Mesoamerican history can tell us, no other similar cases exist among the Nahuas, the Maya in the Classic period, the Mixtecah, or Zapotecah about the transmission or loss of power of a living ruler in favor of other rulers.[50] The situation gets even more tangled because the case under analysis would be a supposed voluntary transmission of power from the main Mesoamerican ruler of the time in favor of a foreign figure, in this case, Charles I, through Cortés, of whom the Nahuas knew very little and who, as we have seen, they did not consider to possess sacral powers equivalent to those of Moteuczoma.

MOTEUCZOMA BEFORE STRANGERS

To evaluate the feasibility of the surrender of power in the first place, we must take notice that the huey tlahtoani was imprisoned along with other rulers belonging to the Excan Tlahtoloyan. In fact, the Spanish leader, following the tradition of Renaissance warfare, not only imprisoned Moteuczoma but also took other important rulers and dignitaries as prisoners. They were undoubtedly under strong political, physical, and psychological coercion by Cortés. Thus, it cannot be claimed that their acts were voluntarily free.

On the other hand, it is necessary to consider whether the Tenochca huey tlahtoani had enough authority to decide on his own such a radical issue as to alienate the power of the whole Excan Tlahtoloyan in favor of a stranger. "The place of the triple seat command" was a very complex political institution. It included two other huey tlahtoque, of Tlacopan and Tetzcoco, which had their own structure and hierarchy of command, in addition to multiple commanders, like the *tlahtocayotl* and *tecuhcayotl*, that formed part of this peculiar institution—all with their own rulers. This complexity has influenced how this political, military, and legal formation has been conceived, whether as an "empire" ruled by an "autocrat," or whether as a confederation, a segmentary state, or some other institution. It can be deduced that Cortés himself lacked a clear notion of the nature of command. Consequently, he imprisoned all the governors and rulers he could to try to control the situation in his favor. As far as is known, major decisions were discussed and made collectively. Therefore, the huey tlahtoani alone most likely lacked sufficient authority to take power away from all the other rulers of the Excan Tlahtoloyan.

Furthermore, although Francisco López de Gómara insisted that Moteuczoma and the Mexicah thought that Cortés was Quetzalcoatl,[51] this allegation is questionable. Many works of both Indigenous and Spanish traditions contain enough elements to doubt such an identification.[52] Cortés says nothing about this subject. It is also very debatable how long such confusion could have lasted, if there was any: if it was only during the first contacts in the Gulf Coast, or until the alliance with Tlaxcala, which was made in terms of a political-military pact between equals,[53] or until the slaughter of Chololan, which, being Quetzalcoatl's main sanctuary in Mesoamerica, made it inconceivable that the deity would have attacked his own community. It should be remembered how, according to the testimony of Cortés, Moteuczoma affirmed that in his conception the Spaniards were, like him, common men and not extraordinary beings: "See me here because I am flesh and blood as you and all are, and I am mortal and physical."[54] Finally, as the lawyers would say, admitting without conceding that such identification existed and was maintained until the supposed handing over of power, it is necessary to acknowledge that although Quetzalcoatl is a god closely linked to political command, he is not the only deity with that nexus. The transfer of power would thus have to be made with the participation of all the deities mentioned above and not just by one. However, there are no references to rites, ceremonies, invocations, calls, prayers, symbols, or simple allusions to these deities in the alleged act of transfer of power.

Then again, hypothetically admitting the identification of Cortés as Quetzalcoatl, one must keep in mind that the latter represented the priestly model in the Nahua world.[55] Consequently, the supposed transition of command, and therefore of functions, would imply that the condition of high priest of the Nahua gods was transmitted to Cortés too. This seems absurd since it would imply a total contradiction of Nahua and Spanish perspectives regarding Cortés's policies, speeches, and actions against the sacred images of the Nahua gods and their places of worship. He tried to destroy the former while intending to convert the latter into spaces of veneration of Christian images. For the Nahuas, such actions were incomprehensible sacrileges, while for the Spaniards they were signs of zeal and devotion.

Moreover, according to the Nahuas, the transfer of power would be not only a matter of a change of political command between mere human beings but of moving the sacral forces that sustain power from one person to another. Moteuczoma, in his duty as huey tlahtoani, could not simply renounce his condition in favor of another person. He would have to dispose himself of the sacral forces that make up his very condition as a leader in the first place. A new ruler who had passed through all the ritual phases was solemnly told to have acceded to a new condition that distanced him from common human beings.[56] For this reason, the rulers had to die so that they would be detached from the forces and soul entities that were concentrated in their bodies. Otherwise, they would continue to be dangerous, as living receptacles of energies that held the basis of power and political command. In this sense, it is worth reflecting that just as the transmission of power in the Nahua world implied a complex ritual, one would expect a similar or equivalent ritual to carry out the transfer of command from Moteuczoma to Cortés. Yet, there is no allusion to it, neither in the Spanish nor in the Indigenous sources.

Gómara and Bernal Díaz state that shortly before the arrival of the expedition of Pánfilo de Narváez, Moteuczoma asked Cortés to leave Tenochtitlan and the whole region. Allegedly, the Mexicah and other inhabitants of the Central Valley as well as the Nahua gods themselves were all very angry, and the death of the Spaniards was already being planned. Gómara writes that the tlahtoani said the following:

> I beg you to leave this my city and land, that my gods are very angry with me because I have you here. Ask me for whatever you want, and I will give it to you, because I love you very much. And do not think that I tell you this mockingly, but very truly. Therefore, let it be done in any case.[57]

If Moteuczoma had indeed transferred his quality of huey tlahtoani to Cortés—that is, his condition of chief ruler, high priest, and supreme judge, among others—such an act would be inexplicable. Moteuczoma would no longer have the authority to execute it. If he did it nonetheless, as the Spanish testimonies claim, it would imply that he still conserved, at least in a nominal way and from his own perspective, sufficient authority and legitimacy to undertake such an act. In other words, either the transmission of power had not occurred, or, at least, it had not been carried out in a way that was complete or acceptable to the rest of the Mexica society. To conclude this discussion: it has become clear that Cortés coerced the imprisoned Indigenous dignitaries to carry out a legal writ of vassalage to justify his actions. This writ, though, was incompatible with the very nature of political command in the Nahua world and completely lacked meaning and value for the Mexicah and their allies.

LOSS OF POWER

From the Nahua point of view, Moteuczoma could not and did not hand over the command to Cortés, nor did he consider himself a vassal of Charles I. In this sense, the questions that remain ask how the tlahtoani lost power and, in a complementary way, at what moment the rupture occurred. To answer we must briefly review some episodes spanning from the kidnapping to the death of the *tlacatecuhtli*, including the massacre at the Templo Mayor. The first signs of a gradual loss of authority appear just after the Spaniards had captured Moteuczoma, first manifested as a resistance of the Tenochca administration to provide the Spanish with the supplies they required. In the Nahuatl text of the *Florentine Codex* it says:

> But when he summoned forth the noblemen, no longer did they obey him. They only grew angry. No longer did they come to him, no longer did they go to him. No longer was he heeded. But nevertheless he was not therefore neglected; he was given all that he required—food and drink, and water [and] fodder for the deer [horses].[58]

This is corroborated by the Jesuit Juan de Tovar in his work:

> And because they strongly suspected that the dealings with the Spaniards, the natives out of fear began to hide and to fail to provide everything that the Spanish needed. They began to suffer hunger, especially the horses and helper dogs that they had brought with them that were very fierce and useful in war; it came to such a state that the native allies and some Mexican went in search of supplies for them.[59]

Another important moment that indicates that the authority of Moteuczoma as huey tlahtoani began to be questioned is the attempt by Cacama, tlahtoani of

Tetzcoco, to liberate the huey tlahtoani. Fernando de Alva Ixtlilxóchitl recounted the scene as follows: "Seen by king Cacama the little spirit and determination of the Mexicans, he left the city and went to Tetzcuco to gather his people, and with them to liberate his uncle and Mexican nobility from the servitude and affront in which they lived."[60] Shortly thereafter, Cacama was captured before he could carry out his intentions.

Additionally, according to Bernal Díaz, Moteuczoma said the following during the aforementioned request to Cortés to leave Nahua lands:

> Oh, Mister Malinche and Mister captains, how much it weighs on me of the answer and command that our teules have given to our fathers and to me and to all my leaders! And we give you war and kill you, or make you go away via the sea. I have learned from this and it seems that, before they start the war, you should leave this city and none of you should remain here. And this, Mr. Malinche, I tell you to do in every way that suits you; otherwise, they will kill you. And look how you lose your lives.[61]

This implies that the ruler's position was being questioned by various sectors of the Tenochca society and possibly also by the rest of the political forces of the Excan Tlahtoloyan.

When Cortés left for the Gulf Coast to confront and finally defeat Narváez, Pedro de Alvarado was left in charge of Tenochtitlan and the hostages. As is well known, the local inhabitants asked for permission to celebrate the feast of Toxcatl. This was one of the most important festivals, since it celebrated Tezcatlipoca, the ancient trickster god and one of the main gods linked to political power, and Huitzilopochtli, the patron deity of the Mexicah. Whether it was because Alvarado thought that an ambush was being prepared against him and he panicked as suggested by the conquistador-chroniclers, or because he was as mad and evil as some Indigenous sources say, or for some other reason, the fact is that the Spaniards killed the Mexicah during the latter's ritual. This caused great human losses in the commanding elite and provoked a violent reaction. As soon as the word of the incident had spread, the enraged population attacked the Spanish-Tlaxcalteca forces and besieged them in their quarters.[62]

Once the counterattack of the inhabitants of Tenochtitlan against the Spanish-Tlaxcalan occupation began, it was no longer possible to stop it. After defeating Narváez, Cortés returned to Tenochtitlan. The Mexicah allowed Cortés and his men to enter Tenochtitlan, then immediately isolated them and cut off their supplies. This again implies a deterioration of the tlahtoani's power. Cortés asked him to normalize the activities in the city, especially on the market of Tlatelolco, to guarantee the supply of food. The tlahtoani said that he had to send someone he trusted to take charge of the matter. Cortés agreed and, according to Francisco Cervantes de Salazar's *Crónica de la Nueva España*, "Motezuma sent his brother, the lord of Itztapalapa, whom, as they saw outside the Mexicans... did not let him return to the prison nor did they do the *tianguez* [sic]; rather they chose him as their leader and Captain."[63] That refers to Cuitlahua, who neither complied with Cortés's orders nor returned to the Spanish camp. Rather, the hostilities against the Spaniards resumed. Torquemada corroborates the account that once free, Cuitlahua coordinated the Tenochca resistance against the occupying Spanish-Indigenous forces.[64] On the other hand, Bernardino Vásquez de Tapia, in his testimonies in Cortés's evaluation of office (*juicio de residencia*), lets shine through that the tlahtoani, before Cortés treated him badly, arranged the attack of the Mexicah against the Spaniards without worrying about his personal security:

> And when the said Motunzuma saw how little means the said Don Hernando Cortés had, he sent to tell the Indios—as a man who was unhappy and desperate to see himself imprisoned and the way things were going—that they should do whatever they wanted and not show any consideration for him. And from then on the Indios began to kill the Christians wherever they could. And the city and the whole land rose up against the Christians.[65]

Thus, despite Cortés's efforts, his men were still under siege. Therefore, he asked Moteuczoma to go out on the roof and calm down the crowd. The first to speak was the lord of Tlatelolco, who asked for the cessation of hostilities and announced the presence of the huey tlahtoani. However, according to Sahagún, when Moteuczoma appeared, the effect was very different:

> When the Mexicans and Tlatelolcans heard these voices, they began to confront and curse at Motecuçoma among themselves saying: "What does that bugger Motecuçoma have to say and you scoundrels with him? We will not stop the war." Then they began to raise the cry and to throw arrows and spears toward where he spoke, beside Motecuçoma.[66]

Beyond the dispute over who killed Moteuczoma, whether the Spaniards with a sword or the Mexica with stones, what is relevant for this study is that this scene is a visible rupture between the imprisoned huey tlatoani and the political institutions of Mexica society. From this moment on, the Mexicah no longer obeyed him. That they reviled him makes evident the severe erosion of his authority and legitimacy. Without these indispensable conditions for exercising political command, the effective loss of power itself happens.

In this regard it should be noted that since his captivity, Moteuczoma has incurred in serious failures in his responsibilities as huey tlahtoani, mainly in what touches four fundamental aspects: First, he neglected the waging of war: not only did he not undertake new campaigns, but several villages had rebelled and their bitter enemies, the Tlaxcaltecah, had settled in the city. Second, he had not complied with the administration of justice according to Nahua rules and principles. Cortés had judged and even executed high dignitaries, such as Cuauhpopoca, without following the rules. Third, Moteuczoma had not fulfilled his religious obligations, especially the official public cult and the sacrifices to the gods had not been continued in a scrupulous manner, since they had been hindered by the Christians. Fourth, the mere presence of a Spanish-Indigenous military force put the security of the city in question, particularly due to the attendance of the Tlaxcalans. All these aspects played into the loss of power among the ancient Nahuas.[67]

The works of Spanish tradition, due to their own perspective, do not speak of the matter; while the works of Indigenous tradition, although they give clues about what happened among the commanding elite, only allow us to glimpse that it is a more complex process of Moteuczoma's gradual political weakening that is catalyzed by the massacre of Templo Mayor, before which, it can be inferred, the priests of Huitzilopochtli expressed a divine mandate by which the forces of the gods abandoned the tlahtoani.

The Spanish sources offer two possibilities for understanding what happened with the succession: A first version indicates that Cuitlahua was elected *after* the death of the huey tlahtoani. Other versions say that the former was elected the successor while the latter was still alive. This testimony of Cortés supports the first version:

> Of those whom they captured in the city of Buacachula [Huaquechula], specially the wounded one, I knew completely about the things of the great city of Timixtitlan [Tenochtitlan] and how after the death of Muteçuma a brother of his had succeeded in the lordship, who was lord of Yztapalapa, called Cuetravaçin [Cuitlahuatzin], who succeeded in the lordship because the son of Muteçuma, who would have inherited, died in the bridges.[68]

Other authors agreed with Cortés; for example, Alva Ixtlilxóchitl said: "The Spaniards left, then the Mexicans made a brother of Moteuczoma called Cuitlahuatzin lord."[69] Torquemada also reiterated it on three occasions: In the first one, he says that they chose Cuitlahua "for their caudillo,"[70] and not as tlahtoani. In the second one, it is Moteuczoma himself who supposedly responded to Cortés's questions regarding a possible succession while they were under siege: "[Moteuczoma] said that they would not dare to elect a king in Mexico, him being alive."[71] Later in his text, the Franciscan specified that the succession process took place after the Native and Spanish warriors had returned to Tlaxcala. He also mentioned that the tlahtocan was renewed, which is an interesting fact because other sources point out that the "supreme council" was renewed precisely at the moment of designation of a new ruler.[72]

For his part, Bernal Díaz in his *True History* stated that Cuitlahua was named the new tlahtoani when Moteuczoma was still alive. According to the author, when the latter tried to appease the Mexicah, the following happened:

> And many captains and principal Mexicans knew him well... and crying they said to him: "Oh lord and our great lord, how all your evil and damage and that of your children and relatives weighs on us! We make you aware that already we have raised a relative of yours as lord." And there he called him as he was named, they said Coadlavaca [Cuitlahua], lord de Iztapalapa.[73]

Considering the characteristics of the ruler, and the nature of power among the ancient Nahuas, the importance of rituality, as well as the mechanisms of deliberation and collective designation developed by the tlahtocan, the version that sustains that a new ruler was designated *after* the death of Moteuczoma is more consistent. As far as we can know, apparently between the lord of Iztapalapa's release from captivity and Moteuczoma's entry on the balcony was the culminating moment when Moteuczoma lost his power.[74] For that reason the designation and the investiture of Cuitlahua as new tlahtoani happened around September 7, 1520. His government was brief, because he fell sick during the smallpox epidemic that broke out in that time. He died around November 25 of that same year after being only four 20-day periods (*veintenas*) in command.[75]

CONCLUSION

For Cortés and the Spanish Crown, the surrender of Moteuczoma's power was fundamental to explaining and justifying the military events that led to the fall of Tenochtitlan, as well as the constitution of New Spain as an integral part of the nascent Spanish dominion overseas. It was even indispensable in the very constitution of the notion of an empire that did not depend on the antecedent of the Holy Roman Empire but on the surrender of an American empire in favor of the Crown of Castile. However, even the Crown doubted both the absolute veracity and complete legality of Cortés's words and deeds. That is why at various times the descendants of Moteuczoma had to endorse the surrender of power in favor of the Castilian kings. In the seventeenth century, Antonio Vázquez de Espinosa said the following in this regard:

> Don Pedro Tesifón Motezuma and his brothers gave the Majesty of King Philip III... in Madrid before Gerónimo Fernández, public notary, on January 26, 1612, the

share and right they might have to the kingdoms and states of New Spain, which had belonged to their great-grandfather, Emperor Motezuma.[76]

In the same sense there was another donation to the next monarch, Philip IV, as expressed by the Jesuit and descendant of the tlahtoani, Diego Luis Motezuma:

> And the title of his right by the renunciation of the Emperor Motezuma has been of such superior esteem, above all others, that, to reestablish and strengthen it, at the request of the lord King Don Felipe IV and his Council of the Indies, the Count of Motezuma, third grandson of that Emperor, made a new renunciation of all his right to the Mexican crown in favor of the royal house of Castile.[77]

Moteuczoma's surrender of power in favor of the Spanish Crown remained relevant until the beginning of the nineteenth century. When Napoleonic troops invaded the Iberian Peninsula and King Charles IV and Crown Prince Ferdinand abdicated in favor of the French, a debate began in the American dominions regarding the legality of the fact and the transmission of sovereignty. The Creoles of New Spain argued that the initial pact between rulers and the ruled was broken and one should return to the very foundations of that relationship.[78] On the other hand, from what is known of the Mesoamerican political world in general and of the ancient Nahuas in particular, such handing over of power, in the terms referred to and assumed by the Spaniards, appears as frankly impossible, impracticable, or at least as extremely doubtful.

Thus, for the Spanish world the surrender of power was a political, legal, and historiographical necessity of the first order. It was indispensable to justify and explain in juridical, political, military, and even personal terms the nascent New Spain. For the Mesoamerican world, it was simply an impossibility from the sacred, ritual, political, and social perspective of the very nature of power and exercise of command. Therefore, based on the existent sources, it seems impossible to fully explain what happened to the Mexica and Excan Tlahtoloyan command structure between the entry of the Spanish-Indigenous forces into Tenochtitlan and the rise to power of Cuitlahua, despite the rivers of ink that have flowed regarding the subject.

NOTES

Translated from Spanish by Vitus Huber. A first version of this essay was published as "La entrega del poder de Motecuhzoma: Una propuesta crítica," *Estudios de Historia Novohispana*, no. 62 (2020): 111–44. I thank the editors of *Novohispana* for their permission to publish this new edition and Patricia Ledesma Bouchan for revising its language.

1. (All quotes were translated by V. H. and John F. Schwaller, except when referenced to English editions.) Hernán Cortés, *Cartas de relación*, ed. Ángel Delgado Gómez (Madrid: Castalia, 1993), 210–11.
2. Cortés, *Cartas de relación*, 227.
3. Cortés, *Cartas de relación*, 228.
4. "Y mucho os ruego, pues a todos es notorio todo esto, que así como hasta aquí a mí me habéis tenido y obedescido por señor vuestro, de aquí adelante tengáis y obedezcáis a este grand rey pues él es vuestro señor natural, y en su lugar tengáis a éste su capitán." Cortés, *Cartas de relación*, 228.
5. "Me respondieron que ya me habían dicho que ellos no eran naturales desta tierra y que había muchos tiempos que sus predecesores habían venido a ella; y que bien creían que podían estar errados en algo de aquello que tenían [creían] por haber tanto tiempo que salieron de su naturaleza [su lugar de origen], y que yo, como más nuevamente venido sabría las cosas que debían tener y creer mejor que ellos, que se las dijese e hiciese entender, que ellos harían lo que yo les dijese que era lo mejor." Cortés, *Cartas de relación*, ed. Delgado Gómez, 239.
6. "Todo pasó ante un escribano público y lo asentó por abto en forma y yo le pedí ansí por testimonio en presencia de muchos españoles." Cortés, *Cartas de relación*, 229.
7. Cortés, *Cartas de relación*, 228, 288.
8. See Silvio Zavala, *Hernán Cortés ante la justificación de su conquista*, in *Hernán Cortés y el derecho internacional en el siglo XVI*, ed. Toribio Esquivel Obregón, 2nd ed. (Mexico City: Porrúa, 1985), 128.
9. See Juan Ginés de Sepúlveda, *Historia del Nuevo Mundo*, ed. Antonio Ramírez de Verger (Madrid: Alianza, 1987), 157–59; William H. Prescott, *History of the Conquest of Mexico and History of the Conquest of Peru* (New York: Modern Library, 1966), 441–53; Manuel Orozco y Berra, *Historia antigua y de la conquista de México*, ed. Ángel M. Garibay and Miguel León-Portilla, 2nd ed., 4 vols. (Mexico City: Porrúa, 1978), 4: 290–92; Carlos Pereyra, *Hernán Cortés*, with the collaboration of Martín Quirarte, 4th ed. (Mexico City: Porrúa, 2006), 153; Juan Miralles, *Hernán Cortés: Inventor de México*, 2 vols. (Mexico City: Folio/ABC, 2002), 1: 184–85; Bernard Grunberg, *Histoire de la conquete du Mexique* (Paris: L'Hartmattan, 1995), 103; Jaime Montell, *La conquista de México Tenochtitlan* (Mexico City: Porrúa, 2001), 513–14; Germán Vázquez Chamorro, *Moctezuma* (Madrid: Algaba, 2006), 235–40.
10. Bartolomé de Las Casas, *De thesauris*, ed. Ángel Losada and Martín Lassegue (Madrid: Alianza, 1992), ch. XXXII, 351; Gonzalo Fernández de Oviedo y Valdés, *Historia general y natural de las Indias*, ed. Juan Pérez de Tudela (Asunción, Paraguay: Atlas, 1959), 4: 259.
11. Eulalia Guzmán, "Prólogo" and "Aclaraciones y rectificaciones," in *Relaciones de Hernán Cortés a Carlos V sobre la invasión de Anáhuac*, ed. Eulalia Guzmán (Mexico City: Libros Anáhuac, 1958), 11–203; Víctor Frankl, "Imperio particular e imperio universal en las

cartas de relación de Hernán Cortés," *Cuadernos Hispanoamericanos* 165 (1963), 443–82; the excellent work of John H. Elliott, "Cortés, Velázquez and Charles V," in *Letter from Mexico*, Hernán Cortés, ed. Anthony Pagden (New Haven, CT: Yale University Press, 2001), 11–37; John H. Elliott, "The Mental World of Hernán Cortés," *Royal Historical Society Transactions. Fifth Series* 17 (1967): 41–58; Anthony Pagden, "Introduction" and "Notes," in *Letter from Mexico*, Hernán Cortés, ed. Anthony Pagden (New Haven, CT: Yale University Press, 2001), 39–71; Susan Gillespie, *Los reyes aztecas: La reconstrucción del gobierno en la historia mexica*, trans. Stella Mastrangelo (Mexico City: Siglo XXI, 1986); Matthew Restall, *Cuando Moctezuma conoció a Cortés* (Mexico City: Taurus, 2019).

12. Hugh Thomas, *La conquista de México*, trans. Víctor Alba (Barcelona: Patria, 1994), 324; Michel Graulich, *Moctezuma: Apogeo y caída del imperio azteca*, trans. Tessa Brisac (Mexico City: Era; Instituto Nacional de Antropología e Historia, 2014), 422–24; Valeria Añón, ed., "Prólogo" y "Notas," in *Segunda Carta de Relación y otros textos*, by Hernán Cortés (Buenos Aires: Corregidor, 2010), 9–88, here 158–59, n. 137.

13. Zavala, *Cortés*, 127.

14. "Se debe de creer que Motezuma, por más que mirase al rey de España como legítimo sucesor de aquel imperio, no tuvo intento de cumplir lo que ofrecía. Su mira fue deshacerse de los españoles." Antonio de Solís y Rivadeneira, *Historia de la conquista de México: Población y progresos de la América Septentrional, conocida por el nombre de Nueva España*, ed. Edmundo O'Gorman and José Valero Silva, 5th ed. (Mexico City: Porrúa, 1990), bk. 4, ch. III, 205.

15. Francisco Martínez Hoyos, *Breve historia de Hernán Cortés* (Madrid: Nowtilus, 2014), 152. For the problem implied by the concept of that "syndrome," see Lucía Ester Rizo-Martínez, "El síndrome de Estocolmo: Una revisión sistemática," *Clínica y Salud* 29, no. 2 (2018), accessed May 1, 2023, http://dx.doi.org/10.5093/clysa2018a12.

16. See Silvio Zavala, *La filosofía política en la Conquista de América*, with the collaboration of Rafael Altamira, 3rd ed. (Mexico City: Fondo de Cultura Económica, 1977); José Valero Silva, *El legalismo de Hernán Cortés como instrumento de su conquista* (Mexico City: Universidad Nacional Autónoma de México, 1965); Víctor Frankl, "Hernán Cortés y la tradición de las Siete Partidas," *Revista de Historia de América* 53–54 (1962): 9–74; and Richard Konetzke, *América Latina II: La época colonial*, trans. Pedro Scaron (Mexico City: Siglo XXI, 1995), 20–33.

17. See Ramón Iglesia, *Cronistas e historiadores de la Conquista de México: El ciclo de Hernán Cortés* (Mexico City: El Colegio de México, 1990).

18. Francisco López de Gómara, *Historia de la conquista de México*, with the collaboration of Jorge Gurría Lacroix, 2nd ed. (Caracas: Ayacucho, 1991), ch. XCII, 145–46; Bernal Díaz de Castillo, *Historia verdadera de la conquista de la Nueva España*, ed. Guillermo Serés and Miguel León-Portilla, 2 vols. (Mexico City: Academia Mexicana de la Lengua, 2014), 1: ch. LXXXIX, CI, 315–16, 375–77.

19. Ramón Iglesia, *El hombre Colón y otros ensayos*, with the collaboration of Álvaro Matute (Mexico City: Fondo de Cultura Económica, 1986), 109–38; see also Guillermo Serés, "Estudio Bernal Díaz del Castillo y la «Historia verdadera»," "Notas," and "Notas complementarias," in Bernal Díaz del Castillo, *Historia verdadera de la conquista de la Nueva España*, ed. Guillermo Serés and Miguel León-Portilla, 2 vols. (Mexico City: Academia Mexicana de la Lengua, 2014), 2: 1131–32 6; 1: 377–78.

20. Francisco Cervantes de Salazar, *Crónica de la Nueva España*, with the collaboration of Juan Miralles Ostos (Mexico City: Porrúa, 1985), bk. 4, ch. XLV, 371–73.

21. Bernardino Vázquez de Tapia, *Relación de méritos y servicios del conquistador Bernardino Vázquez de Tapia*, ed. Jorge Gurría Lacroix (Mexico City: Universidad Nacional Autónoma de México, 1972), 40–41; Andrés de Tapia, "Relación de algunas cosas de las que acaecieron al Muy Ilustre Señor Don Hernando Cortés Marqués del Valle, desde que se determinó ir a descubrir tierra en la Tierra Firme del mar Océano," in *Crónicas de la Conquista de México*, ed. Agustín Yáñez (Mexico City: Universidad Nacional Autónoma de México, 1939), 41–96; Francisco de Aguilar, *Relación breve de la conquista de la Nueva España*, ed. Jorge Gurría Lacroix (Mexico City: Universidad Nacional Autónoma de México, 1980).

22. See *Documentos cortesianos*, 4 vols. (Mexico City: Fondo de Cultura Económica, UNAM, 1990), 2: *1526–1545 Sección IV. Juicio de Residencia*; Thomas, *Conquista*, 699–700, reproduces the testimony of Francisco de Flores, which agrees almost point for point with that of Cortés, which leads us to believe that he had read and followed Cortés's *Second Letter*.

23. Restall, *Cuando Moctezuma*, 120–22.

24. Miguel Pastrana Flores, *Historias de la conquista: Aspectos de la historiografía de tradición náhuatl* (Mexico City: UNAM, 2004), 119–209.

25. Miguel Pastrana Flores, "Códices anotados del centro de México," in *Historiografía novohispana de tradición indígena*, ed. José Rubén Romero Galván (Mexico City: UNAM, 2003), 51–84. In the scene of the *Vatican Codex A*, where in the year *ce ácatl* (one reed) there is the figure of a Spaniard on horseback, who brandishes a sword and carries a standard, in front, according to Patrick Johansson, is an Indigenous apparently offering the Spaniard a necklace. This figure has the name of Moteuczoma, meaning that the ruler is "humiliated" in front of the conquistador. It seems to me that the scene is too schematic to draw such sharp conclusions. Cf. Patrick Johansson, "8 de noviembre de 1519: El encuentro de Cortés con Motecuhzoma," *Arqueología Mexicana* 27, no. 160 (2019): 20–25, here 24.

26. *Lienzo de Tlaxcala*, ed. Alfredo Chavero, *Artes de México: La conquista de México*, special issue 11, no. 51–52 (1964): i–xcii; *Códice Vaticano A. 3738* (Mexico City: Fondo de Cultura Económica; Graz, Austria: Akademische Druck-und Verlagsanstalt, 1996); *Códice Azcatitlan*, ed. Michel Graulich and Robert H. Barlow, trans. Leonardo López Luján, 2 vols. (Paris: Bibliothèque Nationale de France, Société des Américanistes, 1995).

27. *Anales de Tula*, ed. Rudolf van Zantwijk (Graz, Austria: Akademische Druck und Verlagsanstalt, 1979); *Codex en Cruz*, ed. Charles E. Dibble, 2 vols. (Salt Lake City:

University of Utah, 1981); *Tira de Tepechpan: Códice colonial procedente del Valle de México*, ed. Xavier Noguez, 2 vols. (Toluca: Instituto Mexiquense de Cultura, 1996).

28. Pastrana Flores, *Historias de la conquista*, 145–49; Bernardino de Sahagún, *Historia general de las cosas de Nueva España*, ed. Juan Carlos Temprano, 2 vols. (Madrid: Historia 16, 1990), 2: bk. 12, ch. XVI, 969–71; cf. Johansson, in "8 de noviembre de 1519," 21, who thinks that according to Sahagún's text Moteuczoma voluntarily ceded his empire to Cortés.

29. Bernardino de Sahagún, *The Conquest of New Spain, 1585 Revision*, trans. Howard Cline (Salt Lake City: University of Utah Press, 1989), 25; see Miguel Pastrana Flores, "Las cosas mal dichas y mal calladas: Las diferencias entre la primera y la segunda versiones de la *Relación de la conquista de Nueva España* de fray Bernardino de Sahagún," in *El mundo de los conquistadores: La península Ibérica en la Edad Media y su proyección en la conquista de América*, ed. Martín Ríos (Madrid: Silex; Mexico City: UNAM, 2015), 85–95.

30. "Motecuhzoma se le sujetó y se rindió al servicio de Su Majestad desde Ç hora." Diego Durán, *Historia de las Indias de la Nueva España e islas de la tierra firme*, ed. Ángel M. Garibay, 2 vols. (Mexico City: Porrúa, 1984), 2: ch. LXXIV, 541.

31. Pastrana Flores, *Historias de la conquista*, 185–87. The contrasting work is that of Hernando de Alvarado Tezozómoc, *Crónica mexicana*, ed. Gonzalo Díaz Migoyo and Germán Vázquez (Madrid: Historia 16, 1997), but this does not cover the arrival of Cortés in Tenochtitlan; Robert H. Barlow, "'La Crónica X': Versiones coloniales de la historia de los mexica tenochca," in *Los mexicas y la Triple Alianza*, ed. Robert H. Barlow and Jesús Monjarás-Ruiz (Mexico City: Instituto Nacional de Antropología e Historia, Universidad de las Américas, 1990), 13–27; José Rubén Romero Galván, "La Crónica X," in *Historiografía novohispana de tradición indígena*, ed. Romero Galván and José Rubén (Mexico City: UNAM, 2003), 185–95.

32. Fernando de Alva Ixtlilxóchitl, *Historia de la nación chichimeca*, in *Obras históricas*, ed. Edmundo O'Gorman, 2nd ed., 2 vols. (Mexico City: UNAM, 1985), 2: 216, 224–25.

33. Pastrana Flores, *Historias de la conquista*, 203–6.

34. Fernando de Alva Ixtlilxóchitl, "Compendio histórico del reino de Texcoco," in *Obras históricas*, Fernando de Alva Ixtlilxóchitl, ed. Edmundo O'Gorman, 2nd ed., 2 vols. (Mexico City: UNAM, 1985), 1: 417–521, here 452.

35. On this point I rely mainly, in addition to works of indigenous tradition, on the following studies: María del Carmen Herrera Meza, Alfredo López Austin, and Rodrigo Martínez Baracs, "El nombre náhuatl de la Triple Alianza," *Estudios de Cultura Náhuatl* 46 (2013): 7–35; Alfredo López Austin, *La constitución real de México-Tenochtitlan*, with the collaboration of Miguel León-Portilla (Mexico City: Universidad Nacional Autónoma de México, 1961); Alfredo López Austin, "Organización política del Altiplano Central de México durante el Posclásico," in *Mesoamérica y el centro de México: Una antología*, ed. Jesús Monjarás-Ruiz (Mexico City: Instituto Nacional de Antropología e Historia, 1985), 197–234.

36. See Daniel Alatorre Reyes, "El rito de ascenso al poder de los tlatoque mexica y los dioses que participaban" (MA thesis, UNAM, 2014), 16–42.

37. Alfredo López Austin, *Cuerpo humano e ideología: Las concepciones de los antiguos nahuas*, 2 vols. (Mexico City: UNAM, 1984), 1: 83–85.

38. "No es fábula decir que a sus señores tenían por dioses, porque en realidad de verdad, los adoraban como a dioses." Durán, *Historia de las Indias de la Nueva España e islas de la tierra firme*, ed. Ángel M. Garibay, 2 vols. (Mexico City: Porrúa, 1984), 2: ch. XXII, 188.

39. "Y como nos juntamos yo me apeé y le fui a abrazar solo, y aquellos dos señores que con él iban me detuvieron con las manos para que no lo tocase." Cortés, *Cartas*, 208–9. See also Bernal Díaz del Castillo, *Historia verdadera de la conquista de la Nueva España*, ed. Guillermo Serés and Miguel León-Portilla, 2 vols. (Mexico City: Academia Mexicana de la Lengua, 2014), 1: ch. LXXXVIII, 312. Again, the works of indigenous tradition do not mention the matter.

40. [Annotations by V.H. and J.F.S.]. "Cortés... fuéle a abrazar a nuestra costumbre. Los que le traían del brazo lo detuvieron, que no llegase a él, que era pecado tocarle." Gómara, *Historia de la conquista*, ch. LXV, 109.

41. [Annotations by V.H. and J.F.S.]. "Los que le llevaban del brazo le detuvieron porque les pareció que eran gran pecado que hombre alguno le tocase, porque le tenían como a cosa divina." Juan de Torquemada, *Monarquía Indiana, de los veinte y un libros rituales y monarquía indiana, con el origen y guerras de los indios occidentales, de sus poblazones, descubrimiento, conquista, conversión y otras cosas maravillosas de la mesma tierra firme*, ed. Miguel León-Portilla, 7 vols. (Mexico City: UNAM, 1975–83), 2: ch. XLVI, 152.

42. Although the tlahtoani is said to have later led Cortés by the hand, this was not done in front of the crowd but in private.

43. Alfredo Chavero, "Historia Antigua y de la conquista," in *México a través de los siglos: Historia general y completa del desenvolvimiento social, político, religioso, militar, artístico, científico y literario de México desde la antigüedad más remota hasta la época actual*, 3 vols., ed. Vicente Riva Palacio et al. (Mexico City: Cumbre, 1987), vol 2: bk. 4, ch. III, 234. Chavero relies on the works known as *Origen de los mexicanos* and *Relación de la genealogía y linaje* that were published in the nineteenth century by Joaquín García Icazbalceta.

44. On the tlahtocan, see Tezozómoc, *Crónica mexicana*, ch. XVII, 109; Durán, *Historia de las Indias*, 2: ch. XI, 103; Sahagún, *Historia general*, 2: bk. 8, ch. XVIII, 596.

45. "Los reyes y señores que te eligieron y señalaron y ordenaron por inspiración y ordenación de nuestro señor Dios, cuya elección no se puede casar [abrogar] ni variar por haber sido por ordenación divina." Sahagún, *Historia general*, 1: bk. 6, ch. X; 517.

46. Sahagún, *Historia general*, 1: bk. 6, ch. X; 518.

47. Miguel Pastrana Flores, "'Para que descanse su corazón y su cuerpo': Reflexiones en torno a la ejecución de los gobernantes en el mundo náhuatl," in *El gobernante en Mesoamérica: Representaciones y discursos del poder*, ed. María Elena Vega Villalobos and Miguel Pastrana Flores (Mexico City: UNAM, 2019), 121–58.

48. Sahagún, *Historia general*, 2: bk. 6, ch. V, 497–99.

49. Pastrana Flores, "Corazón," 130–39.
50. Pastrana Flores, "Corazón," 130–39. See Alfonso Caso, *Reyes y reinos de la Mixteca*, ed. Ignacio Bernal, 2 vols. (Mexico City: Fondo de Cultura Económica, 1984), esp. the *Diccionario biográfico*, which includes more than 300 entries. For the Classic Maya: María Elena Vega, personal communication; and Simon Martin and Nikolai Grube, *Crónica de los reyes y reinas mayas*, trans. Lorenzo Ochoa Salas and Fernando Borderas (Mexico City: Planeta, 2002).
51. Gómara, *Historia de la conquista*, ch. XXVI, 47.
52. Pastrana Flores, *Historias de la conquista*, 65–117. For an opinion in favor of López de Gómara's claim, see Miguel León-Portilla, "Quetzalcóatl-Cortés en la conquista de México," *Historia Mexicana* 24, no. 1 (1974): 13–35.
53. Miguel Pastrana Flores, "El inicio de la alianza hispano-tlaxcalteca: Una reinterpretación," in *Descubrimiento, conquista e institucionalización: De las expediciones al Yucatán a la consolidación de la Nueva España. Reflexiones a quinientos años del encuentro de dos mundos*, ed. Luis René Guerrero Galván and Alonso Guerrero Galván, 2 vols. (Mexico City: UNAM, Universidad Anáhuac, 2022), 1: 277–83.
54. "Veisme aquí que so [*sic* por soy] de carne y hueso como vos y cada uno, y que soy mortal y palpable." Cortés, *Cartas*, 211.
55. Miguel Pastrana Flores, *Entre los hombres y los dioses: Acercamiento al sacerdocio de calpulli entre los antiguos nahuas* (Mexico City: UNAM, 2008), 67–68.
56. Sahagún, *Historia general*, 1: bk. 6, ch. X; 462–63.
57. "Ruégoos que os vayáis de esta mi ciudad y tierra, que mis dioses están de mí muy enojados porque os tengo aquí; pedidme lo que quisiereis, y dároslo he, porque mucho os amo; y no penséis que os digo esto burlando, sino muy de veras. Por ende, que así se haga en todo caso." Gómara, *Historia de la conquista*, ch. XCIV, 149; Díaz de Castillo, *Historia verdadera*, 1: ch. CVIII, 396.
58. Bernardino de Sahagún, *Florentine Codex*, trans. Charles E. Dibble and J. O. Anderson (Salt Lake City: University of Utah Press, 1975), XII, 47. For a critical review of the Spanish version of the apprehension, see Francis Brooks, "Motecuzoma Xocoyotl, Hernán Cortés, and Bernal Díaz del Castillo: The Construction of an Arrest," *Hispanic American Historical Review* 75, no. 2 (1995): 149–83.
59. "Y así tomaron vehementemente sospecha del trato de los Españoles começando los Yndios de temor a esconderse y faltar en acudir a lo necesario por los Españoles. Començavan a padecer hambre, especialmente los caballos y perros de ayuda que trayan consigo que eran muchos muy feroces y diestros en la guerra; llegó a tanto que fue necesario fuesen los Yndios amigos con algunos Mexicanos a buscar bastimentos." Juan de Tovar, *Manuscrito Tovar: Origines et croyances de los indies du Mexique*, ed. Jacques Lafaye (Graz, Austria: Akademische Druck-u. Verlagsanstalt, UNESCO, 1972), 80.
60. "Visto por el rey Cacama el poco ánimo y determinación de los mexicanos, se salió de la ciudad y se fue a Tetzcuco para juntar sus gentes, y con ellas libertar a su tío y nobleza

mexicana de la servidumbre y afrenta en que vivían." Ixtlilxóchitl, *Historia de la nación*, ch. LXXXVI, 223.

61. "¡Oh, señor Malinche y señores capitanes, cuánto me pesa de la respuesta y mando que nuestros teules han dado a nuestros papas e a mí e a todos mis capitanes! Y es que os demos guerra y os matemos, o os hagamos ir por la mar adelante. Lo he colegido dello y le paresce es que, que antes que comiencen la guerra, que luego salgáis desta cibdad y no quede ninguno de vosotros aquí. Y esto, señor Malinche, os digo que hagáis en todas maneras, que os conviene; si no mataros han. E mirá que os va las vidas." Díaz de Castillo, *Historia verdadera*, ch. CVIII, 396; Gómara, *Historia de la conquista*, ch. XCIV, 149.

62. Sahagún, *Historia general*, 2: bk. 12, ch. XX, 117.

63. "Invió Motezuma a su hermano, el señor de Eztapalapa, al cual, como vieron fuera los mexicanos . . . no le dexaron volver a la prisión ni hicieron el tianguez; antes le eligieron por su caudillo y Capitán." Cervantes, *Crónica*, ch. CIV; 466. See Genaro García, *Carácter de la conquista española en América y en México según los textos de los historiadores primitivos*, with the collaboration of Andrés Henestrosa (Mexico City: Fundación Miguel Alemán, 1990), 211–14.

64. "Cortés (sin pensamiento de malicia) soltó a un hermano de Motecuhzuma, señor de Itztapalapa y los mexicanos le eligieron por su caudillo." Torquemada, *Monarquía indiana*, 2: bk. 4, ch. LXVIII, 209.

65. "E visto por el dicho Motunzuma el poco remedio quel dicho don Hernando Cortés ponía, envió a decir a los indios, como hombre questaba descontento e desesperado de verse preso e las cosas como iban, que hiciesen lo que quisiesen e que no hiciesen cuenta dél, e desde allí en adelante los indios comenzaron a matar de los cristianos por do quiera que podían e se levantó la cibdad e toda la tierra contra los cristianos." "Algunas respuestas de Bernardino Vázquez de Tapia," in *Documentos cortesianos*, ed. José Luis Martínez, 4 vols. (Mexico City: Fondo de Cultura Económica, UNAM, 1990), 2: 31–46, here 35.

66. "Oídas estas vozes por los mexicanos y tlatlilulcas, començaron entre sí a bravear y maldezir a Motecuçoma, diciendo: '¿Qué dize el puto de Motecuçoma, y tú vellaco con él? No cesaremos la guerra.' Luego començaron a dar alaridos y a tirar saetas y dardos hacia donde estaba que hablava, junto con Motecuçoma." Sahagún, *Historia general*, 2: bk. 12, ch. XXI, 975. See Tovar, *Manuscrito Tovar*, 81.

67. Pastrana Flores, *Historias de la conquista*, 128–35; Pastrana Flores, "Corazón," 127–29.

68. "De los que en la cibdad de Buacachula [Huaquechula] se prendieron, en especial de aquel herido, supe muy por extenso las cosas de la grand cibdad de Timixtitlán, y cómo después de la muerte de Muteeçuma había subscedido en el señorío un hermano suyo señor de la cibdad de Yztapalapa que se llamaba Cuetravaçin [Cuitlahuatzin], el cual suscedió en el señorío porque murió en las puentes [*sic*] el hijo de Muteçuma que heredaba el señorío." Cortés, *Cartas*, 305.

69. Fernando de Alva Ixtlilxóchitl, *Sumaria relación de todas las cosas que han sucedido en la Nueva España*, in *Obras históricas*, ed. Edmundo O'Gorman, 2 vols. (Mexico City: UNAM, 1985), 1: 263–393, here 390.

70. Torquemada, *Monarquía indiana*, 2: bk. 4, ch. LXVIII, 209.

71. Torquemada, *Monarquía indiana*, 2: bk. 4, ch. LXX, 212, 232.

72. "The first thing was that they chose for their king and lord a younger brother of Motecuhzuma, called Cuitlahuatzin and four other senators, who were always at the king's side in all business." Torquemada, *Monarquía indiana*, 2: bk. 4, ch. LXX, 212, ch. LXXIV, 232.

73. "Y muchos principales y capitanes mexicanos bien le conoscieron . . . y llorando le dijeron: «¡Oh, señor e nuestro gran señor, y cómo nos pesa de todo vuestro mal y daño y de nuestros hijos y parientes! Hacemos os saber que ya hemos levantado a un vuestro pariente por señor». E allí le nombró cómo se llamaba, que se decían Coadlavaca [*sic* por Cuitláhuac], señor de Iztapalapa." Díaz del Castillo, *Historia verdadera*, 1: ch. CXXVI, 472–73.

74. These events took place between June 24 and 28, 1520.

75. Orozco y Berra, *Historia antigua*, 4: 493.

76. "Hicieron a la Magestad del Rey Felipe III . . . en Madrid ante Gerónimo Fernández escribano en 26 de enero del año de 1612, de la acción y derecho que pudieran tener a los Reinos y estados de la Nueva España, que habían sido de su bisabuelo el emperador Motezuma." Antonio Vázquez de Espinosa, *Compendio y descripción de las Indias Occidentales* (Madrid: Historia 16, 1992), 1: 235.

77. "Y ha sido sobre todos los demás, de tan superior aprecio el título de su derecho por la renuncia del Emperador Motezuma, que, para restablecerle y más fijarle, a instancia del señor rey don Felipe IV y de su Real Consejo de Indias, hizo nueva renuncia de todo su derecho a la corona mexicana en la real casa de Castilla el conde de Motezuma, tercer nieto de aquel Emperador." Diego Luis Motezuma, *Corona mexicana o Historia de los nueve Motezumas*, ed. Lucas de la Torre (Valladolid, Spain: Maxtor, 2012), 452.

78. Juan López Cancelada, "La verdad sabia y buena fe guardada," in *Colección de documentos para la historia de la guerra de independencia de México de 1808 a 1821*, ed. Juan E. Hernández y Dávalos (Mexico City: UNAM, 2008), 1–35, here 3: doc. 147, accessed May 1, 2023, https://www.pim.unam.mx/catalogos/hyd/HYDIII/HYDIII147.pdf. According to this author, an Indigenous man claimed that "he was a descendant in the straight line of the *emperor Moctezuma*; that by virtue of there no longer being a sovereign in Spain, the crown of the Mexican empire fell to him."

8

The Forty *Teteuctin*

Nahua Bodies in the Mediterranean

ERIKA ESCUTIA

> Go with God, for I've tattooed my face and pierced my ears. What would those Spaniards say of me should they see me like this!
> —Gonzalo Guerrero to Jerónimo de Aguilar

ARRIVING AS A GREAT LORD

It was May 1528. Hernán Cortés disembarked in the port of Palos, where he was eagerly awaited.[1] His *Letters to Emperor Charles V*, published in Spanish and Latin, had been read with astonishment by intellectuals and nobles, turning his figure into a legend among his European contemporaries.

The conquistador "filled the whole kingdom with his name and arrival, and everyone wanted to see him."[2] Martin de Salinas, ambassador of Archduke Ferdinand of Habsburg, assured his regent that he would visit Cortés on his behalf so that he could give him "all the explications about there [New Spain] since he is the best author there could be."[3] The notable Venetian Baldassare Castiglione reported to Giovanni Battista Ramusio the arrival of Cortés;[4] and the humanist Jan Dantyszek, representative of Zygmunt I of Poland, would do everything possible to establish a relationship with Cortés that would allow him to obtain reliable news about the activities of the Spanish overseas.[5]

Despite the captain's great fame, his permanence in power was uncertain. The trip to Castile followed, among other secondary matters, his aim to defend himself personally against the accusations raised against him. Even with his constant attempts to demonstrate his loyalty to the king, the suspicion of treason and illicit enrichment had fallen upon him. The effect of his gifts, missives, and representatives had not been powerful enough to convince the monarch of his arguments.

As is so often true, his most helpful tool for transforming calamity into victory was political astuteness. Knowing that magnanimity was a means to gain the favor of the Castilian Crown and of any possible intercessor before the king, he spared no expense. He carried a lot of gold, silver, and jewels, hoping to project an image of prosperity.

The famed leader also understood the role of signs and gestures associated with the generosity and kindness he intended to embody. With this in mind, he embarked with those things from New Spain that had established the imaginary of the distant and prosperous lands to show and present as gifts to whomever necessary: jaguars, opossums, armadillos, gannets, liquid amber, balsam, and colorful birds were among those selected. To this were added "a large sum of feather and fur blankets, fans, shields, feather works, stone mirrors, and the like,"[6] exceptional artifacts in European material culture.

With his paraphernalia and riches, Cortés disembarked "like a great lord."[7] Charles V, from Monzón, ordered his vassals to receive him with solemnity and respect wherever he went. On his journey inland, the man from Extremadura aroused admiration, interest, and envy among nobles and courtiers. He did so not only through solemnity and grace but also through spectacle. As is well known, Cortés "carried dwarfs[8]; and he carried Indios and Indias whiter than Germans."[9] Devoid of the prestigious functions they had in the Mesoamerican world,[10] the extraordinary individuals were treated like objects of astonishment, as becomes evident in the description of Francisco Duarte, a member of the Casa de Contratación of Seville:

> [Cortés] brings four Indio men, very dwarfed, who are said to be from a province where they are all of that size. The biggest one is not more than three palms tall or a little more, according to the paintings they sent us of them. Moreover, they do not have beards, none of them has one, and by age, they should already have them; one is over 70 years old. The hairs of the head are sparse and very black and not disheveled and so fat and more than horsehair.[11]

Their physiognomic differences were read as a sign of the *Other*, perhaps of the monstrous and marvelous. Maybe Cortés brought them along as a counterpoint to himself because, in his premeditated exhibition, there was "the suspicion that he liked them for the enhancement they lent to his figure."[12] These people were objectified and used as "the main ornament of the Court and necessary entertainment"[13] for festivals and amusements, so much so that a Polish diplomat asked to receive one of them as a gift.[14]

Cortés embarked more "people of pleasure,"[15] who appeared before the king at the imperial court. Dexterous men performed an exhibition of *ullamaztli*, a ball game of ritual and warlike background, as well as games of *patolli*, a ceremonial game associated with Macuilxóchitl that was played on a *petate* (a mat of palm leaves), using small colored stones as counters.[16] However, undoubtedly what was most impressive were the skillful displays of *xocuahpatollin*, described as

> a game of one stick in a way never heard of or seen in Spain until now. They made very subtle turns very lightly, while one of them turned the stick to the sound of a song (*areíto*) and, in the other direction, other eight Indios walked around with rattles and small tabors: when that one finished turning, another of the same ones entered, until one by one all eight or nine that were there, had made their turns all different from the others.[17]

The presence of these human beings was not a whimsical extravagance of the conqueror. Nor was it Cortés's sole purpose to create a picturesque triumphal scene with the "curious exotic subjects who were exhibited in a sort of *Völkerschau* [human zoo],"[18] presenting "bizarre games and dances"[19] to the admiration of those present. His exhibition was a premeditated symbolic act. Cortés materially concretized Moteuczoma's possessions described in the *Second Letter*: the flora, fauna, rich objects, and even the people that made up his belongings. People could imagine the game players entertaining the "court and palace" of Mexico and the "dwarfs" in the houses that the *huey tlahtoani* had given them,[20] the caged animals being tended by their keepers, and the rich jewels and feathers being sold in the lively markets. Thus, what was narrated became palpable. What was read corresponded with what was seen. Cortés's invention of Moteuczoma's Empire and the nascent New Spain took shape through the objects and people objectified.

The power of this symbolic act resides not only in the fact that Cortés materialized New Spain's territory before European eyes through the objects but, above all, in the fact that his European contemporaries, when looking at the objects, saw them from the worldview offered by the conquistador.[21] The difference is subtle but significant. The conquistadors commonly supported their discourses by shipping to the Crown the objects they considered most peculiar, valuable, or economically exploitable of a region under the logic of booty, gifts, the royal fifth, enslavement, and samples.[22] Nevertheless, Cortés's *Letters* went further; through the epic narrative, they served as the first great epistemic framework for looking at and thinking about Nahua/New Spanish objects.

In this sense, Cortés's trip to Castile allowed him to fashion his figure as a "paragon and perfect example of virtue,"[23] with "great wit and singular eloquence and smoothness in speaking and writing,"[24] consolidating the indisputable authority that his voice had in order to constitute the first idea of New Spain.

THE CROSSING OF THE FORTY *TETEUCTIN*

Despite the languid reference of the Hispanic chroniclers, a key piece is still missing in the story of the journey: the forty "cavaliers and lords of Mexico, Tlaxcallan, and other cities,"[25] who, in the company of Cortés, met with the emperor. Only colonial Nahua chroniclers partially recovered their names, lineages, and domains. Not exempt from preferences and animosities, they name some local leaders who traveled with the conquistador.[26]

Among that group of men were the two surviving sons of Moteuczoma,[27] Martin and Pedro, and other relatives of the lineages of Tenochtitlan and Tlatelolco.[28] Along went Hernando de Tapia, "son of the ruler of Mexico" Andrés de Tapia Motelchiuh, and some teteuctin from Tetzcoco, Tlacopan, Xochimilco, and Culhuacan.[29] Also, leaders from Cempoala and the partialities of Tlaxcala attended,[30] who already enjoyed the special privilege of the exemption of tributes and the preservation of their lands given by Cortés in 1524.[31]

The biographies traced by scholars suggest that the group was made up of men from the most powerful families of the Anahuac, from defeated followers, and *Indian conquistadors*, without whom the Spaniards would probably never have triumphed in that unknown land and would have lacked the support and stability offered by the allied and subdued peoples.[32]

Some authors say that they went as part of the spectacular triumphal procession of the conquistador, "as one of many gifts,"[33] or that they were carried along for Cortés to show them to the king as part of the consolidation of Cortés's figure and conquest.[34] Others argue that they were sent in exile by the New Spain authorities because of "the fear that the descendants of the pre-Hispanic rulers could lead a revolt"[35] or that they were conceived as "Aztec tourists."[36]

López de Gómara wrote that Cortés offered these men "free passage and sustenance" to Castilla,[37] although never revealing the motives. However, it is clear that they were not taken by force or coercion.[38] Even Bernal Díaz points out that they contributed to the expenses of Cortés.[39] He said that in the months prior to the voyage, "all the Mexican and Texcoco caciques and from all the other towns around the lagoon were in Tlaxcala,"[40] in the company of Cortés, who was banished from Mexico-Tenochtitlan by the new governor, Alonso de Estrada. They were so many and so influential that Estrada feared that they were allying with Cortés not to cross the Atlantic but to make war on the governor.

The Nahua elite joined Cortés to confront the crown officials who sought to strip them of their power. In recent years, several authors have shown that the Nahuas used the meeting with Charles V to negotiate their rights, privileges, lands, and tributes without discarding their support for Cortés, to consolidate their discourses.[41] These scholars have resorted to documents of petitions, reports of merits and services, royal decrees, and concessions of noble coats of arms to demonstrate that in this early period, a political negotiation of the "Indigenous nobility" within the new spaces of power took place. Furthermore, these studies argue that the teteuctin's stay at the imperial court, between August 1528 and April 1529, gave them enough time to elaborate the necessary documents to conserve their power, or at least to get an idea of the juridical-administrative system and procedures to prepare their petitions in the immediately subsequent years.

Although legal writing was a tool of great importance for incorporating the Nahua elites into the European political system, this chapter explores the ceremonial presentation of the teteuctin before the king and the pope as the very first acts of political negotiation codified not only in the protocolary procedure but in the *performatively displayed Nahua bodies*.[42] As in other diplomatic meetings of Charles V with other non-Christian rulers subjected to vassalage, the oath ceremony to the emperor and the Christian faith was "an illocutionary and performative act of the highest binding value."[43] In this light, the ritual was an essential element not only to negotiate but also display both their vassalage and the continuity of their power in New Spain.

First, it is crucial to stress that the embassies of the Nahua leaders in the Mediterranean are unique in European diplomacy. Indeed, the monarch had already had encounters with "Indian ambassadors"[44] from Cempoala,[45] and with Tlaxcalteca dancers and ball players;[46] but he had never met the *rulers* of those latitudes.[47]

Also, a king appearing before another without a mediator was highly unusual. Depending on the journey's outcome, the decision to go personally to another kingdom on a diplomatic or warlike mission was considered risky; on such voyages, control of the temporarily abandoned territory, and even life was at risk. The teteuctin thought this act could help them, presumably weighing the possible consequences of abandoning their lands for a long time.[48]

We know of only one testimony by an eyewitness of the presentation of the teteuctin at the imperial court, recently found in a German family archive.[49] It describes the meeting with the monarch as a solemn ceremony of cooperation organized under the Spanish protocol in Madrid on the first Sunday of August 1528.[50] Charles V enjoyed a messianic and promising time due to his imminent coronation in Italy, the oath of Prince Philip, and the recent birth of his daughter Maria.[51] Before him, the forty "dukes, counts, and great lords,"[52] dressed in rich clothes, demonstrate their status as vassals of the Crown and the church. They performed the traditional ceremony of hand kissing.[53] They presented the king with "their weapons, shields, and helmets, strangely and exquisitely crafted with bird feathers, subtle work never seen before, and exquisite gold jewelry such as turtles, snakes, and other animals that they attend and wear."[54] Then "they knelt before his imperial majesty to celebrate the Christian faith, which they received and swore to in their manner."[55] It being Sunday, after the liturgical ceremony, the festivities, music, and games began, where the ball, log, and patolli "players" were presented.

Royal ceremonies in early modern Europe were codified in an unwritten way. The dignitaries enacted their identities, hierarchies, and social places in the balance of political power throughout the ceremonial acts.[56] As in the entry of Cortés to Castile, each phase of the ceremony had a highly symbolic significance. Reverential gestures such as kissing the king's hand and kneeling before him, as well as the presentation of arms, sealed the commitment of the Nahuas to the emperor's service. The liturgical celebration affirmed them as an Indio-Christian elite, and the display of games allowed them to participate in the royal festival. From the solemn to the festive ceremony, the Nahua elite were incorporated into imperial practices and exhibited their own while gaining legitimacy as a mediator between the European Christian world and the Nahua world to be Christianized.

After the ceremony, the teteuctin remained at court until March 1529, while the future administration of the *indios* of New Spain was being discussed. Then the group traveled to Seville, except for a few dignitaries who continued to accompany the imperial family's entourage.[57] Benito Mazatlaqueme and another principal Nahua even undertook the journey to Rome,[58] the epicenter of Christianity, shortly after it had been sacked in 1527.

Bernal Díaz, recounting this passage of the New-Spanish delegation through the Holy City, omitted to mention the presence of the Nahua leaders and focused his story on the conquistadors Juan de Herrada and Campos as Cortés's representatives who negotiated his petitions and delivered to Clement VII "a whole report by a memorial of the lands, how great they are and the way they are, that all the Indios were idolaters and that they had become Christians, and many other things that should be said to our holy father."[59] The chronicler mentioned, on the other hand, the performance of "log players," or xocuahpatollin, in the Sacred College that, "as they said, . . . His Holiness and the sacred cardinals were very pleased to watch."[60] Unlike Díaz del Castillo, the historian and humanist Paolo Giovio saw the "two illustrious figures" who left the delegation to "pay homage" in Rome to Pope Clement VII in 1529 directly and recalled that episode in his written work, emphasizing the exchange of rich gifts between the pontiff and the teteuctin.[61]

Giovio—and the anonymous German—dedicated a few lines to the phases of the ceremony, but their texts do not end there. The authors paid great attention to the performatively displayed Nahua bodies in the social arena of the diplomatic ceremonies. They conceived the Nahua bodies as a *site of interpretation* to assign them a human and political nature by interpreting three aspects: (1) their physiognomy, (2) their bodies medialized by the attire and artifacts, and (3) the dynamics enacted by their bodies (gestures, body language, and cultural practices).

PERFORMATIVELY DISPLAYED BODIES: THE TETEUCTIN BEFORE THE EMPEROR AND THE POPE

In Renaissance philosophy, the world was a system of signs carefully designed by God that the human being interpreted—as Michel Foucault noted—guided by certain features of the surface of things that would enclose the hidden similarities pointed out as "visible marks of invisible analogies."[62] Especially the male human body was the main system of signs where God had inscribed the character and nature of the human soul, the deposit of the vital breath, the incarnation of the humors, a visible sign of the anima.

In diplomacy, the graceful body was obviously important. Baldassare Castiglione, so admired by Charles V, described such a body as the fundamental pillar of the ideal courtier. In his work, published precisely in 1528, he stated:

> The Courtier therefore, beside noblenesse of birth, I will have him to be fortunate in this behalfe, and by nature to have not only a wit, and a comely shape of person and countenance, but also a certain grace, and (as they say) a hewe [trad. it. *sangue*], that shall make him at the first sight acceptable and loving unto who so beholdeth him.[63]

Imagining the body as a mirror of the soul, the humanist Lucio Marineo Sículo described Cortés's "body and attire" on the occasion of that voyage. He portrayed him as that of an affable and temperate man, "of a body neither too thin nor too thick, of medium height, of good face, . . . all the limbs from head to feet very well proportioned," inferring that from "the gifts and graces of nature, [Cortés was] most highly adorned and most blessed with the goods of his condition and virtues of the spirit."[64]

The anonymous German, who witnessed the arrival of the teteuctin at the imperial court, focused his attention similarly on those signs on which the decipherment of the unknown human being in front of him depended: the skin, the hair, and the proportion of the body. From this, he indicated that they were "strong people, short and fat, very dark, and their hair is strong and black like that of a horse."[65] The color of the skin and hair—understood as excretion produced by the brain[66]—was analyzed according to the humoral theory of the constitution of the body. In this case, their darkness was interpreted as evidence of a melancholic mood from which could come both their great imaginativeness and the pusillanimity that Fernández de Oviedo attributed to them.[67]

The anonymous informant's comparison of the Nahuas' hair with the horse's mane, in addition to his allusion to their short and strong bodies, emphasized potency and virility. Beyond his comparison with a domesticated animal, it also echoes the Aristotelian theory regarding serfs by nature who would be happier being dominated and whose bodies were "strong for the necessary work."[68] They shared with the domesticated animal "the usefulness for the master, the robust constitution of the body and the need to be guided in their work by their incapacity for rational self-initiative."[69]

Paolo Giovio was deeply imbued by medical knowledge and put physiognomy at the center of the biographies in his *Elogia* and *Vitae*.[70] He wrote that "in color, hair, and cheerful ingenuity, they [Nahuas] were very similar to our dark-skinned men,"[71] tying the appearance of the body to the nature of the Indio.

The dark-skinned men to whom Giovio compared the Nahuas were eventually heterogeneous groups present on the Italian peninsula mainly due to slavery. Also, the Venetian ambassador, Andrea Navagero, who had seen the Nahuas in Castile in 1526, described them as having a hue "almost like the Circassians, but their color is most ashen."[72] The Circassians (*adygekher*) were enslaved in the Italian peninsula before the Africans replaced them after the fall of Constantinople.[73] Ippolito de' Medici—nephew of Clement VII and close friend of Giovio—kept at his court, precisely as servants, a heterogeneous group of "barbarians," "perfect specimens" of their lineages: excellent riders related to the king of Numidia, incomparable Tartar archers, strong Ethiopian fighters, expert swimmers from India,[74] and Turkish hunters who accompanied the cardinal on his hunting expeditions.[75]

The teteuctin could not control that their physical appearance resembled the Aristotelian idea of a natural servant's body. Nonetheless, the Nahuas were great experts in the refinement of their clothing, understanding its relevant role in the transforming the *body* into a *persona* as a codified expression of a social site.[76] On their dark skins shimmered the gold pendants, bangles, and jewels of precious stones, the iridescent feathers of their cloaks (*tilmas*) and breechcloth (*maxtles*). The anonymous German witness described all these artifacts as pieces created with rich and singular materials. They moreover impressed him for their strangeness (*selzam* in the original German) and, above all, for their exquisite (*köstlich*) and subtle (*subtil*) craftsmanship.[77]

The excellency, delicacy, and dexterity of the objects were not only a sign of manual skill but also of ingenuity, an inherent nature of a prolific inventive and human sensitivity toward beauty and goodness.[78] Precisely *subtle* is the word most evocative of this sense. Its etymological origin is in textile art. *Subtĭlis*, from the Latin locution *sŭb tela*, was a term weavers used to refer to that which passes under the warp and remains hidden to the eye but founds the artifact.[79]

The apparent contradiction between the strong physiognomy of the Nahuas that made them prone to less noble jobs and the refinement of the artifacts carried by the teteuctin opened a possibility of sustaining the existence of a subtle soul of the Nahuas. Aristotle had already admitted that "some slaves have bodies of free men, and some free men have souls of slaves. . . . Nevertheless, it is not as easy to see the beauty of the soul as that of the body."[80] The materiality of the artifacts and the beauty of their work allowed the European elites to see that soul endowed with the skill for the most refined works. As Stefan Hanß has noted, "Intricate artisanal skills were not simply considered a symbol of cultural refinement, but they were integral categories of how people experienced subjectivity, community, and the divine in relation to materials, things, and the making of objects."[81] Hence, their favorable judgment was a fundamental piece in the early construction of the imaginary of the groups of New Spain.

The bodily artifacts worn by the teteuctin for the occasion were already well known to the emperor, his family, his enemies, and his allies. Since 1519, their senders had inscribed them in narratives of wealth and power while canceling, exalting, reusing, or misrepresenting the primary functions and meanings that the pieces had for their producers.[82] Particularly, the kings of Castile, the Habsburg family, and the pontiffs used them as symbols of their military and evangelical triumph and, consequently, as forms of legitimization and appropriation of the conquered territories.[83]

However, unlike the pieces of the remittances and booty, the jewelry and feather cloaks placed on the bodies of the teteuctin looked different. They were used in the practices of long Mesoamerican tradition and those founded in the convulsive changes of the preceding years. Thus, they created a diverse chain of signifiers, articulating another *imaginary*; that is, a new specific set of images before the European eye that expanded, contradicted, or juxtaposed the episteme of the nature of the "Indio of New Spain" built by the Hispanic written narratives.[84]

Through the use of clothing, body adornment and permanent physical modifications, the teteuctin turned their bodies into the bearers of objects and the means to assert an image.[85] In doing so, their bodies were "subtracted from nature and inserted into a symbolic order."[86] In that performative act of fluid interactions between their bodies and attire, a new interpretative space opened for their observer. Although the Nahua objects, in isolation, were always praised for their artfulness, the testimony offered by the Nuremberg archives stands out for its scathing reprobation of the Nahuas use of the precious objects. It indicates that the teteuctin only wore "a white cloth rolled up to cover their shame"[87] and that, in the street, they covered themselves with a beautiful "coat" or "cape" of feathers, but hanging "it badly over the back, in such a way that it falls over the left shoulder and the right side is uncovered, in short, that it covers a little the buttocks."[88]

The witness did not realize that the tilma worn by the teteuctin was a textile piece with a purpose different from that of the European cloak. It was not an overcloak but something more similar to a dress. The author of the German missive felt he had complete authority to write that the Nahuas misunderstood its correct use.

This misunderstanding of the tilma also occurred with the first shipments of Cortés, when inventories recorded them as capes, coats, blankets, or quilts. In 1522, the humanist and first chronicler of the Indies, Pietro Martire, saw how the Nahua servant of Juan de Ribera used a tilma and understood for the first time that it was not a blanket but attire. He then undermined the textiles that he had previously admired for their subtle craftsmanship, stating that

> The shape of these garments is laughable. They call them garments because they use them to cover their bodies, but they in no way, nearly or remotely, resemble ours. . . . Having seen these garments, I ceased to marvel that they had presented such a number to Cortes as I said: for they are of small value, and most of them occupy little space.[89]

Even if European elites valued the Mesoamerican lip and ear plugs, the teteuctin were criticized for piercing their noses, ears, and lower lips, with holes "so large that they cannot cover the lower row of teeth when the stones fall into their mouths."[90] A similar opinion was held by a European spectator of the Cempoaltecah who appeared in Valladolid in 1520. He stated that "they [the Cempoaltecah] make themselves ugly because they make holes in their nose, ears, and lips and hang jewels and gold rings in them."[91]

The European witnesses were embodied actors who communicated about the other bodies from their own experience. When Lucio Marineo described Cortés as having a harmonious and moderate body, he did nothing more than painting the ideal soul of Renaissance humanism. The extraordinary individuals exhibited by the conquistador were rarities that, from their liminality, irritated the canon. The teteuctin's body, apparently built like that of a natural serf, contradicted the overwhelming evidence of their artifacts' subtle materiality, which could prove that they had a kind and beautiful soul. The discussion about the nature of the Nahuas was fundamental to charting their destiny.

THE NAHUA BODY AND THE BODY POLITIC

In descriptions, the performative body is hard to grasp. Maybe, for this reason, the anonymous German promised his addressee to send paintings about what he related. It is thought that such paintings correspond to the drawings in the *Trachtenbuch*[92] (Book of Costumes) from the sculptor and medalist Christoph Weiditz.[93] The *Trachtenbuch* compiles 154 plates illustrating various types of dress that Weiditz drew between 1529 and 1532. It depicts customs and cultures that the artist had probably seen directly as he traveled with the court of Charles V through Spain, Italy, the Holy Roman Empire, and the Netherlands. The watercolored pen-drawings reflect the cosmopolitan character of the imperial court and Charles's power as ruler of the world.[94] According to the gloss, twelve of the plates represent "the Indians that Fernando Cortés brought from India to His Imperial Majesty and who played in front of His Majesty with wooden logs and ball." They include a woman, "players," and "nobles."

Although some authors emphasize the truthful and testimonial character of these drawings,[95] when looking at the images glossed as those of the "nobles" (figure 8.1), we see—as noted by Elizabeth Hill Boone[96]—that there are many inaccuracies and misrepresentations in the images. Beyond the objects that the characters hold in a scenographic position—which could be explained by a pose of the teteuctin in front of the artist—there are many important divergences in the clothing that make their bearers unrecognizable as Nahua leaders.

In Weiditz's drawings, the men are barefoot. The hair lacks any headdress, which was a fundamental piece in the attire of a principal Nahua to distinguish his social rank before and after the *Conquista*.[97] Although the feather skirt was added by another hand years later,[98] the breechcloth was illustrated as a breeches instead of as a long knotted textile piece with two long and flat hanging strands in the center of the thighs.

It is also interesting to note that, in plate 4 of the *Trachtenbuch*, the "nobleman" wears the tilma like a European cloak or coat, placing it over both shoulders but knotting it over the left shoulder and barely covering the upper thigh, echoing the German testimony that the tilmas were admired because they were "badly put on" and too short.[99] In contrast, the textile pieces depicted in Mesoamerican and colonial sources reach to the knee or ankle, regardless of their placement.[100]

Regarding the jewels, Weiditz represents the lip plug (*bezote*) in the right place under the mouth but draws the nose jewel too high, inserted in the middle cartilage and not in the *septum* (see figure 8.1). Likewise, in plate 5, he draws the man with the ear pierced with only a tiny hole, from which hangs a thin ring set with a large round stone. Conversely, the Nahua practice resorted to lobular expansion with

Figure 8.1. Christoph Weiditz, *Trachtenbuch*. Hs. 22474. Lam. 4–5. Courtesy of Germanisches Nationalmuseum Nürnberg

an inserted stone. Finally, the forehead and cheeks appear with encrusted jewels, something inconceivable in the Mesoamerican tradition.

So distant is the representation of Nahua practices of pre- and post-conquest attire that Casado and Soler have argued Weiditz had never actually observed a Nahua individual in person.[101] From my point of view, the artist's images seem not to illustrate the Nahua group in their documentary character but the anonymous German's perspective on bodies, gestures, and uses of artifacts.[102] As an extension of the impressions of this eyewitness, the images not only emphasize how the "Indians" inappropriately placed rich and beautiful objects on their strong and dark bodies but also represent the character of the people of New Spain.

In the eyes of the embassy's witness, there was no doubt that the population in New Spain was wealthy, that their lords were powerful and strong, and that they had a born nature (ingenuity) for the creation of artifacts derived from fruitful thinking.[103] However, the recognition of this natural ability was only a human potentiality. It had to be developed to complete what God had placed as a seed.[104]

As we have seen, Giovio assigned a "cheerful ingenuity" to the Nahua people. He also said that after bowing to and venerating the pope, "they returned joyfully to their land, and according to what I have been informed, they told their folks the many grandiosities of Rome and the ceremonies and customs of our people."[105] His physiognomic comparison between the teuctin and enslaved people in Europe completed his perception of the Nahuas' nature, which he believed inclined them to be a people happily incorporated as dominated subjects to the body politic of the empire and the church. Nonetheless, the incorporation of the Nahua people was far from being a merely happy process. The same year that Hernando de Tapia ingratiated himself with the emperor and the pope, Fray Juan de Zumárraga denounced the extortions of which Tapia's father suffered.[106] Giovio's impression resulted from the effective political alliance between the Franciscan friars, Cortés, and the Christianized teuctin. They displayed their physical bodies in the diplomatic embassies during 1528 and 1529 and unified the body politic that each one represented. Together, they forged the coherent figure of a "witty Indio," detached from the narrative of the "bestial Indio" dominant in these years to define American peoples.[107]

In the interpretation of the Nahua bodies, the European contemporaries believed they discovered the nature of the New Spanish Indio. There was a relative consensus about the "capacity" of Nahua people to live "civilly and Christianly." Consequently, the colonial authorities ordered them to do everything to "keep their good uses and customs in what were not against our Christian religion."[108]

Before legal writing, political negotiations of the Nahua elite occurred in the first diplomatic encounters. The vassalage to the emperor and the acceptance of Christianity were established in the phases of the ceremonies. Ana Díaz pointed out that Nahuas' "contact with the court allowed them to push forward the process of their annexation to the body politic of the Catholic Monarchy as heads of the indigenous societies, through the direct negotiation with the Crown."[109] As a symbol of their belonging to a transatlantic body politic, the teuctin also transformed their physical body when returning to New Spain.

During the months of their stay in Europe, they received luxurious clothes from the emperor,[110] but they disliked dressing in them in Europe, according to the anonymous witness. The pope gave them clothes, golden spades, horse-riding saddles, and jewels. Paolo Giovio insisted on how they had returned "to their people with blissful gifts."[111] The offered clothes were an essential sign of their status upon their return.

The Franciscans who embarked with the teuctin on the return voyage considered them fundamental pieces in integrating their peoples into the structures of the monarchy and, above all, Christianity.[112] The friars immediately exalt the Nahuas' capacity to produce the admired artifacts to demonstrate—always within the Aristotelian logic—that the Nahuas were possessors of a subtle and kind soul, as was admitted, in the bull *Sublimis Deus*, almost a decade later.[113]

Franciscans also provided education in European Christianity, considering that "the Indios were children, of soft wax, who could be modeled in any desired form."[114]

Figure 8.2. *Cuetlaxcohuapan Codex* (detail), ca. 1530. Biblioteca Nacional de Antropología e Historia, Dr. Eusebio Dávalos Hurtado. Courtesy of Instituto Nacional de Antropología e Historia, Secretaría de Cultura INAH, Mexico.

Franciscans' guidance would, according to their conviction, lead the Indios to the Universal Christian Kingdom. Clothing was an essential part of the *policía*[115]—a set of rules to keep them away from vices and bring them closer to the virtues of Christianity.[116] Furthermore, the Spanish Crown ordered the Franciscans to persuade the Indios to "wear clothes, for more honesty and decency of the people."[117] It even prohibited ornaments, arguing that such "badges and signs on the clothes and heads" would "demonstrate that they offer them and commend them to demons."[118]

The *performatively displayed body* was again a crucial resource to communicate political power. The self-representation of the Tlaxcalteca elite in the *Cuetlaxcohuapan Codex* (figure 8.2), dated between 1531 and 1533 (only a few years after the voyage), is diametrically opposed to Weiditz's representation of the "nobleman."

In it, eleven Tlaxcalteca rulers are glossed with the honorific title of "Don." The main one is Don Francisco, brother of Don Lorenzo Maxixcatzin, one of the *teuctli* who traveled with Cortés and died in Seville in 1529. His body, long and tall, is far from the German description. One can see the remanences of some Mesoamerican signs of power, such as the scarlet and white headdress around the forehead, adorned on the back with the *tecpilotl* of quetzal feathers.[119] However, he is also recognized as a subject legitimized by the Castilian Crown to wear the doublet, a privilege "of clothes," only granted to some. His face, undoubtedly, underwent more transformations because of the absence of piercings, the Spanish haircut, and the beard. In both worlds, the change of face equaled a change of being, as the well-known Nahua pairing of two terms into a metaphoric unit (*difrasismo*) of "face and heart" reminds us, or the studies of physiognomy in Europe.

The codex, intended for a dispute between scribes and painters, the so-called *tlahcuilos*, and governors from Tlaxcala, presented the rulers as similar and assimilated to the Spanish nobles, the new physical prototype of the politically powerful man in Anahuac. By controlling the signs that authorized them in the face of ancient and recent traditions, the teteuctin were more feared, admired, and respected. Onward, "the initiative to look for attire adequate to courtly customs came from the Indios themselves who traveled to the Peninsula and spent considerable sums of money on fabrics and tailors."[120] This allowed these Indios to embody a new body politic, display their preeminence, and generate social distinction in their territories.

To conclude, the earliest power negotiation of the Nahua elites with the Crown, the papacy, and their local subjects happened during this transatlantic journey. In later years, some of the teteuctin obtained privileges through juridical writings, but the first power adjustments occurred already in the material and symbolic realms. The New Spanish Indio's imaginaries, nature, and construction as a political subject emerged from the representations and interpretations of the performatively displayed Nahua body.

NOTES

Translated from Spanish by Vitus Huber. Epigraph: Bernal Díaz del Castillo, *Historia verdadera de la conquista de la Nueva España* (The true history of the Conquest of New Spain), 1568.

1. Bernal Díaz relates that they disembarked at the end of 1527, but he confused the dates, because Cortés was banished in September or October 1527. In fact, on April 5, 1528, Charles V signed instructions to Cortés to travel to Spain. A few days later, Cortés must have left the port of Veracruz. Cf. Bernal Díaz del Castillo, *Historia verdadera de la conquista de la Nueva España* (Mexico City: Academia Mexicana de la Lengua, 2016), 2: ch. CXCV, 946.

2. Francisco López de Gómara, *Historia de la Conquista de México* (Caracas: Biblioteca Ayacucho, 2007), ch. CXCII, 367.

3. Martín de Salinas, *El Emperador Carlos V y su corte según las cartas de Don Martín de Salinas, Embajador del Infante Don Fernando 1522–1539* (Madrid: Establecimiento tipográfico de Fortanet, 1903–5), 410.

4. Julia Mary Cartwright Ady, *Baldassare Castiglione the Perfect Courtier, His Life and Letters, 1478–1529* (London: John Murray, 1908), 390.

5. Ryszard Tomicki, "Una carta desconocida de Hernán Cortés a Jan Dantyszek (Juan Dantisco)," *Estudios Latinoamericanos* 15 (1992): 319–26, here 323.

6. López de Gómara, *Historia de la Conquista*, ch. CXCII, 367.

7. López de Gómara, *Historia de la Conquista*, ch. CXCII, 367.

8. This would be the historically equivalent English term.

9. Fernández de Oviedo, *Historia general y natural de las Indias: Islas y tierra-firme del mar océanico* (Guadalajara: Ediciones Facsímiles Ponton, 2006), 3: bk. 33, ch. IX, 528.

10. Elena Mazzetto, "Amusement and Symbolic Functions of Dwarfs and Hunchbacks in Mexica Society," *Memoria Americana: Cuadernos de Etnohistoria* 29, no. 1 (2021): 27–53. The author points out their function as sacrificial offerings, emissaries, companions, and confidants of the rulers (*tlahtoque*), in addition to their participation as dancers, musicians, and acrobats.

11. "Letter from Francisco Duarte to Juan Rena, archdeacon of His Majesty and vicar general of the kingdom of Navarre in Pamplona, Villarejo de Salvanés, June 24, 1528." Text transcribed and published by Esteban Mira Caballos, "Hernán Cortés returned to Spain in 1528, causing astonishment and admiration." Esteban Mira Caballos (blog), May 20, 2022, accessed May 1, 2023, https://estebanmiracaballos.com/2022/05/20/hernan-cortes-regresa-a-espana-en-1528-causando-asombro-y-admiracion/, document in Archivo General del Reino de Navarra, caj. 5, n. 24.4.

12. José Moreno Villa, *Locos, enanos, negros y niños palaciegos: Gente de placer que tuvieron los Austrias en la Corte española desde 1563 a 1700* (Mexico City: Presencia, 1939), 34.

13. Moreno Villa, *Locos, enanos, negros y niños palaciegos*, 32.

14. In mid-1529, from Krakow, the Polish chancellor Krzysztof Szydłowiecki wrote a letter to Jan Dantyszek: "I hear that Indios from the island that Hernán Cortés found have arrived at the emperor's court. If Your Lordship can conveniently do so, bring us one, which he would give me as a gift because no one can give me a more generous gift at this time." Translated text in Corpus of Ioannes Dantiscus's Texts & Correspondence, "Letter #368," Cracow, 1529-07-23, accessed January 12, 2021, http://dantiscus.ibi.uw.edu.pl/?f=letterSummary&letter=3468.

15. The term "people of pleasure" referred to people who were used for courtly entertainment, as objects of mockery and astonishment, of affection and distraction. Moreno Villa, *Locos enanos, negros y niños palaciegos*; Fernando Bouza, "El uso cortesano de la 'improporción' bufonesca," in *Mentalidad e ideología del antiguo régimen*, ed. León Carlos Álvarez Santaló and Carmen María Cremades Griñán (Murcia, Spain: Universidad de Murcia, 1993), 27–36.

16. The games had sacred implications. In the context of war, they served as an anticipatory or divinatory method for military encounters. Sahagún indicates that patolli and

ullamaztli were played by the principal lords "as a pastime" but also says that "this game [patolli], and that of the ball, have left them for arousing suspicion of some idolatrous superstitions that exist among them." Bernardino de Sahagún, *Historia general de las cosas de Nueva España*, 1577, bk. 8, ch. X, fol. 191r, *Codex* digitized by the Biblioteca Medicea Laurenziana, accessed March 20, 2023, https://www.loc.gov/item/2021667853/.

17. Fernández de Oviedo y Valdés, *Historia general*, 3: bk. 33, ch. IX, 528.

18. Dietrich Briesemeister, "Sobre indios, moriscos y cristianos 'a su manera': Testimonios pictóricos en el Trachtenbuch de Christoph Weiditz," *Jahrbuch für Geschichte Lateinamerikas* 43 (2006): 1–24, here 5.

19. Briesemeister, "Sobre indios, moriscos y cristianos 'a su manera," 6.

20. Hernán Cortés, *Cartas de Relación*, ed. Mario Hernández Sánchez-Barba (Madrid: Historia 16, 1985), 139.

21. Alessandra Russo, "Cortés's Objects and the Idea of New Spain," *Journal of the History of Collections* 23, no. 2 (2011): 229–52. Although I respectfully differ from the author that the artifacts had been materially modified by the direct or indirect intervention of the conquistador since 1519, it is indisputable that they were essential in the construction process of creating Cortés's idea of New Spain in the eyes of his European contemporaries. For the visual-material characteristics of the objects sent by Cortés in 1519, 1522, 1524, and 1526, see Erika Escutia, "Poseer e inventar: Los objetos y la interpretación de las prácticas estéticas americanas en las casas reales europeas (1493–1565)" (PhD diss., Universitat Pompeu Fabra, 2021), 109–38, 153–66, 196–207.

22. Vitus Huber, "Die Ordnung geraubter Dinge: Materielle Kultur in der *Conquista Amerikas*," in *MEMO Medieval and Early Modern Material Culture Online*, Special Issue 2 (2022), Mona Garloff and Natalie Krentz, eds., *Objektordnungen zwischen Zeiten und Räumen: Verzeichnung, Transport und die Deutung von Objekten im Wandel*, accessed May 1, 2023, https://memo.imareal.sbg.ac.at/wsarticle/memo-sonderband/02-2022-huber-ordnung-geraubter-dinge/.

23. Lucio Marineo Sículo, *Obra compuesta por Lucio Marineo Siculo Coronista d[e] sus Magestades de las cosas memorables de España* (Alcalá de Henares, Spain: Miguel de Eguía, 1530), fol. 208v. The biography of Cortés and other "distinguished men of Spain" does not appear in later editions, due to Crown censorship.

24. Marineo Sículo, *Obra compuesta por Lucio Marineo Siculo Coronista*, fol. 209v.

25. Standardized spelling of the plural of *teuctli*, the name of the men who had finished their studies in the *calmecac*, an educational institution for priests and warriors. Among them were chosen the political and military leaders. After the *Conquista* and throughout the sixteenth century, the word was used by the Crown in its Castilian version, *tecles* or *teules*, to refer to the "principal lords" of the Nahua provinces. I prefer not to use the term *pipiltin* because, in many cases, their parents were already deceased, and they covered the functions of *señores*. I do not use the term "noble" because they had not yet acquired such status

within the Castilian system. Quotation from López de Gómara, *Historia de la conquista*, ch. CXCII, 367.

26. Domingo Francisco de San Antón Chimalpahin Cuauhtlehuanitzin, *Historia de las conquistas de Hernando Cortés* (Mexico City: Imprenta de la testamentaria de Ontiveros, 1826), 2: 433–34; Fernando Alvarado Tezozomoc, *Crónica mexicayotl* (Mexico City: UNAM, 1998), 151; Juan Buenaventura Zapata y Mendoza, *Historia cronológica de la noble ciudad de Tlaxcala* (Tlaxcala: Universidad Autónoma de Tlaxcala, Secretaría de Extensión Universitaria y Difusión Cultural, 1995), 137.

27. The most complete list of the Nahuas is in "Libro manual de cargo y data de la Tesorería de la Casa de la Contratación," October 2, 1528, Archivo General de Indias (henceforth AGI), Contratación, 4675-B, L. 4, fol. 29v; see also Howard Cline, "Hernando Cortés y los indios aztecas en España," *Norte* 244 (1971): 58–70, here 63.

28. From Tenochtitlan: Moteuczoma's relatives were Francisco de Alvarado Matlaccohuatzin and Gaspar Toltequitzin. Don Juan Coatl Huitzilihuitl, nephew of the last tlahtoani, Cuauhtémoc, also attended. From Tlatelolco: Damián Tlacochcalcatl, Jerónimo Conchano, and Martín Auelitoc. Also listed in the papers of the Casa de Contratación is a "Francisco Eca," who may have been a relative or was himself Martín Ecatzin. "Libro manual de cargo y data" 29v; Chimalpahin, *Historia de las conquistas*, 2: ch. LXII, 164.

29. From Tetzcoco: "Baltasar de Tescuco," from Tlacopan: Gaspar Tequepal and Gabriel Totoquihuaztli, from Xochimilco: Martín Serón, also Felipe de Castilla Momalquiatzin, lord of Cuitláhuac; and Baltasar Tuzquecoazuyl, ruler of Culhuacan. "Libro manual de cargo y data" 29v; Chimalpahin, *Historia de las conquistas*, 2: ch. LXII, 164.

30. From Cempoala, came "Baltasar" and "Don Juan Tgihuacmitl," son of the so-called fat cacique. From Tlaxcala, Don Lorenzo Maxixcatzin, Valeriano Castañeda, and Pedro Castañeda, Julián Quauhpilzintli, Juan Citlalihuitzin, and Antonio Huatlalotzin. "Libro manual de cargo y data," fol. 29v.

31. Hernán Cortés, "Cuarta carta de Relación," in *Cartas de relación* (Mexico City: Porrúa, 2005), 268.

32. Armando Martínez Garnica, "La incorporación jurídica del vencido: La nobleza aborigen de la Nueva España," in *Modernidad iberoamericana: Cultura, política y cambio social*, ed. Francisco Colom González (Madrid: Fundación ICO, CSIC, 2009), 96–104; Castañeda de la Paz and Miguel Luque Talaván, *Para que de ellos e de vos quede memoria: La heráldica indígena novohispana del Centro de México*. Libro segundo (Mexico City: UNAM, 2021), 59–67, 121–24.

33. Briesemeister, "Indios," 6.

34. "This spectacle allowed Cortés to establish his objectives and succeed in establishing new norms of behavior towards the Amerindians." Eric Taladoire, *De América a Europa: Cuando los indígenas descubrieron el Viejo Mundo (1493–1892)* (Mexico City: Fondo de Cultura Económica, 2017), 53.

35. José Luis de Rojas, "Boletos sencillos y pasajes redondos: Indígenas y mestizos americanos que visitaron España," *Revista de Indias* 69, no. 246 (2009): 185–206, here 186.
36. Cline, "Cortés," 63.
37. López de Gómara, *Historia de la conquista*, ch. CXCII, 367.
38. López de Gómara and Díaz del Castillo coincide in pointing out that Cortés took all the lords who requested to be able to go with him, including the Indian lords. See López de Gómara, *Historia de la conquista*, ch. CXCII, 367; Díaz del Castillo, *Historia verdadera*, 2: ch. CXCIV, 944.
39. Díaz del Castillo, *Historia verdadera*, 2: ch. CXCIV, 942.
40. Díaz del Castillo, *Historia verdadera*, 943.
41. Martínez Garnica, "Incorporación jurídica," 96–104; Jovita Baber, "Empire, Indians, and the Negotiation for the Status of City in Tlaxcala, 1521–1550," in *Negotiation within Domination: New Spain's Indian Pueblos Confront the Spanish State*, ed. Susan Kellogg and Ethelia Ruiz Medrano (Boulder: University Press of Colorado, 2010), 19–44, here 22–23; María Castañeda de la Paz, *Conflictos y alianzas en tiempos de cambio: Azcapotzalco, Tlacopan, Tenochtitlan y Tlatelolco (siglos XII–XVI)* (Mexico City: UNAM, Instituto de Investigaciones Antropológicas, 2013), 222; Caroline Dodds Pennock, "Aztecs Abroad? Uncovering the Early Indigenous Atlantic," *American Historical Review* 125, no. 3 (2020): 787–814, here 800; Caroline Dodds Pennock, *On Savage Shores: How Indigenous Americans Discovered Europe* (New York: Alfred A. Knopf, 2023), 23–26.
42. I develop this notion following Erving Goffman. In his interaction theory, the sociologist uses dramaturgical metaphors. He considers that humans build props "behind the scenes" (clothing, gesture, and others) that are displayed "on stage" as visible resources to perform social acts and negotiate their identity with a specific audience in a social arena. See Erving Goffman, *The Presentation of Self in Everyday Life* (Edinburgh: University of Edinburgh, 1956).
43. Rubén González Cuerva, "La historia global de la diplomacia desde la Monarquía hispana," *Chronica Nova* 44 (2018): 21–54, here 32.
44. Jorge Gurría Lacroix, ed., *Provincias y regiones nuevamente descubiertas en las Indias Occidentales, en el último viaje* (Mexico City: Juan Pablos, 1972), 56.
45. Gurría Lacroix, *Provincias y regiones nuevamente descubiertas en las Indias Occidentales, en el último viaje*, 56. In that source they are described in "Pequeño tratado acerca de los embajadores indios y los regalos presentados a la cesárea majestad mencionada según el intérprete Fernando Flores." See also *Nueva noticia del país que los españoles encontraron en el año de 1521 llamado Yucatán*, Facsimile ed. (Mexico City: UNAM, 1940).
46. "Libro manual de cargo y data. 1525–1530," AGI, Contratación, 4675-B, L. 4, fol. 16v. The episode is also recounted in Andrea Navagero, *Viaje a España del magnífico señor Andrés Navagero (1524–1526): Embajador de la República de Venecia ante el Emperador Carlos V* (Valencia, Spain: Castalia, 1951), 274–75. Diego de Valadés notes, without indicating

a precise date, that the Tlaxcaltecah danced in front of the emperor, who "as he heard the number of dancers and how synchronous that they stayed in the changes of rhythms, could not be persuaded of it until a demonstration was made in his presence in Valladolid, to which he was present for a whole afternoon in the company of his nobles and principal confidants." Diego de Valadés, *Rhetorica Christiana* (Mexico City: Fondo de Cultura Económica, 1984), 168–69. For more on the 1520 Valladolid presentation and the use of artifacts from New Spain in the context of the imperial wedding in Seville, see Escutia, "Poseer e inventar," 115–22 and 204–5.

47. The "caciques" traveled to Castile, but it was not customary to meet with the emperor. Martín Moctezuma had already traveled (1525) to be indoctrinated in a monastery, following the practice implemented since Ferdinand the Catholic. In 1529, at least twenty-four caciques were instructed in Sevillian monasteries by royal mandate: twelve from La Española, eight from La Fernandina, and four sons of *mburuvicha*, or Guarani "caciques," from the Río de la Plata. AGI, Indiferente, 421, L. 11, fols. 308r–311r; L. 12, fols. 207r–208r and 211v; AGI, Indiferente, 1952 L. 1, fols. 25v–27v, 50r–51r, 81v, 89v–91r, and 147r–v; AGI, Santo Domingo, 1121, L. 1, fol. 33r; AGI, Indiferente, 1961, L. 2, fols. 13v–14r and 168v–169r.

48. In 1525, Cortés took the most potent tlahtoque of the Altiplano with him on the journey to the Hibueras. See Julia Madajczak's and María Castañeda de la Paz's chapters in this volume. The absence of such influential figures and the rumors of the possible death of any of them on the trip allowed other Nahuas to take over their lands. Therefore, in 1528, the risk that their absence implied was evident to the teteuctin. For Mesoamerican political change after the journey to the Hibueras, see Castañeda de la Paz, *Conflictos y alianzas*, 181–84. See also the case of Martín, the eldest son of Moctezuma, sent by imperial orders to receive Christian instruction in the convent of Santo Domingo de Talavera de la Reina in 1525 while the Spanish were distributing the tribute of his people. He could not exercise the rights promised by the Crown, as he was poisoned when he returned from Spain for the third time in 1539. Alvarado, *Crónica mexicayotl*, 151.

49. Stephanie Armer, "Augenzeugenbericht über den Aufzug des Hernán Cortés vor Kaiser Karl V: in Madrid im Jahr 1528," supplement in *Welt im Wandel 1500–1600*, ed. Thomas Eser and Stephanie Armer (Nuremberg: Germanisches Nationalmuseum, 2017), n/p. The referenced manuscript is in Freiherrlich Scheuerlsches Familienarchiv, Codex B2, fols. 122r–123r.

50. José Manuel Nieto Soria, "Ceremony and Pomp for a Monarchy: The Trastamara of Castile," *CEMYR Notebooks* 17 (2009): 51–72, here 61.

51. Manuel Fernández Álvarez, ed., "Historia del invencible emperador Carlos Quinto, rey de España, compuesta por su majestad cesárea, como se ve por el papel que va en la siguiente hoja," in *Corpus documental de Carlos V* (Salamanca: Universidad de Salamanca, 1981), 4: 483–567, here 495.

52. Armer, "Augenzeugenbericht," n/p.

53. The teteuctin, in their later documents, usually introduce themselves and mention that they went to Castile "to kiss the hands of Your Majesty." Kissing the king's hand was a ceremonial gesture, introduced by the Catholic Monarchs, of adhesion and vassalage that every person before the monarch had to perform.

54. Armer, "Augenzeugenbericht," n/p.

55. Armer, "Augenzeugenbericht," n/p.

56. Anna Kalinowska and Jonathan Spangler, eds., *Power and Ceremony in European History: Rituals, Practices and Representative Bodies since the Late Middle Ages* (London: Bloomsbury Academic, 2021).

57. "Libro manual de cargo y data," AGI, Contratación, 4675-B, L. 4, fol. 29v.

58. According to the documents of the Casa de Contratación ("Libro manual de cargo y data," AGI, Contratación, fols. 30r–32v), it could be Don Juan Coatl Huitzilihuitl, grandson of Ahuizotl, or Hernando de Tapia. I believe it was the latter, due to the high merits that he obtained, including the appointment as knight of the Order of the Golden Spur of San Pedro in August 1533. See Guillermo Fernández de Recas, *Cacicazgos y nobiliario indígena de la Nueva España* (Mexico City: Instituto Bibliográfico Mexicano, 1961), 231.

59. Díaz del Castillo, *Historia verdadera*, ch. CXCV, 955–56.

60. Díaz del Castillo, *Historia verdadera*, 957.

61. Paolo Giovio, *Elogia virorum bellica virtute illustrium: Septem libris iam olim ab authore comprehensa* (Basle, Switzerland: Petri Pernae Typhographi, 1575), bk. 6, 351.

62. Michel Foucault, "La prosa del mundo," in *Las palabras y las cosas: Una arqueología de las ciencias humanas* (Mexico City: Siglo XXI Editores, 1968), 26–52, here 35.

63. Baldassare Castiglione, *The Courtier of Count Baldessar Castilio: Deuided into foure bookes* (London: Iohn Wolfe, 1588), bk. 1, ch. III, 28–29.

64. Marineo Sículo, *Obra compuesta*, fol. 208v.

65. Armer, "Augenzeugenbericht," n/p.

66. Of hair, "doctors say that it is the excrement that the brain makes at the time of its nutrition." Juan Huarte de San Juan, *Examen de ingenios para las ciencias* (Barcelona: Daniel Cortezo y Compañía, 1889), 265.

67. Huarte de San Juan, *Examen de ingenios*, 141. Regarding the discussion of the Indios as melancholic, phlegmatic, or "choleric dour," and its political implications, see Germán Morong and Víctor Brangier, "El 'humor' de los indios en el saber médico de los siglos XVI–XVII," *Revista Médica de Chile* 145, no. 7 (2017): 920–25; Carlos López Beltrán, "Sangre y temperamento: Pureza y mestizajes en las sociedades de castas americanas," in *Saberes locales: Ensayos sobre la historia de la ciencia en América Latina*, ed. Frida Borbach and Carlos López Beltrán (Mexico City: El Colegio de Michoacán, 2008), 313–23.

68. Aristotle, *Politics* (Madrid: Gredos, 1988), bk. 1, ch. II, 58.

69. Christian Schäffer, "La política de Aristóteles y el aristotelismo político de la conquista," *Ideas y Valores* 119 (2002): 109–34, here 113.

70. Franco Minonzio, "Il Museo di Paolo Giovio e la galleria degli uomini illustri," in *Testi, immagini e filologia nel XVI secolo: Atti della giornata di studio, Pisa (30 settembre–1° ottobre 2004)*, ed. Eliana Carrara and Silvia Ginzburg (Pisa, Italy: Scuola Normale Superiore di Pisa, 2007), 130–33.

71. Giovio, *Elogia*, bk. 6, 351.

72. Andrea Navagero, *Viaje*, 274–75. The greenish-black or ashen color was also associated with melancholy. Huarte de San Juan, *Examen*, 204.

73. Sergio Tognetti, "Note sul commercio di schiavi neri nella Firenze del Quattrocento," *Nuova revista storica* 86, no. 2 (2002): 361–74.

74. It is plausible that this is an "Indio" from the Caribbean area, since their fame as great swimmers ran from the first accounts of Paria, where they swam to the depths to get the largest pearls. See Pietro Bembo, *Della istoria viniziana di m. Pietro Bembo cardinale da lui volgarizzata (Venice: Antonio Zatta, 1790)*, 1: bk. 6, 268; cf. Pietro Martire d'Anghiera, *De Orbe Novo: The Eight Decades of Peter Martyr d'Anghera*, vol. 1 (New York: G. P. Putnam's Sons, 1912), Third Decade, bk. 2, 295–96.

75. Giovio, *Elogia*, bk. 6, 310.

76. Catherine Richardson, *Clothing Culture, 1350–1650* (Aldershot, UK: Ashgate, 2004), 8–9.

77. Armer, "Augenzeugenbericht," n/p.

78. For the earliest European impressions of Cortés's early envoys, see Bartolomé de Las Casas, *Historia de las Indias* (Caracas: Biblioteca Ayacucho, 1986), 3: bk. 3, ch. CXXI, 443; Martire, *De Orbe Novo*, 2: Fifth Decade, bk. 4, 114; Christian Feest, "Una evaluación europea del arte mexicano," in *Destinos cruzados: Cinco siglos de encuentros con los amerindios*, ed. Jöelle Rostkowski and Silvie Deveres (Mexico City: Siglo XXI, 1996), 93–103. Albrecht Dürer, Las Casas, and Anghiera appreciated Mesoamerican art based on their proximity to the European elites' material, technical, or aesthetic canons. See Escutia, "Poseer e inventar," 126–38.

79. Roque Bárcia, *Primer diccionario general etimológico de la lengua española* (Barcelona: F. Seix, 1894), 4: 1132.

80. Aristotle, *Política*, bk. 1, ch. II, 58.

81. Stefan Hanß, "Material Encounters: Knotting Cultures in Early Modern Peru and Spain," *Historical Journal* 62, no. 3 (2019): 583–615, here 588.

82. To learn about different intentions and strategies of Diego de Velázquez, Hernán Cortés, and Fray Domingo de Betanzos, see Erika Escutia, "Antes de Cortés: La historia de los primeros objetos preciosos de Motecuzoma que llegaron al rey Carlos I de España," in *Tornaviaje: Tránsito artístico entre los virreinatos americanos y la metrópolis*, ed. Fernando Quiles, Pablo Amador, and Martha Fernández (Seville: Andavira, Enredars, Universidad Pablo de Olavide, 2020), 111–34; Russo, "Cortés's Objects," 229–52; Davide Domenici and Laura Laurencich Minelli, "Domingo de Betanzos' Gifts to Pope Clement VII in 1532–1533:

Tracking the Early History of Some Mexican Objects and Codices in Italy," *Estudios de Cultura Náhuatl* 47 (2014): 169–209.

83. The Catholic monarchs exhibited Taino sacred sculptures called *cemis* at the University of Alcalá with this intention, Bishop Alessandro Geraldini sent others to be exhibited at the Vatican, and Catherine of Aragon received artifacts from caciques in England. Later, the pieces from the first of Cortés's shipments were distributed among Margaret of Austria, Ferdinand of Habsburg, Charles V, his wife, and children. Likewise, the second Cortesian shipment reached Francis I when Fleury stole it. See Carina L. Johnson, "Aztec Regalia and the Reformation on Display," in *Collecting across Cultures: Material Exchanges in the Early Modern Atlantic*, ed. Daniela Bleichmar and Peter C. Mancall (Philadelphia: University of Pennsylvania Press, 2011), 83–98; Deanna MacDonald, "Collecting a New World: The Ethnographic Collections of Margaret of Austria," *Sixteenth Century Journal* 33, no. 3 (2002): 649–54, here 651; Lauran Toorians, "Het 'Azteeks Museum' van Margaretha van Oostenrijk," *Ons Erfdeel* 35 (1992): 727–34; Escutia, "Poseer e inventar," 32–69, 151–86.

84. Gilbert Durand, *Las estructuras antropológicas del imaginario* (Mexico City: Fondo de Cultura Económica, 2004); for its particular development in the case of Cortés, see Tzvetan Todorov, *La conquista de América: El problema del otro* (Mexico City: Siglo XXI, 2003), 106–36; see, furthermore, Russo, "Cortés's Objects."

85. Hans Belting, *Antropología de la imagen* (Buenos Aires: Katz, 2002), 44–49.

86. Belting, *Antropología de la imagen*, 45–46.

87. Armer, "Augenzeugenbericht," n/p.

88. Armer, "Augenzeugenbericht," n/p.

89. Martire, *De Orbe Novo*, 2: Fifth Decade, bk. 10, 414–15.

90. Armer, "Augenzeugenbericht," n/p.

91. Henry R. Wagner, "Three Accounts of the Expedition of Fernando Cortés, Printed in Germany between 1520 and 1522," *Hispanic American Historical Review* 9, no. 2 (1929): 176–212, here 197.

92. Germanisches Nationalmuseum, Nuremberg, Hs. 22474, "Trachtenbuch/Christoph Weiditz," 1530–40.

93. Armer, "Augenzeugenbericht," n/p.

94. Theodor Hampe, *Authentic Everyday Dress of the Renaissance: All 154 Plates from the "Trachtenbuch"* (New York: Dover Publications, 1927), 22–23; Jean Michel Massing, "Early European Images of America: The Ethnographic Approach," in *Circa 1492: Art in the Age of Exploration*, ed. Jay Levenson (Washington, DC: National Gallery of Art, 1991), 515–20.

95. Briesemeister, "Indios," 7; Russo, "Cortés's Objects," 243–44; Helen Burgos-Ellis, "Innocents Abroad? Representations of Aztecs Traveling in Europe in the Age of Discovery," in *Tornaviaje: Tránsito artístico entre los virreinatos americanos y la metrópolis*, ed. Fernando Quiles, Pablo F. Amador, and Martha Fernández (Seville: Andavira, Enredars, Universidad Pablo de Olavide, 2020), 100–105.

96. Elizabeth Hill Boone, "Seeking Indianness: Christoph Weiditz, the Aztecs, and Feathered Amerindians," *Colonial Latin American Review* 26, no. 1 (2017): 39–61.

97. VV.AA, "Tocados y peinados en el México antiguo: Catálogo visual," *Arqueología Mexicana* 66 (2016): 8–90; Justyna Olko, "Traje y atributos del poder en el mundo azteca: Significados y funciones contextuales," *Anales del Museo de América* 14 (2006): 61–88.

98. Hill Boone, "Seeking Indianness," 46.

99. Armer, "Augenzeugenbericht," n/p.

100. Patricia Rieff Anawalt, *Indian Clothing before Cortés* (Norman: University of Oklahoma Press, 1981), 30–31, 69–70; Frances Berdan and Patricia Rieff Anawalt, *The Essential Codex Mendoza* (Berkeley: University of California Press, 1997), 2: 14–25.

101. On the first point, see Justyna Olko, "Supervivencia de los objetos de rango prehispánicos entre la nobleza colonial nahua," *Revista Española de Antropología Americana* 41, no. 2 (2011): 455–69. On the second point, see José Luis Casado Soto and Carlos Soler d'Hyver de las Deses, *Christoph Weiditz, The Costume Codex: Trachtenbuch* (Valencia, Spain: Grial, 2001), 104.

102. Armer speculated that the author of the missive is Weiditz himself. The author could also be Weiditz's companion, the armorer Kolman Helmschmid, or one of the Welser diplomats, who corresponded with Hernán Cortés in the context of his presence at the imperial court for the cession of Venezuela to the powerful family. Armer, "Augenzeugenbericht," n/p.

103. According to Alfonso de Palencia's *Universal Vocabulario* of 1490, "ingenious is said because it contains the strength or vigor to generate some artifice. Ingenuity is the inner strength of the mind with which we often invent what we did not learn from another: said ingenuity is almost engendered within: or by genius that is natural. Ingenuity is natural wisdom." Alfonso de Palencia, *Universal vocabulario en latín y en romance: Edición facsímil* (Madrid: Comisión permanente de la Asociación de Academias de la Lengua Española, 1967), 1: 214r.

104. Ingenuity and knowledge were very different ideas. The first was only a primary condition for the second. Gasparo Contarini expresses this idea well. Between 1521 and 1525, he informed the Venetian state that the Germans were "not of sublime wit, but they apply themselves with such fixity and perseverance that they succeed in various manual trades as well as in letters." The same author, present at the reception of the Cempoaltecah in Valladolid, said that what he had seen—the gold and silver discs, clothing, and tiny lapidary—"truly proves in those places to have people of wit." Gasparo Contarini, *Relazioni degli ambasciatori Veneti al senato* (Cambridge: Cambridge University Press, 2012), 4: 21; Contarini in Henry Harrisse, *Bibliotheca Americana Vetustissima: A Description of Works Relating to America Published between the Years 1492 and 1551* (Paris: Tross, 1872), 39.

105. Giovio, *Elogia*, bk. 6, 351.

106. "Carta de Juan de Zumárraga a Carlos V. 27 de agosto de 1529," in *Colección de documentos inéditos, relativos al descubrimiento, conquista y colonización de las posesiones españolas*

de América y Oceanía, ed. Luis Torres de Mendoza (Madrid: Imprenta de José María Pérez, 1870), 13: 142.

107. Those ideas revived after the *Parecer* written by Fray Tomás Ortiz, an "Enumeration of the reasons why the Indians are unworthy of liberty," affirming, among harsh accusations, that the Indios are "brutal," "they exercise none of the humane arts or industries," "God has never created a race more full of vice and composed without the least mixture of kindness or culture (policía)." Martire, *De Orbe Novo*, 2: Seventh Decade, bk. 2, ch. IV, 274–76.

108. Vasco de Puga, *Provisiones, cédulas, instrucciones para el gobierno de la Nueva España* (Madrid: Cultura Hispánica, 1945), 54.

109. Ana Díaz Serrano, "La República de Tlaxcala ante el rey de España durante el siglo XVI," *Historia Mexicana* 61, no. 3 (2012): 1049–107, here 1052.

110. "Libro manual de cargo y data," AGI, Contratación, 4675-B, L. 4, fol. 30r; Giovio, *Elogia*, bk. 6, 351.

111. Giovio, *Elogia*, bk. 6, 351.

112. For the journey of the teteuctin and Franciscans, see Ignacio Bernal, "Vida y obra de fray Bernardino de Sahagún: Dos cartas de Paso y Troncoso a García Icazbalceta," *Estudios de cultura náhuatl* 15 (1982): 247–90. It is no coincidence that precisely in 1529 and 1530, the massive conversion to Christianity of the Nahuas began. See Baber, "Empire," 24; Guy Stresser-Péan, *El sol-dios y Cristo: La cristianización de los indios en México vista desde la Sierra de Puebla* (Mexico City: Centro de Estudios Mexicanos y Centroamericanos, 2011).

113. Lewis Hanke, "Pope Paul III and the American Indians," *Harvard Theological Review* 30, no. 2 (1937): 65–102.

114. John Leddy Phelan, *El reino milenario de los franciscanos en el Nuevo Mundo* (Mexico City: UNAM, 1972), 12.

115. "The people are more political, so in their buildings of many planks of wood, *and in the dress of their people*" (my italics), "Carta de Fray Juan de Zumárraga a su sobrino. México, 23 de agosto de 1539," in *Nueva colección de documentos para la historia de México*, ed. Joaquín García Icazbalceta (Mexico City: Antigua librería de Andrade y Morales, successors, 1889), 2: 281–83, here 283.

116. In 1569, Friar Jerónimo Román wrote: "The good laws have only two effects they intend to induce in the *policía*: the first is to straighten every man and member in the whole community and republic by doing good. And the second is to prevent men from doing evil and from all injury to the whole community and to any part or member thereof." Jerónimo Román, *Repúblicas de Indias idolatrías y gobierno en México y Perú antes de la conquista* (Madrid: Victoriano Suárez editor, 1897), 1: 275. The association between virtues and vices with clothing can be seen in Olmos's *Sermonario* and *Tratado de hechicerías y sortilegios*. It includes face painting, embroidery, and clothing associated with the sins of being susceptible to idolatry. Furthermore, the tenth book of the *Florentine Codex* expresses several virtues and vices through gestures and clothing.

117. Antonio de León Pinelo and Juan de Solórzano, *Recopilación de leyes de los reinos de las Indias*, bk. 6, title 1, law 21, digital version, accessed May 1, 2023, https://leyes.congreso.gob.pe/leyes_indias.aspx.

118. Edmundo O'Gorman, "Una ordenanza para el buen gobierno de los indios: México, 1546," *Boletín del Archivo General de la Nación* 9, no. 2 (1990): 63–67, here 66.

119. Justyna Olko, "Convenciones y estrategias en la iconografía del rango de la nobleza indígena del centro de México en el siglo XVI," *Revista Española de Antropología Americana* 38, no. 2 (2008): 207–40.

120. Díaz Serrano, "República," 1087.

Part IV

Representations and Iconic Figures

9

Beyond Malinche

Other Native Women in the Conquista

LORI BOORNAZIAN DIEL

Though women played a key role in the history and politics of pre-Hispanic Mexico, they were infrequently included in Nahua histories, both pictorial and alphabetic, recorded after the imposition of Spanish colonial rule. When they were included, it was typically because they signaled political messages that were important to send in the colonial era when the histories were created.[1] Women were also seldomly mentioned in Nahua accounts of the *Conquista*. Even Malinche, also known as Doña Marina, Hernán Cortés's Native translator and a key participant in the Spanish invasion, is often left out of accounts of the war painted by native scribes. Nevertheless, though portraits of Malinche that attempt to elucidate her position, actions, and motivations during the *Conquista* can never be complete, she has become a potent symbol and literary trope, a singular actor who, despite the extraordinary circumstances of her life and experiences, has taken on the mantle of female identity and potential power at the moment of contact and beyond.[2]

Of course, other women also participated in the *Conquista*, but for the most part their identities and experiences are poorly known as they were so rarely referenced in records of the Spanish invasion. On one level, the lack of information on women in these sources owes to gender bias, with the experiences of women being largely unremarkable to the vast majority of male chroniclers. Moreover, as in the histories about the pre-Hispanic past, when women were included in accounts of the war, it was often because of the larger symbolic role they served, signaling alliances or conflicts that were important to assert in the colonial era, well after the defeat of Tenochtitlan.

By looking beyond Malinche for other women in Nahua accounts of the *Conquista*, we can come to a more nuanced understanding of the roles, actual and symbolic, played by native women in war and diplomacy at this time.[3] Indeed, as Federico Navarrete has written, without the labor of women, the Spaniards could never have survived nor been victorious in their war of invasion.[4] And yet, as Navarrete also points out, our idea of the *Conquista* has been constructed with an active negation and ignorance of the female experience. Moreover, as Karen Vieira Powers notes, much of the scholarship on Indigenous women has tended to oversimplify their experiences and to be limited by what she describes as a "whore/victim" dichotomy, wherein on the one hand, native women are seen as consensual partners to Spanish conquistadors, and on the other hand, they are seen as victims of rape and sexual abuse.[5] While these opposing views certainly encompass the experiences of some women during the war, they do not adequately convey the range and variability in the experiences of women in general. These experiences were largely dictated by a woman's status and ethnicity. For example, many lower-class women were given as slaves to the Spanish conquistadors, just as Malinche was, while noblewomen were given to Spaniards as presumed marital partners and to build alliances, though some of their experiences may have mimicked those of enslaved women. Other women were targeted by the Spaniards in acts of intimidation, and still others took up arms and attempted to fight the Spaniards. And a few women even managed to retain power as high-ranking members of Nahua society after the Spanish invasion, if not always for themselves, then for their children.

ENSLAVED WOMEN

Many of the women who were made to participate in the Spanish-Mexica war did so as slaves, sexual and otherwise. Slavery was closely linked with warfare in ancient Mesoamerican society. Men, women, and children were often enslaved in the aftermath of war, either taken in battle or provided by defeated towns to their conquerors in acts of appeasement. While some of these enslaved individuals were destined for sacrifice, many others were forced to work for their enslavers. Indeed, based on the jobs enslaved people were said to have performed in pre-Hispanic society, jobs largely related to food and textile production, the majority must have been women.[6] There was even a genre of Nahuatl songs that lamented the plight of women taken in war and enslaved, revealing anxiety that the singers' wives and daughters might someday meet such a fate.[7] The association of war with slavery continued through the Spanish invasion, with many women being subsumed into this system and being forced into lives of precarity.

In Hernán Cortés's *Letters*, he makes frequent references to Native lords presenting enslaved women to the Spaniards, often listing them with accounts of food and gifts that were also received. For example, Cortés wrote that one native leader from a village not far from the Panuco River had sent "some women, and chickens and other things to eat" to a newly arrived Spanish ship. He said that two rulers from other towns "gave me several gold necklaces of little weight and value and seven or eight female slaves." Some villages within Huexotzingo gave him "some female slaves and clothing and some small pieces of gold." And when staying in Itztapalapa, the ruler of that city and the ruler of Coyoacan together "gave me some clothing and slave girls, and made me very welcome."[8] The Spanish conquistador and chronicler Bernal Díaz also mentions the provision of women to the Spaniards by some native communities, noting that they were meant to grind corn for them.[9] Queen Isabel had outlawed the enslavement of native peoples in 1501, and this was reiterated in the Laws of Burgos of 1512. However, the practice of *rescate*, or ransom, allowed a loophole in that native peoples who were already enslaved by other native peoples could be legally exchanged with Spaniards.[10] This likely explains why the conquistadors would so openly discuss the acquisition of these women at the start of the invasion.

Though the Spaniards do not directly reference the expectation of sexual services from these women, this was surely demanded of them. As Richard Trexler notes, Spanish soldiers in Europe were accustomed to women's participation in military society through mundane domestic tasks, such as cooking and sewing, but they were also accustomed to women providing sexual services.[11] The Spaniards must have expected women to serve in these same roles in the New World. In fact, Spanish conquistadors came to be perceived as sexually violent toward native women by other European nations, who used this as evidence of their lack of civility.[12]

References to the beauty of the young women given to the Spaniards suggests that sex was an expectation of them. For example, the Spanish friar Diego Durán, writing in the later sixteenth century, notes that native rulers understood that the Spaniards desired beautiful women. Recounting their stop in Tlaxcala, he writes,

> The Tlaxcalteca willingly and rapidly gave the Spaniards a number of soldiers as well as carriers for their belongings and presented them with women to serve them. The latter were accepted by the soldiers with pleasure. Our chronicle narrates that from that time on, wherever the Spaniards arrived, they were given young, beautiful maidens, daughters of men of high position, to serve them.[13]

When the gifting of women to the Spaniards is mentioned in native accounts of the *Conquista*, some also stress that the Spaniards desired beautiful women. For example, the *Anales de Tlatelolco* notes that Cortés sent a message to Cuauhtemoc, ruler of Tenochtitlan, demanding that beautiful women, along with corn, eggs, and other provisions, be sent to him.[14] Even Spanish chroniclers, such as Díaz, reveal that women were not always voluntarily given, as he recounts how the Spaniards took native girls from their communities, specifically targeting beautiful ones. The consistent references to the beauty of these women suggests that they were expected to do more than just grind corn.[15]

While the gifting of enslaved women to the conquistadors may have been a common occurrence, they are rarely included in the pictorial histories that record the Spanish invasion. For example, a well-known image from the *Codex Azcatitlan*, likely painted in Mexico City in the late sixteenth or early seventeenth century, shows the Spanish advance toward Tenochtitlan with Malinche at the fore and native porters at the back. Except for Malinche, the enslaved women who would have also accompanied the group are absent. The same is true in sources from Tlaxcala. The *Lienzo de Tlaxcala*, known only through copies, and its cognate, the *Texas Fragment*, depict the arrival of the Spaniards and their journey to Tlaxcala and from there to Tenochtitlan and other territories, but no enslaved women are shown as a part of their contingent, again except for Malinche. This omission was likely because the presence of enslaved women on military expeditions was largely unremarkable and not worthy of mention.

When women were included as a part of a military expedition, then, it must have been because they were necessary in asserting a particular message. For example, the *Lienzo de Quauhquechollan* does feature Indigenous women, though they are far outnumbered by men. Likely created in the 1530s, this *Lienzo* records in pictorial form the aide the people of Quauhquechollan provided the Spaniards in their invasion of Guatemala. It depicts some women as porters or grinding corn, and a scene of battle includes two Quauhquechollan women.[16] While this pictorial provides information on women's roles on military expeditions, as food preparers, porters, and even combatants, the *Lienzo* is both a story of conquest and migration, establishing the settlement of these Nahua people in Guatemala. Thus, the presence of women on this expedition underscores the strength of their settlement in this foreign land, as women from Quauhquechollan would have been necessary to maintain the ethnic identity of this group of settlers in Guatemala.

NOBLEWOMEN AND MARRIAGE ALLIANCES

At the start of the Spanish invasion, when Nahua lords gave their own daughters to the Spaniards, they expected them to be accepted as wives. The provisioning of royal daughters as wives to political allies was a pre-Hispanic tradition. Such marriages sent political messages, being used to secure loyalties between cities or to break free from another city's control.[17] Accordingly, it makes sense that some Nahua rulers would follow this same pattern to secure an alliance with the Spaniards and break free of Mexica control. Moreover, when a noblewoman was given to the ruler of another city, she would enter that ruler's household, giving her an opportunity to keep watch over her husband and serve as a link between her new homeland and her old one. The same was surely expected of the young women who were given to the Spaniards; they would have joined them on their military campaign and acted as conduits between the Spaniards and their own people, both those on the expedition and at home. The disruption these women would have experienced, being separated from their homelands and kin and immersed into a new culture, must have been a disconcerting experience.[18]

The use of noblewomen as a means of forging an alliance with the European invaders in an act of political maneuvering likely first took place during the Spaniards' stop at Cempoala along the Gulf Coast.[19] Bernal Díaz notes that its ruler gave the Spaniards eight girls, all the daughters of chiefs, with the ruler's own daughter being given to Cortés.[20] Díaz noted that these women were given "to bear our children," which shows that he was aware that these women were intended to solidify unions with the Spaniards through their children. Additionally, to the Nahuas, these marriages and their offspring would have been seen as a public statement of Cempoala's new alliance with the Spaniards and break from Tenochtitlan, to which Cempoala had been subject. According to Díaz, the Spaniards oversaw the baptisms of these young women. Moreover, Díaz notes that the women came dressed in rich clothing, jeweled in gold, and accompanied by young maids. For the Nahuas, this would suggest a marriage ceremony and the belief that these women would now be entering new Spanish households, though under the auspices of the new Christian God. Díaz notes that the noblewomen did indeed leave with the Spaniards upon their departure and that this pleased the leaders of Cempoala, who must have felt that this cemented their alliance. Nevertheless, for Díaz these women seem to have been of little additional import, as he does not mention them again. Nor do we learn of these women in Nahua records.

The people of Tlaxcala also provided noblewomen to the Spaniards to seal their alliance. A description offered by Díaz reveals that he was well aware of the political significance of this gift. As he writes,

> It appeared that it had been decided among the Caciques that they would give us the most beautiful of their daughters and nieces who were ready for marriage. Therefore Xicotenga the Elder said: "Malinche, to prove still more clearly how much we love you and wish to please you in all things, we want to give you our daughters for wives to bear your children. For you are so good and brave that we wish to be your brothers.

I have one most beautiful daughter who is as yet unmarried, and I should like to give her to you." At the same time Mase Escasi and all the other Caciques said they would bring their daughters and asked us to accept them as wives.... As for the gift of the women, Cortés answered that he and all of us were very grateful, and that we would repay them by good deeds in course of time.[21]

According to Díaz, the next day the rulers presented to Cortés five of their daughters with maids to serve them. This event is also recounted in pictorial narratives associated with Tlaxcala. The most detailed representation is included in a partial manuscript owned by the Benson Latin American Library at the University of Texas, Austin, and known as the *Texas Fragment*. Likely created in the mid-sixteenth century, the *Texas Fragment* consists of one sheet of paper that was folded in half, creating four leaves, and painted on the back and front. It shows the Tlaxcaltecah reacting to the arrival of the Spaniards and forging an alliance with them.[22] In each of the leaves, Malinche acts as a conduit between the Tlaxcaltecah and the Spaniards. In the first two leaves, the ruler of Tlaxcala and his followers peacefully receive the Spaniards. The third leaf shows the ruler of Tlaxcala, Xicotencatl, seated in power next to Cortés and with an array of food beneath them, representing the aid the people of Tlaxcala provided to the Spaniards.

The record ends with the gifting of noblewomen to Cortés, a record of a marital alliance between the Tlaxcaltecah and the Spaniards (figure 9.1). The alliance is communicated by an image of Cortés seated on a European folding chair, symbol of Spanish authority, at the top center of the page. A number of Spanish conquistadors stand behind him and hold steel-tipped lances and swords. Four rulers from the Republic of Tlaxcala, representing each of the four divisions of the *altepetl* (city-state), stand in front of Cortés. Each is distinguished by clothing and identified by a name tag. At the front is Xicotencatl, ruler of Tizatlan, and most senior of the four rulers, as suggested by his placement closest to Cortés and the twisted red and white headband only he wears, symbol of rulership for the Tlaxcaltecah. Behind him is Maxixcatzin, ruler of Ocotelulco, followed by Tziuhcohuacatl of Quiahuitztlan and Tlehuexolotzin of Tepeticpac.

Malinche is placed directly below Cortés. She is dressed in an elaborate *huipil*, or shirt, and skirt and wears red shoes, as she does throughout these pages. She looks up toward Cortés and gestures to five women who face her. The painter of this image paid a great deal of attention to the rendering of these women. They too wear ornate *huipiles* and skirts, each with her own intricate and individualized design. Moreover, each of the first four women holds a mantle and a loincloth, while the fifth woman just holds a loincloth. These are traditional garments for Nahua men, and each of them is also decorated in its own unique and embellished

Figure 9.1. *Texas Fragment*, page 4. Courtesy of LLILAS Benson Latin American Studies and Collections, University of Texas at Austin.

design, revealing their high value.[23] The implication is that the women are presenting these garments to the Spaniards, presumably because they would have expected the Spanish men to wear these during their marriage ceremony. The final section of the *Codex Mendoza*, which details life in the Nahua world, includes an image of a marriage ceremony that shows the garments of the marital couple tied together, suggesting this was a key event in a traditional Nahua marriage ritual. The painting then indicates that the women would need to provide these to the Spaniards so that the marriage could be complete according to Nahua custom.

The images at the bottom of the page of the *Texas Fragment* reinforce the message that this is indeed a precursor to marriage. Arrayed to the left are a series of valuable gifts, including golden sheets and jewels, jade necklaces, a feather standard, and cloths decorated in a variety of patterns. Such gifts would be offered as a part of an elite marriage ceremony. Moreover, eight additional women are shown kneeling to the right of the gifts and gesturing toward them. One more woman stands to the left and also gestures; she is likely an elite woman who oversees these other women. The kneeling women are dressed in more simplified and sheer garments, with the outlines of their bodies underneath indicated by the artist. The sheerness of these garments suggests that they are not as fine as those of the noblewomen above and points to these women being the maidens who would have accompanied the noblewomen as a part of the marriage and creation of a new household. The four maidens at the bottom are shown in a more diminutive scale, perhaps suggesting their youth. The breasts of one of the women in the group of four above are delineated under her sheer garment, perhaps as a means of marking these women as slightly older and past puberty. Taken together, the offering of gifts, garments, and young women helpers of a variety of ages reveals that the painter of this image intended for this scene to show the preparations for a marriage ceremony to take place between the daughters of the Tlaxcalteca rulers and the Spanish conquistadors. This marriage, in turn, would signify the alliance between Tlaxcala and Spain, hence its record in this document.

Alphabetic glosses were added later to clarify the imagery, suggesting the historical importance of this event. Cortés, Marina, and the Tlaxcalteca rulers are all identified by name and so are three of the women. The first is identified as Luisa Tecuiluatzin. She was a daughter of Xicotencatl, who is the highest ranking of the Tlaxcalteca rulers shown above. The next woman is named Tolquequetzaltzin. She is likely another daughter of Xicotencatl.[24] The last one is named Couaxochtzin, and she was likely a daughter of Maxixcatzin, second in rank after Xicotencatl. A longer annotation was added below the women. Translated from Nahuatl, it reads, "And here are painted the noblewomen who were the children of rulers who were given to the captain. And necklaces, earplugs, bracelets, lip stones, and also gold. They also gave clothing with stepped frets and other clothing to the captain and to the lords."[25] Thus, the annotation summarizes what is shown visually. As Camilla Townsend notes, it behooved the Tlaxcaltecah of the altepetl of Tizatlan specifically to present this particular version of their past, as the son of Xicotencatl (Xicotencatl the Younger) was the one who held out the longest against the Spaniards, and at the time this document was painted, the Tlaxcaltecah "clearly still believed in the significance of the politically motivated marriages and wanted to advertise them at home and abroad."[26]

Indeed, news of this marriage must have quickly spread and served its intended function. Bernal Díaz claimed that Moteuczoma was not pleased when he heard of it, writing that Moteuczoma had learned that the Tlaxcalteca rulers had cemented their friendship with Cortés by giving him their daughters. As he put it, "The Mexicans thoroughly understood that this alliance could do them no good."[27] The marriage of the Tlaxcalteca women is also mentioned in the Nahuatl text of the *Florentine Codex*, which notes that the Tlaxcaltecah gave the Spaniards "whatsoever they required; they attended to them. And then they gave them their maidens."[28] This last line suggests that the receipt of the Tlaxcalteca women was the final way their alliance was secured. The Texcoca historian Fernando de Alva Ixtlilxochitl also refers to this event, even naming the five noblewomen who were given to the Spaniards and referring to them as "wives."[29] The record of this event in a variety of sources confirms that this act publicly communicated the alliance between Tlaxcala and Spain.

So expected was the gifting of royal daughters to the Spaniards that one Nahua chronicler seems to have made up such an account. In a letter written in Latin in 1552, Don Antonio Cortés Totoquihuatzin, a nobleman from Tlacopan, embellished the welcome his father had provided Cortés upon his arrival in the city. He claimed that his father had welcomed Cortés with open arms and proclaimed, "Here are my daughters—the men who have come with you can take them as wives, so that we may share grandsons and granddaughters."[30] However, as Andrew Laird notes, the extant genealogies for Totoquihuatzin only mention sons and not daughters, making this claim a "strategic fabrication."[31] Indeed, Don Antonio Cortés seems to have been working against a prevailing narrative about Tlacopan not helping the Spaniards. After the death of Totoquihuatzin, his son Tetlepanquetzatzin was said to have joined in alliance with Cuauhtemoc of Tenochtitlan and Coanacochtzin of Tetzcoco to defeat the Spaniards. After the fall of Tenochtitlan, Cortés took these three lords on his expedition to Honduras, where Cortés had Cuauhtemoc and Tetlepantquetzatzin hanged. He claimed that they were planning a rebellion against him.[32] Thus, a marriage alliance would counter claims that Tlacopan had rebelled against the Spaniards. Royal daughters, then, must have come to signify alliance with the Spaniards, necessitating the insertion of these into Tlacopan's petition.

Doña Luisa Tecuiluatzin Xicotencatl specifically must have become a key signifier of Tlaxcala's alliance with Spain, and, as such, it was important that she be protected.[33] When the Spaniards left Tlaxcala, she joined their expedition, gaining entry

Figure 9.2. "Tlacopan," *Lienzo de Tlaxcala*, copy from 1773, Juan Manuel Yllanes de Huerto, Museo Nacional de Antropología (photograph by author).

with them into Tenochtitlan, where they remained until the Noche Triste, when the Spaniards were forced to flee the island city in the night. So necessary was Doña Luisa to the Spanish mission that 300 Tlaxcaltecah and thirty Spaniards were ordered to protect her and Doña Marina, according to Bernal Díaz, who also stresses the joy he felt at seeing Doña Luisa's survival after their hasty departure from Tenochtitlan, which left many Nahuas and Spaniards dead.[34] The survival of Doña Luisa is also depicted in other versions of Tlaxcala's conquest history. There are two copies of the now-lost *Lienzo de Tlaxcala*, which was likely originally created in mid-sixteenth-century Tlaxcala and was either a copy or a close cognate of the *Texas Fragment*. One of the copies, housed at the Museo Nacional de Antropología, was created in 1773. Events on the lower register of its first cloth closely mimic the *Texas Fragment*. The second cloth depicts the events surrounding the Spaniards' flight from Tenochtitlan and subsequent arrival at Tlacopan. The Tlacopan vignette includes two women, who must be Doña Marina and Doña Luisa (figure 9.2). Both women are also shown in the copy of the *Lienzo* that was commissioned in the late nineteenth century by Alfredo Chavero and that also closely follows the *Texas Fragment*.

Nevertheless, though Doña Luisa is included in these works, Malinche is the one given visual prominence. An attribute of Malinche in the *Texas Fragment* and Chavero version of the *Lienzo de Tlaxcala* is her red shoes. Therefore, Malinche must be the figure placed closer to Cortés in the copies of the *Lienzo*. Moreover, in both her face is shown in frontal view instead of the profile view of Doña Luisa, which again points to Malinche's significance, as frontal views are typically reserved for more important people. In fact, yet another copy of the *Lienzo* or a close cognate, this one made to accompany Muñoz Camargo's *Descripción de Tlaxcala* and most likely created in Tlaxcala in the early 1580s, fails to include Doña Luisa in the representation of the arrival at Tlacopan; only one woman, presumably Doña Marina, is shown.[35] The implication is that as time progressed, Doña Luisa lost her significance in Tlaxcala's history.

This diminution of Doña Luisa's significance is also evidenced by how the three later versions of Tlaxcala's conquest history minimized the marriage alliance between Tlaxcala and the Spaniards.[36] Though each of these works includes a scene similar to the marriage alliance representation in the *Texas Fragment*, they deviate from the earlier work, making it unclear if the scene is to be read as a marriage at all. For example, the illustration in Muñoz Camargo's work shows two women below the Tlaxcalteca rulers labeled Xicotencatl and Maxixcatzin, suggesting that these are their daughters (figure 9.3). However, the other women and ladies in waiting are omitted, and the women do not hold the garments that presumably would have been necessary for a marriage ceremony. The annotation, added in Spanish and likely by a scribe in Spain, suggests that the scene's association with marriage was lost, "Presente que hicieron los cuatro señores a Cortés de ropa y oro y piedras de valor, y de comida y mujeres y esclavas de servicio que le dieron." The gloss effectively equates the Tlaxcalteca noblewomen to the other gifts of enslaved women, gold, and clothing.[37] The *Lienzo* copy from 1773 includes a similar scene. It shows the five women given to Cortés, but they do not hold garments to be given to the Spaniards nor do they arrive with their maids. The Chavero copy includes many more women, with the ones in the front being more individualized by their ornate garments, but only one holds a cloth (figure 9.4). Both copies show an array of gifts, and both include the same gloss, *quitlautique*, which again suggests the giving of gifts without reference to marriage.

In her study of the pictorial histories from Tlaxcala, Travis Kranz has argued that the later historians deemphasized the marriage of the Tlaxcalteca women because they found other visual arguments, such as an emphasis on their military assistance and acceptance of Christianity, to be more effective in establishing their alliance with the Spaniards.[38] The implication is that these marriage alliances held little import to the Spaniards. Another implication is that Doña Luisa specifically

254 LORI BOORNAZIAN DIEL

Figure 9.3. *Descripción de Tlaxcala*, Diego Muñoz Camargo, folio 255r. Courtesy of University of Glasgow Archives and Special Collections.

mattered less to Tlaxcala and its historians as the sixteenth century progressed. This may be because she established herself in Guatemala with Pedro de Alvarado, to whom she was partnered and with whom she had children, rather than in Tlaxcala.

Figure 9.4. "Quitlauhtique," *Lienzo de Tlaxcala*, copy from 1892, in Alfredo Chavero, *Antigüedades mexicanas* (photograph by author).

Even though Doña Luisa was not given the same prominence as Doña Marina in the later pictorials from Tlaxcala, she must have served as important a role to the Spaniards as Doña Marina.[39] Doña Luisa would have been a link to the Tlaxcalteca forces that were assisting the Spaniards in their defeat of Tenochtitlan, helping to rally them and keep them obedient to Cortés, as suggested by Bernal Diaz's claim that the Spaniards gave her extra protection when fleeing Tenochtitlan. Moreover, her survival at this moment was crucial to Cortés since he needed to return to Tlaxcala and receive aid from the Tlaxcaltecah before returning to battle Tenochtitlan, a request that may have been denied if the Tlaxcalteca princess did not survive.[40]

Doña Luisa remained a key ally to the Spaniards even after the defeat of the Mexicah. Her daughter, Doña Leonor, submitted a *probanza* (proof) in 1573 detailing the alleged aid her mother, and specifically her father, Pedro de Alvarado, provided the Spaniards, during and after the Spanish invasion. A number of Spanish witnesses concurred. Some mentioned how Doña Luisa was given by Cortés to

Pedro de Alvarado and that they were always together. One even credited Cortés's defeat of Tenochtitlan to Doña Luisa's help with the Tlaxcalteca forces.[41] Moreover, in Alva Ixtlilxochitl's *Thirteenth Relation*, he indicates that when the Spanish forces were strategically placed before the final assault on Tenochtitlan, Pedro de Alvarado was sent to set up a station in Tlacopan and he was accompanied by the Tlaxcalteca forces.[42] If Doña Luisa accompanied Alvarado to Tlacopan, as is likely based on her accompanying him on future expeditions, then she would have been the one communicating between him and the Tlaxcalteca forces, just as Malinche helped Cortés communicate with the Nahua forces helping him.

After the defeat of the Mexicah, Doña Luisa continued to be a significant presence in Alvarado's life.[43] She accompanied him on his military expeditions to Oaxaca and Guatemala. As Robinson Herrera argued, she was clearly more than a "mere concubine."[44] She would have "embodied the alliance between Spaniards and the Tlaxcalteca auxiliaries along with the traditional authority of her father the tlatoani Xicotencatl," and as such she would have provided incentive to Tlaxcalteca forces to continue helping the Spaniards on their military expeditions far from Tlaxcala. Doña Luisa and her daughter even accompanied Alvarado to Peru, perhaps so that she could ensure the loyalty of the Tlaxcalteca allies brought by Alvarado to aid him in subduing yet another foreign land.[45]

Despite Doña Luisa's support of Pedro de Alvarado, she was never considered his principal wife. While Doña Luisa was still alive, Alvarado took a Spanish woman as his wife. She died soon after arriving in New Spain in 1529. Doña Luisa herself died soon after her return to Guatemala from Peru, in 1536. The probanza submitted by her daughter decades later emphasized her mother's relationship with Pedro de Alvarado and her own relationship with her father. Nevertheless, the Spaniards did not value these relationships as the Nahuas did. As Pedro Carrasco notes, at the start of the Spanish invasion, the rulers of Tlaxcala had been acting in accordance with Nahua ideals of marriage alliances, but based on the outcome of Doña Luisa's relationship with Pedro de Alvarado, they "must have soon realized that pre-Hispanic matrimonial practices did not necessarily produce the same desired results in colonial times."[46]

"GIFTING" OF NOBLEWOMEN

Native women provided by Nahua lords to serve the Spaniards were likely taken from the commoner ranks. However, some sources reveal a fear on the part of Nahua rulers that the Spaniards also desired noblewomen to serve them, sexually and otherwise, and that noblewomen given to the Spaniards were not accorded the same status as a noblewoman given in pre-Hispanic times, as suggested by

Doña Luisa's life. This apprehension becomes clear when comparing how three different sources referenced the gifting of young women to the Spaniards by the rulers of Amaquemeca Chalco. In his letters, Cortés dryly notes that the ruler of Amaquemeca Chalco gave him "as many as forty slave girls."[47] Durán writes that in this same province Cortés was "offered many young girls, all beautiful, well dressed and handsomely adorned.... The soldiers received them with thanks, being grateful for this gift."[48] Chimalpahin, a Native of Chalco, mentions this same gift in his *Eighth Relation*.[49] Here he notes that two rulers from this province prepared to receive Cortés by gathering forty beautiful young women, all daughters of *macehuales*, or commoners. However, they ordered the women to be dressed and adorned as if they were the daughters of *tlahtoque*, or noble rulers. The implication is that the leaders of Chalco believed that the Spaniards desired noblewomen, but they did not want their own daughters to be forced into servitude and concubinage, which came to be the fate of many of the noblewomen offered to the Spaniards in presumed marriage alliances. Evidently, they were not as concerned with the fates of the commoner women.

The *Codex Aubin*, created in late sixteenth-century Mexico City, also suggests a fear of the corruption of Nahua noblewomen in an oblique reference in its record of the Spanish invasion. The *Codex* typically gives a sparse pictorial note of important events with a fuller explanation written alphabetically in Nahuatl. For the year 1519, the *Aubin's* author wrote, "In this year the prostitutes who were supposed to be daughters of Moteuczoma died. The Christians said, 'Let women be brought, your daughters.' Moteuczoma said 'Let the Mexica hear.'"[50] The text then switches topics and makes no more references to these women. However, as Matthew Restall writes, this brief mention suggests a fear for Nahua noblewomen, evoking "community memory of how Spanish demands for sex slaves turned Aztec girls into concubines and perverted the purpose of diplomatic marriage alliances. Above all, the line reminds Nahua readers that the ultimate victims were *mochpochuan*, 'your daughters.'"[51] An account by Durán suggests the same fear. He explains how women related to Moteuczoma were hidden from the Spaniards. He writes,

> But the Spaniards, still possessed of that unsatisfied hunger for riches, did not leave a corner or chamber unsearched or undisturbed. In this way they discovered a secret apartment where the women of Moteuczoma were kept, together with their ladies and duennas who served them and looked after them. These women had hidden in those chambers out of fear of the Spaniards.[52]

For Moteuczoma, it must have become clear that the Spaniards would not honor his daughters as wives. During Cortés's stay in Tenochtitlan, he references a night wherein he went to Moteuczoma's palace, and, as they had done on other occasions, they "joked and exchanged pleasantries" and then Moteuczoma had given him "some gold jewelry and one of his daughters and other chiefs' daughters to some of my company."[53] Cortés makes this comment in an off-handed way, in reference to his interrogation of Moteuczoma for the killing of Spaniards in Nautla, a pivotal event in the Spanish-Mexica war that ended with Moteuczoma's imprisonment. In the version of this story recounted by Francisco López de Gómara and copied by Chimalpahin, he told Moteuczoma that "he was married and could not take Moteuczoma's daughter as his wife, as Christian law did not allow a man more than one wife."[54] As polygyny was common among the Nahuas before the *Conquista*, there was often the chance that a noblewoman provided to another ruler would not be the principal wife but a more secondary wife, but this should not have been the fate of Moteuczoma's daughters, as they would have been the highest-ranking women in the Aztec realm and ideal marriage partners.

Noblewomen marrying into other communities did not always do so for the same reasons—some might do so to cement an alliance, others because their hometown was conquered or about to be conquered—but their status within their new households was also permeable depending on shifting alliances. The Nahuatl term for nonprincipal wives was *mecatl*, which is often translated as concubine, but a woman of this status was not necessarily seen as an illegitimate member of a household nor were her children, at least until the Spaniards made them so.[55] Thus, the accounts about the women of Chalco and Moteuczoma's daughters reveal an increasing fear that Nahua noblewomen who were made to join the Spaniards on their expedition and eventually enter into new Spanish households were not treated in the manner to which they would have been accustomed based on pre-Hispanic precedent nor were they given the proper respect due their station, as also evidenced by the life of Doña Luisa of Tlaxcala. Thus, the lives of noblewomen during and after the *Conquista* were oftentimes just as precarious as women of a lower status.

The mestizo historian affiliated with Tetzcoco Fernando de Alva Ixtlilxochitl also references the provision of noblewomen to the Spaniards, and he does so in such a way as to highlight the greed of the Spaniards and reinforce Nahua fears about their treatment.[56] For example, in his *Sumaria relación*, Alva Ixtlilxochitl tells of Cortés sending a group of Spaniards to Tetzcoco to amass gold and jewels.[57] After ransacking the treasury of Texcoco's former ruler, Nezahualcoyotl, the Spaniards still were not satisfied and asked the *principales* (nobles) of Tetzcoco to bring their own gold and jewels to them. Then, presumably not satisfied with that, they demanded that they also bring women, specifically the daughters of the principales. Back in Tenochtitlan, Cortés demanded that Cacama, leader of Tetzcoco, have four of his sisters brought there and given to him. He made a similar request that principales of Tenochtitlan and Tlacopan bring their daughters to him. As Susan Kellogg notes,

Alva Ixtlilxochitl emphasized the involuntary nature of the "gifting" of these noblewomen to the Spaniards.[58] The sisters of Cacama are mentioned in another account of Alva Ixtlilxochitl that highlights the cruelties of the Spaniards even more. He writes that a witness told him that three of the sisters of Cacama were killed by the Spaniards before they fled Tenochtitlan on the Noche Triste.[59] No reason is provided for these deaths, suggesting their pointless nature.

WOMEN ON THE BATTLEFIELD

According to some Nahuas, the Spaniards actively targeted women in acts of intimidation and threatened violation. For example, when describing the massacre that happened at Tenochtitlan during the Toxcatl festival, when Cortés had departed Tenochtitlan and left Pedro de Alvarado in charge of the Spaniards in the city, the writers and painters of the *Florentine Codex* highlight the presence of women. At the start of the festival, women who had fasted for a year came to the courtyard to grind amaranth. The Spaniards then arrived. According to the Nahuatl text, "They were elaborately attired in battle gear; they were arrayed for battle, arrayed as warriors. They came to [the women]: they came among them; they circled about them; they looked at each one, they looked into the faces of each of the grinding women."[60] This description, with Spanish men in battle attire looking directly into the faces of vulnerable women, who must have been weakened from a year of fasting and seclusion, suggests an act of intimidation that the accompanying image also makes clear (figure 9.5). One Spaniard stands on the woman's amaranth and leans into it with his spear. Another walks out of the picture plane, but his sword is clearly rendered.

Some women were also actively targeted during battles. For example, Alva Ixtlilxochitl recounted how Spanish forces captured a noblewoman at Cohuatzacualco in order to force the province to surrender.[61] He also complained of how cruel the Tlaxcaltecah were to women and children, writing of how they took vengeance upon Mexica women and children in battles and during the sacking of Tenochtitlan.[62] Moreover, in its image of the aftermath of the Noche Triste, the painters of book 12 of the *Florentine Codex* show women being fished out of Lake Tetzcoco, suggesting that they too were targeted.

Other accounts reveal women's participation in battle. Chimalpahin writes of a principal from Amaquemeca who was allied with the Spaniards and captured a man and two women during battle.[63] The capture of these two women suggests the presence of women at battles. Chimalpahin also provides their names, Matlacihuatzin and Xahualtzin, pointing to their historic significance. Another woman is credited with warning the Mexicah that the Spaniards were trying to flee Tenochtitlan, thereby starting what came to be known as the Noche Triste. Out getting water

Figure 9.5. *Florentine Codex*, Book 12, folio 30r. Courtesy of Biblioteca Medicea Laurenziana.

when she noticed the Spaniards attempting to escape, she cried out to warn the Mexicah and spur them to action. Her cry is noted in the *Florentine Codex*.[64] Sahagún's Nahua informants also mention the active role one woman played in a battle that took place during the Spanish siege of Tenochtitlan. The Spaniards had attacked again and surrounded the Mexicah, "And when they reached close to us a woman threw water upon them; she threw water into their faces; she made water run from the faces of our foes."⁶⁵ Unfortunately, the space left for imagery remains unfinished. Durán also explains how Cuauhtemoc exhorted women to take up shields and swords against the Spaniards.⁶⁶ The *Anales de Tlatelolco* too mentions women taking up the battle when it had reached Tlatelolco and after the men had been defeated: "That was when the Tlatelolca women all let loose, fighting, striking people, taking captives. They put on warriors' devices, all raising their skirts so that they could give pursuit."⁶⁷ The implication is that women intervened during the Spanish-Mexica war and were prepared to physically engage in battle.⁶⁸

Women remained targets of the Spaniards even after Tenochtitlan fell. Book 12 of the *Florentine Codex* was written largely from the point of view of Sahagún's informants from Tlatelolco, who present an ambivalent view of the Spaniards, with their actions toward women pointing to their ungodly nature.⁶⁹ After detailing the surrender of Cuauhtemoc to Spanish forces, the Nahuatl text relates how the Spaniards targeted women in search for treasure:

> And [the Spaniards] seized, they selected the women—the pretty ones, those whose bodies were yellow: the yellow ones. And some women, when they were taken from the people, muddied their faces, and clothed themselves in old clothing, put rags on themselves as a shift. It was all only rags that they put on themselves.⁷⁰

The *Anales de Tlatelolco* recounts a similar story that points to the lasciviousness of the Spaniards: "The Christians searched all over the women; they pulled down their skirts and went all over their bodies, in their mouths, on their abdomens, in their hair."⁷¹ These records stress the vulnerability of women as they were violated by the Spaniards and the steps some women took to avoid such a fate.

TECUICHPOTZIN, OR DOÑA ISABEL

A daughter of Moteuczoma, named Tecuichpotzin and later baptized and renamed Doña Isabel, surely lived as extraordinary a life as Doña Marina and Doña Luisa Xicotencatl. In pursuit of maintaining what he argued was her rightful patrimony, Juan Cano, Tecuichpotzin's final husband, left a rich archival record about her.⁷² However, she has surprisingly not received as much scholarly attention as Doña Marina.

While Moteuczoma certainly had many children from multiple wives, Tecuichpotzin is often noted as being the most noble, as her mother was said to have been a daughter of the former Mexica ruler Ahuitzotl. At the time of the Spanish arrival, she was perhaps eleven years old, approaching marriageable age.⁷³ As mentioned earlier, Cortés wrote that Moteuczoma had offered a daughter to him; this may have been Tecuichpotzin. Even though Cortés said that he could not take her as

Figure 9.6. "Icpoliuhque mexica," *Lienzo de Tlaxcala*, copy from 1892, in Alfredo Chavero, *Antigüedades mexicanas* (photograph by author).

a wife, this daughter, along with some other children of Moteuczoma, must have been sent to the palace where the Spaniards were stationed. Cortés writes that upon the Spaniards' flight from Tenochtitlan during the Noche Triste, he took with him a son and two daughters of Moteuczoma.[74] He later says that they had died. While he may have been referencing Tecuichpotzin and believed her to have perished at this time, she survived the event, most likely saved by her countrymen due to her parentage. Indeed, her significance to the Mexicah is suggested by the fact that she was said to have married her father's successor, Cuauhtemoc, in order to secure his legitimacy to the throne.[75]

Tecuichpotzin may have been with Cuauhtemoc when he surrendered to Cortés. The Chavero copy of the *Lienzo de Tlaxcala* includes her in a group of Mexica prisoners being presented to Cortés (figure 9.6). For the Tlaxcaltecah, the inclusion of Doña Isabel at this pivotal moment may have further stressed the Mexicah's refusal to submit to Spanish forces and bolstered their argument about the singular alliance the Tlaxcaltecah had with the Spaniards. The *Codex Azcatitlan* may also reference this moment (figure 9.7). After the image of the march to Tenochtitlan, its painter shows the battle at Huitzilopochtli's temple and then later around Lake

Figure 9.7. *Codex Azcatitlan*, folio 24r. Courtesy of the Bibliothèque Nationale de France.

Texcoco. Unfortunately, some pages are missing, but the next image in the *Codex* shows men rowing in canoes with women as passengers, presumably representing families fleeing Tenochtitlan.[76] More women are shown on top of some houses. They are elaborately dressed, which suggests that these are noblewomen. Angela Herren Rajagapolan interprets this scene as the evacuation of Mexica noblewomen from Tenochtitlan and likely including Doña Isabel, whom she identifies as the woman on the roof at the far right, based on her huipil, which is decorated in a similar pattern to a *tilma* (mantle) worn by Moteuczoma elsewhere in the *Codex*.[77] If so, the *Codex Azcatitlan* would be stressing the need for these women to escape the capital, which may point to fear of their violation by the Spaniards and their native allies.

These are the only native pictorials to include Doña Isabel in depictions of the final siege of Tenochtitlan, though she is included in pictorial genealogies, which speaks to her significance for the Mexica royal line. For example, in the *Codex Cozcatzin*, she sits across from her father and in front of her brother. She carries the *xihuitzolli* (diadem) name tag, in reference to her father and as a sign that she, rather than her brother, is the chief heir to her father.[78] She also wears a garment similar to that of her father and distinct from her brother, further signifying her link with the ruler. She actively points, again signaling her power. Isabel is also recorded in an extensive genealogy preserved in the *Codex Mexicanus*, where she is the only woman of her generation to be pictured.[79] She and her brother Pedro are linked to their father, and lines from each of them extend outward to the fraying edge of the page, suggesting the continuity of the royal Mexica lineage into the colonial era.

After the death of Cuauhtemoc, Isabel married another Spaniard, Alonso de Grado. Together, they were given Tlacopan in encomienda.[80] This was a major altepetl, being one of the three cities of the Triple Alliance; the other two cities were Tenochtitlan and Tetzcoco. Isabel's stewardship of this encomienda made her the wealthiest native woman in New Spain. Isabel's husband died soon after they were married. Cortés then invited Isabel into his household, for her protection, as he claimed.[81] She soon became pregnant with his child, but he still did not marry her, arranging instead a marriage between her and another Spaniard, Pedro Gallego de Andrade. The daughter of Cortés and Isabel was raised in the household of a cousin of Cortés.[82] A few years into her marriage with Gallego, Isabel gave birth to a son, Juan de Andrade Moctezuma, but Gallego himself died soon after. Isabel then married yet again, this time to a Spaniard named Juan Cano, with whom she had four more children. Evidencing her independence, Isabel drafted her will in 1550, leaving the most generous amount to her first-born son, which displeased her husband, who successfully contested the will. Ultimately, her encomienda was divided among her heirs.[83] Through the drafting of her own will, Doña Isabel attempted to assert her independence; however, at the end, her Spanish husband essentially overruled her.

CONCLUSIONS

Though there is a lack of reference to women in the vast majority of primary accounts of the *Conquista*, a close reading of the available sources does reveal the actions and experiences of quite a few women. Nevertheless, with the exception of high-status women like Doña Luisa and Doña Isabel, for the most part, references to women are fleeting and allow mere glimpses into their worlds at the time of the Spanish invasion, a time when their precarity became even more enhanced. And yet, the lives of women were unremarkable to many chroniclers, with the day-to-day struggles of women being left out of most accounts of the *Conquista*.

One final image gives a sense of their difficult responsibilities at this time, with a different kind of combat being undertaken, this one against a deadly disease. In its book on the *Conquista*, the *Florentine Codex* includes an image of smallpox victims that shows one woman taking care of five men covered in pockmarks (figure 9.8). Speech scrolls issue from her mouth and she actively gestures, visual cues of her

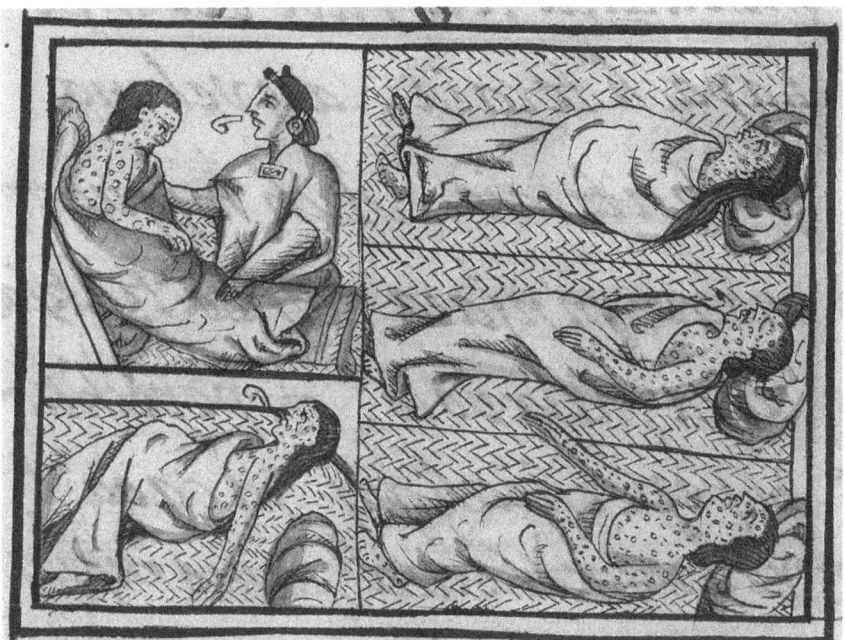

Figure 9.8. *Florentine Codex*, Book 12, folio 53v. Courtesy of Biblioteca Medicea Laurenziana.

authority and labor at this moment. Nevertheless, the Nahuatl text laments that "there was no one to take care of another; there was no one to attend to one another," a statement contradicted by the image and again indicative of how so much of the work done by women was largely unnoticed by others.[84]

NOTES

1. Lori Boornazian Diel, "Till Death Do Us Part: Unconventional Marriages as Aztec Political Strategy," *Ancient Mesoamerica* 18, no. 2 (2007): 259–72. No Nahua pictorial histories survived the Spanish-Mexica war, though many that were recorded during the early colonial period adhere to pre-Hispanic traditions, albeit modified based on their colonial contexts of creation.

2. Deena J. González, "Malinche Triangulated, Historically Speaking," in *Feminism, Nation, and Myth: La Malinche*, ed. Rolando Romero and Amanda Nolacea Harris (Houston: Arte Público Press, 2005), 6–12, here 6–7; Sandra Messinger Cypess, "Malinche and Gendered Histories," in *Feminism, Nation, and Myth: La Malinche*, ed. Rolando Romero and Amanda Nolacea Harris (Houston: Arte Público Press, 2005), 14–57, here 14. For other

studies of Malinche, see Sandra Messinger Cypess, *La Malinche in Mexican Literature: From History to Myth* (Austin: University of Texas Press, 1991); Frances Karttunen, "Rethinking Malinche," in *Indian Women of Early Mexico*, ed. Susan Schroeder, Stephanie Wood, and Robert Haskett (Norman: University of Oklahoma Press, 1997), 290–312; Camilla Townsend, *Malintzin's Choices: An Indian Woman in the Conquest of Mexico* (Albuquerque: University of New Mexico Press, 2006); Federico Navarrete, *Malintzin, O la conquista coma traducción* (Mexico City: UNAM, 2021); and Victoria Lyall and Terezita Romo, *Traitor, Survivor, Icon: The Legacy of La Malinche* (New Haven, CT: Yale University Press, 2022).

3. For more on the lives of women in pre-Hispanic Mexico and colonial New Spain, see Pilar Gonzalbo Aizpuru, *Las mujeres en la Nueva España: Educación y vida cotidiana* (Mexico City: Colegio De Mexico, 1987); María Rodríguez-Shadow, *La mujer azteca* (Toluca, Mexico: Universidad Autónoma del Estado de México, 1997); Susan Toby Evans, "Sexual Politics in the Aztec Palace: Public, Private, Profane," *Res* 33 (1998): 167–83; Susan Toby Evans, "Concubines and Cloth: Women and Weaving in Aztec Palaces and Colonial Mexico," in *Servants of the Dynasty: Palace Women in World History*, ed. Anne Walthall (Irvine: University of California Press, 2008), 215–31; Karen Vieira Powers, *Women in the Crucible of the Conquest: The Gendered Genesis of Spanish American Society, 1500–1600* (Albuquerque: University of New Mexico Press, 2005); Camilla Townsend, "'What in the World Have You Done to Me, My Lover?': Sex, Servitude, and Politics among the Pre-Conquest Nahuas as Seen in the *Cantares Mexicanos*," *Americas* 62 (2006): 349–89; and Lisa Sousa, *The Woman Who Turned into a Jaguar, and Other Narratives of Native Women in the Archives of Mexico* (Stanford, CA: Stanford University Press, 2017).

4. Navarrete, *Malintzin*.

5. Vieira Powers, *Women*, 9–10.

6. Townsend, "Sex," 358.

7. Camilla Townsend, "Slavery in Pre-Columbian America," in *Cambridge World History of Slavery*, ed. Craig Perry, David Eltis et al. (New York: Cambridge University Press, 2021), 2: 553–70, here 561.

8. Hernán Cortés, *Letters from Mexico*, ed. and trans. Anthony Pagden (New Haven, CT: Yale University Press, 1986), 54, 56, 79–80, 82.

9. Bernal Díaz del Castillo, *The Conquest of New Spain*, trans. J. M. Cohen (New York: Penguin Books, 1963), 138, 140, 156–57.

10. Nancy van Deusen, *Global Indios: The Indigenous Struggle for Justice in Sixteenth-Century Spain* (Durham, NC: Duke University Press, 2015), 5.

11. Richard C. Trexler, *Sex and Conquest: Gendered Violence, Political Order, and the European Conquest of the Americas* (Ithaca, NY: Cornell University Press, 1995), 52.

12. Jennifer L. Morgan, "Male Travelers, Female Bodies, and the Gendering of Racial Ideology, 1500–1700," in *Bodies in Contact: Rethinking Colonial Encounters in World History*, ed. Antoinette Burton et al. (Durham, NC: Duke University Press, 2005), 54–66, here 59.

13. Diego Durán, *The History of the Indies of New Spain*, ed. and trans. Doris Heyden (Norman: University of Oklahoma Press, 1994), 523.

14. VV.AA., *Anales de Tlatelolco*, trans. Rafael Tena (Mexico City: CONACULTA, 2004), 117.

15. Matthew Restall, *When Montezuma Met Cortés: The True Story of the Meeting That Changed History* (New York: Harper Collins, 2018), 308–9.

16. Florine Asselbergs, *Conquered Conquistadors: The Lienzo De Quauhquechollan, A Nahua Vision of the Conquest of Guatemala* (Boulder: University Press of Colorado, 2004), 159, 163, 195.

17. For fuller studies of the significance of marriage alliances and wives in Aztec politics, see Pedro Carrasco, "Royal Marriages in Ancient Mexico," in *Explorations in Ethnohistory: Indians of Central Mexico in the Sixteenth Century*, ed. H. R. Harvey and Hanns J. Prem (Albuquerque: University of New Mexico Press, 1984), 41–81; Susan Gillespie, *The Aztec Kings: The Construction of Rulership in Mexica History* (Tucson: University of Arizona Press, 1989); Diel, "Till Death"; and Ross Hassig, *Polygamy and the Rise and Demise of the Aztec Empire* (Albuquerque: University of New Mexico Press, 2016).

18. Townsend, "Sex," 358–59.

19. The Maya at Potonchan also gave the Spaniards a gift of native women, which included Malinche. Though the Spaniards interpreted these women as slaves, they could also have been intended as a marriage alliance. Hassig, *Polygamy*, 105.

20. Díaz del Castillo, *Conquest of New Spain*, 121–25.

21. Díaz del Castillo, *Conquest of New Spain*, 175–76.

22. Detailed analyses of this work can be found in Travis Kranz, "Visual Persuasion: Sixteenth-Century Tlaxcalan Pictorials in Response to the Conquest of Mexico," in *The Conquest All Over Again*, ed. Susan Schroeder (Portland: Sussex Academic Press, 2010), 41–73; Jeannie Gillespie, *Saints and Warriors: Tlaxcalan Perspectives on the Conquest of Tenochtitlan* (New Orleans: University Press of the South, 2004); and Townsend, *Malintzin's Choices*, 67–76.

23. Barbara Mundy (personal communication, May 2019) pointed out how the woman at the far right feels like a later addition. She is not as united compositionally as the other four women are, and her face, along with that of the standing woman below, is drawn in a distinctive manner, without a line delineating her face from her neck as the other women exhibit. If she were indeed added later, one wonders if it could have been because the tradition about this marriage held that there were five women, necessitating a later artist to add the fifth woman.

24. This may be a woman who was later called Doña Lucía and became partnered with Jorge de Alvarado, the brother of Pedro de Alvarado, with whom her sister Luisa was linked. Details on Doña Lucía's life are rather sketchy; see Robinson Herrera, "Concubines and Wives: Re-Interpreting Native-Spanish Intimate Unions in Sixteenth-Century Guatemala,"

in *Indian Conquistadors: Indigenous Allies in the Conquest of Mesoamerica*, ed. Laura E. Matthew and Michel R. Oudijk (Norman: University of Oklahoma Press, 2012), 127–44, here 134. As Vitus Huber has shown, her son-in-law, Francisco de Girón, even omitted her from his *Información de méritos y servicios*, presumably because her ethnic identity and ties to Tlaxcalteca nobility did not bolster his prestige. Vitus Huber, "The Fabrication of Lineage: Genealogical Manuscripts and the Administration of the Spanish Empire (Fifteenth–Eighteenth Century)," in *Genealogical Manuscripts in Cross-Cultural Perspective*, ed. Markus Friedrich and Jörg Quenzer (Berlin: DeGruyter, 2025), 271–298. Nevertheless, over a century later, descendants of Francisco proudly declared their descent from Doña Lucía. Laura Matthew, *Memories of Conquest: Becoming Mexicano in Colonial Guatemala* (Chapel Hill: University of North Carolina Press, 2012), 219.

25. In Nahuatl, the gloss reads, "Yn nican yhcuiliuhtimani ciuatzitzitin ynpilhua nitlatotoque quimacaque nicapitan / yuan cozcatl necochtli mahuextli tentetli yuan ocequi teocuitlatl / yuan tlaquemitl quipach xicalcoliuhqui yuan … tlaquemitl quimacaque capitan notlatoque" (translation by author).

26. Townsend, *Malintzin's Choices*, 68, 74.

27. Díaz del Castillo, *Conquest of New Spain*, 186.

28. Bernardino de Sahagún, *Florentine Codex, Book 12: The Conquest of Mexico*, trans. Arthur J. O. Anderson and Charles E. Dibble (Salt Lake City: University of Utah Press, 1955), 29. The Spanish translation of the Nahuatl text included in the *Florentine Codex* gives a different reading of the event, as it states that the Spaniards "received them and used them as their women," which suggests that they were used for labor and/or sex, something not implied by the original Nahuatl phrasing. Kevin Terraciano, "Reading between the Lines of Book 12," in *The Florentine Codex: An Encyclopedia of the Nahua World in Sixteenth-Century Mexico*, ed. Jeanette Favrot Peterson and Kevin Terraciano (Austin: University of Texas Press, 2019), 45–62, here 46. This speaks to how the Spaniards did not accept the gifting of noblewomen as signifiers of marriage alliances.

29. Fernando de Alva Ixtlilxochitl, *Obras Históricas*, ed. Edmundo O'Gorman (Mexico City: Universidad Nacional Autónoma de México, 1997), 2: 214.

30. Andrew Laird, "Nahua Humanism and Political Identity in Sixteenth-Century Mexico: A Latin Letter from Antonio Cortés Totoquihuatzin, Native Ruler of Tlacopan, to Emperor Charles V (1552)" *Renaessanceforum* 10 (2016): 127–72, here 163.

31. Laird, "Nahua Humanism and Political Identity in Sixteenth-Century Mexico," 142.

32. For details on this incident, see Julia Madajczak's chapter in this volume.

33. Herrera, "Concubines," 133.

34. Díaz del Castillo, *Conquest of New Spain*, 297, 302.

35. Diego Muñoz Camargo, *Descripción de la ciudad y provincia de Tlaxcala de las Indias y del Mar Océano para el buen gobierno y ennoblecimiento dellas*, University of Glasgow Archives and Special Collections, MS Hunter 242, fol. 261r.

36. Kranz, "Visual Persuasion," 59.

37. The text of the *Descripción* says that the Tlaxcaltecah at first gave the Spaniards 300 enslaved women and then later decided to also provide them with noblewomen so that if they were to become pregnant, their children could remain in Tlaxcala. Muñoz Camargo, *Descripción de Tlaxcala*, fol. 186r.

38. Kranz, "Visual Persuasion," 59.

39. Herrera, "Concubines," 133.

40. Townsend, *Malintzin's Choices*, 246.

41. "Probanza del Adelantado D. Pedro de Alvarado y Doña Leonor de Alvarado su hija (1573)," *Anales de la Sociedad de Geografía e Historia* 11 (1934), 483–84.

42. Amber Brian, Bradley Benton, and Pablo García Loaeza, *The Native Conquistador: Alva Ixtlilxochitl's Account of the Conquest of New Spain* (University Park: Pennsylvania State University Press, 2010), 37.

43. Witnesses in the probanza mention that she was always in his company, but the exact nature of the relationship between Doña Luisa and Alvarado is impossible to reconstruct. Mercedes Meade de Angulo provides a rather romanticized analysis of their relationship in *Doña Luisa Teohquilhuastzin: Mujer del Capitán Pedro de Alvarado* (Puebla: Gobierno del Estado de Puebla, 1992). Lovell et al. question whether Alvarado may have prolonged his stay in Utatlán, Guatemala, because of Doña Luisa's pregnancy and imminent birth of Leonor, who was named after Alvarado's mother, which suggests a strong connection between the two. W. George Lovell, Christopher H. Lutz, and Wendy Kramer, *Strike Fear in the Land: Pedro de Alvarado and the Conquest of Guatemala* (Norman: University of Oklahoma Press, 2020), 19. At the same time, Pedro de Alvarado was also known as one of the most notoriously cruel of the conquistadors. For example, Bartolomé de Las Casas lamented, "Oh, if one were to catalogue all those orphaned by him, all those whose children he stole, all those whose wives he took, all the women he widowed, and all the adultery, violence and rape that could be laid at his door, as well as those he deprived of liberty and all the torment and calamity that countless people suffered because of him!" Bartolome de Las Casas, *A Short Account of the Destruction of the Indies*, ed. Nigel Griffin (London: Penguin Group, 1992), 63–64.

44. Herrera, "Concubines," 133.

45. Matthew, *Memories*, 217.

46. Pedro Carrasco, "Indian-Spanish Marriages in the First Century of the Colony," in *Indian Women of Early Mexico*, ed. Susan Schroeder, Stephanie Wood, and Robert Haskett (Norman: University of Oklahoma Press, 1997), 87–104, here 103.

47. Cortés, *Letters*, 80.

48. Durán, *History of the Indies*, 524.

49. Domingo Chimalpahin Cuauhtlehuanitzin, *Las ocho relaciones y el memorial de Colhuacan*, ed. and trans. Rafael Tena (Mexico City: Consejo Nacional para la Cultura y las Artes, 1998), 2: 331.

50. James Lockhart, *We People Here: Nahuatl Accounts of the Conquest* (Berkeley: University of California Press, 1993), 275.

51. Restall, *Montezuma*, 309.

52. Durán, *History of the Indies*, 532–33.

53. Cortés, *Letters*, 88–89.

54. Domingo Chimalpahin Cuauhtlehuanitzin, *Chimalpahin's Conquest: A Nahua Historian's Rewriting of Francisco López de Gómara's* La Conquista de México, ed. and trans. Susan Schroeder (Stanford, CA: Stanford University Press, 2010), 214.

55. Townsend, "Sex," 366, 371.

56. Amber Brian, "Don Fernando de Alva Ixtlilxochitl's Narratives of the Conquest of Mexico: Colonial Subjectivity and the Circulation of Native Knowledge," in *The Conquest All Over Again*, ed. Susan Schroeder (Portland: Sussex Academic Press, 2010), 124–43, here 133.

57. Alva Ixtlilxochitl, *Obras Históricas*, 1: 388–89.

58. Susan Kellogg, "Alva Ixtlilxochitl's Marina and Other Women of Conquest," in *Fernando de Alva Ixtlilxochitl and His Legacy*, ed. Galen Brokaw and Jongsoo Lee (Tucson: University of Arizona Press, 2016), 209–34, here 213.

59. Alva Ixtlilxochitl, *Obras Históricas*, 1: 454.

60. Sahagún, *Florentine Codex*, 51.

61. Brian, Benton, and García Loaeza, *Native Conquistador*, 63.

62. Alva Ixtlilxochitl, *Obras Históricas*, 1: 476, 478; 2: 252; Brian, "Don Fernando de Alva Ixtlilxochitl's Narratives," 134; Kellogg, "Alva Ixtlilxochitl's Marina," 214.

63. Chimalpahin, *Ocho relaciones*, 2: 156.

64. Sahagún, *Florentine Codex*, 67.

65. Sahagún, *Florentine Codex*, 116.

66. Durán, *History of the Indies*, 555.

67. Lockhart, *People*, 267.

68. Sousa, *Woman*, 263–65.

69. Kevin Terraciano, "Three Views of the Conquest of Mexico from the *Other* Mexica," in *The Conquest All Over Again*, ed. Susan Schroeder (Portland: Sussex Academic Press, 2010), 15–40, here 32–33.

70. Sahagún, *Florentine Codex*, 122.

71. Lockhart, *People*, 269.

72. For transcriptions and analyses of these sources, see Emma Pérez-Rocha, *Privilegios en lucha: La Información de doña Isabel de Moctezuma* (Mexico City: Instituto Nacional de Antropología e Historia, 1998); Rodrigo Martínez Baracs, *La Perdida* Relación de la Nueva España *y su conquista de Juan Cano* (Mexico City: Instituto Nacional de Antropología e Historia, 2006); and Anastasia Kalyuta, "La casa y hacienda de un señor mexica: Un estudio analítico de la 'Información de doña Isabel de Moctezuma,'" *Anuario de Estudios Americanos* 65, no. 2 (2008): 13–37.

73. Donald E. Chipman, *Moctezuma's Children: Aztec Royalty under Spanish Rule, 1520–1700* (Austin: University of Texas Press, 2005), 50.

74. Cortés, *Letters*, 138, 178.

75. Martínez Baracs, *Perdida* Relación, 104–9. See also Gillespie, *Aztec Kings*, 106–15.

76. María Castañeda de la Paz and Michel Oudijk, "La conquista y la colonia en el *Códice Azcatitlan*," *Journal de la Société des Américanistes* 98, no. 2 (2012): 59–95, here 70.

77. Angela Herren Rajagapolan, *Portraying the Aztec Past: The Codices Boturini, Azcatitlan, and Aubin* (Austin: University of Texas Press, 2019), 83–84.

78. Gillespie, *Aztec Kings*, 109.

79. Lori Boornazian Diel, "The Codex Mexicanus Genealogy: Binding the Mexica Past and Colonial Present," *Colonial Latin American Review* 24, no. 2 (2015): 120–46, here 138.

80. Chipman, *Moctezuma's Children*, 48–49.

81. Townsend, *Fifth Sun: A New History of the Aztecs* (New York: Oxford University Press, 2019), 143.

82. Chipman, *Moctezuma's Children*, 102–3, 147. This daughter was named Leonor, and she was well provided for in the wills of her parents. She eventually married a wealthy silver mine owner in Zacatecas, Juan de Tolosa, and became the matriarch of a prestigious family in northern New Spain.

83. Chipman, *Moctezuma's Children*, 145.

84. Sahagún, *Florentine Codex*, 83.

10

Between Victor and Vanquished

The Metamorphosis of Moteuczoma in a Painted Biombo

PATRICK HAJOVSKY

A rare and chance discovery I made during the mid-2000s brings together six of ten original panels of a *biombo*, or room-sized folding divider screen with painted scenes. At some unknown date the biombo was split up, so that today one of its panels resides in storage at the Museo de Américas in Madrid (figure 10.1). Perhaps it was singled out from the other panels because it is a portrait of Moteuczoma during his last public appearance alive, standing on his balcony facing the Ceremonial Precinct in order to calm restless warriors and lords who were seeking to expel the Spaniards from Tenochtitlan. The remaining extant five panels of this biombo form a group of scenes narrating the events following the king's tragic death, and these are in the private collection of Rodrigo Rivero Lake, also indefinitely in storage (figure 10.2).[1] Biombos were a form of painting in New Spain with a genealogy extending to East Asia, and gained popularity as they were suited for Baroque-era pageantry in the high courts of the Spanish king's viceroys during the late seventeenth and early eighteenth centuries. Though we do not know who painted most of them or exactly where they were originally displayed, biombos are generally understood to have been produced by small workshops of skilled artists who came from multiple ethnicities in the viceregal capital of New Spain, Mexico-Tenochtitlan, presumably to be presented as gifts at other viceregal courts in their efforts of political solidarity.[2] Whereas a complete biombo usually consists of ten panels, only six so far have been located, and while these blanks still occlude a full understanding of the biombo's meaning, the inclusion of the Madrid panel with the extant five panels

BETWEEN VICTOR AND VANQUISHED 273

Figure 10.1. Portrait of Moteuczoma. Courtesy of Museo de América, Madrid

in the Rivero Lake collection shows a dramatic turn away from the narrative of the *Conquista* as witnessed in all other extant biombos.

While the Madrid panel can be called a portrait because it focuses considerably on the king's features and expressions, when rejoined with the extant panels of

Figure 10.2. Partial biombo of the *Conquista* of Mexico. Private Collection. Courtesy of Rodrigo Rivero Lake. International Art & Antiques.

the biombo the portrait enacts the king in a way not seen anywhere else. The full biombo (henceforth called the Madrid-Lake biombo) reveals a wholly new kind of *Conquista* narrative. As both portrait of Moteuczoma and historical portrayal, this fusion of genres theatricizes a pathos of the Indigenous king, casting him as a fallen hero of the *Conquista* in ways that depart from the messages that are presented in all other known portraits and biombos of the *Conquista*. In its effects, this emergence also anticipates the European projection of the "Noble Savage" that crystallized in the mid-eighteenth century especially with the Enlightenment philosophers Jean-Jacques Rousseau and Voltaire. The concept pervades and continues to be developed out of a romanticized notion that ancient New World inhabitants (and other non-Western ethnicities) were/are somehow closer to nature and therefore freer from the servitude and corruption of human laws.[3] The notion was primarily invested from a European fascination with the New World that gained traction especially during this era and facilitated by stage performances of the Amerindian, particularly the characterization of Moteuczoma. The term was first circulated by the English playwright John Dryden's *The Conquest of Granada by the Spaniards* when referring to Muslims in al-Andalus, performed beginning in 1670 and published in 1672. While Dryden's earlier work *The Indian Emperor* (1665)[4] did not coin that term, that play ends with Moteuczoma's criticism of the Spanish zeal for religious conversion while reflecting on the sorrow of his demise. Above all, Dryden's Moteuczoma is both knowledgeable of natural law and able to critique the moral inferiority of his Spanish adversaries.[5] At least from this point forward, the personification of the king by Europeans elevates the moral and political superiority of Amerindians, and this captivated the imagination of Europeans who sought a pure notion of reason to overcome their own human corruptions. The Madrid-Lake biombo visually initiates this notion, which was otherwise experienced ephemerally in local performances and social intercourse in the late seventeenth and early eighteenth centuries, by presenting a new enactment of the *Conquista* narrative.

THE MADRID-LAKE BIOMBO

Several biombos and other series of paintings depict the *Conquista* as a linear narrative that begins with the famous Encounter between Hernán Cortés and Moteuczoma on the southern causeway, and most end with the Capture of Cuauhtemoc. They were all produced in the late seventeenth into the early and mid-eighteenth centuries, forming a short-lived genre in reaction to Antonio de Solís's widely held *Historia de la conquista de México* (1684 and with multiple editions in other languages thereafter).[6] Many of the paintings are complete with keys to legends that describe major episodes of the *Conquista*, following the contours set forth in Solís's new history. The four known biombos of the *Conquista* depict the events from the eyewitness view of the Valley of Mexico from above, into which are woven the battles and turns of events that led to Spanish capture of Cuauhtemoc and the subsequent fall of Tenochtitlan. Two of these examples are painted on the reverse side with the same elevated view of the city re-presented as an ordered grid plan of streets and architectural details that signal its religious and royal affiliations as the loyal city of Mexico-Tenochtitlan.[7] In the tableaus that convey the chaos of the *Conquista*, the narrative follows a meandering pattern along two registers of the painting, beginning on the upper right with the first encounter of Hernán Cortés and Moteuczoma, then toward the left upper register, before continuing from the lower left toward the lower right, usually climaxing in the lower right with the Noche Triste and the Capture of Cuauhtemoc.[8]

Because both ends of the Madrid-Lake biombo appear to be intact (as evidenced by their borders), there can be no doubt that the narrative focuses on the last quarter of *Conquista* as depicted in other biombos—its climax and conclusion—which are marked by the final appearances of Moteuczoma and Cuauhtemoc. Yet, rather than a tableau emphasizing the geographic space wherein the *Conquista* occurred and whereupon the Spanish could claim to have imposed order over chaos, the surviving narrative produced by the Madrid-Lake biombo draws the critical Native actors to the foreground space, staged and accompanied by props that convey their particular plight.[9] Instead of presenting a sense of ordered society brought about by the *Conquista*, the Madrid-Lake painting aligns with Solís's narrative not by adhering to the heroism of Cortés but by focusing on the Indigenous kings during moments of personal circumspection preceding their deaths at the hands of the Spanish, who, in this case, make their first appearance at the end as Cuauhtemoc's captors.[10]

Other biombos of the *Conquista* depict Spaniards in Moteuczoma's palace, when, according to most narratives of the *Conquista*, the Indigenous king attempted to convince his people to end the mounting defense against the Spaniards. Fortunately, the panels that were adjacent to the Madrid panel survive, completing a composition that was only suggested by the agitated crowd before the Madrid and Lake panels were brought together. Now we can fully see that Moteuczoma appears on the balcony of his palace during the famous incident (figure 10.1).[11] Unlike other paintings that depict this scene, however, the king gazes wistfully into the distance and seems to pay no attention to the confused and angry crowd below, nor does he notice the arrow flying straight for his heart. In the left panel, a warrior wearing an unidentifiable animal suit reminiscent of Mexica warriors has just shot the fatal arrow, which flies toward Moteuczoma in the central panel (see figure 10.2) along the archer's trajectory. Another warrior in the right panel (figure 10.2) holds an open sling, suggesting that he has just launched a stone, though no mid-air stone is discernable. Other lords and warriors gather below, and two important percussive instruments used in Indigenous rituals, a *huehuetl* (upright drum) and *teponaztli* (two-toned horizontal drum), are on the ground, without musicians to play them. Their silence is underscored by the tambourines dangling on the corner of the cage and are no doubt a metaphor for Moteuczoma's captivity, as surely as is the dog trapped inside the cage. Notably, the Spanish conquistadors are nowhere to be seen; however, a fire can be seen through the ground entrance of Moteuczoma's palace, alluding to the moment they retreated from the palace, following the Mexica resistance that also precipitated Moteuczoma's death. Neatly, a cartouche on the upper left of the composition (figure 10.2) explains, "Moteuczoma wants to harangue his subjects, and they [become] more irritated and kill him with three arrows and a stone."[12] This explanation adheres with the official Spanish explanation of Moteuczoma's death that is described in this image: at the hands of his own people and not by the Spanish when they abandoned the besieged palace. Accordingly, the text calls us to witness the three panels together, with the haranguing, the resistance, and the assassination happening simultaneously. Moteuczoma's dejected expression, inserted into its original context, carries the weight of a historical tragedy.

At least four of the panels of this biombo are missing, perhaps forever, and so it is difficult to discern the details that once unfolded between Moteuczoma and Cuauhtemoc. In the panel to the left of the balcony scene, a costumed warrior can be found in the mid-ground whipping a dark-skinned male figure, while a crowd of Indigenous onlookers, or as Marita Martínez del Río de Redo suggests, "accusers," seem to escalate the violence.[13] However, it is not entirely clear how or why this scene would fit into this particular pictorial narrative; it could have been a background scene related to another figure in the foreground, and/or in a composition of two or three panels like those that include Moteuczoma and Cuauhtemoc. To the left (figure 10.2) is another panel that is difficult to interpret. A Mexica warrior-priest stands in the foreground between a row of banners and an altar, languidly holding an arrow that seems to accidentally or providentially point toward a *tzompantli* (skull rack) filled with the heads of Spanish men and horses. A group of Mexica lords look over his shoulder as he stares into the distance, mirroring Moteuczoma's and Cuauhtemoc's introspection. The arrow he holds echoes the arrow flying toward Moteuczoma's heart. Is this the same fatal arrow? Is he the assassinator? Is he also being captured and punished?

Unlike any other biombo, the Madrid-Lake employs an Orientalist iconography that may one day lead to a better understanding of its production, for it is difficult to fathom that the artist was from New Spain. For one, the Indigenous warrior costumes are of unrecognizable creatures, also blended in the portrait of the priest in the penultimate panel toward the left. There also one can see that the tzompantli victims are strung up by their topknots rather than through the temple of the skull, which is inconsistent with Mexica practices. Such errors may be attributed to the faded memories of these traditions almost 200 years after the *Conquista*. However, this logic falls short when considering that Moteuczoma holds a feather fan made of peacock feathers, which is inconsistent with all other known depictions of the king, where he either wears an arm device or holds a feather fan made of the tailfeathers of the quetzal bird, an ancient Indigenous symbol of royalty in Mesoamerica and colonial New Spain. Peacocks, of course, are not indigenous to the Americas but to the Near East, yet the bird's proud display of colorful plumes conveyed a broad notion of luxury and exoticism to be seen on par with the quetzal. The artist's ignorance of this belies a critical separation from Indigenous knowledge that can be tied to the other paintings of *Conquista*, and this hybridity is further enhanced by one more element that appears to be more from the near east: the panel of cloth that covers Moteuczoma's chin, which I call here a *pañuela*, or handkerchief, perhaps referring to a garment worn in the desert for protection. In addition to signifying a non-European, the pañuela obscures another controversial aspect of Moteuczoma's identity: whether or not he grew a beard. Overall, this subject matter is a theatrical portrayal that departs from Spanish histories of the *Conquista* and instead focuses on the tragic heroism of Moteuczoma at the moment of his death.

PORTRAITURE AND MOTEUCZOMA

In Mexica Tenochtitlan, only the highest lords were allowed to look directly at Moteuczoma, and so any true likeness of him would have been impossible to recognize any more widely than by those in his inner circle.[14] The most authoritative portrait of the king, in the sense of representing his physical appearance, was commissioned by Moteuczoma himself in 1519 to be carved at the base of Chapultepec Hill overlooking Tenochtitlan, on the eve of the *Conquista*. Unfortunately, most of this stone body is now missing, destroyed through one or more iconoclastic events into the eighteenth century.[15] Some of the earliest verbal descriptions of the king came from the Spanish conquistadors and Indigenous eyewitnesses during the *Conquista*, yet they disagree on some of the details, in particular the tone of Moteuczoma's skin and whether or not he had facial hair. Furthermore, no known portraits were taken from life, and none have been connected to the patronage of any of his descendants.[16] Certainly, then, every posthumous portrait of him is an invention that reflects more the interests of its patrons rather than the king's actual physiognomy. Therefore, the earliest creators of portraits probably relied on verbal testimonies from the few eyewitnesses of the conquistadors.

At least one early portrait claimed to capture the likeness of the Moteuczoma, appearing in André Thevet's *Les vrais pourtraits et vies des hommes illustres* (True portraits and lives of illustrious men) (1584) (figure 10.3).[17] Although Thevet claimed that his portrait was as meticulously "true" as the other 200+ portraits in his book, Moteuczoma's was, in a way, reverse-engineered from theories associating a person's character with their physical features and facial expressions. This method resulted in a somewhat haggard image of a serious or solemn king.[18] Thevet's authority to produce this portrait was bolstered by his status as eyewitness of the New World (even though he never traveled to New Spain) and his collection of Indigenous treasures that included one of the earliest surviving Indigenous manuscripts from the early colonial period: the *Codex Mendoza* (ca. 1541).

The *Codex Mendoza* was created by Nahua artists who were undergoing religious conversion and learning Renaissance painting techniques of illusionism. Such transformation of Indigenous pictographic systems of writing to pictorial illustration can be witnessed across the pages of this single manuscript. The book contains three parts—a Mexica kings list detailing their years of rule and the conquests during their reign, a list of tribute collected supposedly every eighty days from conquered towns, and a detailed ethnography of Mexica life from raising children to ascending into careers as adults. Whereas the first two sections of this manuscript were based on pre-Columbian recording practices of kings lists and tribute rolls (figures 10.4 and 10.5), the third is an unprecedented reflection set down on paper. Accordingly, the figural and pictorial styles shift more toward naturalism in this part, except in instances where pictographic meaning is retained within the new naturalistic iconography. This shift is most salient in the only figure of the manuscript that is not seen in profile: a view of Moteuczoma in his palace (figures 10.6 and 10.7). Here, the king's body is rendered as he appears in the king's list, though now his *tilma* (cloak

Figure 10.3. Portrait of the Moteuczoma. André Thevet, *Les vrais pourtraits et vies des hommes illustres grecz, latins et payens, recueilliz de leurs tableaux, livres, médalles antiques et modernes*, 1584. Wikimedia Commons.

knotted on one shoulder) is colored turquoise to match his turquoise miter. With a nod toward naturalism, the artist at first attempted to show the legs folded up to the chest underneath his turquoise robe, but the result is awkwardly flattened to match his pictographic form. Yet, the king's face turns to three-quarters, capturing

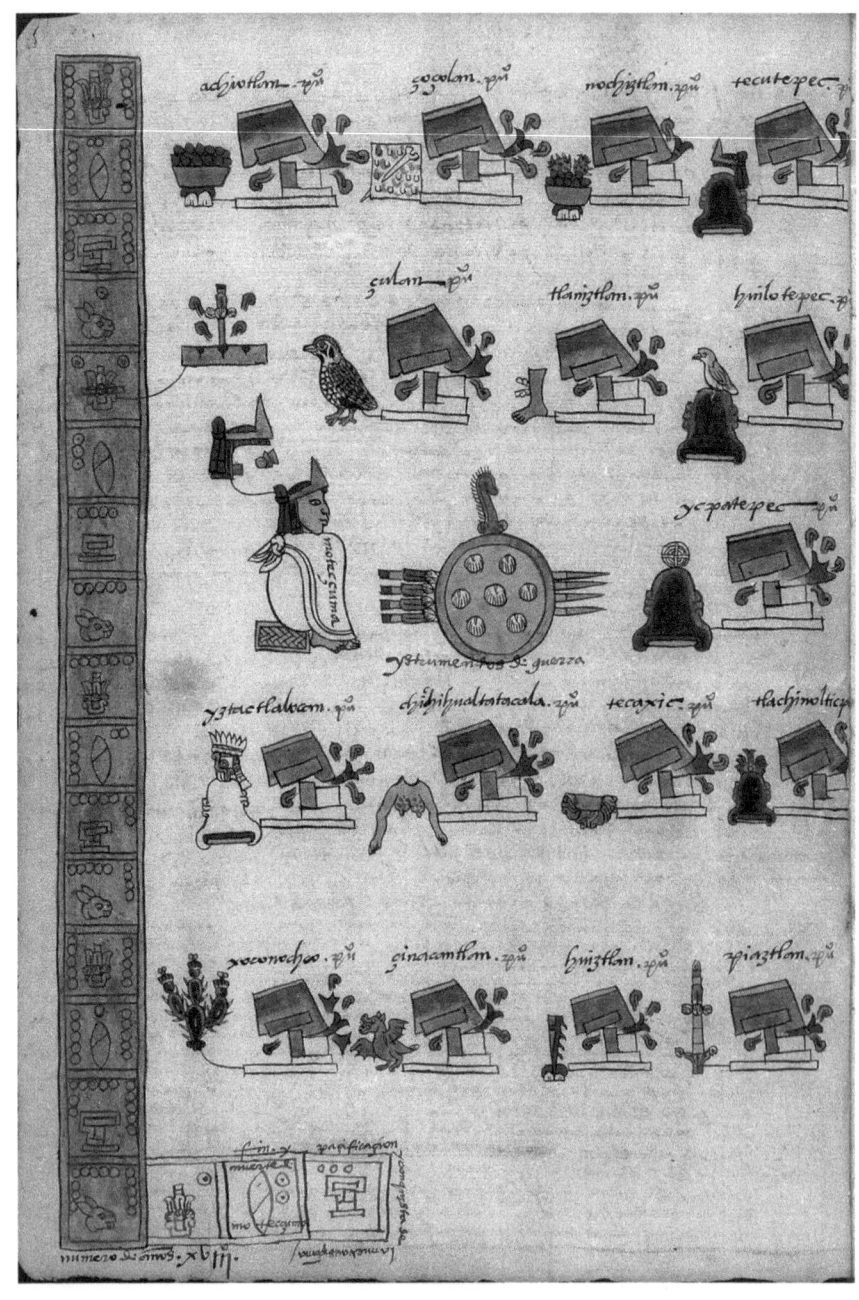

Figure 10.4. *Codex Mendoza*, folio 7v, ca. 1541–1650. Bodleian Libraries, University of Oxford, MS. Arch. Selden. A1 (CC-BY-NC 4.0).

Figure 10.5. Detail of Moteuczoma and name glyph. *Codex Mendoza*, folio 7v, ca. 1541–1650. Bodleian Libraries, University of Oxford, MS. Arch. Selden. A1 (CC-BY-NC 4.0).

a surprising detail: that he sports a beard, which is rendered somewhat heavily due to the width of the artist's pen. Nonetheless, upon seeing this manuscript firsthand in 2010, I can confirm that the lines that compose his beard are the same as those that compose the outlines of the figure, as are those that rotate the crown to follow the turn of the head.

Curiously if not surprisingly, the artist of Thevet's portrait copied what he may have perceived as heraldic ornaments from other parts of *Codex Mendoza*, but he does not seem to have followed this more realistic portrait in the third part of that manuscript. Notably, Thevet's artist effectively ignored the king's beard, which was described in several sources. This is presumably because Thevet wanted to contrast Moteuczoma with Cortés, who sports a heavy beard in *Les vrais pourtraits* (figure 10.8).[19] The written pages accompanying Moteuczoma's image in *Codex Mendoza* describe his kingship in positive terms, but they do not describe his physical countenance. But even Cortés's secretary, Francisco López de Gómara, described a sparse beard on Moteuczoma in his *Historia de las Indias y Conquista de México* (*History of the Indies and Conquest of Mexico*) (1552), and this account was widely circulated by Thevet's time.

> Moteuczoma was a man of medium size, thin, and, like all Indians, of a very dark complexion. He wore his hair long and had no more than six bristles on his chin, black and about an inch long. He was of an amiable though severe disposition, affable, well-spoken, and gracious, which made him respected and feared. Moteuczoma

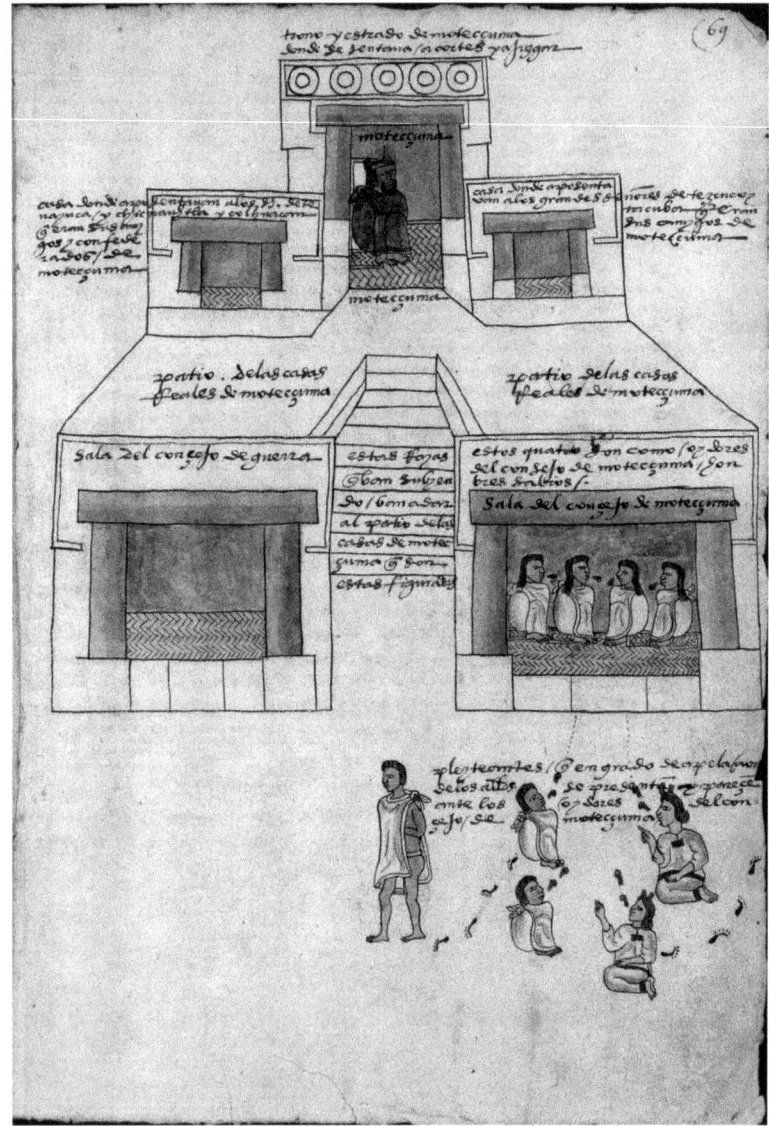

Figure 10.6. *Codex Mendoza*, folio 69r, ca. 1541–1650. Bodleian Libraries, University of Oxford, MS. Arch. Selden. A1 (CC-BY-NC 4.0).

means a furious and solemn man.... His people endowed him with such majesty that they would not sit in his presence, or wear shoes, or look him in the face, with the exception of only a few great lords.[20]

Figure 10.7. Detail of Moteuczoma in his palace. *Codex Mendoza*, folio 69r, ca. 1541–1650. Bodleian Libraries, University of Oxford, MS. Arch. Selden. A1 (CC-BY-NC 4.0).

Even without the beard, the physiognomy and expression of Moteuczoma in *Les vrais pourtraits* seem to reproduce the haggard and lonely king in the *Codex Mendoza* portrait, where the king sits in his empty palace, a fact emphasized by the orthogonal lines that position the vanishing point behind him. Thevet did not copy Moteuczoma's portrait directly from *Codex Mendoza*, and his engraving, despite all its detail, did not inspire portraits outside of France or Spain.[21] Instead, he allowed verbal descriptions to stand in for his own eyewitness, and yet their contradictions point to early essentialist notions of Moteuczoma's racial characteristics.

Such characteristics manifest over a century later in a widely influential new history by Antonio de Solís, *Historia de la Conquista de México*, in an era when the portrait was constructed through baroque dualisms of his and his adversary's character. Since his fall, as Thevet makes explicit verbally, Moteuczoma was the medium from which was made Hernán Cortés's fame, and so the ancient king was most often compared with Cortés according to predetermined European concepts of heroism. Accordingly, the physical differences between the Indigenous king and the conquistador were recognized as signs of moral or spiritual fortitude, cast in terms of opposing abilities to govern and their divine fates, as prophesized through their faiths. Moteuczoma continued to be remembered in terms of his disillusionment and downfall in the colonial histories, as an untold number of historical plays were enacted based on the intersections of Solís's narrative and its visualization in art generated from New Spain of the waning years of the Hapsburg Empire. Benjamin Keen observes that Solís's narrative emerged at the time with "a haughty aristocratic spirit, a fervent piety, and the same somber *desengaño*, disillusionment with the

Figure 10.8. Portrait of Cortés. André Thevet, Les vrais pourtraits et vies des hommes illustres grecz, latins et payens, recueilliz de leurs tableaux, livres, médalles antiques et modernes, 1584. Wikimedia Commons.

things of this world, that pervades the plays of Calderón. Over the work broods an unspoken awareness of Spain's melancholy plight in the reign of the imbecile Charles II."[22] In this regard, Solís's revised account of the *Conquista* was favored by *criollos* who by and large sought to simultaneously tie themselves to the Indigenous past and glorify themselves as purveyors of colonial order.

Comparison with Solís's sources reveals some of the distortions and inconsistencies concerning Moteuczoma's physical appearance. His sources included López de Gómara's *History*, introduced earlier, and the conquistador Bernal Diaz del Castillo's posthumous *La Historia verdadera de la conquista de la Nueva España* (*True History of the Conquest of New Spain*) (written by 1576, first published in 1632). More than his predecessors, Solís remarks upon the opulence of Moteuczoma and his court, including its ceremonial pomp and processional order, rather than over the king's physical appearance. Such aspects reflected on his own notions of royal courtly behavior and a nostalgia projected onto the Indigenous American past. Solís describes Moteuczoma even more briefly than his sources as he leaves out key details: "He was of strong presence, around forty years old, of medium height, [and] more thin than robust. His face [was] aquiline, colored less dark than most Indians, his hair long to the lower part of the ear, [with] lively eyes, [a] majestic air, [and] with some intention."[23] He ignores the critical detail provided by López de Gómara, a point that the Nahua historian Domingo de San Antón Muñon Chimalpahin Quauhtlehuanitzin had already doubled down upon by emphasizing it in his own recopying of López de Gómara's text, commemorating the centennial of the Spanish invasion, when he wrote, "he was dark skinned with a very dark-brown complexion."[24] Equally interesting, all other accessible sources prior to Solís stressed the presence of Moteuczoma's beard, however sparse. Díaz del Castillo repeated much of López de Gómara's details, noting that the king had a "scanty black beard [that] was well shaped and thin."[25] Chimalpahin amends López de Gómara's description by omitting "no more than six bristles" and adding "long hairs measuring a *jeme*, or about six inches in length."[26] Yet, Solís ignored these details altogether in his description, as Thevet had similarly left out Moteuczoma's beard even though he possessed a portrait with a beard, the only three-quarter figure in that manuscript, which happens to be glossed twice with Moteuczoma's name (figure 10.7).

Solís repeats much of the other details provided in the earlier descriptions, but his text instead waxes on Moteuczoma's opulence, a trait that López de Gómara described both in terms of personal daily habits and public festivals. Furthermore, unlike those before him, Solís also elaborates on Moteuczoma's clothing and adornment, re-dressing him in the process.

> For his apparel, he wore a mantle of the finest cotton, tied casually on his shoulders, covering the greatest part of his body, with the end trailing on the ground, adorned with different jewels of gold, pearls, and precious stones, in such number that they seemed rather a weight than an ornament. His crown was a miter of light gold,

ending in a point before, the hinder part was made rounder. On his feet, he wore shoes of hammered gold, whole scraps, studded with the same, bound them to his feet, and came round part of his leg, like the Roman military sandals.[27]

Not only does Solís intentionally lighten Moteuczoma's skin tone, but also he dresses the Aztec king like a Roman lord; later in his description, he even creates an *escudo* (coat of arms) for the Moteuczoma family, crediting a bit of artistic license to its imagery, which he described as emblazoned above the entrance to Moteuczoma's palace:

a griffin, half eagle, and half lion, with the wings extended for flight, and a tiger in his talons. Some maintain that this griffin was an eagle, because there were no griffins in that country, as if there were reason to believe that other parts of the world produced them.

Whereas naturalists place them in the number of fabulous birds, and we shall rather choose to suppose this sort of monsters, the production of fancy through a liberty allowed to poets and painters.[28]

As far as can be discerned, Solís is the first to use such artistic license to invent this heraldic device for Moteuczoma, though one might argue that Thevet culled one together in his portrait. Nonetheless, Solís's invention appeared around the same time that members of the Moteuczoma family were inventing their own blazons as part of their petitions for hereditary rights under the Spanish Crown.

Solís's inventions extend into gendered allusions of masculinity, which he found in the feminization of Moteuczoma, a character who is pompous at best and corrupt at worst. Matthew Restall discusses the death of Moteuczoma as a continuation of the narrative outlined by Solís. In fact, Moteuczoma is impaled (penetrated by the arrow or stoned) when he appears weakest to his public. In the Solís account, the emperor's fatal wounding by arrows and stones is framed by his plea to Mexica warriors "to put down their arms," their dismay at seeing him "so humiliated" and "calling him coward, made a woman and a vile prisoner of his enemies."[29] Upon his captivity, the Mexica king supposedly moved through stages of anger and depression as he is proven impotent to quash a rebellion that grew from his captivity, though, of course, the rebellion was ultimately blamed on his weakness. This rejection by his people allowed Solís a space to pin Moteuczoma with a certain complicity in his own death. Notwithstanding the symbolism of spears and stones, Moteuczoma proved himself impotent on the balcony as his own people rebelled, and especially afterward when he refused to have his wounds dressed by the Spanish soldiers. This gave rise to yet another myth—whether he was baptized before his death—an important point raised by his descendants in almost all of their petitions for escudos, and a central focus of some controversy among early modern scholars.[30] As mentioned, Solís also lightened Moteuczoma's complexion and removed his sparse beard in order to contrast that king's lack of virility and his disgrace with those of Cortés, a point that is emphasized in Solís's text and can be traced back to Thevet's portrait more than a century earlier. Knowing that the rabble was growing, Moteuczoma asked Cortés and his men to leave. Cortés, noting the opportunity to safely escape and with intention of regrouping, agreed, but it was already too late. As a crowd mounted outside of Moteuczoma's palace, Cortés and his men and Tlaxcalan allies are described as strategically defending the walls while the king asked to go to his balcony to calm his people down. What happens next is impressive.

> He caused himself to be adorned with his royal robes, called for his crown and imperial mantle, not forgetting the jewels which he was accustomed to wear upon public occasions, nor other affected formalities, which sufficiently published his diffidence; making it appear by all this care, that he stood in need of exterior show to gain respect, and that the assistance of purple and gold was necessary to cover and conceal the interior weakness of majesty.

In one fell swoop, Solís feminizes Moteuczoma in order to show his ridiculousness—owing to his ridicule—to the point that his subjects were stunned to "see their monarch so humble," a "disrespect [that] immediately was converted into contempt," and so they called him derogatory names. Then, two soldiers, who had been placed at his side by Cortés and who apparently foresaw the rebellion, tried to protect him with their armor. "But all their care was not sufficient to prevent his being touched by some arrows, and very rigorously by a stone which wounded him in the head, breaking part of his temple, with which blow he fell down senseless to the ground." As he recovered, he dithered from anger to confusion and grief, losing all strength and spirit in the process. "A barbarous recourse of cowardly minds, who sink beneath calamity, and are only valiant against that which can least oppose them."[31] Once again, Solís effectively invents a new identity for Moteuczoma that is based on his opposing characteristics when pitted against Cortés. In such acts of comparative analysis, Cortés remained the defining arbitrator of divergent fames and fates, and Moteuczoma's portrayal was subordinate to those rules.

ALTERNATIVE PORTRAITS

At least in the early years of the colonies, viceroys were considered like vicars, or stand-in representations of the king, rather than as independent agents in the New World. However, late seventeenth-century images of the viceroy's palace and portraits assert their agency through the use of local emblems in their escudos and a tradition of portraiture that expresses loyalty to the crown while expressing their individuality. Produced around the same time and place as the articulation of criollo identity, the disillusionment between loyalty and obeyance is apparent in the late seventeenth-century portraits, which "assert themselves as individuals and transgress the spatial boundary of the parapet."[32] Escudos became more prominently displayed as emblems of the viceroy's identity and as such fused together Indigenous and European emblems. Such notions of identity, invested in heraldry and genealogy, were also mapped onto the image of Moteuczoma. Paul Scolieri also observes that through both pictorial practices and staged performances, the colonizers attempted to shape the image of the Indigenous king into one that resembled the Spanish noble court. They did so in order to embody him with an idea of difference and hierarchy—a kind of hybridity that is, like a coat of arms, a European form that can be specified with symbols particular to the individual or family.[33]

This heraldry held Moteuczoma to be like a vicar, who in the Spanish imagination held the throne for the Spanish sovereign, manifested dialogically with the figure of Cortés. At least three series of *enconchados*, or panel paintings encrusted with mother-of-pearl, visualize episodes of the *Conquista*, in which one finds images of the Moteuczoma as a "vicar": for Cortés in the narrative, and the viceroy who commissioned it. Dating to the same time period as biombos, the enconchados were likely among gifts sent to Charles II and by the Viceroy José Sarmiento de Valladares (1696–1701), who carried the title of count of Moctezuma y Tula, inherited by marrying into a branch of Moteuczoma family.[34] His arrival in Mexico-Tenochtitlan marked a turning point to the previously unending legal battles of the Moteuczoma family in the middle colonial period, capitulating the name and situating it within the highest Spanish authority—the office of the viceroy—in New Spain. In two of the three enconchado series, one scene depicts Moteuczoma showing Cortés an imagined Mexica court, where he shows the Spaniard the throne he reserved for his "true" sovereign, presumably to sit alongside him (figure 10.9).[35] In one of these versions, he is seated on his throne, apparently ready to receive the king, and in another, he stands with Cortés and gestures toward dual thrones, apparently ready to sit alongside him. As seen elsewhere, the enconchado artists were experimenting with the rhetorical limits of iconography in the pictorial narratives. The dual thrones suggest an equal status between the kingdoms of the colonizer and colonized, at least as long as Moteuczoma willingly submitted everything under his power to the Spanish.

The event in which Moteuczoma "donated" his throne, and by extension his empire, is one of the major myths to have spun out of the *Conquista* and to have enabled the subsequent colonization of the Americas, for it fit with early Spanish

Figure 10.9.
Enconchado of
the *Conquista*,
Moteuczoma shows
Cortés his throne.
Courtesy of Museo
de América, Madrid.

ambitions and later criollo experiences within a growing white population in New Spain. In this narrative, Moteuczoma recognizes the divine prophesy of Spanish sovereignty in the New World, and so he willingly donated his empire to Cortés.[36]

The donation myth was also important to Moteuczoma's descendants in the late seventeenth century, as they repeatedly proclaimed in documents sent to the king of Spain in order to receive their state benefits, or *mercedes*, in addition to professing that Moteuczoma was baptized and that they have always been good Christians. This nominal identity persisted to the count of Moteuczoma, who held no blood relation to Indigenous America and, as has been remarked, also considered himself a "vicar" of the king of Spain.[37] Furthermore, Viceroy Sarmiento represented a shift in focus from state pageantry through a reunion of heraldic lines that came full circle, as embodied by his title.

As with most of the other painted images, in the Madrid-Lake biombo Moteuczoma wears Roman military or festival dress, fulfilling the role of intermediary for the Spanish sovereign and precursor to Spanish Catholicism through his voluntary conversion. Such is also the case in a portrait bearing the label at the bottom, "El Monarca Montesuma" (figure 10.10). This textual announcement positions the painting as a royal portrait in line with those of the Spanish nobility, including New Spanish viceroys.[38] Pablo Escalante Gonzalbo considers the resemblance between this portrait and a description of a portrait that was commissioned to José Rodríguez Carnero by the criollo polymath Carlos Sigüenza y Góngora.[39] Escalante suggests that Sigüenza y Góngora's description of Carnero's portrait of Moteuczoma resembles the Mexico portrait, in which Moteuczoma was "bedecked with extremely lavish, imperial garb, drawing many pearls, much silver, [and] gold from the mouth of a lion, which he scattered everywhere."[40] There is some overlap, but we may never know whether the portrait at hand was created to stand alongside other portraits of colonial magistrates or Mexica kings in a triumphal arch. More interesting, any irony of presenting the Indigenous king in European clothing appears to have escaped the criollo's attention. Such a portrait could have fulfilled the king's place in the palace alongside the portrait of the count of Moteuczoma and Tula, but there is no known record of such an event. In his *Teatro de virtudes políticas* (1680), Sigüenza describes the portrait as part of a triumphal arch for the grand entrance of the viceroy Tomás de la Cerda in 1680. Sigüenza's arch featured paintings of the Mexica kings from Acamapichtli to Cuauhtemoc, preceded by the Mexica titular god Huitzilopochtli instead of the heroes and kings of Rome and Spain. By breaking from precedent, the criollo sought to disrupt the control of the viceregal government and provide a space for the growing population of Spaniards born in the Americas. As Escalante argues, "Sigüenza's genealogy credited the Nahua kings—and not Hernán Cortés—with the foundation of the kingdom of New Spain, and he presented the colonial rulers as its successors."[41]

The characteristics of the portrait were under negotiation at the time it was painted, as it was repainted over another that changes significant details (figure 10.11).[42] It is

Figure 10.10. Portrait of Moteuczoma, attributed to the Arellano family, ca. 1690. (Private Collection), with x-ray view (right) and color reconstruction (left) of underpainting.

interesting to consider why there was such a dramatic change in the positioning of the head, which became adorned with his *xiuhuitzolli*, or Mexica royal miter, occupied by the Hapsburg double eagle, in the final version. In the earlier version, Moteuczoma gazes upward at an empty space much like that of the Madrid portrait. When his head was tilted downward in the final version, that space is occupied by the Hapsburg eagle emblazoned on his xiuhuitzolli. The emblem served as a visible sign of blood lineage that ran alongside the physiognomic traits of blood relations. The heraldic elements found in this painting may have derived in part from Solís's description, but certainly the double-headed eagle was incorporated later into his Indigenous crown. The artist also changed the position of his hands and their symbolic import. Moteuczoma originally was holding two keys on a plate, apparently as an offering, but in the final version he listlessly holds a scepter downward. Whereas he once had his left hand on the hilt of his *macuahuitl*-sword, he instead closes his hand over his heart. The final iteration of this palimpsest of symbols suggests a shifting attitude toward the king. In fact, the shadowy haze obscures the chin of the figure, where it appears that the artist reconsidered his mustache and beard. The earlier version also appears to have had a prominent mustache and thin strip of a

Figure 10.11. X-Ray of portrait of Moteuczoma. Private collection. Photographer: Laura Cohen.

beard as well, thus departing from Solís but following most other sources, including perhaps Carrera's now-lost painting.

According to Jaime Cuadriello, the downward gaze of this (final) portrait represents the full acceptance of the Christian religion through Moteuczoma's recognition of the "King of Kings."[43] That meaning clearly shifted as more political overtones were conveyed by the later version, which folded out of the same wistful look in the first version as found in the Madrid-Lake biombo. This notion that Moteuczoma was only the vicar for the Spanish Crown, of course, relies on a linear sense of time rather than Mexica cyclical thought. Thus, Moteuczoma was considered the vicar of Quetzalcoatl, the famed ruler of ancient Tollan, who Sigüenza equated with Saint Thomas Aquinas.[44] Cortés, whom criollos considered a vicar of Charles V, arrived in the momentous year that Quetzalcoatl was prophesized to return to reclaim his throne in Mexica legend. Thus, according to divine law, Moteuczoma "was forced to suffer imprisonment and resignation, and to return to his legitimate owners that credential of power."[45] In the painting, his twin crowns—one on his head and the other at his foot—connote the changing political power from the *huey tlahtoani* to the Hapsburg royal line. In a gesture that simultaneously acknowledges the myth of the prophesy of Spanish dominance and Moteuczoma's donation of his empire, the Mexica king bows down to his Spanish sovereign. His cuirass appears to be made of feathers arranged in a paisley design within a baroque version of Roman military garb. If one were to argue that the painting presents a notion of criollismo, it makes its point with these symbols of power in the crown, relegated to European heraldic conventions. This was an inchoate visual language, to be sure, as the transition from upward to downward gaze characterizes the melodramatic nature of Moteuczoma's portraits during this era.

In all of these aspects, the Mexico portrait is a striking contrast to another created at about the same time, perhaps around a decade later, and probably with the influence of Sigüenza y Góngora (figure 10.12). The ultimate beneficiary of this portrait was Cosimo III de' Medici in Florence, where it resides today in the Museo degli Argenti, Florence.[46] Though this portrait does not carry an inscription, it was recopied soon after its arrival in the port of Venice by the engraver Sister Isabella Piccini, who inscribed the label upon it, "Portrait of Moteuczoma, engraved from the original sent from Mexico to the Most Serene Grand Duke of Tuscany."[47] Cosimo's interest in a portrait of Moteuczoma may have stemmed from long-standing Florentine connections to the Americas. Florence held pride as home to the sixteenth-century cosmographer Amerigo Vespucci, the namesake of the Americas. In 1661, Cosimo's wedding to Margarita of Orleans included a procession of allegorical figures of the Americas, which performed in a prominent position alongside those of Europe on the terrace of the Pitti palace gardens of Boboli. Consistent with Lucrezia Buti's Uffizi painting and the later portrait, the figures were described as dressed "in the style of their country, on their naked skin, adornments of multicolored feathers, dressed with gold and precious stones that abound in their region."[48] Nudity and feathers are the most stereotypical assemblage that represented Amerindians and

Figure 10.12. Portrait of Moteuczoma attributed to Antonio Rodríguez, ca. 1660–90, Museo degli Argenti, Florence. Courtesy of Ministero della Cultura.

allegories of the Americas in Europe at this time.[49] Nonetheless, it cannot be stated that this portrait was inspired by Thevet's, which came out over a century before and otherwise referenced in some of Buti's images.[50]

In the Medici portrait, Moteuczoma's gaze out to the viewer is matched only by Thevet's rendition, and though the differences are quite notable, both carry the emblems of shield and spear. These were standard tropes in European portraiture, especially of noble heraldry, and new meanings about their value were attached to Indigenous nobility. Nevertheless, like Thevet's portrait, the Medici portrait was based on Indigenous sources in the collection of Sigüenza y Góngora in Mexico-Tenochtitlan. Cuadriello first noted that at least one inspiration for the portrait came from a manuscript now known as *Codex Ixtlilxochitl*, in which a portrait of Nezahualpilli strikes a similar pose.[51] Escalante stylistically attributes the painting to Antonio Rodríguez, and stresses that it was produced through the agency of Giovanni Francesco Gemelli Careri, an Italian traveler who was in Mexico in 1697.[52] While its codical sources have been established convincingly, the Medici portrait is a synthesis that could have included a model dressed in the stereotypical role of the king for dances and festivals in and around Mexico City, especially the *mitote*, or "Dance of Moteuczoma." The artist's close attention to the characteristics of the face suggests that he was paying attention to a new model, and one that, incidentally, appealed to Chimalpahin's claim about the king's tawny skin more than all of the others. The artist's attention to the king's gaunt features, aquiline nose, and large, deep-set eyes, suggests that this portrait was not from textual descriptions or the imagination alone. Perhaps we are meeting a live model who was chosen for the festival role, thus offering a bridge between the portrait and its portrayal in the background. As shown earlier, Thevet's "true" portrait of Moteuczoma was constructed from *Codex Mendoza*, but that includes only the costume and ornaments, not the king's physiognomy, which derives from another experience altogether.[53] In that case, his likeness was developed from Renaissance theories of physiognomy and descriptions of his character. Since it is certain that this portrait was destined for Cosimo III in the late seventeenth century, its production likely stems from the Renaissance preference for the most accurate portrait from life, one in which the pose conflated ideas of Spanish and American sovereignty.

BETWEEN VICTOR AND VANQUISHED

The Madrid-Lake biombo reinvents Moteuczoma's role in the *Conquista* in at least two important ways that are different from other representations. First, it crops the narrative down to one quarter of the narrative in the panorama views of the *Conquista*, so it can severely reduce the number of figures and focus on their qualitative expressions. Moreover, there are no Spaniards present in the scene on the balcony. Moteuczoma thus appears less engaged with the crowd and more introspective, as he gazes into the distance and appears to be preparing a soliloquy. The palace architecture interacts with the spatial layout of the folding screen, creating a more interactive relationship between the viewer and painted dramatic scenes. This is no more evident than with the palace, which functions and is given the illusion of a stage set. The outer wall of it leads the eye up the orthogonal lines of the bricks to the king on the balcony, which occupies the narrow wall parallel to the screen, which is enclosed by a wall in the foreground of the adjacent panel to the right. Second, by shifting the meander pattern to a dynamic foreground-background composition in three or four clusters of foregrounded figures, it participates in a visual interplay also seen in the Medici portrait, and thus expanding the painting's role to place the portrait within specific roles in the *Conquista* narrative and its performance in the colonial period, whether through written histories or in plays and dances such as the mitote, a topic for later discussion.

The Madrid-Lake biombo highlights some of the remaining quarter of the *Conquista* narrative in order to reshape the historical narrative, of which Indigenous voices are notably absent, into an image of a passive and tragic hero. Moteuczoma's death occurred at the same time that the Spanish retreated from Tenochtitlan in the cover of night, an event that is represented in the lower right of the biombos of the *Conquista*, which ends in many of the pictorial narratives with the capture of Cuauhtemoc. The Madrid-Lake biombo begins with the penultimate scene before Moteuczoma's death and turns it into a melancholy, interior reflection—the tragic hero observed more acutely in the narrative of Solís (figures 10.1, 10.10). This expression was still guided by Spanish notions of prophecy and the myth of the donation, to be sure, but the narratives and paintings center upon Moteuczoma's vitality as well as that of the Mexicah, who are represented by the wistful stares of the other figures, from the priest who stands before beheaded Spanish men and horses on the tzompantli, to the capture of Cuauhtemoc.[54] Solís's revisionist history was able to initiate a new era of baroque festival production by providing a verbal-visual narrative to accompany some fluid perceptions of the Indigenous past. Powerfully, its accompaniment was the mitote because the dance could mediate the trauma of the *Conquista* by reinventing Moteuczoma within the colonial order.

The silence of the drums in the Madrid-Lake painting allows pause for Moteuczoma's soliloquy, and his embodiment of this allegory is rife with Orientalist projections from Europeans who too often blended the proximal religious and political "other" into a singular ethnic category, especially as it was bound for a critique embodied in the Noble Savage. It is perhaps for these reasons that in Cosimo's portrait, Moteuczoma appears younger and with more agency than previous renditions of him. Instead of the Romanized costume, which was part and parcel of colonial Spanish control of the Indigenous body, he is dressed in Indigenous attire as he gazes defiantly at the viewer. Thus, the portrait emerges from a confluence of Cosimo's interests as a patron, the information relayed through Careri and interpreted by Sigüenza, and the translation of these into the painted form by the artist, who, with Sigüenza's help, relied on Indigenous codices as his source material and also his witness and experience as part of the artist community who contributed to decorating the mitotes. Thus, it would make sense that the background scene was significant in positing a relation of truth to visual and performed characterizations of Moteuczoma. The background scene presents the moment in the mitote, when the king arrives on a litter, an observation backed up by the presence of the huehuetl and teponaztli drums in the scene. However, his outfit in the foreground is not the Romanized outfit associated in all other cases with the mitote, and it is not clear whether or not this would have presented a contradiction to the minds of the artists or patrons.

The Medici portrait does not conform with most representations of Moteuczoma, including the Museo Nacional de Arte (MUNAL) and Madrid portraits, and all of the biombos. If this were a portrait informed by actual performances of the king's identity by later figureheads, we can imagine that the scene in the background has just happened, and we are presently confronted with the living embodiment of Moteuczoma in the foreground. If the subject of the portrait is an Indigenous performer of the mitote, there is nothing to indicate that individual depicted here was related to Moteuczoma. It does tie into the symbolism embedded in the balcony scene, where in most cases there are teponaztli and huehuetl drums for the dance either with or without musicians playing them. Because of their proximity to this scene and its correlation to the *Conquista* narrative, they evoke the Toxcatl massacre as they silence its violence. Their silence may be a reminder of when the Spanish famously cut off the hands of the drummers as a prelude to the widespread massacre, but that is not what these paintings depict.[55] Yet these instruments would otherwise not make much sense in this context; in the balcony scenes they also disguise the massacre as they make apparent the conjunction between the dance and the "rebellion" against Moteuczoma.

Like Thevet a century earlier, Cosimo may have sought an image of the king that was not derived from Roman models but from those portraits in Sigüenza's collection that were created by the hands of Indigenous artists. Thevet's portrait had been in circulation for over a century and was even revived in contemporary Spanish imperial histories. Even though Thevet claimed his portrait to be true and accurate, Cosimo had his portrait of Moteuczoma inserted into Italian editions of Solís's history. In these, the king is posed with the tilma and carrying feathered ornaments and a spear, an arrangement that derived from Indigenous painted sources. Nevertheless, Moteuczoma's frontal gaze in Cosimo's portrait emerges from a similar interest that Thevet had with his *True Portrait*.[56] Since there was no more authentic model than the person chosen to dance the mitote, and perhaps because Thevet's not-so-flattering portrait was already derivative as a print that degenerated each time it was copied, Cosimo may have communicated his desire to construct it anew from Indigenous sources as well as a live model who could stand in for the king. It makes perfect sense, then, that the model for the Medici was a living performer of the mitote.

The Madrid-Lake biombo is a historical allegory informed by the *Conquista* narrative, presenting a stage onto which the Indigenous defeat of the *Conquista* could be approached as a consequence of a series of tragedies, the fallen heroes of the *Conquista* who represent the fall of naked innocence. Like the other biombos of the *Conquista*, the narrative begins on the right and proceeds toward the left. As seen in the biombos of the *Conquista*, it has the Encounter of Cortés and Moteuczoma, rather than Moteuczoma on his balcony. The Madrid-Lake biombo, though partial, presents a different movement and relationship between spectator and space as one moves to the foregrounded figures from Moteuczoma to Cuauhtemoc. There is a sense of action and interlude, foregrounding the figures and recognizing their interior suffering in wistful gazes afar, caught in a pivotal moment of their mortality within the *Conquista* narrative. The moment is suspended. As the arrow hangs light in the air, the scene is a moment frozen in suspense. A confused arrangement of lords and warriors seem to begin their focus on the fatal act on the left, while on the right a man with a sling has just also let out a stone. The pairing of these two controversial ways that the king died are alluded to in a number of the scenes of the *Conquista*, obfuscating the fact that the king died in Spanish captivity.

All three portraits discussed here participated in Spain's imperial politics because they were quick to attach, even dramatize, Moteuczoma's similarities and contrasts as they fit European precepts of sovereignty. Through costume and other visual details, their perceptions of Moteuczoma, the Indigenous past, and the Indigenous present paralleled theatrical displays and ephemeral images and performances. The scene in the Madrid portrait is the final dramatic moment of Moteuczoma's political hold, when he was last seen in public, with the fall of the Mexica Empire likened to his death by an arrow. The painting represents a battle in which he was already cast as the loser, yet awestruck, it seems, by his fate. Cosimo's portrait presents a defiant king, whose body and ornaments represented another thread of colonial intellectual activity in which their fates could parallel broader human affairs. With the transition to more Romanized ceremonial garb, which spun out of Solís's whitening of the king, the guilty conscious of the Crown and colonial officials was offset by narratives that repositioned Moteuczoma in more palatable ways, not as victim of Spanish aggression but as tragic hero of his own demise.

The discovery that this portrait fits within a biombo reveals a king between victor and vanquished, caught between his global presence as an allegory of New Spain and his local presence in festivals. The painting is also unusual in that it rests upon a notion of portraiture to convey an allegorical concept within a drama of the fallen king. No other biombo examines Moteuczoma's physiognomy so intimately, and it adds a level of ambiguity as to Moteuczoma's identity in many imaginations. The surviving portraits are contrasting portrayals of Moteuczoma's acquiescence to Spain, or triumphant leader of an imagined Mexica past. The sorrowful gaze on the king's face foreshadows his tragic fate, which critics of Spanish colonialism point out was in a state of purity, unfettered by human-made institutions that are inherently corrupt. The images thus participated in the rhetoric of the Noble Savage, a term that appears in full force in Europe by the eighteenth century, fulfilling some of the reflections of European philosophers to come. While the concept first applied to Muslims of Granada, that identity is relevant to his portrayal of the Madrid-Lake biombo. The term was rather fluidly transferred to Amerindians, and more narrowly to Moteuczoma, for 1492 marked the fall of Granada as well as the discovery of the Americas.

NOTES

1. According to museum records, the panel was transferred from the Museo Arqueológico Nacional (number 189) in 1888 and accessioned to the museum by Manuel Pérez for 1175 pesetas. While I am the first in recent history to assert the connection of the Madrid panel with those in the Rivero Lake collection—an observation facilitated by the latter's publication within the exhibition catalog *Imágenes de los naturales en el arte de la Nueva España* (Mexico City: Fomento Cultural Banamex, 2005)—I have presented my findings at several conferences during this interim. I was first introduced to the panel in 2003, during dissertation research on a Fulbright-Hays, and was able to examine it again in 2015 and 2019, as well as the panels in the Rivero Lake collection in 2015.

2. Sofía Sanabrais, "From Byōbu to Biombo: The Transformation of the Japanese Folding Screen in Colonial Mexico," *Art History* 38, no. 4 (2015), 784–86, finds that Mexican biombos entered the inventories and collections of Spain in the seventeenth century, including those of ship captains, viceroys, artists, the nobility, members of the church, and merchants.

3. Ter Ellingson, *The Myth of the Noble Savage* (Berkeley: University of California Press, 2001), 8.

4. John Dryden, *The Indian Emperor, or, The Conquest of Mexico by the Spaniards. Being the sequel of the Indian queen* (London: H. Herringman, 1670).

5. Anthony Pagden, "The Savage Critic: Some European Images of the Primitive," in *The Yearbook of English Studies, "Colonial and Imperial Themes"* (London: Modern Humanities Research Association, 1983), 32–45, here 34.

6. Antonio de Solís, *Historia de la conquista de México* (Madrid: Bernardo de Villa-Diego, 1684); Antonio de Solis, *The History of the Conquest of Mexico by the Spaniards*, trans. Thomas Townsend (New York: AMS Press, 1973); Antonio de Solís, *Historia de la conquista de la Nueva España* (Barcelona: Linkgua Historia, 2015).

7. Richard Kagan, *Urban Images of the Hispanic World, 1493–1793* (London and New Haven, CT: Yale University Press, 2000); Michael Schreffler, *The Art of Allegiance: Visual Culture and Imperial Power in Baroque New Spain* (University Park: Pennsylvania State University Press, 2007).

8. The four biombos include the ones in the Franz Mayer collection, Fundación Banamex, Museo de Historia del Castillo de Chapultepec, and the collection of Vera Da Costa Autrey. The series of eight paintings in the Kislak Collection in Washington, DC, also follow these contours.

9. Pictorially, its only parallel are the allegories of the four continents, seasons, and liberal arts as found in other biombos known by the hand of Juan Correa, one of the most prominent painters.

10. The textual inscription on this painting stating that he was killed with "three arrows and a stone" is unusual. Solís states that some arrows shot grazed him, but it was a stone that cracked his skull. The conquistador Bernal Díaz del Castillo, who wrote his *True History of the Conquest of Mexico* to counter Solís's account with his own memory of the events, states that the king was attacked with a barrage of stones and darts but that he was hit with three stones—one to his head, another to his arm, and one to his foot. Other accounts vary further on the details, and none directly correlate with this one. Almost all sources agree that he did not die from the arrows, which, they say, only grazed him, but instead from a blow from a stone to the head (Hernán Cortés, Bernardo Díaz del Castillo, Antonio Solís, Juan Cano [Oviedo], and Fernando de Alva Ixtlilxochitl). The *Anales Tolteca-Chichimeca* claim that Cuauhtemoc himself threw the stone, while the *Relación del origen de los indios que habitan esta Nueva España* suggests that Cuauhtemoc shot him with an arrow. Other sources claim that the real fatal wound was exacted by the Spanish, either through stabbing or strangulation (*Historia de los Chichimecas*, Bernardino de Sahagún, Diego Durán, Fernando de Alvarado Tezozomoc). The *Relación del origen de los indios* and José de Acosta's *Historia natural y moral de las indias* suggest all three possibilities.

11. While the panels have not been physically reunited, their size, materials, and painting style match without doubt, and I have brought them together in this article by digitally inserting the Madrid panel in its supposed place among the Rivero Lake panels.

12. It reads: "Quiere Moteuczoma arengar a las suyos y más irritados lo matan con tres flechas y una piedra." Marita Martínez del Río de Redo, "Una visión singular de la conquista de México," in *Imágenes de los naturales en el arte de la Nueva España: Siglos XVI al XVIII*, ed. Elisa Vargaslugo (Mexico City: Fomento Cultural Banamex, 2005), 124–35, here 133. It

must be remarked that several Indigenous sources have accused the Spanish of actually killing Moteuczoma following this scene.

13. del Río de Redo, "Una visión singular de la conquista de México," 135. This may refer to a rumor that can be found in Fray Juan de Torquemada's *Monarquía indiana*, first published in 1615 and again in 1723, that cast the blame of the *cocoliztli* plague (probably smallpox) on a slave named Francisco Eguía.

14. There is ample evidence of this. See, for instance, Bernal Díaz del Castillo, *The Conquest of New Spain*, trans. J. M. Cohen (Baltimore: Penguin Books, 1963).

15. Patrick Hajovsky, *On the Lips of Others: Moteuczoma's Fame in Aztec Monuments and Rituals* (Austin: University of Texas Press, 2015).

16. A fruitful discussion of the rhetorical framing of "painting from life" during early contact can be found in Michael Schreffler, "'Their Cortés and Our Cortés': Spanish Colonialism and Aztec Representation," *Art Bulletin* 91, no. 4 (2009): 402–25, esp. 411–15.

17. André Thevet, *Les vrais pourtraits et vies des hommes illustres* (Delmar: Scholars' Facsimiles and Reprints, 1973; orig. pub. 1584).

18. Patrick Hajovsky, "André Thevet's 'True' Portrait of Moteuczoma and Its European Legacy," *Word and Image* 25, no. 4 (2009), 335–52.

19. Hajovsky, "André Thevet's 'True' Portrait of Moteuczoma and Its European Legacy," 338, 341–46.

20. Francisco López de Gómara, *Cortés: The Life of the Conqueror by His Secretary*, trans. and ed. Lesley Byrd Simpson (Berkeley: University of California Press, 1960), 142.

21. It was reproduced rather poorly for a reedition of his book in 1670, which was in turn reproduced as an even more inferior version in Prudencio de Sandoval's *Historia de la vida y hechos de Carlos V (History of the Life and Deeds of Charles V)* (1681). Hajovsky, "Thevet," 348–50. There I also note that it appears that Thevet's portrait of Atahualpa was adapted for at least some of the colonial period portraits. Notably, this immediately precedes the first publication of Antonio de Solís's *Historia de la conquista* (1684), though that edition does not contain a portrait of Moteuczoma. Interestingly, Solís criticizes Sandoval's work as overly invested in a philosophical question of divine providence invested in Hernán Cortés, whereas the historian's regard is for the vitality of the individual spirit to make history.

22. Benjamin Keen, *The Aztecs in Western Thought* (New Brunswick, NJ: Rutgers University Press, 1985), 176.

23. Solís, *Historia de la conquista*, 205. "Era de buena presencia, su edad hasta cuarenta años, de mediana estatura, más delgado que robusto; el rostro aguileño, de color menos oscuro que el natural de aquellos indios, el cabello largo hasta el extremo de la oreja, los ojos vivos, y el semblante majestuoso, con algo de intención."

24. Susan Schroeder et al., *Chimalpahin's Conquest: A Nahua Historian's Rewriting of Francisco López de Gómara's* La conquista de México (Stanford, CA: Stanford University Press, 2010), 187.

25. Diaz del Castillo, *Conquest of New Spain*, 143; Hajovsky, "Thevet," 344.

26. Schroeder et al., *Chimalpahin's Conquista*, 187, 183n210.

27. Solís, *Conquest of Mexico*, 2: 57. The Spanish reads, "Su traje un manto de sutilísimo algodón, anudado sin desaire sobre los hombros, de manera que cubría la mayor parte del cuerpo, dejando arrastrar la falda. Traía sobre sí diferentes joyas de oro, perlas y piedras preciosas, en tanto número, que servían más al peso que al adorno. La corona una mitra de oro ligero, que por delante rematada en punta, y la mitad posterior algo más obtusa se inclinaba sobre la cerviz; y el calzado unas suelas de oro macizo, cuyas correas tachonadas de lo mismo, ceñían el pie, y abrazaban parte de la pierna, semejante a las cáligas militares de los romanos." See Solís, *Historia de la conquista*, 205–6.

28. Solís, *Conquest of Mexico*, 2: 65. "Un grifo, medio águila y medio león, en ademán de volar, con un tigre feroz entre las garras. Algunos quieren que fuse águila, y se ponen de propósito a impugner el grifo con la razón de que no los hay en aquella tierra, como si no se pudiese dudar si los hay en el mundo, según los augores que los pusieron entre las aves fabulosas. Diríamos antes que pudo inventor acá y allá este género de monstruos el desvarío artificioso, que llaman licencia los poetas, y valentía los pintores." See Solís, *Historia de la conquista*, 212; for further discussion, see also Schreffler, *Allegiance*, 54–58.

29. *Death of Moteuczoma at the Hands of His Own People* is after Antonio de Solís, *Histoire de la conquête du Mexique par Fernand Cortez*, 2 vols. (Paris: Librairie commerciale et artistique, 1968), 245–46; Matthew Restall, *When Montezuma Met Cortés: The True Story of the Meeting That Changed History* (New York: Harper Collins, 2018), 98–99.

30. Restall, *Montezuma*.

31. Solís, *Historia de la conquista*.

32. Schreffler, *Allegiance*, esp. 72–74.

33. Paul Scolieri, *Dancing the New World: Aztecs, Spaniards, and the Choreography of Conquista* (Austin: University of Texas Press, 2013), 146.

34. For a full expository of this family history, see Donald Chipman, *Moctezuma's Children: Aztec Royalty under Spanish Rule, 1520–1700* (Austin: University of Texas Press, 2005), 119–41. For more on the viceroy and his role in New Spain, see Schreffler, *Allegiance*; Michael Schreffler, "The Conquest of Mexico and the Representation of Imperial Power in Baroque New Spain," in *Invasion and Transformation: Interdisciplinary Perspectives on the Conquest of Mexico*, ed. Rebecca P. Brienen and Margaret A. Jackson (Boulder: University Press of Colorado, 2008), 103–24, here 115; María Concepción García Saíz, "La conquista militar y los enconchados: Las peculiaridades de un patrocino indiano," in *El origen del reino de la Nueva España, 1680–1750* (Mexico City: Instituto Nacional de Bellas Artes, 1999), 113–14.

35. In the Franz Meyer biombo, they carry an additional throne for Moteuczoma.

36. Restall, *Montezuma*, 35–53.

37. Jaime Cuadriello, "El origen del reino y la configuración de su empresa: Episodios y alegorías de triunfo y Fundación," in *Los pinceles de la historia: El origen del reino de la Nueva España 1680–1750* (Mexico City: Instituto Nacional de Bellas Artes, 1999).

38. Schreffler, *Allegiance*, 46–53.

39. Pablo Escalante Gonzalbo, "Moctezuma, Sigüenza, and Cosimo III," in *Images of the Natives in the Art of New Spain, 16th to 18th Centuries* (Mexico City: Fomento Cultural Banamex, 2005), 211–12. Unfortunately, his *Genealogía de los reyes mexicanos* (he also called it *Cronología del imperio mexicano*) is now lost, but he apparently had listed the Mexica rulers up to 1680, and then updated it in 1695.

40. Escalante Gonzalbo, "Moctezuma, Sigüenza, and Cosimo III," 212; "Sea esta, de la que aora Motecuohçuma se recomiende, de la misma manera, que en el Arco se le expressa, que fue assi: Estaba adornado de imperials y riquissimas vestiduras, sacando de la boca de un Leon muchas perlas, mucha plata, mucho oro, que esparcia por todas partes con esta Letra: De forti dulcedo. Jud. P. 14 verf. 14." Carlos Sigüenza y Góngora, *Teatro de virtudes políticas que constituyen a un príncipe, advertidas en los monarchos antiguos del México imperial*, in *Obras* (Mexico City: Sociedad de Bibliófilos Mexicanos, 1680), 76.

41. Escalante Gonzalbo, "Moctezuma," 211.

42. Maria Castañeda de la Paz, "El doble retrato de Moteuczoma Xocoyotzin," *Liber* 3 (2019): 28–37. It was x-rayed in 2015 as part of the exhibition *Yo, El Rey*.

43. Cuadriello, "Origen," 50–107; and David A. Brading, "The Rebirth of Ancient Mexico," in *Moctezuma, Aztec Ruler*, ed. Colin McEwan and Leonardo López Luján (London: British Museum, 2009), 258–287, 285.

44. This thesis was presented in a now-lost work. See Keen, *Aztecs*, 192.

45. "Se vio obligado a sufrir la prisión y la renuncia, y a devolver a sus legítimos dueños esa credencial de poder." (My translation.) Cuadriello, "Origen," 59.

46. Hajovsky, "Portraits"; Pablo Escalante Gonzalbo, *Painting a New World: Mexican Art and Live, 1521–1821* (Denver: Denver Art Museum, 2004), 177, attributes the painting to Antonio Rodriguez based on stylistic grounds, though his relationship with Sigüenza is still unclear.

47. Hajovsky, "Portraits," 285–87. Escalante Gonzalbo attributes the painting to the workshop of Antonio Rodríguez (1636–91).

48. "Al modo de su país, sobre su piel desnuda, adornos de plumas multicolores, aderezos de oro y piedras preciosas que abundan en su region." Huguette Zavala, "América inventada: Fiestas y espectáculos en la Europa de los siglos XVI al XX," in *Arte, historia e identidad en América: Visiones comparativas*, ed. Gustavo Curiel et al. (Mexico City: UNAM, 1994), 33–50, here 37; Giovanni Moniglia, *Il Mondo Festeggiante: Balletto a cavallo fatto nel teatro congunto a Palazzo di serenis, Gran Duca per le reali nozza de Serenissimi Princip Cosimo Terzo di Toscaana e Margherita Luisa d'Orleans* (Florence: Stamperia di S.A.S., 1661).

49. Hugh Honour, *The New Golden Land: European Images of America from the Discoveries to the Present Time* (New York: Pantheon Books, 1975); Keen notes that the "composite portrait of the Indian drawn by the Spanish literary imagination assigned him great strength, ferocity, and the practices of cannibalism and human sacrifice, dressed him in a feathered headdress and a belt of feathers, and placed a bow and arrows in his hands." Keen, *Aztecs*, 179–80.

50. Lia Markey, *Imagining the Americas in Medici Florence* (University Park: Pennsylvania State University Press, 2016).

51. Cuadriello, "Origen," 59; Escalante Gonzalbo, "Rodríguez"; Escalante Gonzalbo, "Moctezuma," 214–17.

52. Escalante Gonzalbo, "Rodríguez," 218, finds that Zelia Nuttall noted a now-lost painting in a Franciscan convent that, according to an inscription, suggests it was sent by Cosimo. Zelia Nuttall, ed., *Book of the Life of the Ancient Mexicans* (Berkeley: University of California Press, 1983), xiii–xiv. See also Detlef Heikamp, *Mexico and the Medici* (Florence: Edam, 1972), 23. Sigüenza y Góngora's connections to the Jesuit order are well established. See Keen, *Aztecs*, 189–90; Escalante Gonzalbo, "Rodríguez," 176–77.

53. Hajovsky, "Thevet."

54. See Scolieri, *Dancing*, 101.

55. This detail is especially highlighted in Diego Durán, *The History of the Indies of New Spain*, trans. Doris Heyden (Norman: University of Oklahoma Press, 1994); and Bernardino de Sahagún, *Florentine Codex: General History of the Things of New Spain*, ed. and trans. Arthur J. O. Anderson and Charles E. Dibble (Santa Fe, NM: School of American Research; Salt Lake City: University of Utah, 1951), both of which were constructed out of Indigenous perspectives.

56. Hajovsky, "Thevet."

Epilogue

Conclusions

JOHN F. SCHWALLER

> I do not much wish well to discoveries, for I am always afraid they will end in conquest and robbery.
> —SAMUEL JOHNSON AND JAMES BOSWELL, ED.,
> *LIFE OF JOHNSON* (1765–1766), VOL. 2

The scholars whose works appear in this volume each attempt to come to grips with the encounter controversially called "Conquest of Mexico" and with the implications of the way this complex encounter is and was described. The starting point for all these chapters was the recognition of the quincentenary of the conflict between the Spanish and the Natives of what is now central Mexico in the period 1519–21. Each author approached this commemoration by looking at a different feature. One goal has been to better understand the encounter and all the players involved in light of the most recent scholarship. Another important feature of this collection has been the dialogue between practitioners from Europe, Mexico, and the United States. We also have included scholars based in different disciplinary traditions to provide as broad a perspective on the central issues as possible. In principle, we believe that there must be a better name. At the same time, we know that countering 500 years of tradition calling it the "Conquest of Mexico" is a nearly impossible task.

The first chapter of the collection, by Stephanie Wood, tackles the issue head on. Rather than blithely accepting the term "conquest," she engages us with reconsidering the different perspectives that can be brought to bear on the period. The Native peoples who survived after the European invasion were not eradicated. Neither do they characterize their own history as that of victims. The very term "conquest" implies a winner and a loser. Wood notes that it is more a case of the history having been written by the victors. The Spanish and Europeans in general view their triumph in absolute terms, and that serves as a justification for their actions. Specifically, in the last few decades, more sources have become available for scholars to use to consider the Native side of the battle. Many scholars now work comfortably with Native languages, opening a wealth of information to better understand this confrontation. As a result, the notion of invasion and colonization better describes the events of the sixteenth century. Native sources written in the decades following the arrival of the Spanish, at least in central Mexico, do not refer to conquest. When the term does appear in the late decades of the century, it is as a borrowed word from Spanish and generally referred to Spaniards, although a few instances exist where Natives took credit for their alliance with the Spanish and called themselves conquerors. Wood then explores in detail the manners in which Nahuatl language authors described that event labeled by the Spanish as "conquest." Through her essay, she carefully leads the reader through the changes in language and in attitude toward the concept of the conquest.

Vitus Huber takes us to a crucial phase of the Spanish invasion and studies the transition from warfare to Spanish settlement. Having taken possession of the regions through military force, the Spanish began to settle on the land to exercise a more immediate control over its resources, in a pattern that had begun several centuries earlier. On the Iberian Peninsula, nominally Christian forces in the northern regions fought to regain lands that had fallen under nominal Muslim control after 718. Using the case of a Spanish "conquistador," Francisco de Granada, Huber explores all the nuances behind the Spanish actions related to the various rewards offered to participants in the *Conquista*. The grants and gifts, distributions and assignments, had as their goal the need to tie the Spanish population to the New World. In general, they were seen as features of the Spanish royal patrimony to reward good and faithful service. Huber also explores the vocabulary of the requests for grants and gifts, seeing the infusion of terms related to conquest and battle that bleeds over into requests by Native allies of the Spanish as well. In short, he traces the legal and psychological process whereby the Spanish conquistadors came to consider themselves as settlers.

Justyna Olko analyzes the trauma unleashed by the *Conquista* not just on the Natives of what is now Mexico but its damning repercussions through the ages. In the twentieth century, in Mexico there began a revalorization of the ancient Native past. The event was depicted as an invasion by the Spanish and became more sinister and an example of European exploitation of lands that were not their own. Over the centuries of colonial rule, the Natives of Mexico had been despised by their overlords, at the same time that the colonists came to rely on their labor and creativity. While at the national level since the Mexican Revolution (1910–17), the state harked back to its Native roots, the reality is that Native communities are continuing to be oppressed by the state, in spite of an official ideology that valorizes the Natives and nominally makes them the equals of all other racial and ethnic groups. As Olko points out, the Indigenous people of the Americas continue to be subject to colonial relationships that originated in the time of the *Conquista* and were further extended and perpetuated after the creation of the nation-states. But even on top of this marginalization, there are deep divides among Native communities. With the rise of the national origin myth that emphasized the Spanish-Tlaxcalteca alliance defeating the Mexicah, modern-day Tlaxcalans are subject to discrimination from their fellow Mexicans as heirs of what is considered treason during the battles. Taken as a whole, the *Conquista* of Mexico left a bitter legacy that continues to have negative repercussions even today.

In the next part, we consider the narratives of the *Conquista* and how both individuals and communities recounted its events and impact. In her chapter, Julia Madajczak provides a meticulous analysis of the accounts of the death of the last Mexica *tlahtoani*, Cuauhtemoc, by looking at the various sources that narrate the events surrounding his tragic demise. In particular, she focuses on the account provided in the manuscript source known as the *Anales de Tlatelolco*. Her analysis demonstrates that the confusing story is a recasting of the general story of Cuauhtemoc's death, using pre-contact models, colonial legends, and even mid-colonial tropes. While modern readers might see the story as an odd amalgam of sources and images, the developers must have felt that it provided a compelling narrative based on cultural traditions, powerful images, and more recent historical events. As she puts it: "They still actively used this story to bolster their interests and cultivate pride in their ancestry. Far from being an old grandma's tale, it juxtaposed two critical founding moments in Central Mexican history: the fall of Tollan and the end of the Mexicah's power."

Don Zacarias de Santiago, from Tlaxcala, is the focus of the essay by Robert Haskett. Although in the eighteenth century, Don Zacarias was remembered as a Native conqueror who fought with Hernán Cortés and the Spanish to defeat the Mexicah, Haskett demonstrates that this was probably not the case. While he was a leading political figure in the latter sixteenth century, his contributions had less to do with the field of battle and more to do with political alliances. He even traveled to Spain as part of a delegation to the Spanish monarch. He was undoubtedly born after the Spanish invasion. Yet to later generations, the time frame was blurred. Don

Zacarias was remembered as an important political figure generations earlier, and so over time his role was reified by scribes and authors until he became a leading figure from the time of the Spanish invasion, not its second-generation aftermath. Haskett traces the real and mythic life of Don Zacarias to demonstrate the important role that his figure came to play in the later colonial period.

The role of the *Conquista* narratives lies at the center of the essay by María Castañeda de la Paz. She notes that the narratives produced by the Native nobles tended to erase some aspects of the events, those that might put them in a bad light with the new European overlords, while embracing other details. Since these narratives emerged in the colonial period, they respond to the pressures of the new political condition. Some of the larger narratives clearly borrowed from one another, and from yet unknown sources. Taken together, however, they provide a rich set of sources to assist historians and others in piecing together the events and implications of the *Conquista*. These essays are examples of the critical analysis of sources that looks not simply at the texts themselves but also at the possible functions of the documents. Each of the three authors has explained internal contradictions and inconsistencies by looking at how the narratives functioned in the societies that relied on them.

The next part of this collection continues the dialogue among scholars by addressing issues of power and the negotiations between the Spanish and the Natives, a topic that flows from Castañeda's piece. In particular, just as Madajczak explored the legends and history surrounding the last journey of Cuauhtemoc, Miguel Pastrana Flores focuses critically on one of the key events of the *Conquista*, Moteuczoma's surrender of power and eventual death. Using a broad set of sources and methodologies, Pastrana argues that there never really was such a relinquishing of power but that, as with some many other nuances of the *Conquista*, it was a fiction created by the Spanish to partially justify their establishment of lordship over the land. Here, as in most cases, a close analysis of different sources allows scholars to revisit established opinions and the alleged victors' narratives. In this way, these studies of the *Conquista* reach beyond simple recountings of victors' tales to a deeper understanding of the panoply of events, actors, and repercussions.

For her chapter, Erika Escutia focuses on the role of the forty lords who accompanied Cortés in his triumphal return to Spain in 1528. These lords, while important representatives of their people in the Americas, became part of an imperialist window dressing, players in a victory parade reminiscent of ancient Rome. The importance of the voyage and mission differed radically depending on the point of view of the observer, Escutia notes. For the nobles of the Spanish court, and representatives from elsewhere in Europe, the lords were colorful pagans having a certain entertainment value. But for their subjects, back in what was becoming

New Spain, their rulers had gained an aura of prestige and power. They had successfully negotiated with the new political elite across the ocean and returned with gifts and privileges. Others also took part in applying their own interpretation to the visit, such as the Franciscans who would use it in their defense of the Natives from exploitation by colonists and others. Indeed, Escutia points out that viewed from all angles, the trip had tremendous symbolic value; it became a question of how the symbolism was read.

The fourth part considers how different individuals were represented in depictions of the *Conquista*. This builds directly on themes already established and used in Escutia's essay. The role of Native women in the battles of the *Conquista* is the theme of Lori Boornazian Diel's essay. Of course, Doña Marina / Malinche is by far the best known of the female participants, but large numbers of women served on both sides of the conflict. The chronicles written by the Spanish almost completely ignore the role of women. Native accounts, both written in European characters and in picture writing, present a very different story. Native women both supported and fought on both sides of the conflict. Female slaves were gained by the Spanish to help with daily chores. Native women in Mesoamerica continued to support their families throughout the armed phase of the invasion, frequently appearing on the front lines. Noblewomen played a political role, frequently as pawns in a game of marriage alliances, among the Natives and linking the Spanish to important Native polities. In fact, a noblewoman was concocted after the fact to symbolize the alliance between the Spanish and the Tlaxcaltecah, in the form of Doña Luisa Tecuiluatzin, also known as Doña Luisa Xicotencatl.

Patrick Hajovsky focuses his attention on the depiction of the tlahtoani Moteuczoma Xocoyotzin as he is represented in a mid-colonial painted folding screen, known as a *biombo*. The folding screens became important pieces of furniture in Mexico following the opening of the trade with Asia. Artists used their several panels as vehicles for narratives, and the *Conquista* of Mexico was a very popular theme. But as Hajovsky points out, this particular panel became separated from its fellows. According to his reconstruction, the full screen, of perhaps five or six 2-sided panels, focuses on the pathos of Moteuczoma from the time of his capture by the Spanish until his death and the captivity of Cuauhtemoc, his successor. Hajovsky considers it an allegory of the *Conquista* focusing on the two last rulers and their fall. Clearly, the artist wished to examine triumphalist Spanish notions of conquest in light of the more human reality of the loss of empire felt by the Mexica leaders and serving as an early example of the trope of the "Noble Savage."

These essays, each in its own way, are significant new contributions to the New Conquest History. Each offers enticing glimpses into a reevaluation of what we thought that we knew about the period, the participants, and the events. As is so often the case, new times and new sources bring new interpretations. Each of the essays follows a path that has become more clearly defined in the last decade.

The question of what to call this episode traditionally characterized as the "Conquest of Mexico" has not been widely considered in the literature until the recent day. Quite simply, only a few scholars have questioned the use of the word "conquest" to describe the *Conquista* of the Native civilizations of the New World. Clearly, although the authors of these essays have been working closely with one another over years, there is no real consistency in what to call this event. Some call it the "Conquest of Mexico" and analyze the ways in which contemporaries considered it. Others look at specific aspects of the confrontation and elect slightly different descriptions.

In the introductory chapter to this volume, Vitus Huber has outlined the arguments regarding the use of the term the "Conquest of Mexico," preferring instead to call it the *Conquista* of Mexico. This simultaneously identifies the specific phenomenon and marks a critical distance to it comparable to—though arguably greater than—the use of scare quotes for Conquest. As Huber has already described, publications by Matthew Restall have explored the essential questions regarding the concept of the conquest. Most recently, Restall has described the *Conquista* of Mexico as a "time-loop." Describing this phenomenon, he argues that the confrontation of the Spanish and the Natives beginning in 1519 did not just happen as a discrete event but occurred many times over in different places and contexts, being reanalyzed and serving as a model and as a trope over various epochs. The notion of "conquest" was subject to reinterpretation and reimagination over times, as local conditions required. In his argument, Restall points out that the *Conquista* came to mean different things to different people as local conditions and the needs of different eras focused attention on different features of the event.[1]

In the years prior to the quincentenary of the *Conquista* of Mexico in 1519, Restall and I had a private debate precisely about how to characterize this event. During this conversation, Restall was in the midst of researching his Moteuczoma and Cortés book, and I was working on my book *The First Letter from New Spain*. In this conversation, we tossed out several alternate names for what has been known as the "Conquest of Mexico" since the sixteenth century. Cortés's secretary Francisco López de Gómara published the first chronicle of the military action in 1553. In his book, López de Gómara called it "the conquest of Mexico" (*conquista de México*). Bernal Díaz del Castillo's rejoinder to López de Gómara also referred to the action as the "conquest of Mexico," emphasizing the point that his was "the true history" (*verdadera historia*) about that period.[2] Beyond these two, hundreds of Spanish participants in the warfare referred to it as the "conquest" in their various petitions to the crown and personal accounts of action, as demonstrated by Huber in this collection. These men, and by and large they were men, came to be known collectively as conquerors. Consequently, "conquest" is a term that had currency at the time, at least among the Spanish participants looking back on that series of events.

Restall and I initiated our discussion looking at this long historical tradition. When one refers to the "Conquest of Mexico," a specific set of events and a particular time frame immediately come to mind. What worried us was whether or not this name was completely accurate given that it was so clearly and unquestionably developed from a Spanish/European perspective. Restall went on to explain his thoughts on the issue in the prologue to his book on Moteuczoma and Cortés. He noted that it "evokes a triumphalist narrative" and was "a highly partisan label."

The first ideas that Restall and I considered were imitations of the circumlocutions that were applied to the 1992 commemorations of the arrival of Europeans to the New World, in the form of the voyages of Christopher Columbus. In that epoch, the two labels that emerged as favorites, at least among many academics, were the Encounter of Two Worlds and the Columbus Quincentennial. Certainly, the moniker of the encounter of two worlds could easily be applied to the events unleashed by Cortés's expedition into the lands of the Mexicah. But it is so bland and generic as to have little real value. Likewise, we could call these events the Quincentennial of the Cortés expedition, but as for the Columbus example many scholars feel that it places the emphasis on the European actors (Columbus, Cortés) rather than on the conflict that ensued when the two worlds met. Equally irking were terms like the "discovery" of the New World, since it was only a "discovery" to the Europeans who had been unaware of its existence.

We could agree that the name the "Conquest of Mexico" is flawed on many levels. Perhaps the major issue is that this expression is triumphalist, as Restall indicated. It looks at the events solely from the point of view of the alleged "victors." One quickly sees the difference in perspective looking at the Nahuatl accounts of the conflict. The best-known version, penned by Fray Bernardino de Sahagún, a Spanish Franciscan friar who used Native informants and scribes, described it as "the war which was waged here in the city of Mexico."[3] Of course, even this analysis is flawed because it tends to continue to look at a confrontation of Natives (Mexicah) versus Spaniards.

The term "Conquest" also reinforces several of the myths decried by Restall. The two most important are the myths of the white conquistador and the myth of completion because the term "Conquest" favors the vision of the Spanish and their allies. Moreover, to an uninformed audience, it carries an assumption that only the Europeans were involved and that they were somehow "victorious." Similarly, it assumes that there was a definitive end to the action. The Natives were conquered, full stop. As Restall points out, in most instances this was simply a fiction. Some areas of the west and north of modern Mexico defied Spanish influence for decades, if not centuries. We know from a host of modern sources that the cultures, languages, rituals, and daily traditions of the Native peoples persisted for generations and centuries. To refer to the "Conquest of Mexico" implies that it ended at some point. As a military encounter, conquests have a beginning, middle, and end. Eventually one side defeats the other, and a new regime is imposed. In the case of Mexico, there was no one definitive point in which the fighting ended but rather a series of moments in which Spanish rule was extended incrementally over the region. Looking at the day-to-day reality of events, Restall notes, there was more a gradual shift from a purely Native culture to a hybrid Native-Spanish culture that varied across time and place.[4] Certainly scholarly analysis of this specific topic has clearly demonstrated that the "Conquest" was an ongoing process, as several of the authors in this volume clearly demonstrate in their essays. What was true about scholarship when Restall wrote *The Seven Myths* has been addressed by more recent scholarship.

The term "conquest" is deeply rooted in our perception of the history of Latin America. The event provides a clear line of demarcation between two epochs: pre-conquest and post-conquest. Certainly, the arrival of Europeans on the shores of the New World and the subsequent warfare that ensued disrupted world history. The examples of Cortés and Pizarro provided templates for other powers to invade and hegemonize other regions at other times. But "conquest" is a very loaded word. Perhaps most disturbing is that it tends to encompass all the myths but not provide much clarity. The strongest argument for its continued use is that for 500 years it has been the word that Westerners have used to describe the Spanish military actions against Natives of the New World.

There are alternatives. "Encounter" seems to be too bland given the pain and suffering unleashed by the confrontation. Stephanie Wood proposes "invasion and colonization" as an option, as she explores the way in which Nahuatl-speaking scribes recorded the events and attempted to describe the conflict. There are also various options describing it as a war between the Spanish, in specific, or Europeans, in general, and Native peoples. Restall's option to call it the Spanish-Aztec War, referring to the first phase ending in 1521, is insofar more accurate as it valorizes the participation of the Mexicah who fought against the Spanish. Many of us in the field of Nahuatl and Nahua studies, however, do not like the term "Aztec" or argue that it should be used more precisely. The term "Aztec" is relatively new as an alternative to the name the people gave themselves, which was Mexicah. Over time, scholars have begun to reach a consensus, that when we refer to the people who lived in the Central Basin of what today is Mexico in the cities of Tenochtitlan and Tlatelolco, we should call them Mexicah. The language that they, and their neighbors, spoke was Nahuatl. Thus, referring to any number of groups who spoke

Nahuatl, we use the term the "Nahua." Aztec is a term that is best reserved to encompass all the members of the political entity known as the Triple Alliance, which included the Mexicah, and two other Nahua groups, the Acolhuah of Tetzcoco and the Tepanecah of Tlacopan. This military and political alliance stretched from the Central Basin to both coasts and well to the south into Central America. The west and north of modern Mexico remained outside of its control. Hence, Restall's suggestion that we call it the Spanish-Aztec War can be adequate, if we discuss those phases when the Triple Alliance confronted the Spanish and their allies.[5] The major problems are that it leaves aside the Native supporters of the Spaniards and that the Triple Alliance saw some fracturing, as some elites from Tetzcoco broke away and began to support the Spanish. Yet, as will be seen, to place the Spanish uniquely in opposition to one Native group, or even alliance, is misleading.

Looking at the various options, and considering the benefits and liabilities of each, we have three alternatives. Restall's use of scare quotes, "Conquest," Huber's suggestion of *Conquista* (Spanish, in italics), and "Spanish Invasion of Mexico." One must note that even the term "Spanish" has its shortcomings as well. People from the Iberian Peninsula did use the descriptor Spanish in the New World to characterize themselves as a group; their individual town or region of origin was the primary marker for their personal identity. But an entity known as Spain did not yet exist. As several authors have demonstrated, the expeditions under Cortés and Pizarro, for example, consisted largely of people from what is now Spain but not entirely. In the Cortés expedition, at least eight men came from regions other than Castille and Aragon.[6] Nevertheless, English speakers of the period would recognize the term "Spanish" as appropriate to all the Iberian residents under the crown of Charles or Philip II.[7]

It matters less exactly what we call the military encounter between the Spanish and the Native peoples of the Americas than what is the reality. These essays are following a recent movement to look beyond the writings of the Spaniards and to consider the Native perspective along with that of the European men and women who served in the expeditions and who saw the realities of the war and destruction that surrounded them. Thus, whether we call it the "Conquest," or the *Conquista*, or simply the Invasion, the destruction was real. The cataclysm that befell the Americas was real. It ushered in centuries of mistreatment and exploitation of Native peoples in a colonial system.

NOTES

Epigraph: Accessed May 1, 2023, https://www.gutenberg.org/cache/epub/9072/pg9072.html.

1. Matthew Restall, "The Time Loop of Mexico's Conquests," in *The Conquest of Mexico: 500 Years of Reinventions*, ed. Peter B. Villella and Pablo Garcia Loaeza (Norman: University of Oklahoma Press, 2022), vii–xi.

2. Francisco López de Gómara, *Historia general de las Indias: "Hispania victrix" cuya segunda parte corresponde a la conquista de Méjico*, ed. Pilar Guibelalde, 2 vols. (Barcelona: Iberia, 1966); Bernal Díaz del Castillo, *Historia verdadera de la conquista de la Nueva España* (Mexico City: Porrúa, 1992).

3. Fray Bernardino de Sahagún, *Florentine Codex: General History of the Things of New Spain*, ed. and trans. Arthur J. O. Anderson and Charles E. Dibble (Santa Fe: School of American Research; Salt Lake City: University of Utah, 1951), XII, 1.

4. Matthew Restall, *Seven Myths of the Spanish Conquest* (New York: Oxford University Press, 2003), 44–76.

5. Matthew Restall, *When Montezuma Met Cortés. The True Story of the Meeting That Changed History* (New York: ECCO, 2019), xii.

6. John F. Schwaller and Helen Nader, *The First Letter From New Spain: The Lost Petition of Cortés and His Company, June 20, 1519* (Austin: University of Texas Press, 2014), 122–23.

7. From as early as about 1275 there are references to "Spanish" referring to peoples and things from what are now considered Spain. *Oxford English Dictionary*, "Spanish," A. adj. 1. A. "Of or pertaining to Spain or its people." "Spanish, adj., n.1, and adv.," OED Online, March 2022, Oxford University Press, accessed May 13, 2022, https://www.oed.com/dictionary/spanish_adj?tab=meaning_and_use#21569103.

Index

Note: Many Nahua names appear in the text with the honorific suffix *-tzin* attached to the names (e.g., "Cuauhtemoctzin" for "Cuauhtemoc" and "Coanacochtzin" for "Coanacoch"). These names are indexed according to the base name (e.g., "Cuauhtemoc," "Coanacoch"). The various forms of terms related to the major cities (singular, plural, possessive, and English adjectival forms) are indexed by the city name (e.g., "Tenochca," "Tenochcah," and "Tenochtitlan" appear under "Tenochtitlan"; "Tlaxcalteca," "Tlaxcaltecah," and "Tlaxcallan" appear under "Tlaxcala"; and Tlatelolco, Tlatelolca, and Tlatelolcah appear under "Tlatelolco"). Furthermore, some authors have chosen to use the more correct form "Tlaxcallan." The words "Nahuatl" / "Nahua" and "Mexico" are not indexed, because they appear so frequently that their index entries would encompass most of the book.

Acacingo, 141
Acalan / Acallan, 48, 100–101, 105–8, 110–111, 116, 177
Acamapichtli, 290
Acolhua, 112–13, 170–71, 179, 197, 313
Acxotecatl, 126
Africa, 3, 7, 111, 222
Aguilar, Francisco de, 161, 194–95
Aguilar, Jerónimo de, 215
Al-Andalus, 274
Alcalde, 45, 127–28, 130–31, 134, 140–42, 151–52
Alfonso X, 193
Alguacil, 127–28
Almonte, Juan de, 128
Altepetl, viii, 30–32, 35, 42, 44, 71, 73, 99–101, 103–5, 107, 112–13, 118, 126–35, 138, 141–42, 145–48, 248, 250, 264

Alva Ixtlilxochitl, Don Fernando de, 103–4, 108–9, 112, 114, 171–72, 179, 196, 202, 204, 251, 256, 258–59
Alvarado, Pedro, 47, 163, 202, 254–56, 259
Alvarado Tezozomoc, Don Hernando, 112–14, 167, 170–72, 177
Amanalco, 145
Amaquemeca, 257, 259
Amatlacuilolli, 30
Anahuac, 218–229
Anales de Cuauhtitlan, 105
Anales de Tlatelolco, viii, 10, 73, 99–117, 173–74, 177, 179, 245, 261, 307
Anderson, Arthur J. O., 27
Andrade Moctezuma, Juan de, 264
Annals of Tula, 195
Añón, Valeria, vii, 193

315

Anónimo mexicano, 33–34
Apiaco, 129
Aquiyauhtecuhtli, Don Francisco, 142, 146
Aragon, 313
Aristotle, 222–23, 227
Asia, 272, 309
Atempan, 141
Atempan, Don Julian (Don Julian de Castilla), 142
Atlancatepec, 131
Atlihuetzian, 136, 142
Atzintzintlan, 127–28, 131–32, 147–50
Avila, Alonso de, 48
Axayaca, Don Alonso, 114
Axayacatl, 27, 115
Azcapotzalco, 33, 110, 114, 197
Aztec. *See* Mexica
Aztec empire. *See* Triple Alliance

Badajoz, Gutierre de, 57
Batalla Rosado, Juan José, 109
Bautista, Juan, 27, 145
Benítez, Fernando, 69
Benson Latin American Library, 248
Besote, 225
Biombo, ix, 10, 272–99, 309
Black Legend, 21
Boboli Gardens, 293
Bonfil Batalla, Guillermo, 77
Boone, Elizabeth Hill, 225
Borgia Group, 110
Boswell, James, 305
Briones, Pedro de, 47
Broken Spears, 13, 18, 21
Buti, Lucrezia, 293–94

Cabildo, 9, 18, 129, 132, 141, 143–45
Cacama, 201–2, 258–59
Cacique / cacicazgo, 29, 35, 112, 127, 130, 133, 148, 165, 167, 173, 218, 247–48
Calderón de la Barca, Pedro, 284
Calpan, 127, 143, 148
Calpultin, 198
Campeche, 48
Cano, Juan, 261, 264
Cantares mexicanos, 105–6
Caqchikel, 28
Cardenas, Lázaro, 77
Carlos. *See* Charles

Carr, David Wright, 22–23
Carr, Edward, 70
Carrasco, Pedro, 256
Casa de Contratación, 54–55, 216
Casado Soto, José Luis, 226
Casas, Bartolomé de las, 193
Castañeda de la Paz, María, viii, 10, 100, 102–4, 109, 112, 134, 308
Castiglione, Baldasare, 215, 221
Castilla, Don Pablo de (also Castilla y Galicia), 138–40, 143, 146, 150
Castilla, Don Pedro, 146, 150
Castille. *See* Spain
Castillo, Cristóbal del, 113
Castillo, Juan del, 14
Catholic Church, 15, 57, 126–27, 130–33, 145, 148, 150, 220, 227
Cazonci (Purépecha leader), 113
Ceiba. *See* Pochotl
Cempoala, 218–19, 224, 247
Central Basin, 163, 191, 200, 275, 312
Cerda, Tomás de la, 290
Cervantes de Salazar, Francisco, 194, 202–3
Chalco, 31, 34, 167, 195, 257–58
Chapultepec, 278
Charles I (V), ix, 6–7, 57–58, 30, 162, 164, 191–92, 194, 197–98, 201, 215, 219, 221, 225, 293, 313
Charles II, 284, 288
Charles IV, 206
Chavero, Alfredo, 197, 252–53, 262
Chiapas, viii
Chichimeca, 29, 31, 33, 36, 71, 85, 142, 146
Chicomoztoc, 106
Chimalpahin Quauhtlehuanitzin, Domingo Francisco de San Antón Muñón, 25, 28, 31, 103, 106, 112–13, 167, 172, 179, 195, 257–59, 285, 295
Chimalpopoca, 114
Cholollan, 48, 199
Chronicle X, 195
Cincalco, 115
Cihuacoatl, 196
Circassian, 222
Clement VII, 220, 222
Coanacoch, 101, 163, 166–67, 171–72, 177, 251
Cochiztlan, 48
Codex Aubin, 257
Codex Azcatitlan, 195, 246, 262–63

Codex Cozcatzin, 26, 263
Codex en Cruz, 195
Codex Ixtlilxochitl, 295
Codex Mendoza, 20–22, 250, 278, 281, 283, 295
Codex Mexicanus, 264
Codex Telleriano Remensis, 195
Codex Vaticanus A, III, 195
Codex Xolotl, 110, 114
Codice municipal de Cuernavaca, 139
Cohuatzacoalco, 259
Colegio de Santa Cruz, 6
Columbus, Christopher, 4, 311
Compendio histórico del reino de tescoco, 112
Congreso de Constituyentes, 75
Conquistadora, La, 126
Constantinople, 222
Cortés, Hernán, vii, ix, 1, 6–9, 26–27, 45, 48–54, 57, 60, 69, 72, 99–105, 108–9, 112–16, 125–29, 131, 134, 137, 142, 144, 146, 148–50, 161–63, 165–67, 170–73, 176–79, 191–95, 197–202, 203–5, 215–22, 224–25, 243, 245, 248, 251, 255–59, 261–62, 264, 275, 281, 283, 287–90, 293, 298, 307, 311–13
Cortés, Don Toribio, 125–26, 131, 142, 145, 147
Cortés Acaxochitl, Doña Ana, 30
Cortés Totoquihuaztli, Don Antonio, 165–66, 251
Cosimo III de' Medici, 293, 295–98
Cotztemexi, 99, 101, 111–15, 167, 171–72, 177
Couaxochtzin, 250
Council of Four, 197
Coyoacan, 51, 163, 245
Crónica mexicayotl, 112
Cuadriello, Jaime, 292, 295
Cuauhpopoca, 204
Cuauhtemoc, viii, 8, 10, 99–117, 163, 165–67, 170–71, 173–74, 176–77, 180, 245, 251, 261–62, 264, 275, 277, 296, 298, 307–9
Cuetlaxohuapan Codex, 228
Cuernavaca, 125–26, 131, 139–40, 142, 145, 147
Cuitlahua, 103, 163, 203–5
Culhuacan, 218

Dance of Moteuczoma, 295, 297–98
Dantyszek, Jan, 215
Departamento de Asuntos Indígenas, 77
Descripción de Tlaxcala, 253
Díaz, Ana, 227
Díaz, José de la Cruz Porfirio, 74–75

Díaz, Don Juan, 137
Díaz del Castillo, Bernal, 6–7, 112–13, 126, 161, 167, 171–73, 179, 194, 200, 202, 205, 218, 220, 245, 247–48, 251–52, 255, 285, 310
Dibble, Charles, 27
Diel, Lori Boornazian, ix, 10, 309
Difrasismo, 229
Dryden, John, 274
Duarte, Francisco, 216
Dueños, Dr., 127
Durán, Alonso, 129
Durán, Diego, 104, 195–96, 245, 257, 261
Dyckerhoff, Ursula, 102

East Asia, 272
Ecatl, Don Martín, 100, 102–5, 113, 177–78
Ehecatepetl, 197
Elliott, John H., 193
Encarnación, Pasqual de la, 127
Encomienda, 50–51, 55–61
Enconchados, ix, 288
Encuesta Nacional, 82
Enslaved Indigenous people, 244–46
Entrada, ix, 45, 47–49, 56
Epcoatl, 103
Escalante Gonzalbo, Pablo, 290, 295
Escutia, Erika, ix, 10, 308–9
Estrada, Alonso de, 218
Ethiopia, 222
Excan Tlahtoloyan. *See* Triple Alliance
Extremadura, 192, 195, 197

Ferdinand VII, 206
Ferdinand of Hapsburg, Archduke, 215
Fernández, Gerónimo, 205
Fernández de Oviedo, Gonzalo, 222
Fernández de Recas, Guillermo, 133
fiscal, 127
Florence, 293
Florentine Codex, 18, 21–22, 27, 73, 110–111, 115, 126, 195, 201, 251, 259–61, 264
Flughöhe, 8
Forjando Patria, 76
Foucault, Michel, 221
Franciscan Order, 57–58, 227–28, 309
Frankl, Victor, 193
French, 206
Frizzi, Romero, 161–62

Galicia, Don Antonio de, 127–28
Galicia, Don Pablo de, 136, 138, 140–47
Galicia, Don Pedro de, 141–43, 150
Gallego de Andrade, Pedro, 264
Gallegos, José Antonio Zacarias de Santiago y, 131
Gallegos, Mariano Zacarias de Santiago, 131
Gallegos, Pedro Nolasco Zacarias de Santiago y, 131
Gamio, Manuel, 76
García, Don Lucas, 136
García Loaeza, Pablo, vii
García de Mendoza Moctezuma, Don Diego, viii, 102–3, 113, 116, 174, 180
Garrido, Juan, 54
Gemelli Careri, Giovanni Francisco, 295–96
General History of the New Things of New Spain, 195
German, 216, 219, 221–22, 224–25, 228
Gibson, Charles, 129, 144
Gillespie, Susan, 193
Ginés de Sepúlveda, Juan, 193
Giovio, Paolo, 221–22, 226–27
Gómez, Don Alonso, 136, 138
González, Pedro, 48, 141
González Dávila, Gil, 130
Grado, Alonso de, 264
Granada, 299
Granada, Francisco de, 45–47, 49, 51–53, 56, 60–61, 306
Graulich, Michel, 107, 110–11, 193
Grunberg, Bernard, 193
Guatemala, 8, 28, 45, 47, 51, 166, 246, 254, 256
Guerrero, Gonzalo, 215
Guevara, Antonio de, 129–30
Gulf Coast, 107, 199, 202
Gullo Omodeo, Marcelo, 79
Guzman, Don Diego de, 134
Guzman Itztlolinque, Don Juan de, 164
Guzman, Eulalia, 193

Hajovsky, Patrick, ix, 10, 309
Hanss, Stefan, 223
Hapsburg Empire, 283, 293
Haskett, Robert, viii, 10, 30, 307–8
Hernández Luna, Doña Leonor, 133
Hernández Xochiotzin, Desiderio, 86
Herrada, Juan de, 220
Herren Rajagapolan, Angela, 263

Herrera, Antonio de, 170
Herrera, Robinson, 256
Herrera y Tordesillas, Antonio de, 108, 112
Hespanha, Manuel António, 51
Hibueras, 166, 171–72, 176–78, 180
Hispaniola, 57
Historia de la nación chichimeca, 196
Historia de los mexicanos por sus pinturas, 107, 113
Historia tolteca-chichimeca, 27
Histoyre du Mechique, 106, 111
Hojacastro, Don Juan Martín, 128
Holy Roman Empire, 205, 225
Honduras, 100, 103–4, 107, 128, 166, 251
Huamantla, 131
Huaquechula, 204
Huasteca, 106
Huber, Vitus, ix, 10, 31, 306, 310
Huehue, 106
Huehuetl, 276
Huehuetlahtolli, 198
Huexotzinco, 25–27, 48, 105, 127–28, 148, 245
Hueymollan, 101, 108, 177
Hueyotlipan, 50
Huipil, 248, 263
Huitzilopochtli, 107, 116, 196, 202, 204, 263, 290

Iberian Peninsula, 5, 9, 50, 128, 137, 148, 206, 306, 313
Iglesia, Ramón, 194
Indigenous noblewomen, 244–56
Indio, deprecatory term, 75–77
Isabel, Doña, ix
Isabel, Queen, 58, 245
Italy, 219, 222, 225, 295
Itzamkanah, 8, 108
Itzcuauhtli, 103–4, 176
Itztapalapa, 165, 171, 197, 203–5, 245
Ixiptla, 107
Ixtlilxochitl, 32

Jalisco, 113, 142, 146
Jiménez, Juan, 140–41
Johnson, Samuel, 305
Jonacatepec, 32
Juárez, Benito, 85
Just War, 58

Karttunen, Frances, 20, 26
Keen, Benjamin, 283

Kellogg, Susan, 258
Klaus, Susanne, 173
Kranz, Travis, 253

Laird, Andrew, 251
Lamana, Gonzalo, 6
Laws of Burgos, 245
Legend of the Suns, 106
León-Portilla, Miguel, 7, 18
Lesbre, Patrick, 109, 170–71
Les vrais pourtraits, 278, 281, 283
Letters of Cortés, 6, 108, 161–62, 172, 179, 193–94, 215, 217, 245, 257
Ley Lerdo, 75
Lienzo de Quauhquechollan, 246
Lienzo de San Simon Tlatlauhquitepec, 136–40, 146
Lienzo de Tepatlaxco, 29
Lienzo de Tlaxcala, 195, 246, 252–53, 262
Lilly Library, 132, 135
Lockhart, James, 7, 18, 25, 48, 135, 145, 173
López Austin, Alfredo, 110, 196
López de Gómara, Francisco, 108, 112, 170, 194, 196–97, 199–200, 218, 258, 281, 285, 310
López de Palacios Rubios, Juan, 194
López Obrador, Andrés Manuel, 69, 78, 89
Luis, Juan, 133

Macehualli, 6
Macuahuitl, 33, 132, 137, 142, 291
Macuilxochitl, 217
Madajczak, Julia, viii, 8, 10, 307–8
Madrid, 219, 272–73
Madrid-Lake biombo, 274, 276–77, 290–91, 293, 295–99
Malinalco, 22
Mano de Plata, Don Antonio, 136, 138
Mapa de Tepetomatitlan, 125, 131–37, 146
Marina, Doña (La Malinche, Malintzin), ix, 10, 49, 83, 100–101, 167, 177–78, 202, 243–65, 309
Marineo, Lucio, 224
Marriage alliances, 246–56
Martín, Juan, 133
Martínez, Francisco, 193
Martínez del Río de Redo, Marita, 276
Martire, Pietro, 224
Mase Escasi. *See* Maxixcatzin
Matlalcueye, 132
Matlaciahuatzin, 259

Maxixcatzin, 248, 250, 253
Maxixcatzin, Don Juan, 144
Maxixcatzin, Don Lorenzo, 143–44, 228
Maxtla, 114
Maxtle, 222
Maya, 100, 110, 198
Mayor, Diego, 129
Mazatlan, 48
Mazatlaqueme, Benito, 220
Medici, Ippolito de', 222
Mendoza, Don Antonio de, 128
Mendoza Moctezuma, Don Diego de, 33
Mercedes reales, 52–54
Mestizo, vii, 77, 85
Metepec, 30
Mexia, Don Felix, 138, 140
Mexica / Mexicah, 5, 8–9, 11, 20–21, 26, 28, 49, 51, 71–72, 74, 80, 82–83, 85, 99, 103–5, 107, 116, 126, 163, 165, 191–92, 197, 199, 201–3, 205–6, 247, 255–57, 260, 262–64, 276–77, 286, 288, 290, 293, 298–99, 307, 311–13
Mexicalcingo, 112, 166, 171, 173, 177
Mexicalcingo, Cristobal, 166
Mexican Revolution, 77, 307
Mexicatl, 99, 101, 176
Mexicatl Cotzolotic, 177
Mexico profundo, 77
Michhuaque, 113, 167
Mictlan, 110–11, 115
Miguel, Gaspar, 142–43
Miralles, Juan, 193
Mixtecah, 198
Moctezuma y Tula, Count, 288, 290
Molina, Alonso de, 20–22, 24, 26–27, 144
Moluccas, 53–54
Montejo, Francisco de, 48
Montell, Jaime, 193
Monzón, 216
Moquihuix, 103
Mora, José María Luis, 75
Moreno, Don Joachin, 127
Motelchiuh, 105, 112–14, 116
Moteuczoma, vii, ix, 1, 5, 10, 25, 27, 49, 72, 99, 103, 105, 107, 126, 163, 165, 176, 191–201, 203–6, 217–18, 251, 257–58, 261–63, 272–99, 308–311
Motezuma, Diego Luis, 205
Muñoz Camargo, Diego, 115, 129, 144, 146, 253
Museo de Americas, 272
Museo de la Memoria, Tlaxcala, 74, 83

Museo degli Argenti, 293
Museo Nacional de Antropología, 74, 252
Museo Nacional de Arte, 297
Muslims, 274, 299

Nanahuatl, 107
Narváez, Pánfilo de, 200, 202
Native marginalization, 78–89
Nautla, 258
Navagero, Andrea, 222
Navarrete, Federico, vii, 244
Nacxitl Topiltzin, 106
Netherlands, 225
New Conquest History, 7, 18, 309–10
New Laws, 57
New Philology, 19
Nezahualcoyotl, 258
Nezahualpilli, 295
Niza, Tadeo de, 144
Noble Savage, 274, 296, 309
Noche Triste, 162–63, 166, 192–93, 252, 259, 262, 275
Nonohualca Teotlixca Tlacochcalca Tecpantlaca, 106
Noticonquista, vii
Nuidia, 222
Nuremberg, 224

Oaxaca, 48, 79–80, 148, 256
Ocaña, Diego de, 54–55
Ocotelulco, 128, 138, 140–41, 144, 248
Olid, Cristóbal de, 104
Olko, Justyna, viii, 10, 306–7
Ordenanza de Cuauhtemoc, 102, 174
Orientalist, 277, 296
Orleans, Margarita de, 293
Orozco, José Clemente, 69
Orozco y Barra, Manuel, 193
Oselotl Chalchiuhtecutli, Don Juan, 143–45
Osorio, Blas, 143–44
Otomi, 71, 76
Oudijk, Michel, 50, 146
Oviedo, Gonzalo de, 193

Pacific Ocean, 53
Pagden, Anthony, 193
Pago de Minchaque, 129
Pánuco River, 245
Paredes, Don Diego de, 134

Pastrana Flores, Miguel, ix, 10–11, 308
Patolli, 217, 220
Pedroso, Antonio del. *See* Mano de Plata
Pehua / tepehua / tepehualiztli, 19–22
Pellicer, Carlos, 69, 78
Pereyra, Carlos, 193
Pérez, Dionisio, 127
Pérez, Nicolas, 127
Peru, 53
Petate, 217
Petición al cabildo, 9
Petztetl, Miguel, 140
Philip II, viii, 4, 31, 50, 59, 126, 130, 132–34, 137, 140, 143, 146, 149–50, 165, 220, 313
Philip IV, 206
Pimentel Maxixcatzin, Don Luis, 144
Pintura de San Luis Tecopilco, 138, 141
Pinturas tlaxcaltecas, 196
Pizarro, Francisco, 312–13
Pochotl / pochote, 101, 108–11, 115–16, 167, 170, 172, 177
Pochtecah, 195
Poland, 216
Poloa, 26–27
Porcallo, Vasco, 47
Powers, Karen Viera, 244
Poyauhtecatitlan / Poyauhtecatl, 106, 110–11
Prem, Hanns J., 102
Prescott, William H., 193
Primeros memoriales, 24–25
Puebla, 25, 29, 58, 81, 87, 110, 130–31, 136, 146
Purépecha, 76

Quahuitzatzin, 31
Quauhpopoca, 163–64
Quauhquechollan, 246
Quecholac, 58
Quetzalcoatl, 105–8, 110–11, 115–16, 161, 196, 199–200, 193
Quetzalcoltzin, Don Valeriano, 137
Quiahuitztlan, 138, 248

Ramusio, Giovanni Bautista, 215
Recopiliación de leyes, 129
Reconquista, 50
Repartimiento, 50–51
Requerimiento, 194
Restall, Matthew, vii, 5–7, 18, 50, 193, 257, 286, 310–13

Reyes García, Luis, 139, 142
Reyes Tellez, Diego, 129–30
Ribas, Don Juan de, 129
Ribera, Juan, 224
Ribero Lake, Rodrigo, 272–73
Rivera, Diego, 85
Rodríguez Carnero, José, 290
Rome, 220, 226, 290, 293, 308
Rosenzweig, Ross, 88
Rousseau, Jean Jacques, 274
Rovira Morgado, Rossend, 112–13

Sahagún, Bernardino de, 24–25, 178, 195, 198, 203, 311
Salinas, Martín de, 215
Sandoval, Gonzalo de, 47
Santiago, Alejandro de, 130
Santiago, Doña Pasquala de, 129
Santiago, Don Zacarías de, viii, 10, 30, 125–50, 307–8
Santiago, Order of, 137, 146, 149
Sarmiento de Guzmán, Alonso, 142, 146
Sarmiento de Valladares, José, 288, 290
Sarmiento Guzmán Paredes, Alonso, 131–35, 150
Sarmiento Paredes, Gaspar, 134
Saussure, Ferdinand de, 4
Schirrmacher, Jonas, 59
Schroeder, Susan, 17, 19–20, 26, 31
Schwaller, John F., ix, 11, 71
Scolieri, Paul, 288
Secretaría de Salud, 82
Seven Myths, 312
Seville, 5, 54, 216, 220, 228
Siculo, Lucio Marineo, 221
Siena, Juan de, 129
Siete Partidas, 51, 193
Sigüenza y Góngora, Carlos de, 290, 293, 295–97
Snyder, Timothy, 70
Soler d'Hyver de las Desas, Carlos, 226
Solís, Antonio de, 275, 283–87, 291, 296–97
Spain, 205, 313
Stockholm syndrome, 193
Sublimis deus, 227
Suezo, Pedro de, 128
Sumaria relación, 114
Survivance, 17
Szoblik, Katarzyna, 105

Tapia, 171
Tapia, Andrés de, 194
Tapia, Don Hernando de, 113, 218, 227
Tapia Motelchiuh, Don Andrés de, 112, 167, 173, 218
Tarascan, 113
Tatar, 222
Tayauh, 114
Tecamachalco, 58
Tecapan, 103
Techialoyan, 32–35, 102
Tecopilco, 138–41, 146, 150
Tecpilotl, 228
Tecuichpotzin, ix, 261–64
Tecuiluatzin, Doña Luisa, 250–53, 255–58, 261, 264, 309
Tellez, Don Diego, 129
Tellez, Francisco, 56
Temilotl, Don Pedro, 100, 103–5, 176–78
Templo Mayor, 163, 191, 197, 201, 204
Tena, Rafael, 172, 174
Tenango Tepolula, 148–49
Tenochca / Tenochcah, 99–100, 102, 104–5, 107, 112, 115, 125, 162–67, 171, 173, 177, 195, 201–3
Tenochtitlan, vii, x, 8–9, 19, 22–23, 27, 45, 47, 50–52, 54, 69–72, 77–80, 85, 99–105, 112–14, 126, 144, 146, 162, 164–67, 173, 176–77, 191, 193, 195, 197, 200, 202, 204, 218, 243, 246–47, 251–52, 255–64, 272, 275, 277, 295, 312
Teoatl Tlachinolli / Atl Tlachinolli, 22–24
Teotihuacan, 24
Tepanecah, 197, 313
Tepatlaco, 29
Tepeticpac, 125, 130, 135–38, 142, 248
Tepetomatitlan, 125, 131–33, 135, 137, 139, 146, 148, 150
Teponaztli, 276, 297
Terraciano, Kevin, 100, 102–3, 109, 174
Tetetl, 132
Teteuctin, ix, 215–29
Tetlpanquetzal, 101, 163, 165–67, 177, 251
Tetzcoco, 47, 99, 101, 104, 108, 128, 163, 166–67, 170–72, 177, 191, 196–97, 199, 202, 218, 251, 258–59, 264, 313
Texas Fragment, 248, 250, 252–53
Texcoco, Lake, 259, 263
Tezcatlipoca, 105, 111, 196, 202
Tezozomoc, 110, 114, 197

Thevet, André, 278, 281, 285–87, 294–95, 297
Thomas Aquinas, St., 292
Thomas, Hugh, 193
Tilma, 222–25, 263, 278
Tira de Tepechpan, 195
Título primordial, viii
Tizatlan, 133, 138, 141–42, 248, 250
Tlacahuepan, 105
Tlacopan, 47, 99, 101, 104, 163, 165–67, 177, 191, 197, 199, 218, 251–52, 256, 258, 264, 313
Tlacopanecah, 163, 165
Tlacotzin, 113, 116
Tlacuilo, 229
Tlahtohuani / Tlatoque, 10, 99–101, 103–5, 107–10, 112, 114–15, 128, 173, 191, 196–206, 217, 256–57, 293
Tlahtocan, 197
Tlahuelahualol, Pedro, 143
Tlahuelxolotzin, Don Gonzalo, 135
Tlaloc, 106–7, 196
Tlalocan, 106–7, 110, 115
Tlalmaceuhqui, 20, 31–35
Tlameme, 127
Tlapallan. *See* Tlillan Tlapallan Tlatlayan
Tlatelolca / Tlatelolcah / Tlatelolco, vii, viii, 6, 27, 71, 99–100, 102–4, 112–13, 116–17, 163, 165–67, 171, 173–74, 176–78, 202–3, 218, 261
Tlatlauhquitepec, 136–40, 146, 150
Tlatolon / Telon, 114
Tlaxcala / Tlaxcalteca / Tlaxcaltecah, viii, 5, 8–11, 25–26, 28, 47–48, 50, 71, 82–89, 110, 115, 125–31, 133–34, 136–37, 140–44, 146–49, 199, 204, 218, 229, 245–46, 248, 251–56, 259, 262, 287, 307, 309
Tlayac, 29
Tlehuexolotzin, 137–38, 248
Tlillan Tlapallan Tlatlayan, 106–7
Tlilquiyahuatzin, Don Diego, 127, 144
Tochpan, 143–44
Tollan / Tula, 105, 107–8, 111, 116, 293, 307
Tolquequetzatzin, 250
Toltec, 116, 161, 197
Toluca, Valley, 30, 33
Topiltzin Quetzalcoatl. *See* Quetzalcoatl
Torquemada, Juan de, 108–9, 112–13, 170–72, 179, 197, 203–4
Torres, Don Pedro, 129–30
Totomela, murals, 24
Totonac, 8, 49, 144

Totoquihuaztli. *See* Cortés Totoquihuaztli
Tovar, Juan de, 201
Townsend, Camilla, 26, 250
Toxcatl, 202, 259, 297
Trachtenbuch, 225
Translatio imperii, ix, 194
Trexler, Richard, 245
Triple Alliance / Excan Tlahtoloyan, 8, 10, 34, 47, 79, 85, 89, 126, 148, 163, 165–66, 170–72, 177, 179, 192–93, 198–99, 202, 206, 217, 264, 313
Trueba, Don Martín, 134
Trouillot, Michel-Rolph, 7, 60
Tzaqualtitlan, 31
Tziuhcohuac, 100, 113, 248
Tzompantli, 277
Tzontecomatl, 30

Uffizi Palace, 293
Ullamaztli, 217
Urbano, Alonso, 22

Valiente, Alonso, 127
Valladolid, 55, 224
Valle, Perla, 174
Valley of Mexico. *See* Central Basin
van Deusen, Nancy, 6–7
Vazquez, Germán, 193
Vazquez de Espinosa, Antonio, 205
Vazquez de Tapia, Bernardino, 194, 203
Velasco, Don Luis de, 131
Velázquez, Diego, 162
Velázquez, Juan, 171
Velázquez Tlacotzin, Don Juan, 112, 167, 173
Venezuela, 50
Venus, 105–6
Veracruz, 49, 105–6
Veronica, Doña, 138–40
Vespucci, Amerigo, 293
Villa Alta, 148–49
Villela, Peter, vii
Vizenor, Gerald, 17
Völkerschau, 217
Voltaire, 274

Wankel, Lara, 161
Weiditz, Cristoph, 225–26, 228
Wood, Stephanie, viii, 9, 145, 147, 149, 174, 305–6, 312

Xahualtzin, 259
Xaltocan, 136
Xicotencatl, 72, 133–34, 247–48, 250–51, 253, 256
Xihuitzolli, 263
Xipe Totec, 196
Xiuhuitzolli, 291
Xiuhtecuhtli, 196
Xiuhtonacateotzin, Doña Luisa, 133
Xochimilco, 31, 218
Xochiyaotl, 72
Xochitiotzin Pérez, Ethel, 88
Xocoyotl Cuauhtemoctzin. *See* Cuauhtemoc
Xocuahpatollin, 217, 220
Xolotl, 33, 197
Xotelulco, 132
Xuárez, Alonso, 129
Xuárez Quecehual, Juan, 128

Yannakakis, Yanna, 48, 148–49
Yaotl / Yaoyotl, 24–26
Yucatan, 102, 104–6, 108–9, 113, 116

Zamora, Alejandro de, 129
Zapata Mendoza, Juan Buenaventura, 25, 28, 130–31, 140, 144
Zapatista rebellion, viii, 80
Zapoteca / Zapotecah, 47, 198
Zavala, Silvio, 193
Zempoala, 32
Zócalo, 79
Zuazo, Alonso de, 57
Zumárraga, Juan de, 227
Zygmunt I of Poland, 215

About the Authors

María Castañeda de la Paz is a historian, conducting research at the Instituto de Investigaciones Antropológicas at the Universidad Nacional Autómoma de México since 2006. She did her postgraduate studies at Leiden University and received her PhD from the University of Seville. Her main research involves the pre-Hispanic and colonial Indigenous history in Central Mexico through a historical and philological analysis of various sources, themes about which she has published various books and numerous articles. In 2023, King Felipe VI distinguished her with the Cross of the Order of Isabel la Católica. In 2018 she was elected as associated member of the International Academy of Heraldry for her novel works around the Indigenous heraldry in New Spain.

Lori Boornazian Diel, PhD, is the Kay and Velma Kimbell chair of Art History at Texas Christian University. Her research focuses on Aztec codices created after the conquest. Her book *The Codex Mexicanus: A Guide to Life in Late Sixteenth-Century New Spain* (2018) was awarded the Roland H. Bainton Prize in Art and Music History from the Sixteenth Century Studies Conference. She has also published *The Tira de Tepechpan: Negotiating Place under Aztec and Spanish Rule* (2008) and *Aztec Codices: What They Tell Us about Daily Life* (2020), as well as essays on Aztec pictorial manuscripts and the role of women in Aztec history. Her work has been supported by fellowships from the Dumbarton Oaks Research Library and Collection and the Wenner-Gren Foundation.

Erika Escutia has graduated in art history and holds a master's in art studies from the Universidad Iberoamericana, Mexico City. She has collaborated in teaching, research, communication, and educational curatorship work for several universities, museums, and research centers in Mexico and Spain. She received her PhD in Humanities from the Universitat Pompeu Fabra, Barcelona (2021). Her research, awarded by the Association for Latin American Art in 2023, focuses on the practices of exchanging, gift giving, treasuring, displaying, and collecting of American artifacts in Europe in the sixteenth century, including the ways in which ruling families in Europe employed and interpreted them.

Patrick Hajovsky is an associate professor of art history and contributing member of the Latin American and Border Studies program at Southwestern University in Georgetown, Texas. His research focuses on the intersections of pre-Columbian art and rulership, especially among the Aztec and Inca into the colonial period. His first book, *On the Lips of Others: Moteuczoma's Fame in Aztec Monuments and Rituals* (University of Texas Press, 2015), examines how Moteuczoma's name, and his name glyph, conveyed his living divinity according to an Indigenous duality of fame. Hajovsky's research further shows also how colonial-period representations of the king reframed his identity through a colonized politics of personhood and portraiture. He is currently working on his second book, which investigates Aztec notions of embodiment while regarding the supernatural in sculpture.

Robert Haskett, an ethnohistorian studying Nahua peoples of central New Spain, has published on Indigenous town government and society in Cuernavaca and has written about Nahuatl-language *títulos primordiales* (local histories and land tenure descriptions) from this region as well as the Chalco and Puebla-Tlaxcala areas. A principle aim of this work has been the recovery of later-colonial Indigenous memories of the Spanish invasion and the onset of the colonial regime, and how these recollections of the past had been crafted by the end of the seventeenth and eighteenth centuries to legitimize continuing Nahua sovereignty that, according to such records, had been established in the first half of the sixteenth century, embodied in the persons of heroic Indigenous leaders. Dr. Haskett is an emeritus professor of history at the University of Oregon.

Vitus Huber is professor of early modern history at the University of Fribourg. He is the author of two books on the coercive encounter between the so-called Old and New World: The first, *Beute und Conquista: Die politische Ökonomie der Eroberung Neuspaniens* (Campus 2018), derives from his dissertation at the University of Munich and analyzes the political economy of the *Conquista* of New Spain. By carving out the peculiar role of booty and the prime importance of the notion of distributive justice for the expansive dynamics, Huber provides a new approach to the process of the *Conquista* and of empire formation in Spanish-America. His second monograph, *Die Konquistadoren: Cortés, Pizarro und die Eroberung Amerikas* (C. H. Beck 2019), is a synthesis on the conquistadors.

Julia Madajczak is a historian working with pre-contact and colonial Nahua culture. She obtained her PhD in cultural studies from the University of Warsaw in 2015. She has participated in and directed numerous research projects regarding the Mexican Nahua language, culture, and history. Currently, she runs the project Metaphors as a Key to the

Pre-Hispanic Nahua Worldview: A Multidisciplinary Approach at the University of Warsaw, Poland. She edited and coauthored *Fragments of the Sixteenth-Century Nahuatl Census from the Jagiellonian Library: A Lost Manuscript* (Leiden: Brill, 2021) and coauthored *Loans in Colonial and Modern Nahuatl: A Contextual Dictionary* (Berlin: De Gruyter Mouton, 2020). Recently, she has been particularly interested in pre-contact Nahua deities, the Otherworld, and the afterlife.

Justyna Olko is a professor at the Faculty of "Artes Liberales" of the University of Warsaw and director of its Center for Research and Practice in Cultural Continuity. She specializes in Indigenous history, sociolinguistics, multilingualism, and language revitalization as well as participatory and decolonizing research practices, with a focus on Nahua language and culture. Author of *Insignia of Rank in the Nahua World* (University Press of Colorado, 2014), coeditor of *Revitalizing Endangered Languages. A Practical Guide* (Cambridge University Press, 2021), and coeditor and coauthor of *Living with Nature, Cherishing Language: Indigenous Knowledges in the Americas through History* (Palgrave MacMillan, 2023), she is also a recipient of two European Research Council grants and a 2020 winner of the Falling Walls Science Breakthrough of the Year in social sciences and humanities.

Miguel Pastrana Flores is professor of the bachelor's degree in history and currently coordinator of the master's and doctoral program in history at the National Autonomous University of Mexico (UNAM). Moreover, he is a researcher at the Institute of Historical Research at UNAM. His lines of research are the historiography of Indigenous tradition and religious and political institutions of Mesoamerican tradition. His publications include the following books: *Historias de la conquista: Aspectos de la historiografía de tradición náhuatl* (UNAM, 2004); *Entre los hombres y los dioses: Acercamiento al sacerdocio de calpulli entre los antiguos nahuas* (UNAM, 2008); and *Tula y los toltecas en la historiografía mexicana del siglo XVIII al XXI* (UNAM, 2023).

John F. Schwaller is professor emeritus of history at the University at Albany (SUNY) and a research associate at the University of Kansas. He is known for his work on the secular clergy in early colonial Mexico, Nahuatl-language manuscripts, a history of the Catholic Church in Latin America, and studies on Mexica religion, the Cortés expedition, and the Stations of the Cross. For many years he served as an academic administrator at various universities, including Florida Atlantic University (as associate dean), the University of Montana, (as associate provost and associate vice president), the University of Minnesota—Morris (as vice chancellor for academic affairs and dean), and the State University of New York at Potsdam (as president). He is also the former director of the Academy of American Franciscan History. He was Latin American editor of *Ethnohistory* and is currently editor of the journal *The Americas*.

Kevin Terraciano is professor, Robert Burr Endowed chair of history, and chair of the UCLA Department of History. He specializes in the history of Latin America, especially the Indigenous writings, languages, and cultures of Mesoamerica and Mexico in the postclassic and colonial periods. His many publications include two prize-winning books, *The Mixtecs of Colonial Oaxaca* and *Codex Sierra: A Nahuatl-Mixtec Book of Accounts from Colonial Mexico*. He also coedited *Mesoamerican Voices: Native-Language Writings from Colonial Mexico, Oaxaca, Yucatan, and Guatemala* (with Lisa Sousa and Matthew Restall), and *The Florentine Codex: An Encyclopedia of the Nahua World in Sixteenth-Century Mexico* (with Jeanette Peterson). Terraciano founded the Nahuatl Language program at UCLA in 2015 and is co-founder of the Digital Florentine Codex, sponsored by the Getty Research Institute in Los Angeles, California: https://florentinecodex.getty.edu.

Stephanie Wood is a research associate in the Center for Equity Promotion at the University of Oregon. She has worked with Nahuatl-language manuscripts for forty-five years, seeking Nahua perspectives on their history. She is the author of *Transcending Conquest: Nahua Views of Spanish Colonial Mexico* (University of Oklahoma Press, 2003), and she has coedited four anthologies about Mesoamerican ethnohistory. She may be best known for her open-access digital collections, funded primarily by the National Endowment for the Humanities and aimed at scholars and teachers of Mexican history. For example, her open-access *Online Nahuatl Dictionary*, created in collaboration with John Sullivan and Native speakers of Eastern Huastecan Nahuatl, has 150,000+ users per year. Having most recently held the Kislak Chair at the Library of Congress (2022–23) on the Early Americas, she is currently expanding her *Visual Lexicon of Aztec Hieroglyphs*.

www.ingramcontent.com/pod-product-compliance
Lightning Source LLC
Chambersburg PA
CBHW061744070526
44585CB00025B/2796